AF564399

Trends in Networking and Communication

Trends in Networking and Communication

Edited by

Girish Kumar Srivastava
Charul Bhatnagar

Published by

ATLANTIC

PUBLISHERS & DISTRIBUTORS (P) LTD

7/22, Ansari Road, Darya Ganj,
New Delhi-110002
Phones : +91-11-23273880, 23275880, 23280451
Fax : +91-11-23285873
Web : www.atlanticbooks.com
E-mail : info@atlanticbooks.com

Branch office
5, Nallathambi Street, Wallajah Road,
Chennai-600002
Phones : +91-44-64611085, 32413319
E-mail : chennai@atlanticbooks.com

ISBN: 978-81-269-1052-6

Printed in India at Nice Printing Press, A-33/3A, Site-IV,
Industrial Area, Sahibabad, Ghaziabad, U.P.

Dedicated to

Late Shri Ganeshi Lal Agrawal
A noted philanthropist and social worker with vision and belief that true knowledge should be promoted and spread far and wide

Foreword

Networking & communication has created a global village in terms of the immediacy within which people across the world can share audio, video and text data. The process of making decisions has also increased in speed due to instant access to databanks for information. Due to electronic technology, jobs, working locations and cultures are all changing. The need of the hour is to come up with better, faster, more reliable and cheaper technology which can take India to new frontiers in the field of Science & Technology.

Institutions, industry and teaching faculty are constantly engaged in exploring the possibilities of development in networking and communication so that society at large can reap the benefits. In the present scenario of globalization, one has to constantly strive to keep pace with new avenues and growth in order to be competitive in various endeavors.

This book will be of immense help to people from both the industry and the academics who want to enhance their knowledge in the field of networking and communication.

Prof. (Dr.) Jai Prakash
Director General
GLA Group of Institutions
Mathura

Acknowledgements

We take this opportunity to thank Shri Narayan Das Agrawal, Chairman, GLA Group of Institutions, for providing an excellent academic environment in which one can work to enhance one's skills. We express our heartfelt gratitude to him for his blessings and support rendered during writing the book. Our thanks are also due to Mr. Neeraj Agrawal, Secretary, Society, GLA Group of Institutions and to Mr. Vivek Agrawal, Secretary, Trust, GLA Group of Institutions, for extending all the support and assistance to carry out this endeavor.

We express our sincere thanks and indebtedness to Prof. (Dr.) Jai Prakash, Director General, GLA Group of Institutions, for his guidance and invaluable suggestions. With all the warmth and respect that we can muster, we thank Prof. Anil K. Gupta, Director, GLAITM; Prof. Anoop K. Gupta, Director, GLAIPS; Prof. Masood Hassan, Director, GLAIBM; and Prof Pradeep Mishra, Director, GLAIPR, for sparing their valuable time to give us ideas on how to proceed on this work.

We would like to express our gratitude to the people who saw us through this book—to all those who provided support—read, wrote, offered comments and assisted in the editing, proofreading and designing. Our thanks are due to all our colleagues, specially Prof. M. Ahmad, Prof. S. Basu, Prof. V.N. Nanda, Prof. G.S. Sharma, Prof. A.K. Verma, Prof. G. Chatterjee, Mr. Anil Kumar Singh and Mr. Somesh Dhamija. We would be remised if we do not put on record our gratefulness for the painstaking work carried out by Mr. Rakesh Tiwari, Mr. Saurabh Singhal, Mr. Soumendu Chakraborty, Ms. Divya Saxena and Mr. Tarun Kulshreshta. We are also thankful to Mr. Saurabh Sharma and Mr. Rajendra Singh for providing secretarial assistance in preparation of the manuscript.

Girish Kumar Srivastava
Charul Bhatnagar

Preface

Modern-era technology has the potential to make notable impact on our social and national life. Thus, the tasks of disseminating scientific information and proliferating technological concepts among the masses have assumed paramount importance. The emerging technologies give an impetus to globalization, increase competition and make it imperative for the organization to incorporate and adopt new developments into their manufacturing and service applications. As a result, a large number of research organizations, academic institutions and MNCs worldwide are eagre to make a huge investment in the research and the development activities.

Communication and networking constitutes the nervous system of the information technology-enabled economic scenario. The key areas which will decide and define the parameters of excellence and benchmarks will be dictated by the future trends in the arena of networking and communication. India as a developing economy now requires new domains to be explored, new initiatives to be taken and new regulations to be framed in the realm of networking and communication. The trends towards unified communications, along with richer web-based applications and a wider application of consumer-oriented devices are among the key issues emerging for enterprise network in the next few years.

The present work focuses on the following sub-themes:

- Broadband Wireless Communication System
- Mobile Computing
- Wireless Personal Communications
- Mobile Database
- Wireless ad hoc Sensor and Bluetooth Networks

- Multimedia Communications
- Advances in Satellite Communication
- Networking Protocols, Routing and Algorithms
- Optical Communication
- Parallel and Distributed Architectures and Algorithms
- Antennas, Propagation and Transmission Technology
- Network Security
- Communication Software Techniques
- Wi-fi Systems
- Information Theory and Coding
- Grid Computing

It is hoped that various stakeholders like government, research scholars and industrial houses will come together to promote research work to keep pace with emerging technologies in the field of networking and communication so that its benefits can reach the society at large.

Girish Kumar Srivastava
Charul Bhatnagar

Contents

Cryptographic Protocols: Security and Composition

Sunder Lal, Santosh Kumar Yadav and *Kuldeep Bhardwaj*

ABSTRACT

Capturing the security requirements of cryptographic tasks in a meaningful way is a slippery business: On the one hand, we want security criteria that prevent 'all feasible attacks' against a protocol. On the other hand, we want our criteria not to be overly restrictive; that is, we want them to accept those protocols that do not succumb to 'feasible attacks'. This paper studies a general methodology for defining security of cryptographic protocols. The methodology, often dubbed the 'trusted party paradigm', allows for defining the security requirements of practically any cryptographic task in a unified and natural way. We first review a basic formulation that captures security in isolation from other protocol instances. Next we address the secure composition problem, namely the vulnerabilities resulting from the often unexpected interactions among different protocol instances that run alongside each other in the same system. We demonstrate the limitations of the basic formulation and review a formulation that guarantees security of protocols even in general composite systems.

INTRODUCTION

The goal of this paper is to introduce the reader to the problems associated with formulating and asserting security properties of protocols, and to present a general methodology for modeling protocols and asserting their security properties.

In particular, for the most part it assumes very little prior knowledge in cryptography. Also, while the main focus in on the foundational aspects of specifying security, the text attempts to be accessible and useful to practitioners as well as theoreticians. Indeed, the considered security concerns are realistic ones, and the end goal is to enable analyzing the security of real-world protocols and systems.

Cryptographic protocols, namely distributed algorithms that aim to guarantee some 'security properties' in face of adversarial behavior, have become an integral part of our society and everyday lives. Indeed, we have grown accustomed to relying on the ubiquity and functionality of computer systems, whereas these systems make crucial use of cryptographic protocols to guarantee their 'expected functionality'. Furthermore, the perceived security properties of cryptographic protocols and the functionality expected from applications that use them is being used by lawmakers to modify the ground rules of our society. It is thus, crucial that we have sound understanding of how to specify, develop, and analyze cryptographic protocols. The need for sound understanding is highlighted by the empirical fact that cryptographic protocols have been notoriously 'hard to get right,' with subtle flaws in protocols being discovered long after development, and in some cases even after deployment and standardization. In fact, even *specifying* the security properties required from protocols for a given task in a rigorous and meaningful way has proved to be elusive. There is vast literature describing protocols aimed at solving the problems mentioned above, and many others, in a variety of settings. Out of this literature, let us mention only the works of *Yao* [1] and *Goldreich, Micali* and *Wigderson* [2], which give a mechanical way to generate protocols for solving practically *any* multi-party cryptographic protocol problem 'in a secure way', assuming authenticated communication. But, what does it mean for a cryptographic protocol to solve a given protocol problem, or a cryptographic task, 'in a secure way'? How can we formalize the relevant security requirements in a way that makes mathematical sense, matches our informal intention, and at the same time can also be met by actual protocols? This turns out to be a tricky business.

The Trusted-Party Paradigm

In this section, we motivate and sketch the trusted-party definitional paradigm, and highlight some of its main advantages. More detailed descriptions of actual definitions are left to subsequent sections. We consider, as a generic example, the task of two-party secure function evaluation. Here two mutually distrustful parties want to 'securely evaluate' some known function *f*, in the sense that has value *0P1PiPix* and the parties wish to jointly compute ()01,*fxx* 'in a secure way.' Which protocols should we consider adequate for this task? Two basic types of requirements come to mind. The first is correctness: the parties that follow the protocol (often called the 'good parties' or 'honest parties') should output the correct value of the function evaluated at the inputs of all parties. Here the 'correct function value' may capture multiple concerns, including authenticity of the identities of the participants, integrity of the input values, correct choice of random values, etc. The second requirement is secrecy, or hiding the local information held by the parties as much as possible.

For instance, we consider two parties (say, two databases), each having a list of items, that wish to find out which items appear in both lists. Here, correctness means that the parties output all the entries which appear in both lists, and only those entries. Secrecy means that no party learns anything from the interaction *other than* the joint entries.

However, in general, formalizing these requirements in a meaningful way seems problematic. Let us briefly mention some of the issues. First, defining correctness is complicated by the fact that it is not clear how to define the 'input value' that an arbitrarily-behaving party contributes to the computation. In particular, it is of course impossible to 'force' such parties to use some value given from above. So, what would be a 'legitimate', or 'acceptable' process for choosing inputs by parties who do not necessarily follow the protocol?

Assume that the parties want to toss *k* coins, where *k* is a security parameter; formally, the evaluated function is ().,.*fr*=, where let *f* be a one-way permutation on domain { (i.e., given a random *k*-bit value *x*, it is infeasible to compute {}0,1.*kRr*←□□}0,1*k*()1*fx*-. The protocol instructs to choose and send to both parties output *r*. 0*P*{}0,1.*kRs*←□□()*rfs*=1*P*

This protocol preserves secrecy vacuously (since the parties do not have any secret inputs), and is also perfectly correct in the sense that the distribution of the joint output is perfectly uniform. However, the protocol lets hold some 'secret trapdoor information' on the joint random string. Furthermore, it does not have this information, and cannot feasibly compute it (assuming that *f* is one-way). This 'quirk' of the protocol is not merely an aesthetic concern. Having such trapdoor information can be devastating for security if the output string *r* is used within other protocols. This example seems to suggest that a definition of security should somehow specify also the *process* in which the output is to be obtained. 0*P*1*P*

The trusted party paradigm follows the 'unified requirement' approach mentioned above. The idea proceeds as follows. In order to determine whether a given protocol is secure for some cryptographic task, first envision an ideal process for carrying out the task in a secure way. In the ideal process, all parties secretly hand their inputs to an external trusted party who locally computes the outputs according to the specification, and secretly hands each party its prescribed outputs. This ideal process can be regarded as a 'formal specification' of the security requirements of the task. The protocol is said to securely realize a task if running the protocol amounts to 'emulating' the ideal process for the task, in the sense that any damage that can be caused by an adversary interacting with the protocol can also be caused by an adversary in the ideal process for the task.

In principle, this idea seems to have the potential to answer all the concerns discussed above. Indeed, in the ideal process both correctness and lack of influence are guaranteed in fiat, since the inputs provided by any adversarial set of parties cannot depend on the inputs provided by the other parties in any way, and furthermore all parties obtain the correct output value according to the specification. Secrecy is also immediately guaranteed, since the only information obtained by any adversarial coalition of parties is the legitimate outputs of the parties in this coalition. In particular, no implicit leakage of side-information correlated with the output is possible. Another attractive property of this approach is its apparent generality: It seems possible to capture the requirements of very different tasks by considering different sets of instructions for the external trusted party.

It remains to substantiate this definitional approach in a way that maintains its intuitive appeal and security guarantees, and at the same time allows for reasonable analysis of 'natural' protocols. In this tutorial we describe several formalizations that differ in their complexity, generality and compos ability guarantees. Yet, all these formalizations follow the same outline, sketched as follows. The definition proceeds in three steps. First, we formalize the process of executing a distributed protocol in the presence of adversarial behavior of some parts of the system. Here, the adversarial behavior is embodied via a single, centralized computational entity called the adversary. Next, we formalize the ideal process for the task at hand. The formalized ideal process also involves an adversary, but this adversary is rather limited and its influence on the computation is tightly controlled. Finally, we say that a protocol π securely realizes a task F if for *any* adversary A that interacts with π there *exists* an adversary S that interacts with the trusted party for F, such that no 'external environment,' that gives inputs to the parties and reads their outputs, can tell whether it is interacting with π or with the trusted party for F. (Here the 'environment' represents 'everything that happens outside the protocol execution', including both the immediate users of the protocol and other parties and protocols.)

Very informally, the goal of the above requirement is to guarantee that any information gathered by the adversary A when interacting with π, as well as any 'damage' caused by A, could have also been gathered or caused by an adversary S in the ideal process with F. Now, since the ideal process is designed so that *no* S can gather information or cause damage more than what is explicitly permitted in the ideal process for F, we can conclude that A too, when interacting with π cannot gather information or cause damage more than what is explicitly permitted by F.

Basic Security

Before defining security of protocols, one should first formulate a model for representing distributed systems and protocols within them. Informally, we wish to capture a system of (resource bounded) computing elements that communicate in an arbitrary asynchronous manner. This section sketches such a model; since we only need to capture two-party protocols, the model is somewhat simplified (it is extended later). Still, readers that are satisfied with a more informal notion of distributed systems, protocols, and polynomial-time computation can safely skip this section.

Interactive Turing Machines

Interactive Turing machines (ITMs) are probabilistic Turing machines augmented with mechanisms that allow transferal of data between different machines. Specifically, an ITM is a Turing machine with some externally writable tapes, namely tapes that can be written into by other machines. It will be convenient to distinguish three externally writable tapes: An input tape, representing inputs provided by the 'invoking program', an incoming communication tape, representing messages coming from the network, and a subroutine output tape, representing outputs provided by subroutines invoked by the present program. The input tape represents information coming from 'outside the protocol instance', while the incoming communication tape and the subroutine output tapes provide information that is 'internal to a protocol instance.' In addition, the incoming communication tape models information coming from un-trusted sources, while the information on the subroutine output tapes is treated as coming from a trusted source.

Systems of ITMs

The model of computation consists of several instances of ITMs that can write on the externally writable tapes of each other, subject to some global rules. We call an ITM instance an ITI. Different ITIs can run the same code (ITM); however they would, in general, have different local states.

An execution of a system of ITMs consists of a sequence of activation of ITIs. In each activation, the active ITI proceeds according to its current state and contents of tapes until it enters a special wait state. In order to allow the writing ITI to specify the target ITI we enumerate the ITIs in the system in some arbitrary order, and require that the write instruction specify the numeral of the target ITI. (This addressing mechanism essentially means that each two ITIs in the system have a 'direct link' between them.)

The order of activation is determined as follows: There is a pre-determined ITI, called the initial ITI, which is the first one to be activated. At the end of each activation, the ITI whose tape was written to is activated next. If no external write operation was made then the initial ITI is activated. The execution ends when the initial ITI halts.

In principle, the global input of an execution should be the initial inputs of all ITIs. For simplicity, however, we define the global input as the input of the initial ITI alone. Similarly, the output of an execution is the output of the initial ITI. A final ingredient of a system of ITMs is the control function, which determines which tapes of which ITI can each ITI write on. As we'll see, the control function will be instrumental in defining different notions of security.

Polynomial Time ITMs

In order to model resource-bounded programs and adversaries, we need to define resource-bounded ITMs. We concentrate on polynomial time ITMs. We wish to stick with the traditional interpretation of polynomial time as 'polynomial in the length of the input'. However, since in our model ITMs can write on the tapes of each other, care should be taken to guarantee that the overall running time of the system remains polynomial in the initial parameters. We thus, say that an ITM M is polynomial time (PT) if there exists a polynomial $p(.)$ such that at any point during the computation the overall number of steps taken by M is at most $p(n)$, where n is the overall number of bits written so far into the *input* tape of M, minus the number of bits written by M to the input tapes of other ITIs. This guarantees that a system of communicating ITMs completes in polynomial time in the overall length of inputs, even when ITMs write on the input tapes of each other. (An alternative, somewhat simpler formulation says that the overall running time of an ITM should be polynomial in the value of a 'security parameter'. However, this formulation considerably limits the expressibility of the model, especially in the case of reactive computation.

Protocols

A protocol is defined simply as an ITM. This ITM represents the code to be run by each participant, namely the set of instructions to be carried out upon receipt of an input, incoming message, or subroutine output (namely, output from a subroutine). If the protocol has different instructions for different roles, then the ITM representing the protocol should specify the behaviors of all roles. A protocol is PT if it is PT as an ITM.

Experimental Definition of Security

We flesh out the definitional plan from Section 2, for the case of two-party, stand-alone, non-reactive tasks.

The Protocol Execution Experiment

Let *n* be a two-party protocol. The protocol execution experiment proceeds as follows. There are three entities (modeled as ITIs): an entity *P*, that runs the code of π, the adversary, denoted *A*, and the environment, denoted ε.

The environment (who is activated first) provides initial inputs to *A* and the party *P* running μ; later, it obtains the final outputs of *P* and *A*.

Once either *P* or *A* is activated, with either an input value or an incoming message (i.e., a value written on the incoming communication tape), it runs its code and potentially generates a message to be written on the other party's incoming communication tape, or an output, to be read by ε. Both *P* and *A* can generate only a single output value throughout the computation.

The final output of the execution is the output of the environment. As we'll see, it's enough to let this output consist of *s* single bit.

We use the following notation. Let (),,*AxEXEC*μπε denote the random variable describing the output of environment ε when interacting with adversary *A* and protocol π on input *x* (for ε). Here, the probability is taken over the random choices of all the participating entities. Let, denote the ensemble of distributions. επ,A,EXEC(){}{}*,,0,1*AXEXECx*πε□.

An ideal process for two-party function evaluation is formulated. Let be the (potentially probabilistic) two-party function to be evaluated. {}{}(()*:0,10,1*Rf* □□→

We want to formalize a process where the parties hand their inputs to a trusted entity which evaluates f on the provided inputs and hands each party its prescribed output. For that purpose, we add to the system an additional entity (ITI), denoted *fT*, which represents the trusted party and captures the desired functionality. *P* now runs the following simple ideal protocol for *f*: When receiving input value, *P* forwards this input to *fT*. When receiving an output from *fT*, *P* forwards this output to ε. *fT* proceeds as follows: It first waits to receive input (*b, x*) from *P* and input *x*' from the adversary *A*, where {}1,2*b*□ denotes whether *x* is to be taken as the first or second input to *f*. Once the inputs are received, *fT* evaluates the function, namely it lets 3,*bbxxxx*-'←←, and ()()1212,*yyfxx*←. Next, *fT* outputs to *A*. Once it receives an ok message from *A*, b3y-*fT* output to *P*. by analogously to the protocol execution experiment, let (),,*fAIDEALx*ε denote the random variable describing the output of environment ε when interacting with adversary *A* and the ideal protocol for *f* on input *x* (for ε), where the probability is taken over the random choices of all the participating entities. Let denote the ensemble ε,A,FIDEAL(){}{}*,,0,1*FAxIDEALx*ε□.

Essentially, a two-party protocol π is said to securely evaluate a two-party function *f* if for *any* adversary *A*, that interacts with, if there *exists* another adversary, denoted *S*, that interacts with *fT*, such that no environment will be able to tell whether it is interacting with π and *A*, or alternatively with *fT* and *S*.

To provide a more rigorous definition, we first define indistinguishability of probability ensembles. A function is negligible if it tends to zero faster than any polynomial fraction, when its argument tends to infinity. Two distribution ensembles {}{}*0,1*ia*Xχ□= and {}{}*0,1*ia*Xχ□□= are indistinguishable (denoted χχ≈) if for any the statistical distance between distributions and is a negligible function of *k*.{},0,1*kaa*'□aX'aX^2. Secure evaluation is then defined as follows:

Definition (Basic security for two-party function evaluation)

A two-party protocol π securely evaluates a two-party function f if for any PT adversary A there exists a PT adversary S such that for all PT environments ε that output only one bit:

επε≈,A,,S,fEXECIDEAL

SOME BASIC SECURITY TERMS

Database Intersection

We consider the task mentioned in Section 2: Two parties, each having a list of items, wish to find out which items appear in both lists. Here both parties have private inputs and both have private outputs which are different than, but related to each other. Still, it can be formulated as a function in a straightforward way:

()()()()()()112211221111,...,,,...,,...,,,...,,*DInmnmfxxxxbbbb*=

where if 1*ijb*=*ijx* equals 3*ijx*-' for some j', and 0*ijb*= otherwise. This would mean that a party *P* which follows the protocol is guaranteed to get a valid answer based on its own database *x* and some database *x*', where *x*' was determined by the other party based only on the initial input of the other party. Furthermore, the information learned by the other party is computed based on the same two values *x* and *x*'. Also, if there is reason to believe that the other party used some concrete 'real' database *x*', then correctness is guaranteed with respect to that specific *x*'. Recall, however, that the definition does not guarantee fairness. That is, the other party may obtain the output value first, and based on that value decide whether *P* will obtain its output value. We will see how to express fairness within an extended formalism.

Common Randomness

Next, we consider a task that involves randomness requirements from the outputs of the parties. Specifically, we consider the task of generating a common string that is guaranteed to be taken from a pre-defined distribution, say the uniform distribution over the strings of some length: ()(,*kCRfrr*--=, where *r* is a random *k*-bit string. Here, the parties are guaranteed that the output *r* is distributed (pseudo) randomly over {. Furthermore, each party is guaranteed that the other party does not have any 'trapdoor information' on *r* that cannot be efficiently computed from *r* alone. As mentioned in the Introduction, this guarantee becomes crucial in some cryptographic applications. Finally, as in the previous case, fairness is not guaranteed. }0,1*k*

Zero Knowledge

Let be a binary relation, and consider the bivariate function ()()()()(),,,,,*RZKfxwxRxw*-=- That is, the first party (the 'prover') has input (x, w), while the second party (the 'verifier') has empty input. The verifier should learn or; plus the one-bit value R(x, w), and nothing else. The prover should learn nothing from the interaction. In particular, when R is the relation associated with an NP language L (that is, (){}|s.t.,1*defRLLxwRxw*==□=).

These requirements are very reminiscent of the requirements from a Zero-Knowledge protocol for L: The verifier is guaranteed that it accepts, or outputs (x, 1), only when x □ L (soundness), and the prover is guaranteed that the verifier learns nothing more other than whether x □ L (zero-knowledge).

It is tempting to conclude that a protocol is Zero-Knowledge for language LR if and only if it securely realizes *RZKf*. This statement is true 'in spirit', but some technical caveats exist. Below, we discuss these caveats; readers that are satisfied with a more intuitive notion of Zero-Knowledge or are not familiar with its classic definition may safely skip this discussion.

The first caveat is that define Zero Knowledge so that both parties receive x as input, whereas here the verifier learns x only via the protocol. This difference, however, is only 'cosmetic' and can be resolved via simple syntactic transformations between protocols. The remaining two differences are more substantial: First, securely realizing *RZKf* only guarantees 'computational sound-ness', namely soundness against PT adversarial provers. Second, securely realizing *RZKf* implies an additional, somewhat implicit requirement: When the adversary plays the role of a potentially misbehaving prover, the definition requires the simulator to explicitly hand the input *x* and the witness *w* to the trusted party. To do this, the simulator should be able to 'extract' these values from the messages sent by the adversary. This requirement has the flavor of a proof of knowledge, albeit in a slightly milder form that does not require a black-box extractor.

In conclusion, we have that a protocol securely realizes *RZKf* if and only if a slight modification of the protocol is a computationally sound Zero-Knowledge proof of knowledge for L_R (with potentially non black-box extractors).

The Protocol Execution Experiment

We describe the generalized protocol execution experiment. Let π be a protocol to be executed. As before, the model for executing π is parameterized by an environment ε and an adversary *A*.

Initially, the system consists only of ε and *A*. During the execution, ε invoke as many parties (ITIs) as it wishes, and determine their identities. All of these parties run π. In addition, ε can write on the input tapes of the parties throughout the computation, and parties can hand outputs to ε. In addition, ε can give initial input to *A* and can obtain a single (presumable final) output message from *A*. No other interaction between ε and the system is allowed. Once a party is activated, either with an input value, or with an incoming message, it follows its code and potentially generates an outgoing message or an output. All outgoing messages are handed to the adversary, regardless of the stated destinations of the messages. Outputs are handed to [. Parties may also invoke new subroutines (ITIs), that may run either π or another code. However, these subroutines are not allowed to directly communicate with ε. Once the adversary is activated, it can deliver a message to a party, i.e. write the message on the party's incoming communication tape. In its last activation it can also generate an output, i.e. write the output value on the incoming communication tape of ε. As before, the final output of the execution is the (one bit) output of the environment. With little chance of confusion, we re-define the notation $\mathrm{EXEC}_{\mu,A,\varepsilon}$ to refer to the present modeling.

The Ideal Process

The main difference from the ideal process in Section 3 is that, instead of considering only trusted parties that perform a restricted set of operations (such as evaluating a function), we let the trusted party run arbitrary code, and in particular to repeatedly interact with the parties, as well as directly with the adversary. We say that the code run by the trusted party is the ideal functionality representing the task.In addition, the richer system model allows us to simplify the presentation by formulating the ideal process as a special case of the general protocol execution experiment. That is, given an ideal functionality *F*, we define an ideal protocol I_F as follows: When a party running I_F obtains an input value, it immediately copies this value to the input of F. (The first party to do so will also invoke *F*.) When a party receives an output from F (on its subroutine output tape), it immediately outputs this value to ε.

The notation $\text{IDEAL}_{F,A,\varepsilon}$ it is replaced by $\text{EXECI}_{F,}\text{A},\varepsilon$.

Protocol Emulation and Secure Realization

The notion of realizing an ideal process remains essentially the same. Yet, formalizing the ideal process as an execution of a special type of a protocol allows formalizing the definition of realizing an ideal functionality as a special case of the more general notion of emulating one protocol by another. That is:

Definition (Protocol emulation with basic security)

A protocol π emulates protocol φ if for any PT adversary A there exists a PT adversary S such that for all PT environments ε that output only one bit:

,,,,»*SAEXECEXEC*φεπ

Definition (Realizing Functionalities with Basic Security)

A protocol π realizes an ideal functionality *F* if π emulates I_F, the ideal protocol for *F*.

COMPOSITION OF PROTOCOLS

This section provides a brief taxonomy of the different types of protocol composition operations considered in the literature, namely the various ways of combining together protocols in a single system. Taking another point of view, these operations naturally correspond to different ways of de-composing a complex system into separate pieces, which we would like to view as individual 'protocols.'

Timing Coordination

This parameter refers to the possible ways in which the messages of the individual executions can interleave with each other. Salient option include:

Sequential Composition

Here, no two messages of different protocol executions may interleave. That is, when ordering the events of sending and receiving of messages in the system along a common time axis, then all the events related to each protocol execution must form an uninterrupted sequence.

Enforcing global sequentiality requires each party to locally coordinate the different executions in terms of the timing of message sending. It also requires some level of global coordination among the parties, to guarantee that no party 'gets ahead of the pack' and starts sending messages of a new execution before other parties completed prior executions.

N On-Concurrent Composition

This is a somewhat more general variant that allows 'nesting' of protocol executions, as long as there is no 'interleaving' of messages. That is, assume some message of execution el was delivered, and at a later point a message of execution was delivered. Then, once another message of execution is delivered, messages of execution can no longer be delivered. Also here, guaranteeing global non-interleaving requires global coordination. 2*e*1*e*2*e*

Parallel Composition

Here it is assumed that the messages in each protocol execution are naturally associated with 'rounds', where a 'round *i* message' is sent only in response to receiving a 'round *i* – 1 message'. The composed execution of a given set of protocol executions allows any interleaving of protocol messages, as long as all the 'round *i* messages' of all the executions are delivered before any 'round $i + 1$ message' is delivered. While this composition method is also quite restrictive and requires global timing coordination among the executions, it is natural in synchronous systems where messages are naturally associated with rounds.

Concurrent Composition

Here, any interleaving of messages from different protocol executions is allowed. Clearly, concurrent composition allows both sequential and parallel composition as special cases. It also allows many other special types of interleaving, such as the common case where various executions wait for an external global event to proceed. Concurrent composition is very powerful in that it requires no timing coordination among the various executions. Indeed, the timing of events may of course be adversarially coordinated.

INPUT COORDINATION

This parameter refers to the possible relations between the input values to the various protocol executions. We distinguish three variants:

Same Input

Here each party has the same input value for all the executions. Taking the role of a party in a protocol as part of its input, this means that each party has the same role in all the executions it participates in. Still, different executions may include different parties. (A somewhat more restrictive case is where the same set of parties participate in all executions.)

Fixed Inputs

Here the inputs to different executions can be arbitrarily different from each other. In particular, a party may have different roles in different executions. (For instance a party may be a receiver in one execution of a commitment protocol, and a committer in a different execution.) Still, all inputs, including the set of participants in each execution, are fixed in advance before the execution of the composed system starts.

Adaptively Chosen Inputs

Here each input to each party in each execution can be determined adaptively based on the current state of the composed system. This is, of course, the most general setting of this parameter, and includes the above two settings as special cases. Variants of this setting depend on the amount of information available to the entities that choose the inputs; for instance, the inputs of a given party may be determined only based on the information available to that party, or alternatively based on the current global state of the system.

PROTOCOL COORDINATION

This parameter refers to the possible relations between the *programs,* or *codes,* executed in different executions. We distinguish two main cases:

Self Composition

Here all executions run the same program. A closely related case is where different executions may run different programs, but the set of programs is fixed and known in advance. (Indeed, running a fixed number of programs is equivalent to running a single program that multiplexes between the many programs depending on the input.)

General Composition

Here a given execution of a protocol may be running alongside arbitrary other protocols (i.e., programs) that may not be known in advance. Furthermore, these programs may be determined adaptively, depending on the protocol in question and potentially even on the current state of the composed system. This is indeed a highly adversarial setting. Still, it seems to adequately model the situation in open and unregulated networks such as the global Internet.

STATE COORDINATION

This parameter refers to the amount and type of information that is shared among different executions. We distinguish the following cases:

Independent States

This is the 'classic' case of protocol composition where different executions have no shared state. That is, the local variables of each execution within each participant are seen only by that execution. Also, the random choices made within each execution are independent from those in other executions. (Of course, different executions can still have related inputs).

Joint State

Here, some variables or random choices may be visible to multiple protocol executions. One salient example of such a setting is a protocol where the same secret signing key for a signature scheme is used in multiple protocol executions (say, for generating multiple session keys). Another example is a 'common random string', namely a public string that is drawn from some distribution and is assumed to be globally available in the system. Here the 'joint part' is typically modeled as a 'subroutine protocol' that takes input from and provides output to multiple protocol executions. We note that, although this type of composition is somewhat non-traditional, without it would not be possible to de-compose such systems into smaller components such as a single exchange of a key in a key-exchange protocol.

NUMBER OF EXECUTIONS

This parameter determines the number of protocol executions that run together in the composed system. It is crucial, in the sense that, for most settings of the rest of the parameters and for each i, it is possible to construct protocols that 'compose securely' as long as at most i executions run together, but break as soon as the system involves $i + 1$ execution.

Three salient settings are:

Fixed Number of Executions

Here the number of executions is fixed in advance. In particular, it does not depend on the input, nor on a security parameter.

Bounded Number of Executions

The maximum number of executions may depend on public information, such as the security parameter or some global input, but is known when designing the protocol. In particular, the complexity of the protocol may depend on this bound.

Unbounded Number of Executions

The number of executions is chosen adversarial in an adaptive way, and is limited only by the runtime of the adversary. In particular, it may depend on the execution, and remain unknown to all or some of the parties.

Some studied settings. Almost any combination of the above parameters yields a meaningful setting for the study of security-preserving protocol composition. Yet, some settings have been the focus of much dedicated study, both in the context of specific primitives such as key-exchange, zero-knowledge or commitment, and in more general contexts. We briefly mention some of these settings (For sake of conciseness and brevity, we do not expand here on the specific contributions of the works mentioned below, nor on the notions of security that are obtained in each of these settings.)

CONCLUSION AND FUTURE WORK

This paper addressed the challenges associated with rigorously modeling cryptographic protocols and capturing their security properties. Particular stress was put on guaranteeing security in settings where protocols are composed with each other in a number of ways. We have reviewed a general definitional approach, the trusted party paradigm. We saw two formalizations of this approach: A basic formalization, that is easier to satisfy but provides only limited secure composability guarantees, and a more advanced formalization that is considerably more restrictive in general, but provides very strong secure composability guarantees.

When looking back at the covered material, one thing becomes very clear: It is far from obvious what is 'the right' way to capture and formalize security properties of cryptographic protocols. In fact, there probably is no single good way to do so, and different formalisms have incomparable strengths.

Furthermore, seemingly small differences in the formalisms result in drastic differences - both in the meaningfulness (e.g. in the behavior under protocol composition), and also in the restrictiveness, namely in the ability to assert security of natural protocols.

One consequence of this fact is that finding viable notions of security for cryptographic protocols remains an intriguing and lively research area. Another consequence is that appropriately formulating the security requirements of a given cryptographic task can be a delicate challenge in itself. In fact, this is often the 'hard part' of the security analysis, more so than actually asserting that a given protocol satisfies the formulated property in the devised model.

REFERENCES

1. A. Yao, How to generate and exchange results, FOCS pp. 162-167, 1986.
2. Goldreich. Foundations of Cryptography (Vol. 2) Cambridge Press, 2001.
3. M. Backes, C. Jacobi, B. Pfitzmann. Deriving Cryptographically Sound Implementations Using Composition and Formally Verified Bisimulation. In proceedings of Formal Methods Europe (FME) 2002, pp. 310-329.
4. M. Backes, B. Pfitzmann, and M. Waidner. A composable cryptographic library with nested operations. In 10th ACM conference on computer and communications security (CCS), 2003. Extended version at the eprint archive, http://eprint.iacr.org/2003/015/.
5. J.M. Backes, B. Pfitzmann, and M. Waidner. A general composition theorem for secure reactive systems. In 1st Theory of Cryptography Conference (TCC), LNCS 2951 pp. 336354, Feb. 2004.
6. B. Barak, R. Canetti, Y. Lindell, R. Pass and T. Rabin. Secure Computation Without Authentication. In Crypto'05, 2005.
7. B. Barak, R. Canetti, J. B. Nielsen, R. Pass. Universally Composable Protocols with Relaxed Set-Up Assumptions. 45th FOCS, pp. 186-195. 2004.
8. B. Barak and A. Sahai, How To Play Almost Any Mental Game Over the Net – Concurrent Composition via Super-Polynomial Simulation. 46th FOCS, 2005.
9. D. Beaver. Secure Multi-party Protocols and Zero-Knowledge Proof Systems Tolerating a Faulty Minority. J. Cryptology, (1991) 4: 75-122.

10. D. Beaver and S. Haber. Cryptographic protocols provably secure against dynamic adversaries. In Eurocrypt '92, LNCS No. 658, 1992, pp. 307-323.
11. M. Bellare and P. Rogaway. Entity authentication and key distribution. CRYPTO'93, LNCS. 773, pp. 232-249, 1994.
12. M. Ben-Or, R. Canetti and O. Goldreich. Asynchronous Secure Computation. 25th Symposium on Theory of Computing (STOC), 1993, pp. 52-61. Longer version appears in TR #750, CS dept., Technion, 1992.
13. M. Ben-Or, S. Goldwasser and A. Wigderson. Completeness Theorems for NonCryptographic Fault-Tolerant Distributed Computation. 20th Symposium on Theory of Computing (STOC), ACM, 1988, pp. 1-10.
14. M. Ben-Or, B. Kelmer and T. Rabin. Asynchronous Secure Computations with Optimal Resilience. 13th PODC, 1994, pp. 183-192.
15. M. Blum. Coin flipping by telephone. IEEE Spring COMPCOM, pp. 133-137, Feb. 1982.
16. G. Brassard, D. Chaum and C. Crepeau. Minimum Disclosure Proofs of Knowledge. JCSS, Vol. 37, No.2, pages 156-189, 1988.

Cryptographic Attacks and Steganography

2

Brijesh Kumar Chaurasia and
Rajendra Singh Kushwah

ABSTRACT

An attack plays important roles in network security. In this paper we describe about cryptographic attacks, types of attacks and one step ahead to cryptography i.e. Steganography. We describe about what is stenography and it can be used in media and image encoding techniques to information hiding in images.

INTRODUCTION

An attack is nothing but simple invasion to security through a loose patch or loose fencing. The attacks on e-documents as well as network systems are categories into types of

(1) Theoretical concepts behind these attacks.

(2) Practical approaches used by attackers.

Now in Theoretical concepts we have

(a) **Interception:** It attacks the principle of Confidentiality, which specifies that only the sender, and the intended recipients should be able to access a message and to understand this. Let a email is send between user A and user B but if it is accessed by another user C then it is said to be Interception [1].

(b) **Fabrication:** It breaks the principle of Authentication that establishes the proof of identities.

(c) **Modification:** It breaks the concept of Integrity because modification to information is a loss of message.

(d) **Interruption:** It breaks the principle of Availability which states that resources which are in the form of information should be available to authorized parties at all times.

These attacks are further grouped into two types: PASSIVE and ACTIVE attacks [10].

In **passive** attacks, the attacker aims to obtain information that is in transit and *it does not attempt to perform any modification to the data.* The general approaches to deal with these attack is to prevent it rather than taking detective or corrective actions.

In case of **active** attacks, there is a *modification to the original information in some manner or a creation of false information.* They can be detected with some effort and measures can be taken to recover from them. Generally, these attacks are in the form of interruption, modification and fabrication attack. The interruption attacks are called as masquerade attacks which is caused by when an unauthorized entity pretends to be another entity which is not a valid one. In modification attacks there is further replay attacks and alteration of messages. In replay attacks, a user captures a sequence of events or some data units and then resends them to take malafide advantage from it and alteration to message means change to original message. In fabrication attacks there is a Denial of Service (DOS) by preventing legitimate user from accessing some services [10] which they are eligible for.

There are many types of attacks described in below:

Ciphertext-only Attack

This is the situation where the attacker does not know anything about the contents of the message, and must work from cipher text only. In practice, it is quite often possible to make guesses about the plaintext, as many types of messages have fixed format headers. Even ordinary letters and documents begin in a very predictable way. For example, many classical attacks use frequency analysis of the ciphertext, however, this does not work well against modern ciphers [11, 2]. Modern cryptosystems are not weak against ciphertext-only attacks, although sometimes they are considered with the added assumption that the message contains some statistical bias.

Known-Plaintext Attack

The attacker knows or can guess the plaintext for some parts of the ciphertext. The task is to decrypt the rest of the ciphertext blocks using this information. This may be done by determining the key used to encrypt the data, or via some shortcut [11, 2].

One of the best known modern known-plaintext attacks is linear cryptanalysis against block ciphers.

Chosen-Plaintext Attack

The attacker is able to have any text he likes encrypted with the unknown key. The task is to determine the key used for encryption.

A good example of this attack is the differential cryptanalysis which can be applied against block ciphers (and in some cases also against hash functions).

Some cryptosystems, particularly RSA[8] are vulnerable to chosen-plaintext attacks. When such algorithms are used, care must be taken to design the application (or protocol) so that an attacker can never have chosen plaintext encrypted.

Man-In-The-Middle Attack

This attack is relevant for cryptographic communication and key exchange protocols. The idea is that when two parties, A and B, are exchanging keys for secure communication (for example, using Diffie-Hallman [8, 9]), an adversary positions himself between A and B on the communication line. The adversary then intercepts the signals that A and B send to each other, and performs a key exchange with A and B separately. A and B will end up using a different key, each of which is known to the adversary. The adversary can then decrypt any communication from A with the key he shares with A, and then resends the communication to B by encrypting it again with the key he shares with B. Both A and B will think that they are communicating securely, but in fact the adversary is hearing everything.

The usual way to prevent the man-in-the-middle attack is to use a public-key cryptosystem capable of providing digital signatures. For set up, the parties must know each other's public keys in advance. After the shared secret has been generated, the parties send digital signatures of it to each other. The man-in-the-middle fails in his attack, because he is unable to forge these signatures without the knowledge of the private keys used for signing.

This solution is sufficient if there also exists a way to securely distribute public keys. One such way is a certification hierarchy such as X.509. It is used for example in IPSec.

Correlation

Between the secret key and the output of the cryptosystem is the main source of information to the cryptanalyst. In the easiest case, the information about the secret key is directly leaked by the cryptosystem. More complicated cases require studying the correlation (basically, any relation that would not be expected on the basis of chance alone) between the observed (or measured) information about the cryptosystem and the guessed key information.

For example, in linear (resp. differential) attacks against block ciphers the cryptanalyst studies the known (resp. chosen) plaintext and the observed ciphertext. Guessing some of the key bits of the cryptosystem the analyst determines by correlation between the plaintext and the ciphertext whether she guessed correctly. This can be repeated, and has many variations[9, 11].

The differential cryptanalysis introduced by Eli Biham and Adi Shamir in late 1980s was the first attack that fully utilized this idea against block ciphers (especially against DES). Later Mitsuru Matsui came up with linear cryptanalysis which was even more effective against DES. More recently, new attacks using similar ideas have been developed. Perhaps, the best introduction to this material is the proceedings of EUROCRYPT and CRYPTO throughout the 1990s. There, one can find Mitsuru Matsui's discussion of linear cryptanalysis of DES, and the ideas of truncated differentials by Lars Knudsen (for example, IDEA cryptanalysis). The book by Eli Biham and Adi Shamir about the differential cryptanalysis of DES is the "classical" work on this subject. The correlation idea is fundamental to cryptography and several researchers have tried to construct cryptosystems which are provably secure against such attacks. For example, Knudsen and Nyberg have studied provable security against differential cryptanalysis.

Attack against or Using the Underlying Hardware

In the last few years, as more and smaller mobile crypto devices have come into widespread use, a new category of attacks has become relevant which aims directly at the hardware implementation of the cryptosystem. The attacks use the data from very fine measurements of the crypto device doing, say, encryption and compute key information from these measurements. The basic ideas are then closely related to those in other correlation attacks. For instance, the attacker guesses some key bits and attempts to verify the correctness of the guess by studying correlation against her measurements.

Several attacks have been proposed such as using careful timings of the device, fine measurements of the power consumption, and radiation patterns. These measurements can be used to obtain the secret key or other kind of information stored on the device. This attack is generally independent of the used cryptographical algorithms and can be applied to any device that is not explicitly protected against it.

In real life, attacks come in the form of application level attacks and network level attacks and at application level the attacker attempts to access, modify or prevent access to information of a particular application or the application itself. In the network level these attacks aims at reducing the capabilities of a network by a number of possible means. These attacks make an attempt to either slow down or completely bring to halt a computer network. By using virus, one can launch an application level attack or a network level attack and a virus infected system or network can be repaired or controlled by using good backup procedures worm is similar to virus but different in implementations and it replicates itself again and again. And this leads system or network Overloaded and functionally very slow so that it may come to halt.

Now to ensure secure information in communication of data or information we rely upon Hash Functions [2, 3, 4] which are used to providing data integrity check on stored data and authentication on signed data in digital signatures hash function accepts a variable size message as input and produces a fixed size hash code, called the message digest. The hash code is a function of all the bits of the message and provides error detection capabilities. The attack are not much proficient to break the dedicated hash functions. It has successful applications in stenography.

WHAT IS STEGANOGRAPHY

Steganography concerns itself with the ways of embedding a secret message in a cover object such as audio or video files., this a parameterized with a key and without knowledge of which it is difficult for a third party to detect or remove the embedded material. Steganography should not be confused with cryptography where the message is transformed so as to make it's meaning obscure to a person who intercepts it. There has been a considerable growth in this subject. The publishing and broadcasting industries have become interested in techniques for hiding encrypted copyrights and serial numbers in digital films, audio recordings, books and multimedia products Because of ease of the digital works and it's distribution, there is a ease to copy it. There is difference between classical steganography and copyright marking. In the former, a successful attack consists of the warden's observing that a given object is marked. In the second. all the participants in the scheme are aware that marks are in use so some effects of the marks may be observable. So a successful attack does not mean detecting attack, rather rendering it useless.

Term Used in Steganography

There are some terminology used in steganography which was given at First Hiding Workshop, 1996 held in Cambridge, U.K.

Cover is used to describe the original, innocent message data, audio, video and so on. When referring to audio signal steganography, the cover signal is sometimes called the Host signal.

Embedded data is the information to be hidden in the cover data.

Stego data is the data containing both the cover signal and the embedded information.

Container is the cover image referring to image Steganography.

Steganography in Media-The "Kerckhoff principle" in cryptography states that the security of the system has to be based on the assumption that the enemy has the full knowledge of the design and implementation details of the steganographic system. The only missing information for the enemy is a short random number sequence, key. Without this secret key, the enemy should not have the chance to even suspect that an observed communication channel or hidden communication is taking place. When embedding data, Bender et al [6] remind us that it is important to remember the following restrictions and features:

The cover data should not be degraded by the embedded data and the embedded data should be as imperceptible as possible. The embedded data should be directly encoded into the media, rather than into header or wrapper, to maintain data consistency across formats. The embedded data should be immune as possible to modifications from intelligent attacks or anticipated manipulations such as filtering or re-sampling. Some degradation of the data can be expected when the cover data is modified. To minimize this, error correcting codes should be used. The embedded data should be Self-clocking or arbitrarily re-enterant. This ensures that the embedded data can still be extracted when only portions of the cover data are available. For example, if only a part of Image is available, the embedded data should still be recoverable.

Steganography in Images

In image Steganography, we concern, with exploiting the limited power of the visual system [7]. Within reason, any plain text, ciphertext, other images, or anything that can be embedded in a bit stream can be hidden in a image. Image Steganography has come quite far in recent years with the development of fast, powerful graphical computers and steganographic software is now available in public domain everyday user.

CONCLUSION

We presented details on cryptographic attacks and Steganography techniques that is the science of hidden messages. Cryptanalysis is the art of deciphering encrypted communications without knowing the proper keys. There are many cryptanalytic techniques and attacks described above in this paper. Steganography techniques have a significant role in e-security and we present in brief that it can be used in media and image encoding techniques to information hiding in images.

REFERENCES

1. W. Stallings; Cryptography and Network Security, Principles and practice, Prentice Hall Publications, 1999.
2. Applied Cryptography by Bruce Schneir, Wiley Publication, 2002.
3. R. Anderson; The classification of Hash Functions, Proceedings of IMA conference in Cryptography and coding, 1993
4. R. Anderson and E. Bjham; Tiger: A fast new hash function, Proceedings of Fast software Encryption 3, Cmabridge 1996.
5. S. Bakhtiari, R. Safavi-Naini and J. Piperzyk; Cryptographic Hash Functions, 1995.
6. N. F. Johnson and S. Jajodia, "Exploring Steganography: Seeing the unseen" Computer 31, no. 2 pp. 26-34, 1998.
7. W. Bender, D. Gruhl, N. Morimoto, and A. Lu., "Techniques for data hiding" In IBM Systems Journal Vol. 35, Nos. 3-4, pp. 313-336, 1996.
8. A. Kahate, Cryptography and Network Security, Tata McGraw Hills Publications.

Cryptography: Study on Use of Cryptography Technique in Digital Signature and, an Overview of Legal Framework of Digital Signature in an IT Act

3

Snehalata Bhat (Kaul) and *Hemlata Jankinath Bhat*

ABSTRACT

Cryptography is an application system for network security. This concept has existed for our financial, national and other field's security. In this technique secret data/information will hide its original substance into by some different method like plain text is converted into coding text and later again converted through cryptography in to plain text in data readable form. In this way the security of the data/information can be formed. The process of disguising a message in such a way as to hide its substance is called "encryption". An encrypted message is called "cipher text". The process of turning a cipher text back into the plain text is called "decryption". Cryptography is the art and science of keeping message secure. The 'Cryptography', concept was applicable more frequently in Military. In past, the messages to be encrypted have traditionally been given to poorly paid clerk for encryption and transmission. The sheer volume of messages prevented this work from being done by a few elite specialists. But in the age of computerization, cryptography techniques is used for data security and transmission from head quarter to battle field. Today, Cryptography concepts are also used for detection of forgery in signature. This technique is used in the digital signatures. Digital signatures like other signature authenticate record. Digital signatures are unique to individuals and cannot be initiated.

Hence, in the context of the above information, the aim of this paper is to present the details about the cryptography techniques. The study will also cover:

(*a*) *Use of Cryptography techniques in Digital Signature.*

(*b*) *An overview of legal framework of Digital Signature in an IT Act.*

INTRODUCTION

The process of disguising a message in such a way as to hide its substance is called encryption. An encrypted message is called cipher text. The process of converting a cipher text back in to plain text is called decryption

Cryptography is the art and science of keeping e-banking customer messages or information secure. It uses a 'Key' for encrypting or decrypting a message. Both the mother of encryption and the size of key are important to ensure confidentiality of an e-banking customer's information.

There are two types of encryption.

(1) Symmetric key and

(2) Asymmetric key

In the symmetric key cryptography scheme, the same key is used to encrypt and decrypt the message. Common symmetric algorithms include One-time pad encryption, Data encryption algorithm (DES), Triple DES, LOKI, Twofish, Blowfish, and International Data Encryption Algorithm (IDEA). DES and Triple Des are the commonly used techniques.

Asymmetric key cryptographic scheme is also known as Public key crypto-system. Here, two keys are used. One key is kept secret and therefore it is referred as "private key". The other key is made widely available to anyone who wants it, and is referred as "public key".

The public key and private key are mathematically related so that information encrypted using the public key can only be decrypted by the corresponding private key and vice versa. Importantly, it is near to impossible to find out the private key from the public key. Some common and more popular public key cryptosystem algorithms are Diffie-Hellman, RSA, and Elliptic Curve etc. In all these, the confidentiality is directly related to the key size. Larger the key size, the longer it takes to break the encrypted message. This technique is used in digital signature to secure the important information and control the use of e-banking services in authorized way.

Digital Signature and Certification

A banker has to play a decisive role if frauds through signatures are to be prevented. The banker has to practice identification and adopt preventive measures for successful operations. With modern instruments such as scanner and plotter, it is possible to reproduce every signature perfectly and to copy it. A digital signature system with some technical warnings has a higher degree of security. Digital Signature performs three functions:

(a) Data Integrity

(b) Data Authentication,

(c) Non-repudiation

A digital Signature is a personalized thumb print. It is the encryption of an electronic document by a key. Acceptance of forged signature can be financial hazard to the banker, a bad name and a great irritation to the customer. Signatures of a person are his graphic identity and usually the signatures are names written after abbreviations. Digital signatures authenticate the identity of a sender, through the private, cryptographic key. Every digital signature is different because it is derived from the content of message itself. The combination of identity authentication and singularly unique signature results in a transmission that can not be repudiated. Digital signature can be applied to any data transmission, including e-mail. To generate digital signature, the original, unencrypted message is processed through mathematical algorithms that generate 'message digest' (a unique character representation of data). This process is known as 'hashing'. The message digest is then encrypted with the private key and sent along with the message (which could be encrypted also). The recipient receives both the message and encrypted message digest. The recipient decrypts the message digest using the sender's public key, and then runs the message through the hash function again. If the result message digest matches the one sent with the message, the message has not been altered and data integrity is verified. Because the message digest was encrypted using the private key, the sender can be identified and bound to the specific message.

Certification Authorities and Digital Certificates

Certification Authorities and Digital Certificates are emerging to further address the issues of authentication, non-repudiation, data privacy and cryptographic key management. A Certificate Authority (CA) is a trusted third party that verifies the identity of a party to a transaction. To do this, the Certificate Authority (CA) vouches for the identity of a party by attaching the CA's digital signature to any messages, public keys, etc., which are transmitted. The CA must be trusted by the parties involved, and identities must have been proven to the CA beforehand Digital Certificates are messages that are signed with the CA's private key. They identify the CA, the represented party, and even include the represented party's public key.

Legal Framework on Digital Signature

It is a big headache to the law enforcement agencies throughout the world. Development of signatures is development of handwriting. Advance age and accidents; affect both mental and physical health. The legal provision has been made in the IT ACT, 2000 (Section 47A) to be part of the Indian Evidence Act. The court has to form an opinion on the digital signature, of any person. The opinion of the Certifying Authority which has issued the Digital Certificates is a relevant fact. The process of the proof of verification has been incorporated in Section 73A of the Indian Evidence Act-, a new section in the IT ACT, 2000 (Second Schedule).

Some of the provisions of the act are:

(a) Authentication of Electronic Records

Subject to the provision any subscriber may authenticate an electronic record by affixing his digital signature. The authentication of the electronic record shall be effected by the use of asymmetric cryptosystem and hash function which envelop and transform the initial electronic record into another electronic record.

(b) License to Issue Digital Signature Certificates

(i) Subject to the provisions of Sub-section (2), any person may make an application, to the controller, for a license to issue Digital Signature Certificates.

(ii) No license shall be issued under sub-section (1), unless the applicant fulfils such requirements with respect to qualification, expertise, manpower, financial resources and other infrastructure facilities, which are necessary to issue Digital signature Certificates as may be prescribed by the Central Government.

(iii) A license granted under this section shall:-

(a) Be valid for such period as may be prescribed by the Central Government; not transferable or Heritable;

(b) Be subject to such terms and conditions as may be specified by the regulations;

(c) Receipt occurs at the time when the electronic record enters the designated computer resources; or

(d) If the electronic record is sent to computer resources of the addresses that is not the designated computer resources, receipt occurs at the time when the electronic record is retrieved by the addressee.

(c) Secure Electronic Records and Secure Digital Signatures

(i) **Secure Electronic Record:** Where any security procedure has been applied to an electronic record at a specific point of time, then such record shall be deemed to be a secure electronic record from such point of time to time verification.

(ii) **Note on Clause 14 As Appended to the Bill:** This clause provides for the security procedures which have to be applied to an electronic record for being treated as a secure electronic record.

(iii) **The Digital Signature:** If by, application of a security procedure agreed to by the parties concerned, it can be verified that digital signature, at the time it was affixed, was:

(a) Unique to the subscriber affixing it;

(b) Capable of identifying such subscriber;

(c) Created in a manner or using a means under the exclusive control of the subscriber and is linked to the electronic record to which it relates in such a manner that if the electronic record was altered the digital signature world be invalidated.

Then such digital signature shall be deemed to be a secure digital signature.

(iv) **Security Procedure:** The Central Government shall for the purpose of this Act prescribe the security procedure having regard to commercial circumstances prevailing at the time when the procedure was used, including:

(a) The nature of the transaction;

(b) The level of sophistication of the parties with reference to their technological capacity.

(c) The volume of similar transactions engaged in by other parties;

(d) The availability of alternatives offered to but rejected by any party;

(e) The çost of alternative procedures; and

(f) The procedures in general use for similar types of transactions or communications.

CONCLUSIONS

As per above information, Cryptography is an application system for network security. This concept has existed for our financial, national and other field's security. In this technique, important information will be coded by some different methods like letters in the data replaced by other understanding your data or information. This method was traditionally also applied manually especially in military area for capture and transformation of secret information from one place to another. Today, banks face various problems to find out the authorized person of the account. A banker has to play a decisive role if frauds through signatures are to be prevented. Many cases happen for forgery of signatures. The banker has to practice identification and adopt preventive measures for successful operations. To avoid this, "Digital Signature" Concept is introduced. In Digital Signature, the Cryptography technology is applied. Digital signatures like other signatures authenticate record. In this technique (cryptography), our secret data/information will hide its original substance into by some different method like plain text is converted into coding text and later again convert through cryptography in to plain text in data readable form, therefore in this way the security of the data/information can be formed. The process of disguising a message in such a way as to hide its substance is called "encryption". An encrypted message is called "cipher text". The process of turning a cipher text back into the plain text is called "decryption". The legal provision has been, made in the IT Act 2000 (section 47 A) for the digital signature. The major provisions under this are:

- Authentication of Electronic Records
- License to issue Digital Signature Certificates
- Secure Electronic Records and Secure Digital Signatures.

Hence, the Conclusion of the study is, that Cryptography techniques is useful to secure data at the time of transmission and this is also applied in digital signature. It will be more beneficial for forgery detection.

Acknowledgements

I am very much thankful to My Research Guide, Dr. Syed Abdul Mannan, Reader and Head of the Department of Commerce and Management Science, Mulana Azad College of Arts, Science and Commerce Aurangabad, for guiding me for completion of this paper and providing valuable information about the topic.

REFERENCES

1. URL from RBI Reports of Internet Banking.
2. E-Banking by Vasu Deva for Commonwealth Publishers.

3. Information System for Banks–Indian Institute of Banking & Finance, Taxman Publications (P.) Ltd.
4. e-commerce by C.S.V. Murthy – Himalaya Publishing House.
5. Computer Networks by Andrew S. Tanenabum.

Role of IPTV in Entertainment

Saurabh Pareek

ABSTRACT

With the ever changing scenario of the information sector new inventions and discoveries of the things needed or required by the human being are taking place either for his comfort or for development or for his entertainment.

Nowadays, everything is going to be related with information technology or with electronic technology then how the entertainment sector can be left behind. After the invention of "zoopraxiscope" in 1867 a lot of changes had been done in this field.

In the past, television was only distributed via cable, satellite, or terrestrial systems. The primary models for Internet television are streaming Internet TV or selectable video on an Internet location, typically a website.

Today — with the increase in Internet connection speeds, advances in technology, the increase of total number of people online, and the decrease in connection costs — it has become increasingly common to find traditional television content accessible freely and legally over the Internet. In addition to this, new Internet-only television content has appeared which is not distributed via cable, satellite, or terrestrial systems.

IPTV describes a system capable of receiving and displaying a video stream encoded as a series of Internet Protocol packets. If you've ever watched a video clip on your computer, you've used an IPTV system in its broadest sense. When most people discuss IPTV, though, they're talking about watching traditional channels on your television, where people demand a smooth, high-resolution, lag-free picture, and it's the telcos that are jumping headfirst into this market. Once known only as phone companies, the telcos now want to turn a "triple play" of voice, data, and video that will retire the side and put them securely in the batter's box.

INTRODUCTION

IPTV, short for Internet Protocol Television, is a new method of delivering and viewing television programming using an IP network and high speed broadband access technology. More than simply a new distribution and playback method, IPTV is poised to create an entirely new mindset about the television experience. Whereas current terrestrial broadcast television is the same content sent continuously to all consumers' homes, IPTV removes the fixed television schedule. Similar to how information on the Internet can be downloaded and viewed at any time, IPTV enables television programming to be available whenever each individual consumer demands it. In this way, each household can create their own custom content and viewing schedule.

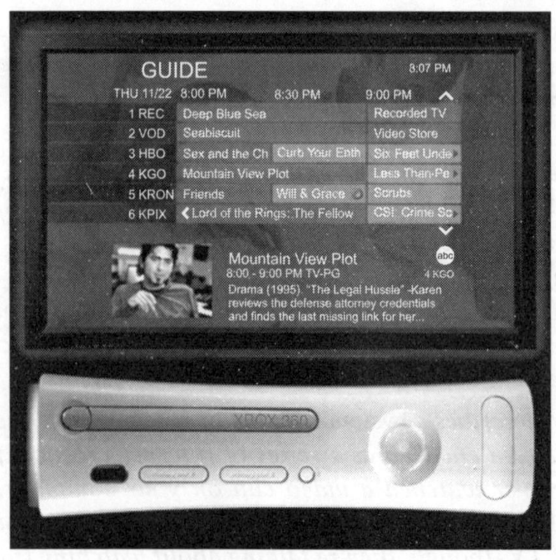

It usually means distribution of television or video content over a controlled IP network, where the end consumer receives the information through a set-top box which is connected to its normal broadband connection. Just because its name is IPTV (Internet Protocol Television) it dose not mean that information is sent over the internet, only that IP protocol is used. So you should not consider streaming video over the internet as IPTV.

Essentially in IPTV broadly encompasses a rich functionality that ranges from the acquisition, encoding and decoding, access control and management of video content, to the delivery of digital TV, movies on demand, viewing of stored programming, personalized program guides, and a host of interactive and multimedia services.

(IPTV) is delivery of digital audio and video content over a broadband connection using the same basic protocols that have traditionally supported internet services. IPTV can deliver live and on demand digital television and radio channels and can be viewed on your TV, a computer, or on a portable device (such as a mobile phone).

It is a system capable of receiving and displaying a video stream encoded as a series of internet protocols packets. It generally satisfies the people demand for smooth, high-resolution, lag-free pictures. IPTV is unlike cable television, which delivers all of its channels concurrently (both analog and digital), using up a good deal of bandwidth. Basic IPTV delivers only one channel at a time, as requested by the user. This, of course, requires much less bandwidth. [**The signal can be received either on a computer with appropriate software, or on a television equipped with an IPTV set-top box.**] The signal can be recorded and/or transferred to other IP-enabled devices.

IPTV technology, integrated with the higher speed digital subscriber line (DSL) access technologies (ADSL2, ADSL2+ and VDSL), offers attractive revenue-generating opportunities for the telecom service providers, enabling them to compete effectively in the "triple play" market space with the delivery of voice, data and video services to residential and business customers.

Internet Protocol

The Internet Protocol (IP) is the method or protocol by which data is sent from one computer to another on the Internet.

Each computer (known as a host) on the Internet has at least one IP address that uniquely identifies it from all other computers on the Internet. When you send or receive data (for example, an e-mail note or a Web page), the message gets divided into little chunks called packets. Each of these packets contains both the sender's Internet address and the receiver's address. Any packet is sent first to a gateway computer that understands a small part of the Internet. The gateway computer reads the destination address and forwards the packet to an adjacent gateway that in turn reads the destination address and so forth across the Internet until one gateway recognizes the packet as belonging to a computer within its immediate neighborhood or domain. That gateway then forwards the packet directly to the computer whose address is specified.

Because a message is divided into a number of packets, each packet can, if necessary, be sent by a different route across the Internet. Packets can arrive in a different order than the order they were sent in. The Internet Protocol just delivers them. It's up to another protocol, the Transmission Control Protocol (TCP) to put them back in the right order.

Triple Play

The biggest thing in telecom today is the "triple play" — in which one provider offers a package deal for voice, broadband Internet, and television i.e. voice, data and video.

Requirements for IPTV

A television set
A set top box
An internet service provider

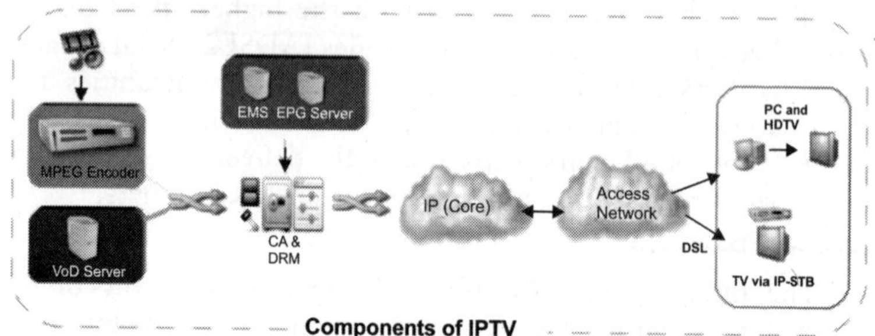

Components of IPTV

If the telco owns the network from end to end then it is beneficial as all the control are in one hand so there is less problems of IP packets trafficking and the quality of service (QoS) tools can prioritize the video traffic to prevent delay or fragmentation of the signal and even can ensure enough bandwidth for their signal at all times.

KEY FEATURES

Digital Broadcast TV

Customers get a conventional digital television through IPTV. This digital broadcast TV is delivered to subscribers via an upgraded cable TV plant or through satellite systems. The initiation of higher-speed DSL technology such as ADSL2, ADSL2+ and VDSL has brought a revolution to this field. This higher-speed technology enables IPTV to be a convincing and highly competitive substitute for customers.

More Channels: The function of conventional broadcast, cable, and satellite TV is to provide all channels simultaneously (i.e., broadcast) to the subscriber home. However, IPTV is unique and different from all conventional groups. IPTV only delivers those channels which are being viewed by the subscriber and has the potential to offer practically an 'unlimited' number of channels. The IPTV consumers will get the freedom to control what they want to watch and also when they want to watch. This is possible because it has a combination of two-way interactive capability. This is inherent in IPTV because of its association with IP. This association is built-in and tied to a robust internal network.

Therefore, subscribers are enjoying the facility to broaden the unique experience at home or in their business.

Video on Demand (VoD)

VoD is a service which provides television programs per the demands of the subscribers. The users interactively request and can receive television channels. These television services are beamed from previously stored media consisting of entertainment movies or education videos. It has a live access through live connection, such as news events in real time. The VoD application provides freedom to the individual subscribers to select a video content and view it at their convenience.

When the initial IPTV infrastructure is in its place, IPTV applications and potential revenue-generating services, such as video telephony and video conferencing, remote education, and home security/monitoring cameras, will be available.

There are also some additional features and services available, which are much more advanced in comparison to traditional broadcast television systems. In addition to providing the basic television services and features, IP Television can provide the following advanced features and services:

- Anywhere Television Service
- Global Television Channels
- Personal Media Channels
- Addressable Advertising

We think of these as VoD, timeshift TV and Network PVR...all based on the Media Server approach.

Anywhere Television Service

Anywhere Television Service uses television extensions, which are the viewing devices that can be connected to the system of a television distribution. There are two options in this regard: (1) these connections may be shared, for example, by several televisions on the same line or (2) they may be controlled independently, such as the case of a private television system.

Conventionally, television extensions have a fixed wire or a connection line. This is because: (1) it allows a television viewing device to either share (i.e., directly connect to) another communication line or (2) it allows an independent connection to a switching point (such as a private company television system).

In IPTV, when an IP television viewer is connected to a data connection for the first time, it sends the request to an assignment of a temporary Internet address from the data network. After its connection to the Internet, it uses the said Internet address to get registered with the Internet Television Service Provider (ITVSP). The reason is that the ITVSP is always aware of the current

Internet address, which is assigned to the IP television each time it has been connected to the Internet. This also allows IP televisions to operate at any connection point that is willing to provide it broadband access to the Internet. In real meaning, this allows an IP television to operate like a television extension, which can be plugged in anywhere in the world.

Global Television Channels

As the name indicates, global television channels are TV channels which can be viewed globally. IP television channels are beamed through the Internet and, as it offers broadband data access, it can, thus, be typically viewed in any part of the globe.

The IP television system is capable of providing video service outside the purview of their local, often regulated, areas. This ability makes IP television a very competitive tool around the world. The typical cost for viewing global television channels is the content media access costs, for example, the cost or fee for watching a movie. Moreover, the cost includes the broadband data access cost, which is a monthly charge for broadband access.

Personal Media Channels (PMC)

PMC is a communication service which is user friendly to subscribers. It allows a media user, for example, to select and view media from different media sources such as video or music.

Here is an example how a PMC may be used for IP television. The control and distribution of mixed media, such as digital pictures and digital videos, can be done through a personal television channel for the service of friends and family members. In this regard, an IP television customer can be assigned a personal television channel. Then, the user can upload media to their personal media channels and can thus allow friends and family to access their pictures and videos. This is done via their IP televisions.

Addressable Advertising

The well-knit communication of a particular message or media content between a specific device and the customer based on their address is called addressable advertising. Here, the said address of the customer may be obtained by scrutinizing the profile of the viewer. This is done in order to determine whether the advertising message is appropriate for the recipient or not. Therefore, addressable advertising allows for speedy and straight measurement of the efficiency of advertising campaigns.

The cooperation of the viewer is the key aspect of addressable advertising. As soon the IP television is turned on, the IP television systems may ask or prompt the viewer to pick their name from a list of registered users. As a reply, viewers will typically want to select their programming name. Here, the programming name has a profile (or, preferences) and the advertising messages can be selected, which are the best match to the concerned viewer profile. Because of the advanced features offered by IP television, such as incoming calls and e-mails and programming guides that remember favorite channels, the viewers can actually do so here.

More Revenue: The generated revenue for addressable advertising messages sent to viewers with specific profiles can be 10 to 100 times higher than the revenue for broadcasting an advertisement to a general audience. The ability to send commercial advertisements to a specific number of viewers allows the advertisers to fix a precise budget for addressable advertising. It also allows the advertiser to experiment a number of different commercial advertisements in the same geographic area at the same time.

Multicast

By using the IP multicast feature in providing an IPTV service, a service provider can conserve bandwidth in their core and access networks. When more than one user is viewing the same channel in a home network, the service provider may only deliver a single video stream. But, at the same time, the home network technology must be competent to distribute this towards multiple users on the home network.

Imagine the core requirements for bandwidth if all customers are watching a different time-shifted channel to when they wanted to watch. Both Multicast and Unicast are needed in the IPTV world, but the former is quicker and easier to deploy in terms of core network capacity than the latter which mostly requires a dedicated one-to-one relationship from customer to server.

Privacy and Security

Let us look at the important aspect of privacy and security of the subscribers. In this regard, the home network must be a closed one. Where is the user's security in this regard? It should be a secure network where access is limited only to users and concerned devices within the home. This is an important factor for the home networks as it uses wireless technologies or shared media technologies such as power line networking. Further, the user data on the home network is protected and no outsiders or intruders have the power to intercept. Unauthorized users do not have the capacity to view it.

Advantages of IPTV

Now, let us have a look at the various advantages of IPTV. It has already been established that IPTV system conserves bandwidth. But there are many more advantages beyond this.

In IPTV, a new level of interactivity among Internet, voice, and video can be established. This enables new types of services which were previously unavailable over stacked networks. For example, in traditional cable TV networks, video transmission is beamed over MPEG streams on an explicit portion of the bandwidth. On the other hand, high-speed data products, such as cable- and modem-based Internet service, are delivered over an IP based network. It is separate from the broadcast TV network that uses MPEG transmission. In this case, both services were delivered via an IP network then, in such a situation, overlapping products are possible. Interactive TV is a good example which often relies on data-centric applications. Today, the delivery of such applications is quite complex due to the separation of IP packets from MPEG streams. These would be missing if such IP packets delivered all video and data.

Education

IPTV can be very helpful in providing web-based training to courses. If we take a case of large size courses, they contain many sections and instructors that can easily share video materials. Therefore, if you own an instructional video which needs to cover ten sections of a course, IPTV can greatly extend its service. The video can be put on IPTV and then all the ten sections could be viewed at one time, or each instructor will have the freedom to schedule a broadcast time for their concerned section. As a result, this removes the scheduling conflicts, if any. Moreover, appearances of any valuable guest lecturers can be recorded and kept for future use. The recording can be used for multiple courses and can be viewed semester after semester. In addition, different orientations, which are given to a large group of people on a regular basis, can be recorded and stored. The recording can be viewed through IPTV, which is possible as long as you have rights from the publishing company to do so.

The point to remember is that video broadcasts made through IPTV is automatically archived in Real Media format, which is stored on a real server. This facility allows the students, who could not view the broadcast or watch the same video, to view it later, either on or off campus. However, Real Media is not a multicast system and, therefore, has a limited bandwidth capacity.

IPTV can report detailed levels of usage and viewer ship which can allow the operator to report statistics of programs/channels/adverts watched as well as be able to bill using various methods of bundled or a-la-carte content....billed by the second, minute, month or par per view.

Disadvantages of IPTV

There are some limitations to IPTV. As IPTV is based on the Internet Protocol, it is sensitive to packet loss and delays if the IPTV connection is not fast enough and it also does not support HDTV at the moment. AT&T is currently experimenting with HDTV and its U-Verse service in the Houston area according to Cable Industry Insider.

Unconventional Remote

Compared to the traditional television remote, the remote of IPTV is more complicated. Therefore, efforts must be made by IPTV providers to teach audiences to get used to it.

Higher Fees

The charge for IPTV includes basic channels plus pay-per-view charges. The fee of access to basic channels is NT 150 per month. An extra charge will be assessed based on the number of channels, videos or movies selected. It is higher than the fee for subscribing to cable television. Therefore, it will be difficult to attract audiences who are more sensitive to price and who are used to paying just one fee to access more than 100 channels.

Voice over IP Security and Law Enforcement

5

Gunjan Verma, Akanksha Rastogi and
Parul Verma

ABSTRACT

Voice over IP is one of the fastest growing Internet based application in today's networking world. As more and more enterprises are moving towards IP based voice network, the payload security has become an important issue. The voice traffic is exposed to the same threats as the normal data traffic. However, with voice traffic, the security and accessibility requirements are different from the data traffic. While it is important to protect the voice packets from spoofing and eves dropping, it is equally important that the law enforcement agencies gain access to these voice packets when legally required. With the deployment of security mechanisms like encryption, it becomes harder for the law enforcement agencies to decipher the information hidden in the IP packets related to voice calls. It would make sense to use standardized encryption techniques with voice over IP, at the same time provide a means to decipher the data as and when needed. This would provide the law enforcement agencies an easier access to the information during critical situations provided they have access to the encryption keys. The emphasis should be placed on the choice of encryption keys making it difficult for intruders to decipher. In this paper, the authors review the security requirements of voice traffic transmitted via Internet with the law enforcement and security perspective. The authors review the requirements of various law enforcement agencies and assess the impact of security mechanisms deployed in VoIP networks on law enforcement.

INTRODUCTION

Voice over IP – the transmission of voice over packet-switched IP networks – is one of the most important emerging trends in telecommunications. As with many new technologies, VOIP introduces both security risks and opportunities.

VoIP has a very different architecture than traditional circuit-based telephony, and these differences result in significant security issues. Lower cost and greater flexibility are among the promises of VoIP for the enterprise, but VoIP should not be installed without careful consideration of the security problems introduced. Administrators may mistakenly assume that since digitized voice travels in packets, they can simply plug VoIP components into their already-secured networks and remain secure. However, the process is not that simple. This publication explains the challenges of VoIP security for agency and commercial users of VoIP, and outlines steps needed to help secure an organization's VoIP network. VoIP security considerations for the public switched telephone network (PSTN) are largely outside the scope of this document.

VoIP Equipments

VoIP systems take a wide variety of forms. Just about any computer is capable of providing VoIP; Microsoft's NetMeeting, which comes with any Windows platform, provides some VoIP services, as does the Apple Macintosh iChat, and Linux platforms have a number of VoIP applications to choose from. In general, though, the term Voice over IP is associated with equipment that provides the ability to dial telephone numbers and communicate with parties on the other end of a connection who have either another VoIP system or a traditional analog telephone.

Traditional Telephone Handset

Usually these products have extra features beyond a simple handset with dial pad. Many have a small LCD screen that may provide browsing, instant messaging, or a telephone directory, and which is also used in configuring the handset to gain access to enhanced features such as conference calls or call-park (automatic callback when a dialed number is no longer busy).

Some of these units may have a "base station" design that provides the same convenience as a conventional cordless phone.

Conferencing Units

These provide the same type of service as conventional conference calling phone systems, but since communication is handled over the Internet, they may also allow users to coordinate data communication services, such as a whiteboard that displays on computer monitors at both ends.

Mobile Units

Wireless VoIP units are becoming increasingly popular, especially since many organizations already have an installed base of 802.11 networking equipment. Wireless VoIP products may present additional challenges if certain security issues are not carefully addressed. The WEP security features of 802.11b provide little or no protection. The more recent WiFi Protected Access (WPA), a snapshot of the ongoing 802.11i standard, offers significant improvements in security, and can aid the integration of wireless technology with VoIP.

PC or "Softphone"

With a headset, software, and inexpensive connection service, any PC or workstation can be used as a VoIP unit, often referred to as a "softphone". If practical, softphone systems should not be used where security or privacy are a concern. Worms, viruses, and other malicious software are common on PCs connected to the internet, and very difficult to defend against. Well-known vulnerabilities in web browsers make it possible for attackers to download malicious software without a user's knowledge, even if the user does nothing more than visit a compromised web site. Malicious software attached to email messages can also be installed without the user's knowledge, in some cases even if the user does not open the attachment. These vulnerabilities result in unacceptably high risks in the use of "softphone", for most applications. In addition, because PCs are necessarily on the data network, using a softphone system conflicts with the need to separate voice and data networks to the greatest extent practical.

In addition to end-user equipment, VoIP systems include a large number of other components, including call processors (call managers), gateways, routers, firewalls, and protocols. Most of these components have counterparts used in data networks, but the performance demands of VoIP mean that ordinary network software and hardware must be supplemented with special VoIP components. The unique nature of VoIP services has a significant impact on security considerations for these networks,

Transmitting Voice over IP

Step 1: Because all transmissions must be digital, the caller's voice is digitized.

This can be done by the telephone company (which is how carriers use IP in their networks), by an Internet service provider (ISP), or by a PC on your desk.

Step 2: Next using complex algorithms the digital voice is compressed and then separated into packets; and using the Internet protocol, the packets are addressed and sent across the network to be reassembled in the proper order at the destination. Again, this reassembly can be done by a carrier, and ISP, or by one's PC.

Step 3: During transmission on the Internet, packets may be lost or delayed, or errors may damage the packets. Conventional error correction techniques would request retransmission of unusable or lost packets, but if the transmission is a real-time voice communication that technique obviously would not work, so sophisticated error detection and correction systems are used to create sound to fill in the gaps. (This process stores a portion of the incoming speaker's voice, and uses a complex algorithm to "guess" the contents of the missing packets and create new sound information to enhance the Communication.)

Step 4: After the packets are transmitted and arrive at the destination, the transmission is assembled and decompressed to restore the data to an approximation of the original form. As this explanation suggests, technology that works fine for sending data may be less than perfect for voice transmissions. The

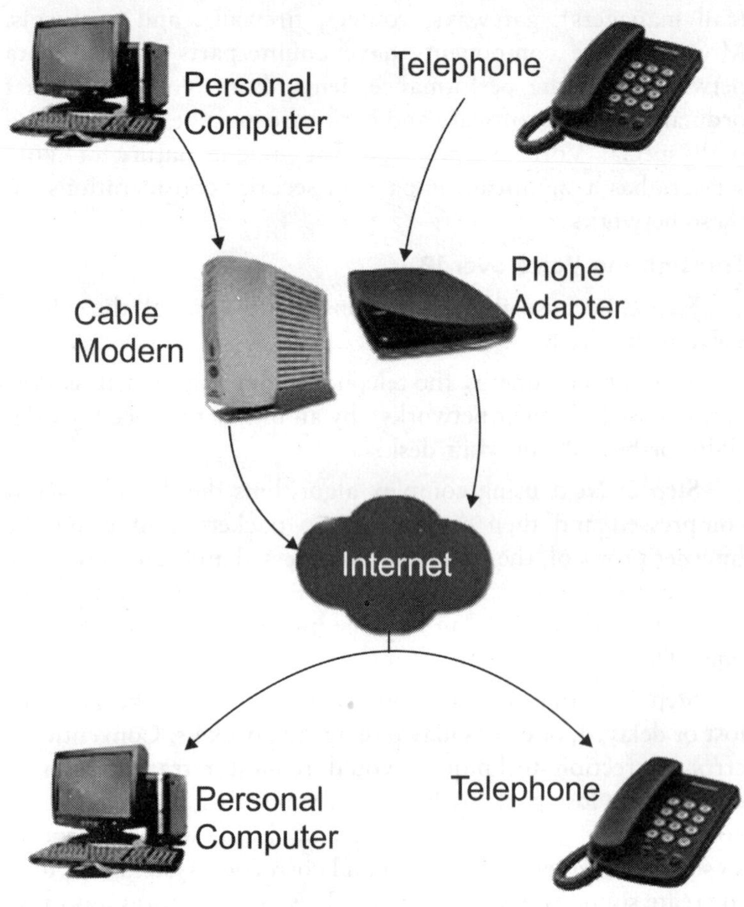

technology is improving, but still the quality of a voice transmission using packet technology is inferior to a circuit-switched connection, and that difference in quality would normally be obvious to any listener. As IP technology improves, the quality advantage for voice communication enjoyed by the circuit-switched will decrease, but most experts see parity in quality as still a distant prospect.

Privacy and Legal Issues with VoIP

Although legal issues regarding VoIP are beyond the scope of this document, readers should be aware that laws and rulings governing interception or monitoring of VoIP lines may be different from those for conventional telephone systems. Privacy issues, including the security of call detail records (CDR) are addressed primarily by the Privacy Act of 1974. In addition, agencies may need to consider the Office of Management and Budget's "Guidance on the Privacy Act Implications of Call Detail Programs to Manage Employees' Use of the Government's Telecommunication System". Because of these guidelines, many federal agencies have Privacy Act System of Record notices for the telephone CDR or usage records. CDR data may be used to reconcile the billing of services and for possible detection of waste, fraud, and abuse of government resources. In addition, NARA General Records Schedule 12, requires a 36-month retention of telephone CDR records (see http://www.archives.gov/records_management/ardor/grs12.html). VoIP systems may produce different types (and a higher volume) of CDR data than conventional telephone systems, so agencies must determine retention requirements for these records. Agencies should review any questions regarding privacy and statutory concerns with their legal advisors.

VoIP Security Issues

The need for security is compounded because now we must protect two invaluable assets, our data and our voice. Federal government agencies are required by law to protect a great deal of information, even if it is unclassified. Both privacy-sensitive and financial data must be protected, as well as other government information that is categorized as sensitive but unclassified. Protecting the security of conversations is thus required. In a conventional office telephone system, security is a more valid assumption. Intercepting conversations requires physical access to telephone lines or compromise of the office private branch exchange (PBX). Only particularly security-sensitive organizations bother to encrypt voice traffic over traditional telephone lines. The same cannot be said for Internet-based connections. For example, when ordering merchandise over the phone, most people will read their credit card number to the person on the other end. The numbers are transmitted without encryption to the seller. In contrast, the risk of sending unencrypted data across the Internet is more significant. Packets sent from a user's home computer to an online retailer may pass through 15-20 systems that are not under the control of the user's ISP or the retailer. Because digits are transmitted using a standard for transmitting digits out of band as special messages, anyone with access to these systems could install software that scans packets for credit card information. For this reason, online retailers use encryption software to protect a user's information and credit card number. So it stands to reason that if we are to transmit voice over the Internet Protocol, and specifically across the Internet, similar security measures must be applied.

The current Internet architecture does not provide the same physical wire security as the phone lines. The key to securing VoIP is to use the security mechanisms like those deployed in data networks (firewalls, encryption, etc.) to emulate the security level currently enjoyed by PSTN network users. This publication investigates the attacks and defenses relevant to VoIP and explores ways to provide appropriate levels of security for VoIP networks at reasonable cost.

Encryption Technology used for Securing the Voice Transmission

An encryption device for a telephone having a handset and a base unit is disclosed. The device includes a handset interface, a first converter, an encryption processor, a second converter, and a host interface. The handset interface receives analog output signals from the handset. The first converter converts the analog output signals into digital output signals. The encryption processor includes a compressor, a key manager, an encryptor, and a modulator. The key manager generates key material for encrypting the digital output signals.The compressor compresses the digital output signals, the encryptor encrypts the digital output signals based on the key material, and the modulator modulates the encrypted digital output signals. The second converter converts the encrypted digital output signals into encrypted analog output signals. The host interface receives the encrypted analog output signals from the encryption processor, and forwards the encrypted analog output signals to the base unit.

VoIP Encryption VoIP networks are highly vulnerable to unauthorized access. Hackers can use easily available applications to decode voice data packets into simple audio files and utilize them for personal benefits. Consequently, voice data packets need to be encrypted. Encryption of voice packets involves camouflaging actual data being transmitted over the VoIP network. Any attempt to decode encrypted voice packets would result in white noise. However, encryption has some disadvantages. Encryption causes a delay in transmitting voice data packets over the VoIP network. Besides, it might also degrade the voice quality. Nevertheless, encryption is an effective means of protecting VoIP data. Companies are gradually coming up with products based on exchange of encryption keys to enable end-to-end encryption. Such devices are effective for VoIP users as they allow conversation only when the assigned keys are correctly identified.

Our secure phone technology uses two steps to encrypt the voice:

1. Key exchange (using a key exchange algorithm).
2. Voice Encryption (using a symmetric algorithm).

These two steps are important for the product security and we can compare this process with a door and it's key. No matter how strong the door (voice encryption) is, if you don't care with its key security, you won't keep it locked against intruders. Below we compare different key exchange technologies, at the left we have the key exchange technologies, at the right we have their securities.Our near competitor (#4) have a 160 bits security. Each bit increased in the symmetric encryption key size doubles the difficulty to break the encryption, for example, from 160 bits to 161 bits you multiply by 2 the difficulty. Comparing the encryption #4 with our encryption (#5), we are

1,000,000,000,000,000,000,000,000,000 times more difficult to break.

Symmetric Algorithms

The encryption key is trivially related to the decryption key, in that they may be identical or there is a simple transform to go between the two keys. The keys, in practice, represent a shared secret between two or more parties that can be used to maintain a private information link.

In cryptography, a **shared secret** is a piece of data only known to the parties involved in a secure communication. The shared secret can be a password, a passphrase, a big number or an array of randomly chosen bytes The shared secret is either shared beforehand between the communicating parties, then it can also be called a pre-shared key. Or it is created at the start of the communication session by using a key-agreement protocol, for instance using public-key cryptography such as Diffie-Hellman or using symmetric-key cryptography such as Kerberos The shared secret can be used for authentication (for instance when logging in to a remote system) using methods such as challenge-response or it can be fed to a key derivation function to produce one or more keys to use for encryption and/or MACing of messages. To make unique session and message keys the shared secret is usually combined with an initialization vector (IV). An example of this is the derived unique key per transaction method.

CONCLUSION

The best way of protecting voice data is by means of the Symmetric algorithm i.e. encrypting the entire voice bit sequence using a fast conventional cryptosystem. If we want to transmit the large amount of data over network at fast rate then we have to use Compression technique before encryption.

REFERENCES

1. European Telecommunications Standards Institute, Recommendation GSM 03.20, "Security Related Network Functions".
2. Hodges, M.R.L., "The GSM Radio Interface," *British Telecom Technology Journal*, Vol. 8, No. 1, January 1990, pp. 31-43.
3. Schneier, B., "Applied Cryptography," J. Wiley & Sons, 1994.

4. Williamson, J., "GSM Bids for Global Recognition in a Crowded Cellular World," Telephony, vol. 333, no. 14, April 1992, pp. 36-40.

5. Cooke, J.C.; Brewster, R.L., "Cryptographic Security Techniques for Digital Mobile Telephones,"

6. Biala, J., "Mobilfunk und Intelligente Netze," Friedr., Vieweg & Sohn Verlagsgesellschaft, 1994.

Voice over Internet Protocol (VoIP) "Why everybody doesn't use it"

Neeraj Varshney and *Juginder Pal Singh*

ABSTRACT

This paper will explain some facts about VoIP systems. Recent development like Internet diffusion at low cost, new integration of dedicated voice compression processors, have changed common user requirements allowing VoIP standards to diffuse

Voice over Internet Protocol (VoIP) is a technology that allows making telephone calls using a broadband Internet connection instead of a regular (or analog) phone line. Some services using VoIP may only allow calling other people using the same service, but others may allow calling anyone who has a telephone number—including local, long distance, mobile, and international numbers. Also, while some services only work over computer or a special VoIP phone, other services allow to use a traditional phone through an adaptor.

More than 30 years ago Internet didn't exist. Interactive communications were only made by telephone at PSTN line cost. Few years ago we saw some interesting things appear: PCs to large masses, new technologies to communicate like cellular phones and finally the great net. Today, we can see a real revolution in communication world: everybody begins to use PCs and Internet for job and free time to communicate each other, to exchange data (like images, sounds, documents) and, sometimes, to talk each other using applications like Net meeting or Internet Phone. Particularly starts to diffusing a common idea that could be the future and that can allow real-time vocal communication: VoIP. We cannot know what the future is, but we can try to image it with many computers, Internet almost everywhere at high speed and people talking (audio and video) in a real time fashion. We only need to know what will be the means to do this: VoIP (with video extension) or other.

INTRODUCTION

Voice over Internet Protocol (VoIP) is a technology that allows to make telephone calls using a broadband Internet connection instead of a regular (or analog) phone line.

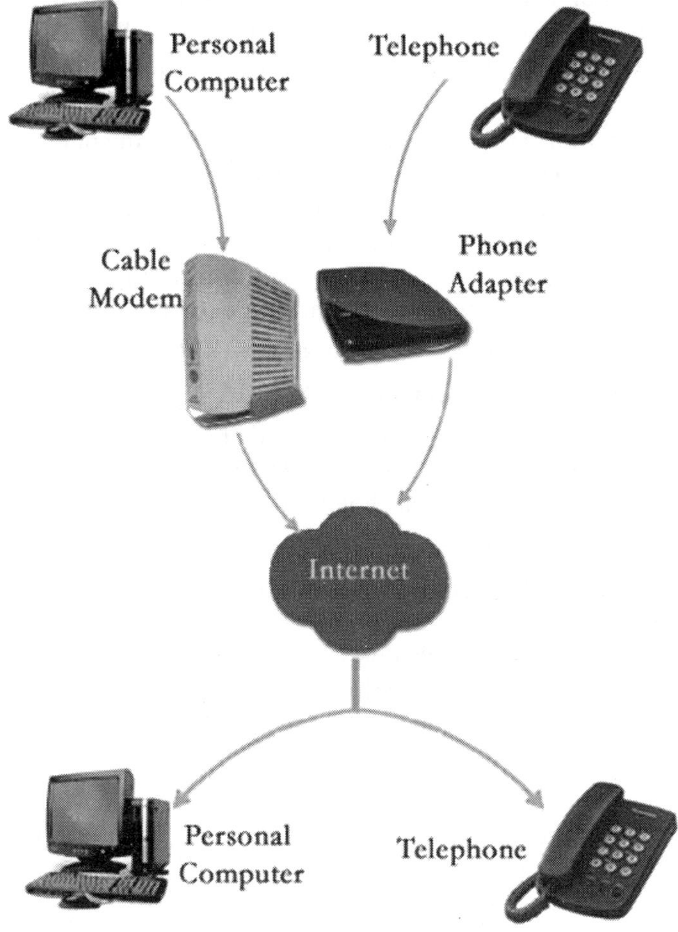

Some services using VoIP may only allow to call other people using the same service, but others may allow to call anyone who has a telephone number—including local, long distance, mobile, and international numbers. Also, while some services only work over computer or a special VoIP phone, other services allow to use a traditional phone through an adaptor.

How does it work?

Many years ago we discovered that sending a signal to a remote destination could have be done also in a digital fashion: before sending it we have to digitalize it with an ADC (analog to digital converter), transmit it and at the end VoIP works like that, digitalizing voice in data packets, sending them and reconverting them in voice at destination.

Digital format can be better controlled: we can compress it, route it, convert it to a new better format, and so on; also we saw that digital signal is more noise tolerant than the analog one. TCP/IP networks are made of IP packets containing a header (to control communication) and a payload to transport data: VoIP use it to go across the network and come to destination.

Voice (source) - - ADC - - - - Internet - - - DAC - - Voice (dest)

TECHNICAL DETAILS

The two major competing standards for VoIP are the IETF standard **SIP** and the ITU standard **H.323**. Initially H.323 was the most popular protocol, though in the "local loop"

Session Initiation Protocol (SIP)

The **Session Initiation Protocol** (**SIP**) is an **application-layer control** (signaling) protocol for creating, modifying, and terminating sessions with one or more participants. It can be used to create two-party, multiparty, or multicast sessions that include Internet telephone calls, multimedia distribution, and multimedia conferences.

SIP has the following characteristics:

- Transport-independent, because SIP can be used with UDP, TCP, ATM & so on.

- Text-based, allowing for humans to read SIP messages transform it again in analog format with DAC (digital to analog converter) to use it.

H.323

H.323 is a recommendation from the ITU-T that defines the protocols to provide. Audio-visual communication sessions on any packet network.

The first version of H.323 was published by the ITU in November 1996 with Videoconferencing capabilities over a Local Area Network (LAN).

In H.323, the data is made up of 3 streams of data:

(1) H.225.0 Call Signaling;

(2) H.245; Control Protocol for Multimedia Communication

(3) Media

Differences between SIP and H. 323

	H. 323	SIP
Philosophy	H.323 was designed with a good understanding of the requirements for multimedia communication over IP networks, including audio, video, and data conferencing. It defines an entire, unified system for performing these functions, leveraging the strengths of the IETF and ITU-T protocols.	SIP was designed to setup a "session" between two points and to be a modular, flexible component of the Internet architecture. It has a loose concept of a call (that being a "session" with media streams), has no support for multimedia conferencing, and the integration of sometimes disparate standards is largely left up to each vendor.
Reliability	H.323 has defined a number of features to handle failure of intermediate network entities. If a gatekeeper fails, the protocols designed to utilize an alternate gatekeeper. If a call that is being routed through intermediate	SIP has not defined procedures for handling device failure. If a SIP user agent fails, there is no means for the proxy to detect that failure except by having the proxy send INVITE messages to the device and waiting for them to timeout. Moreover, if a

	H. 323	**SIP**
	signaling entities fails, H.323 has the wherewithal tore-route the call to an operational entity so that the call is not disrupted.	SIP proxy fails, the SIP user agent has no means of detecting that failure.
Message Encoding	H. 323 encodes messages in a compact binary format that is suitable for narrowband and broadband connections. Most Internet protocols are binary, e.g., IP, TCP, UDP, ICMP, DNS, LDAP, SNMP, RADIUS, NTP, DHCP, and SSH, and for those that are text, there are or have been efforts to provide a binary form, e.g., HTTP and XML.	SIP messages are encoded in ASCII text format, suitable for humans to read. As a consequence, the messages are large and less suitable for networks where bandwidth, delay, and/or processing are a concern. Some argue that message size is not so important because bandwidth is increasing. However, it is a problem because some SIP messages are getting so large that they are reaching the MTU (maximum transmission unit) of the network, risking router fragmentation. As a direct result, it has been at least suggested within the SIP community that UDP be deprecated. TCP would be used instead. Now, however, the scheme is to use UDP or TCP on a message-by-message basis depending on the size of the message.
Call Setup	Il can be established in as few as 1.5 round trips. Setup -> <- Connect Ack ->	A call can be established in as few as 1.5 round trips. INVITE -> <- 200 OK Ack ->
Video and Data Conferencing	H.323 fully supports video and data conferencing. Procedures are in place to provide control for the conference as well as lip synchronization of audio and video streams.	SIP has limited support for video and no support for data conferencing protocols like T.120. SIP has no protocol to *control* the conference and there is no mechanism within SIP for lip synchronization.

What is the Advantage using VoIP rather PSTN?

When you are using PSTN line, you typically pay for time used to a PSTN line manager company; more time you stay at phone and more you'll pay. In addition you couldn't talk with other than one person at a time In opposite with VoIP mechanism you can talk all the time with every person you want (the needed is that other person is also connected to Internet at the same time), as far as you want (money independent) and, in addition, you can talk with many people at the same time.If you're still not persuaded you can consider that, at the same time, you can exchange data with people are you talking with, sending images, graphs and videos.

VoIP Market

The VoIP market is poised for explosive growth. The number of terminal devices that can handle a VoIP call have increased dramatically in number and have come down in price. VoIP is in reach of the average consumer. However, the average consumer needs an incentive to want to switch from circuit-switched voice to VoIP. In order to gain wide scale acceptance in the business community, the business community needs to find a way of finding more value out of an IP network.

The solution is probably one that requires bundling of services. Service bundling is an old concept. Bundling is a very simple concept; people want as much for their money as possible. Consumers and businesses. want many layers of value for the money they spend on telecom services. Bundling in the case of IP means bundled voice, data, and video.

Since the days of ISDN (Integrated Services Digital Network) circa 1976, the telecom industry has been seeking to combine voice, data, and video on a single set of transmission wires to a single terminal. Of course, in 1976 no one had heard of the Internet but there was a vision of a network that would enable people to transact business of some kind using a network.

The term "killer app" is overused. What is good for one person is not good for another. The service that creates enough interest in a mass number of people usually ends up being crowned the "killer app". For years pundits called email the killer app. For a period of time it was the "killer app", but email soon became a "free-bee" or a "flat fee service". Voice will be the next "killer app but it will be one that is bundled with others. Today, there are providers of voice. VoIP is not going to sell unless there is a financial imperative and personal benefit to the consumer. In today's economic environment this situation will call for bundling. People want as much for their money as possible. The mass-market consumer is always looking for a deal.

The technology and critical mass of consumer/user devices have grown and evolved to the point at which bundled VoIP, video, and Internet is not only possible but also cost effective. The recent economic collapse and slow recovery of the telecom industry is forcing the industry and Wall Street moneymakers to put product out into the marketplace at reasonable costs. The first bundled voice services will most likely be sold as audio and video conference services.

However, despite the on set of VoIP, there will be operational support system challenges and marketing challenges. These challenges are being addressed by the industry today.

Network Security Issues and Internet Protocol IPv6

7

Brijesh Kumar Chaurasia

ABSTRACT

Rapid development in the field of communication technologies has increased the need for online and offline security and authentication for the data communication. This paper provides security issues of the data communication using Internet protocol of next generation (IPv6). IPv6, the next generation Internet protocol, has been seen as the best solution for the addressing problems in networks that current Internet protocol faced. In this paper, IPv6 is introduced, including main benefits of IPv6 and related work with IPv6.

INTRODUCTION

As we know that there is no one single security policy for all networks/information system and internet protocol. However, there are a few common issues that are of concern for most network organization and companies that manage information. We are discussing some issues here:

Authentications mechanisms help establish proof of identities. The authentication process ensures that the source of an electronic message or document is correctly identified. It is a mechanism by which the sender identity is expressed and the receiver of a transaction or message can be confident of the identity of the sender. Authentication verifies the identity of a user or a service using certain encrypted information from the sender to the receiver. For example let us assume that a person A wants to send an envelope of a check worth $100 to another person B. then B would like to be assured that the check has indeed come from A, and not from someone else posing as A (as it could be a fake check in that case). This is **Authentication.**

Integrity of a message means that the received message is exactly the same as the message transmitted by the senders. In other words a message that has not been altered in any way, either intentionally or unintentionally, during transmission, is said to have maintained its integrity. For example let us assume that a person A wants to send an envelope of a check worth $100 to another person B. Then A and B will further like to make sure that no one can tamper with the contents of the check (i.e. amount, date, signature, name of the payee). This is **integrity**.

Non-repudiation the term 'repudiation' means to refuse to accept. Non-repudiation prevents either the sender or the receiver from denying a transmitted message. Thus when a message is sent and the sender tries to deny it, the receiver can prove that the alleged sender in fact sent the message. Similarly when a message is received and the recipient denies its receipt, the sender can prove that the message was in fact received by the alleged receiver.

Non-repudiation services are concerned with three types of issues: proof of origin, proof of receipt and proof of content. For example, let us assume that a person A wants to send an envelope of a check worth $100 to another person B. Then what will happen tomorrow if B deposits the check in her account , the money is transferred from A's account to B's account , and then A refuses having written/sent the check? The court of law will use A's signature to disallow A to refute this claim and settle the dispute. This is **non-repudiation**.

Confidentiality means that only the sender and receiver, and not any other party may know the contents of the message. For example let us assume that a person A wants to send an envelope of a check worth $100 to another person B. Then A will like to ensure that no one except B gets the envelope and even if someone else gets it, he does not come to know about the details of the check. This is **confidentiality**.

Access Control the ability to limit and control the access to system and data only to authorized users is the objective of access control. To achieve access control, each entity trying to gain access must first be identified or authenticated and permitted entry only if his details match the access criteria pre-designed for the individual or system. The mechanism used is logins, passwords, and firewalls.

Introduction about Internet Protocol

The Internet Protocol version 4 (IPv4) [1] was developed in the early 1980s. Since then, it has established itself as a primary protocol which enables internetworking thereby allowing a vast array of client/server or peer-to-peer applications to communicate. TCP/IP engineers and designers recognised the need for upgrading in the late 1980s when it became apparent that the existing IP protocol would not be adequate to support the continued exponential growth of the Internet. In 1994, the Internet Engineering Steering Group approved a new Internet Protocol, first called IP next generation (IPng), and later known as Internet Protocol version 6 (IPv6) [2, 3]. The most important issue driving the need for IPv6, but not the only one, is the rapid depletion of IPv4 network addresses. IPv6 main features include: '**plug and play**' which makes it easier for new users with not much TCP/IP knowledge to connect their machines to the network since all configuration will be done **automatically**, '**scalability**' with its **128-bit address space**, '**security**' which includes encryption, '**real-time support**' consideration (using the flow label field) and others, such as '**multicasting**' [4].

Most of the existing protocol stacks, systems and applications run on IPv4-based systems. Changes to these systems can have significant impact on existing applications and must therefore be carefully implemented. While a principal design objective of IPv6 was to ease the transition from and coexistence with IPv4, the migration of IPv4-based systems to IPv6 will be a major challenge despite IPv6's built-in features that are backward-compatible with IPv4 [3]. Options, such as tunnelling of IPv4 packets over IPv6 and tunnelling IPv6 over IPv4, are needed for a smooth transition. In the last few years, network and operating system vendors have started to include support in many of their network applications and communication software products.

Version (4 bits)	priority (4 bits)	Flow Label (24 bits)
Payload Length (2 bytes)	**Next Header** (1 bytes)	**Hop Limit** (4 bits)
	Source Address (16 bytes)	
	Destination Address (16 bytes)	
	Payload Extension Header + **Data Packet from the Upper Layer**	

Fig. 1 IPv6 Header

Migrating from IPv4 to IPv6 in current applications, or implementation of new IPv6 applications, requires the support of many components (application programming interfaces (APIs), protocol stack, routers etc.) of network systems. In this work however, we focus on the end-system which constitutes an important component in the deployment of IPv6-based systems. The IPv6 protocol stack at the end-system is expected to have a definite impact on end-to-end performance of emerging IPv6 applications. We have reported, in previous work [5], an extensive performance comparison between the IPv6 stacks running on Solaris and Windows 2000. Given the wide popularity and acceptance of the Linux operating system, we thought it would be interesting to carry the comparison obtained with Windows 2000 and Solaris further with the IPv6 stack performance delivered by Linux. Windows 2000 had the IPv4 stack as a standard protocol. However, to obtain IPv6 support, an add-on package was installed. There were two choices, both written by Microsoft and they were both in Beta testing. We chose the newer release of the two, 'Microsoft IPv6 Technology Preview for Windows 2000' [6], which is supported by Winsock 2 as its programming API. Solaris 8 and Linux both have dual production level IPv4/IPv6 stacks. The IPv6 protocol stack has been implemented in Linux kernel (version 2.1.8) since 1996 and current 2.2.x and 2.4.x kernel versions fully support IPv6. In this work we use Linux Red Hat version 7.3 (Valhalla) with kernel version 2.4.18-3.

Related Works

The main motivation behind our work was driven by the fact that there are few published performance comparisons (as discussed below) between IPv4 and IPv6 protocol stacks at the end-system. This work differs from previous efforts of other researchers in that we performed a performance evaluation of three IPv6 protocol stack implementations on three widely used operating systems, in contrast to most previous works which compare IPv4 and IPv6 on one platform only or, as in the case of our previous work, on two operating systems [5]. We now briefly present some related work conducted recently and highlight how these efforts differ from ours. Draves et al. [7] presented a performance evaluation of a small subset of tests (actually only throughput) on a prototype IPv6 stack for Windows NT. In [8], a performance comparison was performed between IPv6 and IPv4 on Linux using a gigabit Ethernet adapter. The author conducted only some of the tests we report in this paper and did not compare IPv4/IPv6 stacks for different operating systems. In [9], the authors evaluate the performance of data transmission over IPv4 and IPv6 using various security protocols. They utilised end hosts with FreeBSD 2.2.8 and a KAME [10] IPv6 protocol stack and did not perform detailed testing based on the metrics discussed in this work. In [11], the author presented an evaluation of IPv6 compared to IPv4 using the dual stack implementation of KAME over a FreeBSD operating system using the ping utility and an FTP application; the metrics used were latency and file transfer throughput. They used the FTP application to find out the throughput rates over the IPv6 protocol, and used the ping utility to find the latency. They did not experiment with parameters such as packet size, connection time or protocol type (since they could not perform any UDP tests due to the nature of FTP).

Advantages of Next Generation Internet Protocol IPv6 [2, 12]

Simplified header and flexible extension

IPv6 simplifies the header of the packet to reduce the cost of CPU and to save the network bandwidth. Each IPv6 packet consists of a main header and many extension headers. The IPv6 main header has a fixed 40-bytes long size. six fields and two addresses, while IPv4 had ten fixed header fields, two addresses, and some options. Less header fields can expedite processing rate of router. The checksum field of IPv4 has been removed in IPv6. The main advantage is to diminish the cost of header processing. IPv6 headers do not contain any optional element. This does not mean that we cannot express options for special-case packets. The functions that the variable-sized option field offered in IPv4 are now deployed by a chain of extension headers that follow the main IPv6 header. This makes the IPv6 header more flexible for future use.

Unlimited addresses and more addressing hierarchies

An IPv4 address is 32 bits wide, this means that the theoretical upper bound on the size of the Internet is 2^{32}, consisting of hosts and routers. By extending the size of the address field in the network layer header from 32 to 128 bits, IPv6 raised this theoretical limit to 2^{128}. Therefore, IPv6 could solve the IP address space depletion problem for the foreseeable future. Moreover, the size of IPv6 addresses allows more addressing hierarchies. The improved addressing hierarchy allows smaller routing tables and faster lookups.

Plug and play

Plug and play allows a host to be connected to the network and be immediately ready for use without manual intervention. Plug and play greatly simplifies the work of network administration and control. The necessary parameters that an interface must know in order to be part of the network are its network address, its host name, the local subnet prefix that are determined using the stateful or stateless "auto-configuration" features of IPv6. Moreover, in order to be able to transmit packets over the network, a node needs to know the addresses of local routers and neighbors. The "neighbor discovery" feature of IPv6 does this.

IP layer authentication and security

Security always is the most important issue on Internet. The inclusion of security features in IPv6 can be attributed to the rapid growth of commerce, exchange of intellectual property and security sensitive applications on the Internet. IPsec, which is developed by IETF from 1995, is an optional extension protocol for IPv4, and now is a must in IPv6. Traditionally, network security has been the task of the higher layers in the protocol stack. Adding security to the IP layer extends security to all applications on the Internet. IPv6 provides authentication and encryption, both implemented as extension headers, known respectively as the authentication header (**AH**) and the encapsulating security payload (ESP) hcadcr.

Quality of service guarantees

The "best effort" mechanism of IPv4 is unable to provide sufficient services for some new applications that will be running over the Internet. It is becoming clear that, in the future, applications like FTP, telnet, e-mail, etc. will be running in parallel with a variety of more complex and demanding applications such as video-conferencing and real-time voice etc. These applications require quality of service guarantees to be made by the network. Under IPv6, hosts are able to identify packets that belong to a particular traffic stream using the "flow" field. One can divide flows into different classes based on their quality of service requirements and assign each class to a different priority queue.

Proposed Model Solution

According the previous review, have analyzed following field option suitable for covertness

- 8-bit hop limit field. Initialized to zero for transmission; ignored on reception.
- Extension headers:
- Hop-By-Hop Options
- Destination Options Routing
- Fragmentation
- Authentication Header
- Encapsulating Security Payload

- Destination Options (for options processed only by the final destination)

A technique look at IPv6 secure covert channels and data hiding algorithm that can pass supplementary information through most firewalls and intrusion detection systems. Proposed model solution for secure communication is given below:

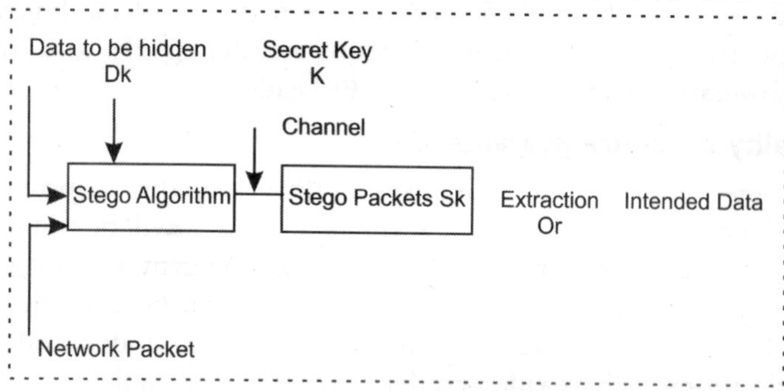

Fig. 2.

CONCLUSION

Ntwork security is always a big issue. Data communication just reflect various problems in the existing network architecture and protocol organization. We just categorize them and list some possible ways to deal with them. We have also listed advantage of next generation protocol IPV6. My work is under process and I will develop some agents for this Network security

REFERENCES

1. Information Sciences Institute, USC: 'Internet protocol'. RFC 791, IETF, September 1981.
2. Deering, S., and Hinden, R.: 'Internet protocol, version 6 (IPv6) specification'. RFC 1883, Internet Engineering Task Force, December 1995.
3. Goncalves, M., and Niles, K.: 'IPv6 networks' (McGraw–Hill, 1998).
4. Huitema, C.: 'IPv6: The new internet protocol' (Prentice Hall, 1997, 2nd edn.).
5. Zeadally, S., and Raicu, I.: 'Evaluating IPv6 on Windows and Solaris', IEEE Internet Comput., 2003, 7, (3).

6. Microsoft Corporation: 'Microsoft IPv6 technology preview for Windows 2000' December 2000, http://www.microsoft.com/
7. Draves, R. et al.: 'Implementing IPv6 for Windows NT'. Proc. 2nd USENIX Windows NT Symposium, Seattle, WA, USA, August 1998.
8. Anand, M.: 'Netperf3 TCP network performance on IPV6 using 2.4.17kernel'.IBM Linux TechnologyCenter,www-124. ibm.com/ developerworks/opensource/linuxperf/netperf/results/may_02/ netperf3_ipv6_2. 4.17resutls.htm, August 2002.
9. Ariga, S., Nagahashi, K., Minami, A., Esaki, H., and Murai, J.: 'Performance evaluation of data transmission using IPSec over IPv6 networks'. Proc. INET 2000, Japan, July 2000.
10. KAME, http://www.kame.net
11. Ettikan, K.: 'IPv6 dual stack transition technique performance analysis: KAME on FreeBSD as the case'. Faculty of Information Technology, Multimedia University, Jalan Multimedia, October 2000.
12. Conta A., Deering and December S., "[RFC 24631-lntemet Control Message Protocol (ICMPv6) for the Internet Protocol Version 6 (IPv6) Specification", 1998.

Nonlinear Equalizers and Near-Maximum Likelihood Detectors for Future Mobile Systems

Mohd. Israil and *M. Salim Beg*

ABSTRACT

This paper describes the performance of adaptive non-linear equalizers (NLE) and Near Maximum Likelihood Detectors (NMLD) in different mobile radio environments. Computer simulation tests have been carried out to assess the performance of both linear as well as non-linear equalizers using the transmission of 4-level Quadrature Amplitude Modulated (QAM) signal. Performance of these two detection techniques (Nonlinear Equalizer and Near Maximum Likelihood Detector) has been assessed in terms of bit error rate versus signal to noise ratio (SNR). In this paper, signal transmission is carried out at two different values of carrier frequency viz. 900 MHz and 1800 MHz. Performance of both NLE as well as NMLD are presented separately for carrier frequency 900 MHz as well as 1800 MHz for slow moving terminals in indoor mobile radio fading environments. A number of different cases of mobile radio channels have been simulated in this work. These channels have different number of reflected paths with different power distribution in the respective paths. The aim of this paper is to take a 'worst case' model of a mobile radio channel in terms of rapidity of fading and ISI, and then to investigate the performance of detectors in the receivers.

INTRODUCTION

The aim of the future mobile communications system is to satisfy the increasing demand of high bit rate services. In order to accommodate new multimedia and Internet application services involving the transmission of text, audio, and image over wideband mobile radio systems, the transmission bit rate over such mobile channels becomes extremely high. In this case, the time delay spread of the channel becomes appreciably large compared to the signal element duration. As the antenna height of a mobile terminal is usually very small, the antenna is expected to have very little 'clearance', so obstacles and reflecting surfaces in the vicinity of the antenna have a substantial influence on the characteristics of the propagation path. Moreover, the propagation characteristics change from place to place and, if the mobile unit moves, from time to time. Thus, the transmission path between the transmitter and the receiver can vary from simple direct line-of-sight (LOS) to one that is severely obstructed by buildings, foliage and the terrain. The radio waves reach at the receiver after reflection from various objects. This type of radio wave propagation is called Multipath prorogation. Due to Multipath propagation, radio waves arrive at the receiver from different directions with different time delays, and they combine vectorially at the receiver antenna to give a resultant signal which can be large or small depending upon whether the incoming waves combine constructively or destructively.

As the mobile station moves from one location to another, the phase relationship between the various incoming waves changes; hence there are substantial amplitude fluctuations and the signal is said to be subject to fading. Multipath fading may also arise due to the movement of the surrounding objects from which the reflection of signals is coming to the receivers. Fading can be flat or of the frequency selective type. In a flat fading channel, all the frequency components are affecting in similar manner [6]. In frequency selective, different frequency components of the signal fade differently. A further cause of fading is the obstruction of the radio signals by buildings and hills, and this is known as 'shadowing'. Although this may lead to sudden deep fades, as when a vehicle passes under a low bridge, the fading rate due to shadowing is typically very much less rapid than that caused by multipath propagation [1]. It is important to note that whenever the relative motion exists there is a Doppler shift of the frequency components within the received signal.

The time difference between first and last replica of the signal at the receiver is called delay spread of the channel. The delay spread may range from a fraction of microsecond to few tens of microseconds [6]. When the delay spread becomes large, the multipath replica of the signal may interfere with other, causing intersymbol interference (ISI), and the resulting overall system performances get degraded.

A technique to employ the baseband equivalent form of the bandpass signal is used here, and this can be used to represent the action of any linear bandpass channel on the modulated carrier signal fed through this channel. The modulator, transmission path and demodulator can now be modeled as a linear baseband channel, where all filters at the transmission path are represented by the corresponding low-pass filter, and similarly at the receiver. In general, all signals here are complex-valued. The 4-QAM signaling is used in this work which is generated by inphase and quadrature phase suppressed carrier modulation. It is assumed here that the detectors know all about the channel i.e. perfect channel estimation is assumed. This assumption is made because the objective of this study is to assess the performance of detection processes in combating signal fading and intersymbol interference.

To improve the overall system performance equalization and Near Maximum likelihood (NML) detection used in this work. Signal is operated at 900 and 1800 MHz carrier frequency and it is assumed here that channel is estimated perfectly. Advantages of adaptive equalization over channel coding and spread spectrum is that adaptive equalization can provide high data rates without any loss of bandwidth efficiency [3, 4]. NML detection is known to have near optimal performance even under worst case model of the channel [5-8].

Channel Model

The fading channel is generated in this paper using tapped delay line model which is based on the model developed by Clark & Jayasinghe [9]. With some appropriate modifications, this narrowband model can be further extended to represent the wideband channel in the IMT-2000 mobile systems.

The channel model is illustrated in Figure 1 where the input signal is fed to a tapped delay line. The delay signals at each of the taps are modulated in amplitude as well as in phase by complex-valued baseband random function Qi(t) in such a way that each of these represents a Rayleigh fading path. The number of taps is equal to the number of reflected signals reaching the receiver via different paths. Each tap gain function is independent of the other, which means that each of the reflected signals arrives via an independently fading path. The delayed and modulated signals are summed with additive noise, which has a Gaussian probability density (AWGN). With the help of this model CH11 and CH21 has been generated. These two channels are two paths with equal power distribution [50%-50%] but the carrier frequency are different. CH11 and CH21 are operated at 900 MHz and 1.8 GHz respectively.

Detection Techniques

The problem of dealing with ISI in the received signal has been overcome by equalizing the received signal before passing it on to the detector, but the performance of such a system is known to be very much sub-optimal [10]. On the other hand, the optimum detection process for a sequence of statistically

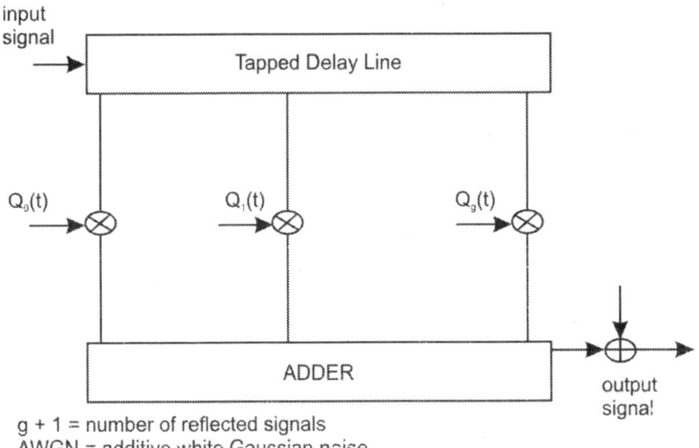

Fig. 1: Tapped Delay Line model of the Channel

independent data symbols transmitted over a non-ideal band-limited channel that introduces ISI and AWGN is Maximum Likelihood Detection (MLD) which can be implemented using Viterbi algorithm but suffer from the problem of excessive storage requirements and high computationally complexity. A class of detectors that reduce this problem to a certain degree, are known as near-maximum-likelihood detectors (NMLD) and are studied in this paper.

Equalization

In the Equalization the signal is multiplied by the inverse of the channel coefficients so that channel and signal get ISI free symbols for detection. It compensates the intersymbol interference (ISI) created by the multipath within time dispersive channel. Equalization must be adaptive in mobile environments, since the channel is generally unknown and time varying [6, 8].

Linear equalizer is generally implemented as a linear feedforward tranversal filter. In Non-linear equalization the detector is used within the feedback path with linear equalizer as shown in Fig. 2. Since the detector is a highly nonlinear device, therefore equalization becomes nonlinear. Non-linear equalizer uses decision directed cancellation of intersymbol interference (ISI). The received sample value at the input before the Equalizer at time t=iT, is

$$r_i = s_i\, y_{i,0} + \sum_{j=1}^{g} s_{i-j}\, y_{i,j} + w_i \qquad (1)$$

The corresponding sample value at the input to the equalizer in fig. 2 is given as

$$r_i/y_{i,0} = s_i + \sum_{j=1}^{g} s_{i-j}\,(y_{i,j}/y_{i,0}) + (w_i/y_{i,0})$$

$$r_i/y_{i,0} = s_i + \sum_{j=1}^{g} s_{i-j} v_j + w_i\,/\,y_{i,0} \qquad (2)$$

Where: $v_j = y_{i,j}/y_{i,0}$

s_i = symbol to be detected

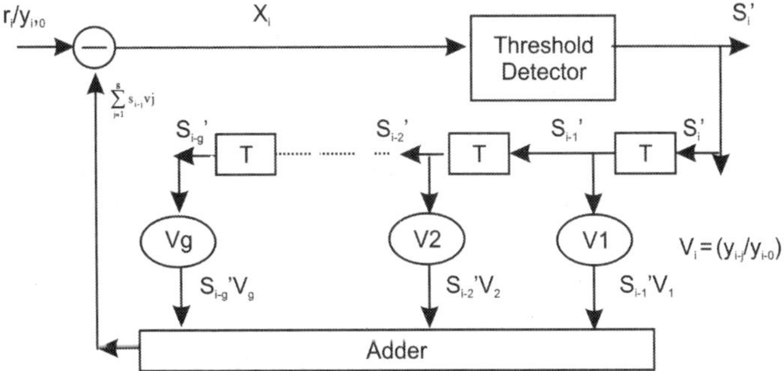

Fig. 2: Nonlinear Equalizer

$w_i / y_{i,0}$ = noise component

$\sum_{j=1}^{g} s_{i-j}v_j$ = ISI

The sampled impulse-response of the baseband channel, sampler and multiplier is

$1/y_{i,0} * V$ = 1 v1 v2 ...... v_g (3)

Assuming that 1/yi, 0 V and the two possible initial values of si are known at the receiver, the output signal from the linear feed forward transversal filter in Fig. 2 is

$\sum_{j=1}^{g} s'_{i-j}v_j$ where is the detected value of s_{i-j}

Thus, the signal at the detector input at t=iT is

$$x_i = r_i/y_{i,0} - \sum_{j=1}^{g} s'_{i-j}v_j \qquad (4)$$

$$xi = s_i + \sum_{j=1}^{g} s_{i-j}v_j + w_i / y_{i,0} - \sum_{j=1}^{g} s'_{i-j}v_j \qquad (5)$$

And with the correct detection of each si-j, such that si-j' = si-j for j=1,2,....g , then equation (5) becomes

$$x_i = s_i + w_i/y_{i,0} \qquad (6)$$

Now detection can be made using the simple threshold detector.

B. Near-Maximum Likelihood Detector

Near-maximum likelihood (NML) detectors are a class of detectors that reduce the problem of complexities and excessive storage faced by the maximum likelihood detectors (MLD). In Maximum likelihood Detector (MLD) the detector stores m^g vector for making the detection of single sample. One method of reducing the complexity of the MLD is to reduce the number of its stored vectors i.e. the number of its survivors. So instead of holding m^g survivors, the detector may hold m' survivors where $m^1 < m^g$. Here m represents the number of levels in the transmitted signal, and the channel sampled impulse response (SIR) is assumed to consist of $g + 1$ components. The criterion for the selection of m' vectors ensures that the degradation in the tolerance to noise is kept to a minimum. The performance degradation relative to the optimum detector is dependent on the ratio of m'/m^g. NML detectors are a derivative of MLD detectors where m' is much smaller than m^g and where all the m' stored vectors need not be survivors [10]. This paper presents a performance analysis of the NML detectors over a number of mobile radio channels simulated for this work.

For near optimum performance of the NML detector, the magnitude of the first few components of the channel SIR should be large relative to other components. If the first component is the largest, the SIR is often referred to as a minimum phase response. If the channel SIR is not a minimum phase (or near minimum phase), then some sort of processing ahead of the detector may be used to make the channel SIR as a minimum phase. This is generally implemented by making use of an adaptive filter ahead of the detector. In the work presented in this paper, however, no adaptive pre-filtering is used in order to reduce the overall complexity of the system. Since the channel used in this work is not a minimum phase (in fact it can be near maximum phase at certain times), the design of the detection algorithms becomes extremely challenging [10]. In this work, the number of stored vectors (k) is 4 and delay in detection (n) is 4.

Results

Simulation results for NLE and NML detector is shown in Fig. 3 and Fig. 4. Fig. 3 shows the BER performance curve for nonlinear equalizer and NMLD when the signal is operated at the carrier frequency 900 MHz, whereas Fig. 4 shows the BER performance for the same detectors but the difference is that the signal is operated here on carrier frequency 1800 MHz. As can be seen from the Fig. 3 and Fig. 4, the NMLD is significantly better in performance compared to the NLE. The channel model consists of two resolvable fading paths with equal power in the two paths. The channel used in this work is verified by checking its mean and variance which is given in the Table 1.

Table 1: Simulation Results of Two-Path Rayleigh Channel (CH 11)

Parameter	Theoretical Value	Practical value
Mean of Rayleigh Path 1	0.6267	0.6230
Mean of Rayleigh Path 2	0.6267	0.6230
Variance of Rayleigh Path 1	0.1073	0.1127
Variance of Rayleigh Path 2	0.1073	0.1127
Mean of q1	0	-0.0014
Mean of q2	0	0.0023
Mean of q3	0	0.0014
Mean of q4	0	0.0023
Variance of q1	0.25	0.25
Variance of q2	0.25	0.25
Variance of q3	0.25	0.25
Variance of q4	0.25	0.25

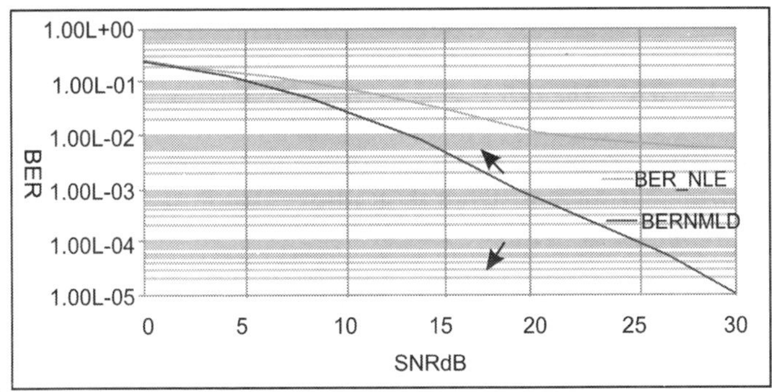

Fig. 3: BER performance curve for channel CH11

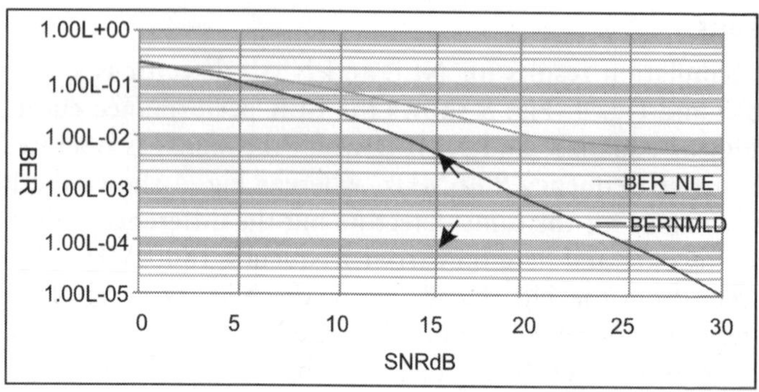

Fig. 4: BER performance curve for channel CH21

CONCLUSION

The results have shown that the NML detector has performed impressively under harsh conditions of fast moving vehicular environment and severe ISI. Even for the case of almost 'maximum phase response' channel, the detector still manages to mitigate the bad ISI effect satisfactorily. Therefore, it can be concluded that since this detector can withstand such a severely distorted channel, then this detector will be unlikely to have poor performance over any practical wideband channel that may be encountered in a vehicular mobile radio environment. It is also seen that by changing the carrier frequency of the signal, performance of the detector remains same so it can be also concluded that the carrier frequency does not affect the performance of the detector, under the assumption of perfect channel estimation.

REFERENCES

1. G.J. Foschini and J. Salz, "Digital Communications over Fading Channels", The Bell System Technical journal, Vol. 62, Feb 1983 Number 2 part 1, pp. 429-456.
2. Adolf J. Giger and Willium T. Barnet, "Effects of Multipath propagation on Digital Radio", IEEE Transaction on Communications, Vol. COM-29 No. 9 , September 1981, pp. 1345-1352.
3. T.A. Sexton and K. Pahlavan, "Channel modeling and adaptive equalization of indoor radio channels", IEEE Journal Selected Areas in Communications, vol. 7, January 1989, pp. 114-121.

4. K. Pahlavan S.J. Howard and T.A. Sexton, "Decision feedback equalization of the indoor radio channel" IEEE Trans. on Communication. Vol. COM-41, 1993, pp. 164-170.
5. M. Bhat and M. Salim Beg, "Computer simulation and modeling of high speed data transmission over mobile radio links", Journal of Institution of Engineers (I), Vol. 77, Sept. 1996, pp. 20-23.
6. T.S. Rappaport, Wireless Communications, Principles and Practice, Prentice Hall, New Jersey, 1996.
7. M. Salim Beg and Mohd Nazri Muhayiddin, "Receiver Signal Processing for Next Generation Wideband Digital Cellular System," Proceeding of International Wireless and Telecommunication Symposium (IWTS 98), Shah Alam, Malaysia, pp. 400-403, May 11-15, 1998.
8. M. Salim Beg, S. C. Tan and Hazemi Hamidi, "Performance Assessment of Some Adaptive Equalizers in Mobile Radio Environments", Proc. Int. Symposium. on Wireless Personal Multimedia. Communications, pp. 761-766, Bangkok, Thailand, Nov. 2000.
9. A.P. Clark and S.G. Jayasinghe, "Channel Estimation for Land Mobile Radio Systems", IEE Proceedings Part F, Vol. 134, N. 4, pp. 383-393, July 1987.
10. M. Salim Beg, "Novel Detection Techniques for data transmission over a fading channel" Ph.D. thesis, Loughborough University, UK 1990.
11. M. Salim Beg and Mohd. Israil, "Adaptive Equalization for Indoor Fading Channel", Proceeding of National Conference on Emerging Trends in Communication and Computing (ETCC-07), 27-28 July 2007, NIT Hamirpur, pp. 382-385.

Demystifying High Speed Wireless Technologies

9

Abha Agarwal and *Abhinav Agarwal*

ABSTRACT

There has been lot of advancement in high speed wireless technologies. Thus, there comes a need of understanding the advancement in major wireless technologies. The paper gives an introduction on Evolution of WCDMA (UMTS) and detailed explanation of WCDMA coding.

Various high speed wireless technologies like:-

WPAN– *Wireless Personal Area Network – blue tooth, NFC (near field communication), ultra wideband, and mm wave.*

WLAN– *Wireless Local Area Network – Wi-Fi (wireless fidelity)*

WMAN– *Wireless Metro Area Network – Wi-Max (world wide interoperability for microwave access)*

WWAN– *Wireless Wide Area Network – UMTS (universal mobile telecommunication system), HSDPA (hi speed downlink packet access), Flash OFDM.*

UMTS *is the broadband, packet-based wireless technology with a core network evolved from GSM and* **WCDMA** *is the air-interface technology behind UMTS.*

The paper introduces the basic CDMA Concepts-Multiple Access Method, UMTS Spectrum, UMTS Bandwidth, Power Control, Closed Loop Power Control, Handover -Soft Handover, Softer Handover, and Hard Handover.

It explains in detail the Orthogonal Codes transmission and reception, Orthogonal Sequences, Orthogonal Spreading in WCDMA. The use of PN codes in WCDMA (UMTS). Generic Physical Layer Procedures in WCDMA like Channel Coding, Interleaving, Mapping data onto physical channels, Spreading using OVSF Channel codes, PN Scrambling, QPSK Modulation.

Lastly, it is concluded by including advantages, disadvantages, competing technologies and future of WCDMA (UMTS).

INTRODUCTION

There has been lot of advancement in high-speed wireless technologies. Thus, there comes a need of understanding the advancement in major wireless technologies. The paper gives an introduction on Evolution of *Wide Band Code Division Multiple*

Access (WCDMA) and detailed explanation of WCDMA coding. The paper introduces the basic CDMA Concepts-Multiple Access Method, *Universal Mobile Telecommunication System (UMTS)* Spectrum, UMTS Bandwidth, Power Control, Closed Loop Power Control, Handover–Soft Handover, Softer Handover, and Hard Handover. It explains in detail the Orthogonal Codes transmission and reception, Orthogonal Sequences, Orthogonal Spreading in WCDMA. The use of PN codes in WCDMA. Generic Physical Layer Procedures in WCDMA like Channel Coding, Interleaving, Mapping data onto physical channels, Spreading using OVSF Channel codes, PN Scrambling, QPSK Modulation. Lastly, it is concluded by including advantages, disadvantages, competing technologies and future of WCDMA (UMTS).

CDMA Concepts – Multiple Access Methods

Overview of CDMA

The CDMA concept is like the situation encountered at a party. At the "CDMA Cocktail Party," all users are talking in the same room simultaneously. Imagine that every conversation in the room is being carried out in a different language that you do not understand. They would all sound like noise from your perspective. But if you knew the language, you could filter out the unwanted conversations and listen only to the conversation of interest to you. Even with the knowledge of the appropriate language, the conversation of interest may not be completely audible. The listener can signal the speaker to speak more loudly and can also signal other people to speak more softly.

In a CDMA system, the network radio equipment has a "conversation" with multiple subscribers at the same time and in the same frequency allocation. But each subscriber is assigned a unique code, so the subscriber equipment only "hears" the conversation that is encoded with that code. The network equipment "hears" all conversations simultaneously and decodes each one using the appropriate code.

UMTS Spectrum

UMTS Frequency Allocations

It would be desirable to have a worldwide frequency allocation for all 3G systems. Unfortunately, individual regulatory agencies control spectrum allocations and there is no universally clear spectrum available. The chart above labeled IMT-2000 shows the desired allocation. In China, the entire spectrum is available. In Europe, Japan, and Korea, portions of it are available. In North America, both CDMA2000 and UMTS systems will be supported in the existing Personal Communications System (PCS) and cellular bands.

UMTS FDD systems are currently specified to operate in the following paired bands:

- 1920 to 1980 MHz (Uplink)
- 2110 to 2170 MHz (Downlink) and
- 1850 to 1910 MHz (Uplink)
- 1930 to 1990 MHz (Downlink)

UMTS Bandwidth

Channel Spacing

The nominal channel spacing is 5 MHz, but this can be adjusted to optimize performance in a particular deployment scenario.

Channel Raster

The channel raster is 200 KHz, which means that the center frequency must be an integer multiple of 200 KHz.

Channel Number

The carrier frequency is designated by the UTRA Absolute Radio Frequency Channel Number (UARFCN),

Where Fcenter = UARFCN * 200 KHz

Power Control

The network radio equipment controls the volume level of each conversation, by requesting more power from those subscribers that are faint and requesting less power from those that are too strong. Similarly, the subscriber equipment can request more or less power from the network. This process is called *power control.* It ensures that each conversation is just loud enough to be heard, but not so loud that it drowns out the other conversations. In a cellular system, there is a "near-far" problem that requires power control. One *User Equipment (UE)* may be 10 kilometers from the Node B, while another UE may be only a few hundred meters away. As a result, UEs can experience greatly differing amounts of path loss due to their varying distance from the Node B and varying multipath environments. CDMA systems use power control on both the Downlink and the Uplink to ensure that the signal sent to and from a UE that is near the Node B is relatively low compared to the signals sent to and from a UE that is far from Node B. Path loss can easily vary by 80 dB. If all UEs attempted to transmit at the same power level, some signals could arrive at the Node B 80 dB stronger than others. Each UE must be carefully power-controlled to ensure that transmissions arrive at the Node B at an appropriate level. Additionally, the UEs' transmissions do not fade together. They typically take different paths and are subject to different propagation conditions.

Closed Loop Power Control

A closed loop process controls transmission power on both the Downlink and Uplink. Closed loop control is basically a three-step process. A transmission is made, a measurement is made at the receiver, and feedback is provided to the transmitter indicating whether the power should be increased or decreased. The closed loop process can eventually correct the mobile's transmit power regardless of the initial transmit level. Significant gain can be achieved, however, if the mobile's initial transmit level is close to the appropriate power.

Selection of a metric is affected by the speed that is required of the closed loop process. Block error rate is a good metric, for example, but measuring block error rate can be a slow process. If faster response is needed, another indicator, such as Eb/I0, may be more appropriate. For quick response to power control commands, multiple commands are sent every radio frame

Handover

Handover is the process of adding or removing cells with which the UE is communicating on a dedicated Traffic Channel. The UE assists in the process by taking measurements of the signal strength of neighbor cells and reporting this to *Universal Terrestrial Radio Access Network (UTRAN)*, but ultimately UTRAN decides when to perform a handover.

Soft Handover

Soft handover allows the mobile to establish a connection with a new Node B before breaking the connection with the previous serving cell. In a WCDMA system, a mobile can be "in soft handover" with two or more cells for an extended period of time. This is a desirable state as it provides path diversity. If the path to one cell experiences a temporary fade, the communication link through the other path or paths may not be affected.

Hard Handover

A hard handover occurs when all existing radio links must be dropped before a new link is established. This causes a brief interruption in voice or data communication, while making the transition from the old serving link to the new.

Coding in WCDMA

Orthogonal functions have zero correlation. Two binary sequences are orthogonal if the process of "XORing" them results in an equal number of 1s and -1s:

Example: - 1 -1 1 1

1 1 -1 1

1 -1 -1 1

Orthogonal sequences

Orthogonal functions (that is, signals or sequences) have zero cross-correlation. Zero correlation is obtained if the product of two signals, summed over a period of time, is zero. For the special case of binary sequences, the values 0 and 1 may be viewed as having opposite polarity. Thus, when the product (XORing in this case) of two binary sequences results in an equal number of 1s and 0s, the cross-correlation is zero. Orthogonal codes in WCDMA are termed *orthogonal variable spreading factor (OVSF)* codes.

Orthogonal spreading

In the diagram, each user input symbol is spread by the orthogonal code 0110 by XORing the symbol with each bit of the code. The resulting sequence is processed and transmitted over the Physical Channel along with other spread symbols.

The principle behind spreading and despreading is when a symbol is XORed with a pattern, and the result is again XORed with the same pattern, the original symbol is recovered.

Recovery of spread symbols

The receiver despreads the chips by using the same orthogonal sequence used at the transmitter. Note that under no noise conditions, the symbols are completely recovered without any errors. In reality, the channel is not noise free, but WCDMA systems employ. *Forward Error Correct (FEC)* techniques to combat the effects of noise and enhance the performance of the system.

Recovery of spread symbols using the wrong sequence

When the wrong orthogonal sequence is used for despreading, the resulting correlation yields an average of zero. This is a clear demonstration of the advantage of the orthogonality property of these sequences. If the wrong code is mistakenly used by the target, or other users attempt to decode the signal using the wrong code, the resulting correlation is always zero, and the original data cannot be recovered.

Pseudorandom noise codes

- M-sequences (maximum length pseudorandom binary sequences)
- Gold codes (produced using M-sequences)

M-sequence properties

- Balance
- Run-Length
- Shift and Add
- Autocorrelation

PN codes

Maximum Length Pseudorandom Binary Sequences

- Pseudorandom – Of, relating to, or being random numbers generated by a deterministic process.
- Binary – Takes on one of two values.
- Maximum Length – Maximum achievable period of a generated sequence – not arbitrary.

Properties

- Balance property – The output sequence has an almost equal number of zeros and ones

  (2r - 1 ones and 2r - 1 - 1 zeros).
- Run-length property – In any period, half the runs of consecutive zeros or ones are of length one, one-fourth are of length two, one-eighth are of length three, etc.
- Shift and add property – The chip-by-chip sum of the output sequence Ck and any shift of itself Ck+t is a timeshifted version of the same sequence.
- Autocorrelation property – It is the measure of correlation between a PN code & a time shifted version of the same code.

Gold Codes

*Generation of Gold code sequence of length 25-1.*Using two preferred M-sequence generators of degree r, with a fixed non-zero seed in the first generator, 2r Gold codes are obtained by varying the seed of the second generator from 0 to 2r-1. All pairs of M-sequences do not yield Gold codes, and those that yield Gold codes are called *preferred pairs*. Gold codes have three-valued autocorrelation and cross-correlation functions.

The Downlink Gold code sequences are of length 218-1. They begin at phase 0, go up to phase 38399, and are repeated. The Uplink Gold code sequences are of length 225-1.

WCDMA DL Gold Codes The scrambling code on the DL uses a Gold code of length 218-1. Gold codes are produced by XORing the outputs of two M-sequence generators. There are 512 possible scrambling sequences used on the DL, which when combined with the other overhead channels completely identify the cell that the UE is listening to.

Cross Correlation of Gold Codes

The ability of the UE to discriminate between multiple cells is achieved through the cross correlation properties of the scrambling codes. For Gold codes the cross correlation is three valued when correlating across the entire length of the sequence. This is not exactly realized in a true implementation. Usually only partial cross correlations are used resulting in slight degradations. The cross-correlation spectrum between any pair of sequences is three-valued, where those three values are–

t(n), -1, t(n)-2 where

Generic Physical Layer Procedures

- Coding
- Interleaving
- Mapping data onto physical channels
- Spreading using OVSF Channel codes
- PN Scrambling
- QPSK Modulation

The Physical Layer needs to take the transport data and put it onto a Physical Channel. In the process, it adds an optional CRC and codes the transport data using either convolutional or turbo coding. Afterwards, it optionally interleaves the data and breaks it into 10 ms radio frames. Rate matching and Transport Channel multiplexing work together to form a Coded Composite Transport Channel that more easily maps multiple Transport Channels to a Physical Channel. The second interleaving provides additional robustness to defeat long-term fades in the mobile environment.

Spreading is done with channelization codes—spreading changes symbols to chips at a particular rate. Scrambling is done with pseudorandom noise (PN) sequences— making the signal look like thermal noise.

Coding

There are two types of coding, convolutional and turbo. Convolutional coding uses Viterbi decoding and has been in practice for many decades. Turbo coding evolved in the early 90s and is now in common practice. Within turbo coding are convolutional coders. Additionally, turbo decoding iterates to converge on a solution.

The convolutional coder has a constraint length of 9 (K=9). This size is typical—a good tradeoff between complexity and performance. Zero tailing of the data means adding zeros to the data stream to flush the encoder/decoder. The turbo coder uses a parallel-concatenated convolutional code with two 8-state constituent encoders.

Turbo coding is most efficient at larger blocks sizes, approximately greater than 1000 symbols. Coding is done on code blocks, where code blocks are formed by first concatenating all transport blocks on a transport channel within a TTI, and then segmenting the resulting concatenation based on maximum code block size. The maximum size of the code block depends on whether convolution or turbo coding used for the transport channel.

Interleaving

Rate matching is required, because transport channels can have different bit rates. The bit rate can also change for a transport channel during different TTIs. Thus, to get the right Physical Channel bit rate, there needs to be rate matching of the individual Transport Channels prior to multiplexing.

Furthermore, the relative importance of each Transport Channel is signaled by the higher layers as Rate Matching Attributes (RMA). A Transport Channel with a higher RMA has more bits repeated (or fewer bits punctured). Rate matching attributes of all the Transport Channels are used together to compute repetition/puncturing factors.

1st Interleaving

(a) #Columns = TTI/10 ms.

(b) #Rows = #bits in the Transport Channel per 10 ms.

(c) Permute columns.

(d) Read by columns. Transport Channel Multiplexing puts the variety of Transport Channels onto a single channel, the Coded Composite Transport Channel (CCTrCh). This occurs in 10 ms radio frame increments.

2nd Interleaving

(a) Write in rows of 30 columns wide. For Physical Channel 'p', up, i are the bits in the 10 ms radio frame.

(b) Permute columns.

(c) Read by columns.

Physical Channel (DL)

The 10 ms CCTrCh, after 2nd Interleaving, is placed into the data bits of the Dedicated Physical Data Channel (UL or DL). Additionally, the TFCI (Transport Format Combination Indicator) is sent on the Dedicated Physical Control Channel (UL or DL). The TFCI specifies the transport formats that are currently used in the CCTrCh over the 10 ms period. Also, Pilot bits, used for synchronization, and the transmit power command, used for power control, are included. Pilot bits are for channel estimation (synchronization) and for signal powerestimation for Downlink power control. The transmit power command is a bit pattern and maps to a single up/down command used in closed loop power control. The rate is 1500 Hz: 15 slots/frame * 100 radio frames/sec.

Physical Channel (UL)

The 10 ms CCTrCh, after 2nd Interleaving, is placed into the data bits of the Dedicated Physical Data Channel (UL or

DL). Additionally, the TFCI (Transport Format Combination Indicator) is sent on the Dedicated Physical Control Channel (UL or DL). The TFCI specifies the transport formats currently being used in the CCTrCh over the 10 ms period. Pilot bits, used for synchronization, the transmit power command, used for power control, and Feedback Indicators, used for some transmit diversity schemes, are also included. Pilot bits are for channel estimation (synchronization) and for signal power estimation for Downlink power control. The transmit power command is a bit pattern and maps to a single up/down command used in closed loop power control. The rate is 1500 Hz: 15 slots/frame * 100 radio frames/sec. When there is no data transmitted on the DPDCH, the DPCCH is still active. The DPCCH is sent on a separate channelization code than the DPDCH.

Spreading and Scrambling (DL)

The Physical Channels (except *synchronization channel SCH)* are spread to the chip rate with individual channelization codes and then scrambled with the same scrambling code. In the DL, each *dedicated physical control channel DPCH* data and control are multiplexed together. For each pair of symbols, one is sent to the I branch and the other is sent to the Q branch. Both are scrambled using the same channelization code. Afterwards, the signal is scrambled using either a primary or secondary scrambling code. The Gs are the DL weight factors: G is for the Physical Channels; Gp, Gs for the Primary and Secondary Synchronization Channels. Cch,SF,m is the channelization code with the m-th code of spreading factor, SF. Sdl,n is the n-th Downlink scrambling code, where n is 1 of 8192 codes.

Spreading and Scrambling (UL)

The Physical Channels are spread to the chip rate with individual channelization codes and then scrambled with the same scrambling code. In the UL, the *dedicated physical control channel DPCCH* is always on the Q branch, while the *dedicated physical data channel DPDCHs* can be on both the I and Q branch; if there is only one DPDCH, it is on the I branch. βs are the UL weight factors. βd is for data and βc is for control. Notice that the DPCCH is on the Q branch and single DPDCHs are either on the I or Q branch. This is really BPSK. Cd is the channelization code for the DPDCH. Cc is the channelization code for the DPCCH. Sul,n is the n-th scrambling code for the UL DPDCH/DPCCH, where n is 1 of 224 codes.

QPSK Modulation

Both the UL and the DL arrive here after scrambling. The signal is split into a real and imaginary part, passed through a pulse-shaping filter, and mixed with an in-phase and quadrature-phase signal. The pulse-shaping filter is a Root-Raised Cosine (RRC) filter.

CONCLUSION

Advantages

- Improvement in spectral efficiency is accomplished with Code Division Multiple Access (CDMA).
- WCDMA systems support increased voice call capacity by using a wider bandwidth.
- GSM is an internationally supported cellular standard; global uniformity will facilitate International Roaming.
- There are several different QoS classes for maximum transfer delay, delay variation, and bit error rate targets, and for four types of traffic: Conversational, Streaming, Interactive, and Background.

Disadvantages

- Increased use of spectrum can complicate deployment and increase costs.
- UMTS currently offers lower data rates than competing technologies.

Future of WCDMA/UMTS

- Release 5, referred to as *High Speed Downlink Packet Access (HSDPA)*, will provide improvements in peak data rate, cell throughput, and round trip delay.
- Release 6 will incorporate the use of Multiple-Input Multiple-Output (MIMO) technologies.

- More carriers are transitioning from *Global System for Mobile Communication (GSM)* to WCDMA/UMTS systems.

REFERENCES

1. 80-W0421-1 Rev D by Qualcomm
2. CDMA (UMTS) Overview 80-W0068-1 Rev B by Qualcomm
3. The cdmaOne Standard 80-13322-1 Rev X6 by Qualcomm

An Introduction to Fuzzy Control Systems

10

Bharat Bhushan Agarwal, Manoj Kumar and
Sumit Prakash Tayal

ABSTRACT

Fuzzy logic is a superset of conventional (Boolean) logic that has been extended to handle the concept of partial truth - truth-values between "completely true" and "completely false". Dr. Lotfi Zadeh of U.C. Berkeley introduced it in the 1960's.This paper introduces fuzzy logic & fuzzy subset theory. Fuzzy controllers with if... then type are considered. examples of fuzzy control systems are also considered.

INTRODUCTION

Fuzzy logic is a superset of conventional (Boolean) logic that has been extended to handle the concept of partial truth - truth-values between "completely true" and "completely false". Dr. Lotfi Zadeh of U.C. Berkeley introduced it in the 1960's.

Fuzzy logic is a powerful problem-solving methodology with a myriad of applications in embedded control and information processing. Fuzzy provides a remarkably simple way to draw definite conclusions from vague, ambiguous or imprecise information. In a sense, fuzzy logic resembles human decision making with its ability to work from approximate data and find precise solutions.

As its name suggests, it is the logic underlying modes of reasoning which are approximate rather than exact. The importance of fuzzy logic derives from the fact that most modes of human reasoning and especially common sense reasoning are approximate in nature. The essential characteristics of fuzzy logic founded by Dr. Lotfi Zadeh are as follows. In fuzzy logic, exact reasoning is viewed as a limiting case of approximate reasoning. In fuzzy logic everything is a matter of degree. Any logical system can be fuzzified In fuzzy logic, knowledge is interpreted as a collection of elastic or, equivalently, fuzzy constraint on a collection of variables Inference is viewed as a process of propagation of elastic constraints. The third statements hence, define Boolean logic as a subset of Fuzzy logic.

Fuzzy Subset Theory

There is a strong relationship between Boolean logic and the concept of a subset. Similarly, there is a strong relationship between fuzzy logic and fuzzy subset theory. A subset U of a set S can be defined as a set of ordered pairs, each with a first element that is an element of the set S, and a second element that is an element of the set { 0, 1 }, with exactly one ordered pair present for each element of S. This defines a mapping between elements of S and elements of the set { 0, 1 }. The value zero is used to represent non-membership, and the value one is used to represent membership. The truth or falsity of the statement x is in U is determined by finding the ordered pair whose first element is x. The statement is true if the second element of the ordered pair is 1, and the statement is false if it is 0. Similarly, a fuzzy subset F of a set S can be defined as a set of ordered pairs, each with a first element that is an element of the set S, and a second element that is a value in the interval [0, 1], with exactly one ordered pair present for each element of S. This defines a mapping between elements of the set S and values in the interval [0, 1]. The value zero is used to represent complete non-membership, the value one is used to represent complete membership, and values in between are used to represent intermediate *degrees of membership*. The set S is referred to as the *universe of discourse* for the fuzzy subset F. Frequently, the mapping is described as a function, the *membership function* of F. The degree to which the statement *x is in F* is true is determined by finding the ordered pair whose first element is x. The *degree of truth* of the statement is the second element of the ordered pair. This can be illustrated with an example. Let's talk about people and "youthness". In this case the set S (the universe of discourse) is the set of people. A fuzzy subset YOUNG is also defined, which answers the question "to what degree is person x young?" To each person in the universe of discourse, we have to assign a degree of membership in the fuzzy subset YOUNG. The easiest way to do this is with a membership function based on the person's age.

young(x) = {1, if age(x) <= 20.,
(30-age(x))/10, if 20 < age(x) <= 30,
0, if age(x) > 30}

A graph of this looks like:

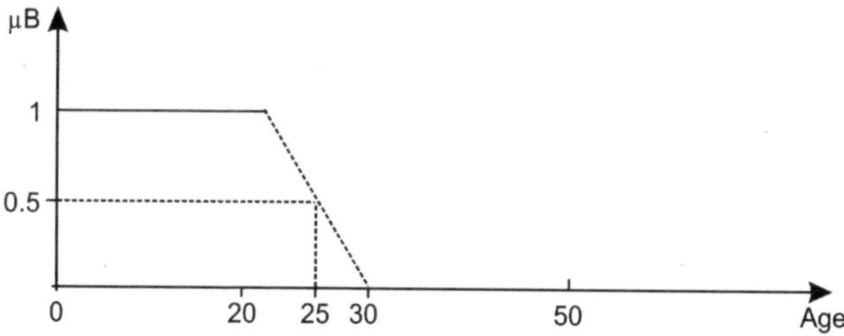

Given this definition, here are some example values:

Person	Age	Degree of youth
Johan	10	1.00
Edwin	21	0.90
Parthiban	25	0.50
Arosha	26	0.40
Chin Wei	28	0.20
Rajkumar	83	0.00

So given this definition, we'd say that the degree of truth of the statement "Parthiban is YOUNG" is 0.50.

Note: Membership functions almost never have as simple a shape as age(x). They will at least tend to be triangles pointing up, and they can be much more complex than that. Furthermore, membership functions so far are discussed as if they always are based on a single criterion, but this isn't always the case, although it is the most common case. One could, for example, want to have the membership function for YOUNG depend on both a person's age and their height (Arosha's short for his age). This is perfectly legitimate, and occasionally used in practice. It's referred to as a two-dimensional membership function. It's also possible to have even more criteria, or to have the membership function depend on elements from two completely different universes of discourse.

Fuzzy Logic Operations

It is clear what the statement *X is LOW* means in fuzzy logic. But, how do we interpret a statement like

X is LOW and Y is HIGH or (not Z is MEDIUM)

The standard definitions in fuzzy logic as suggested by Lotfi are:

(1) *Negate (negation criterion) : truth (not x) = 1.0 - truth (x)*

(2) *Intersection(minimum criterion): truth (x and y) = minimum (truth(x), truth(y))*

(3) *Union(maximum criterion): truth (x or y) = maximum (truth(x), truth(y))*

In order to clarify this, a few examples are given. Let *A* be a fuzzy interval *between 5 and* 8 and *B* be a fuzzy number *about* 4. The corresponding figures are shown below.

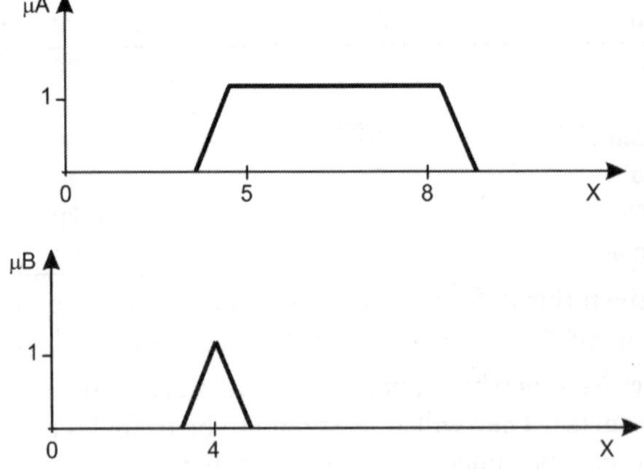

The figure below gives an example for a negation. The blue line is the NEGATION of the fuzzy set A. Note that the *negation* criterion is used.

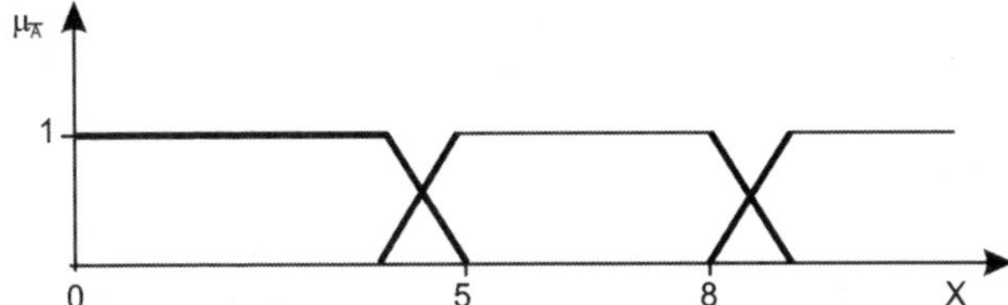

The following figure shows the fuzzy set between 5 and 8 **AND** about 4 (blue line). This time the *minimum* criterion is used

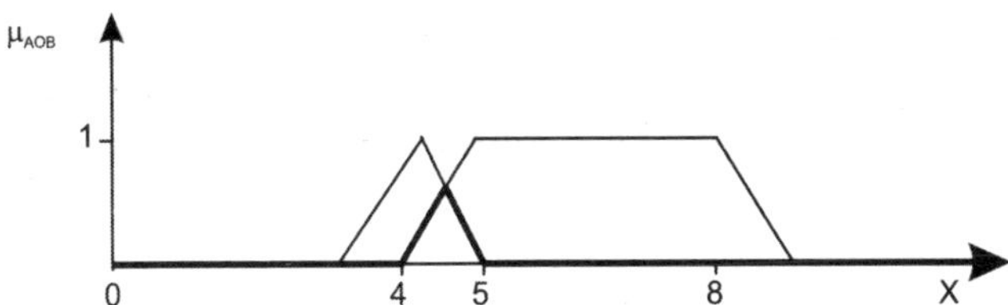

Finally, the Fuzzy set *between* 5 and 8 **OR** *about* 4 is shown in the next figure (blue line). This time the *maximum* criterion is used.

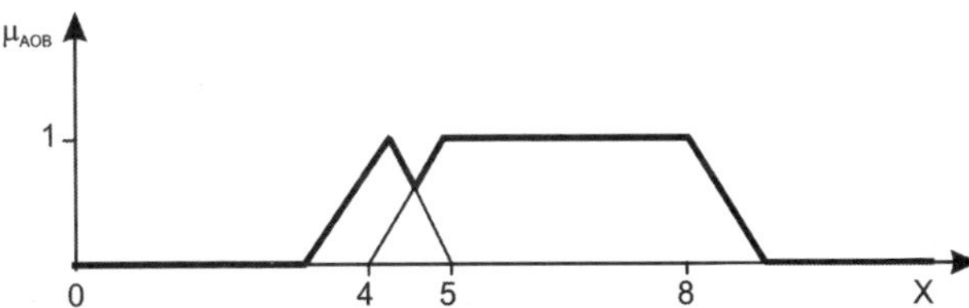

These basic operations, provide guidelines to construct more complex ones which in turn can be used to create fuzzy machines.

Fuzzy Control

* "Fuzzy logic" has become a common buzzword in machine control. However, the term itself inspires certain skepticism, sounding equivalent to "half-baked logic" or "bogus logic". Some other nomenclature might have been preferable, but it's too late now, and fuzzy logic is actually very straightforward. Fuzzy logic is a way of interfacing inherently analog processes that move through a continuous range of values, to a digital computer, that likes to see things as well-defined discrete numeric values.

For example, consider an antilock braking system, directed by a micro controller chip. The micro controller has to make decisions based on brake temperature, speed, and other variables in the system.

The variable "temperature" in this system can be divided into a range of "states", such as: "cold", "cool", "moderate", "warm", "hot", "very hot". Defining the bounds of these states is a bit tricky. An arbitrary threshold might be set to divide "warm" from "hot", but this would result in a discontinuous change when the input value passed over that threshold.

The way around this is to make the states "fuzzy", that is, allow them to change gradually from one state to the next. You could define the input temperature states using "membership functions" such as the following:

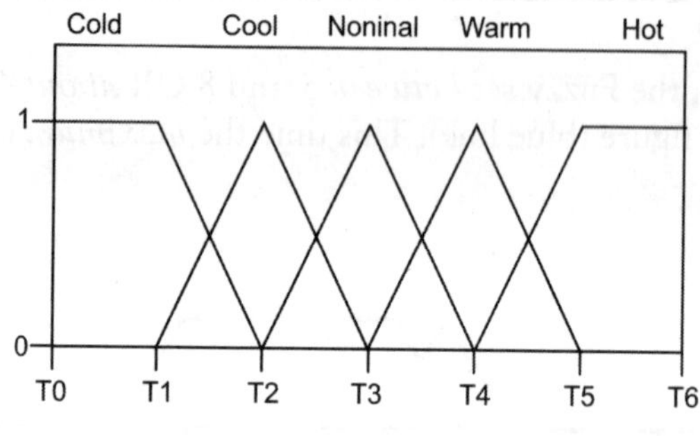

Fig. 1

With this scheme, the input variable's state no longer jumps abruptly from one state to the next. Instead, as the temperature changes, it loses value in one membership function while gaining value in the next. At any one time, the "truth value" of the brake temperature will almost always be in some degree part of two membership functions: 0.6 nominal and 0.4 warm, or 0.7 nominal and 0.3 cool, and so on.

Fuzzification

The input variables in a fuzzy control system are in general mapped into by sets of membership functions similar to this, known as "fuzzy sets". The process of converting a crisp input value to a fuzzy value is called "fuzzification".

A control system may also have various types of switch, or "ON-OFF", inputs along with its analog inputs, and such switch inputs of course will always have a truth value equal to either 1 or 0, but the scheme can deal with them as simplified fuzzy functions that are either one value or another.

Rules

Given "mappings" of input variables into membership functions and truth-values, the micro controller then makes decisions for what action to take based on a set of "rules", each of the form:

IF brake temperature IS warm AND speed IS not very fast

THEN brake pressure IS slightly decreased.

All the rules that apply are invoked, using the membership functions and truth-values obtained from the inputs, to determine the result of the rule.

Defuzzification

This result in turn will be mapped into a membership function and truth-value controlling the output variable. These results are combined to give a specific ("crisp") answer, the actual brake pressure, a procedure known as "defuzzification".

This combination of fuzzy operations and rule-based "inference" describes a "fuzzy expert system". Traditional control systems are based on mathematical models in which the control system is described using one or more differential equations that define the system response to its inputs. Such systems are often implemented as "proportional-integral-derivative (PID)" controllers. They are the products of decades of development and theoretical analysis, and are highly effective.

If PID and other traditional control systems are so well developed, why bother with fuzzy control? It has some advantages. In many cases, the mathematical model of the control process may not exist, or may be too "expensive" in terms of computer processing power and memory, and a system based on empirical rules may be more effective.

Furthermore, fuzzy logic is well suited to low-cost implementations based on cheap sensors, low-resolution analog-to-digital converters, and 4-bit or 8-bit one-chip micro controller chips. Such systems can be easily upgraded by adding new rules to improve performance or add new features. In many cases, fuzzy control can be used to improve existing traditional controller systems by adding an extra layer of intelligence to the current control method.

Fuzzy controllers are very simple conceptually. They consist of an input stage, a processing stage, and an output stage. The input stage maps sensor or other inputs, such as switches, thumbwheels, and so on, to the appropriate membership functions and truth-values. The processing stage invokes each appropriate rule and generates a result for each, then combines the results of the rules. Finally, the output stage converts the combined result back into a specific control output value.

The most common shape of membership functions is triangular, although trapezoids and bell curves are also used, but the shape is generally less important than the number of curves and their placement. From three to seven curves are generally appropriate to cover the required range of an input value, or the "universe of discourse" in fuzzy jargon.

As discussed earlier, the processing stage is based on a collection of logic rules in the form of IF-THEN statements, where the IF part is called the "antecedent" and the THEN part is called the "consequent". Typical fuzzy control systems have dozens of rules.

Consider a rule for a thermostat:

IF (temperature is "cold") THEN (heater is "high")

This rule uses the truth-value of the "temperature" input, which is some truth-value of "cold", to generate a result in the fuzzy set for the "heater" output, which is some value of "high". This result is used with the results of other rules to finally generate the crisp composite output. Obviously, the greater the truth value of "cold", the higher the truth value of "high", though this does not necessarily mean that the output itself will be set to "high", since this is only one rule among many.

In some cases, the membership functions can be modified by "hedges" that are equivalent to adjectives. Common hedges include "about", "near", "close to", "approximately", "very", "slightly", "too", "extremely", and "somewhat". These operations may have precise definitions, though the definitions can vary considerably between different implementations. "Very", for one example, squares membership functions; since the membership values are always less than 1, this narrows the membership function. "Extremely" cubes the values to give greater narrowing, while "somewhat" broadens the function by taking the square root.

In practice, the fuzzy rule sets usually have several antecedents that are combined using fuzzy operators, such as AND, OR, and NOT, though again the definitions tend to vary: AND, in one popular definition, simply uses the minimum weight of all the antecedents, while OR uses the maximum value. There is also a NOT operator that subtracts a membership function from 1 to give the "complementary" function.

There are several different ways to define the result of a rule, but one of the most common and simplest is the "max-min" inference method, in which the output membership function is given the truth-value generated by the premise.

Rules can be solved in parallel in hardware, or sequentially in software. The results of all the rules that have fired are "defuzzified" to a crisp value by one of several methods. There are dozens in theory, each with various advantages and drawbacks.

The "centroid" method is very popular, in which the "center of mass" of the result provides the crisp value. Another approach is the "height" method, which takes the value of the biggest contributor. The centroid method favors the rule with the output of greatest area, while the height method obviously favors the rule with the greatest output value.

Notice how each rule provides a result as a truth-value of a particular membership function for the output variable. In centroid defuzzification the values are OR'd, that is, the maximum value is used and values are not added, and the results are then combined using a centroid calculation.

* Fuzzy control system design is based on empirical methods, basically a methodical approach to trial-and-error. The general process is as follows:

Document the system's operational specifications and inputs and outputs.

Document the fuzzy sets for the inputs.

Document the rule set.

Determine the defuzzification method.

Run through test suite to validate system, adjust details as required.

Complete document and release to production.

As a general example, consider the design of a fuzzy controller for a steam turbine. The block diagram of this control system appears as follows:

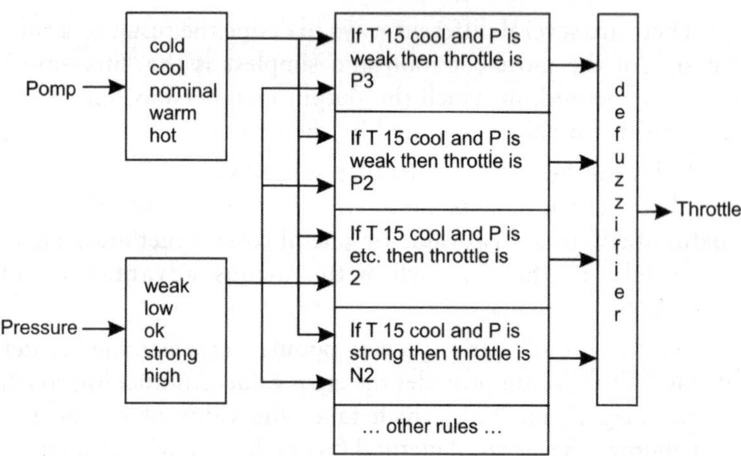

Fig. 2

There are two input variables, temperature and pressure, and a single output variable, the turbine throttle setting. The turbine's operation can be reversed, so the throttle setting can be positive or negative. The fuzzy set mappings are shown below

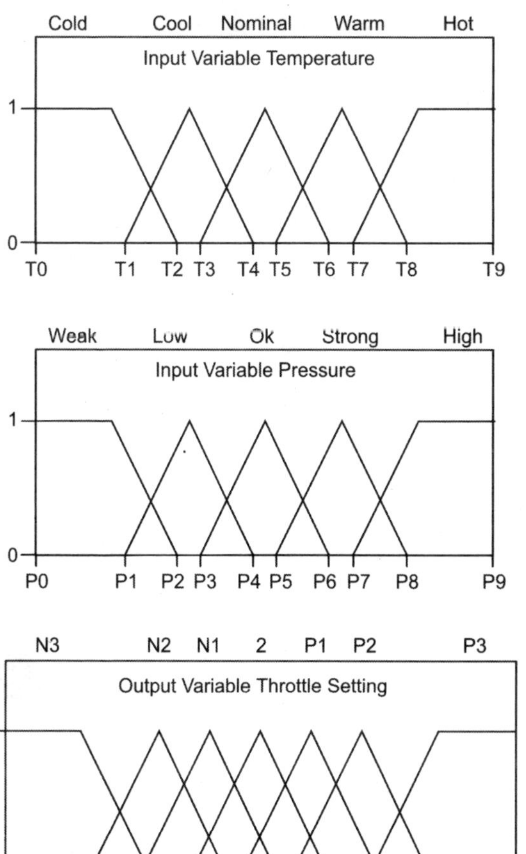

Fig. 3

The throttle settings are defined as follows:

N3: Large negative.

N2: Medium negative.

N1: Small negative.

Z: Zero.

P1: Small positive.

P2: Medium positive.

P3: Large positive.

The rule set includes such rules as:

rule 1: IF temperature IS cool AND pressure IS weak, THEN throttle is P3.

rule 2: IF temperature IS cool AND pressure IS low, THEN throttle is P2.

rule 3: IF temperature IS cool AND pressure IS ok, THEN throttle is Z.

rule 4: IF temperature IS cool AND pressure IS strong, THEN throttle is N2.

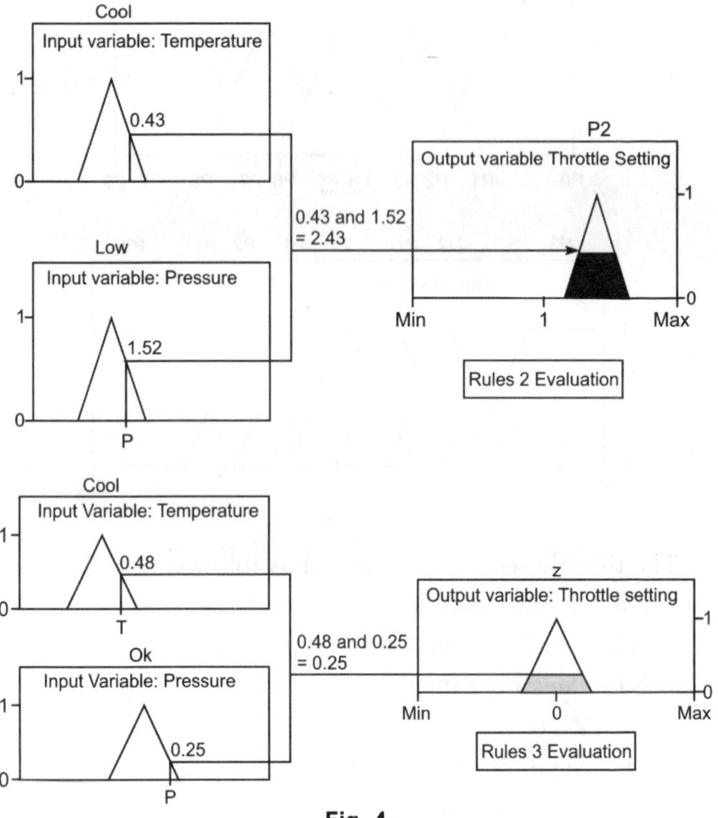

Fig. 4

In practice, the controller accepts the inputs and maps them into their membership functions and truth-values. These mappings are then fed into the rules. If the rule specifies an AND relationship between the mappings of the two input variables, as the examples above do, the minimum of the two is used as the combined truth value; if an OR is specified, the maximum is used. The appropriate output state is selected and assigned a membership value at the truth level of the premise. The truth-values are then defuzzified.

For an example, assume the temperature is in the "cool" state, and the pressure is in the "low" and "ok" states. The pressure values ensure that only rules 2 and 3 fire. Rule 2 is evaluated as follows:

The two outputs are then combined:

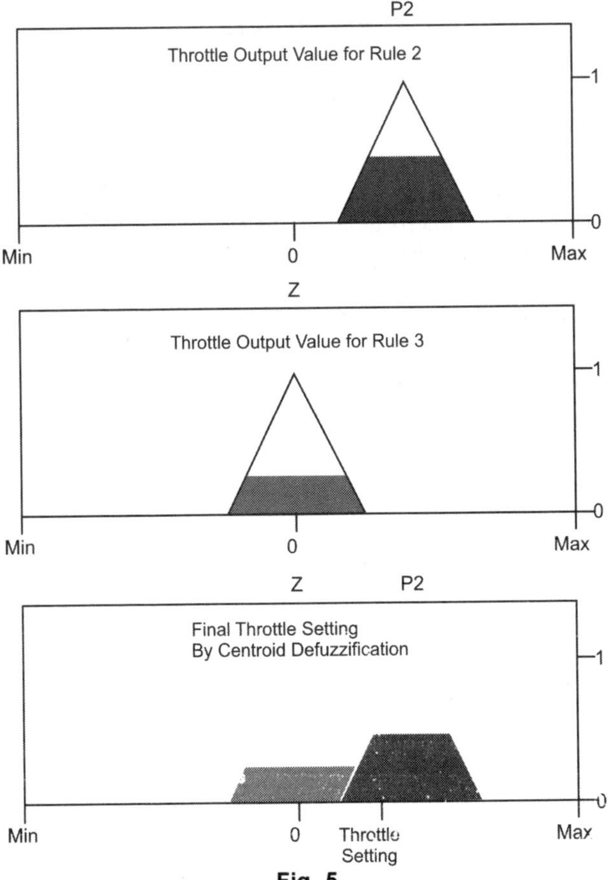

Fig. 5

The output value will adjust the throttle and then the control cycle will begin again to generate the next value.

CONCLUSION

In literature there are many reasoning systems. generally they are classified as conjunctions, disjunctions, and implications. Here only some of them are applied approximate reasoning. Main idea of the paper is to show that behavior of fuzzy controller depend mainly on the rules and a plant parameters, not on reasoning and defuzzification mmethods. It will give best out of it as it is integrated with comuting methods like artificial intelligence etc.

REFERENCES

1. "Designing With Fuzzy Logic" by Kevin Self, IEEE SPECTRUM, November 1990, 42:44, 105.
2. "Fuzzy Fundamentals" by Earl Cox, IEEE SPECTRUM, October 1992, 58:61. Notes from this article constitute the core of this tutorial.
3. "Fuzzy Logic Flowers In Japan" by Daniel G. Schwartz & George J. Klir, IEEE SPECTRUM, July 1992, 32:35.
4. "Clear Thinking On Fuzzy Logic" by Lawrence A. Berardinis, MACHINE DESIGN, 23 April 1992, 46:52.
5. "Fuzzy Controller Challenges 8-bit MCUs", COMPUTER DESIGN, November 1995.
6. "Dishwasher Cleans Up With Fuzzy Logic", MACHINE DESIGN, 23 March 1995.
7. "How To Design Fuzzy Logic Controllers", MACHINE DESIGN, 26 November 1992.

ON-OFF Traffic Model for Simulation for Calculating Threshold in ATM Network using Fuzzy in Multicasing Routing in ATM Networks

Vinita Dutt

ABSTRACT

The ATM (Asynchronous Transfer Mode) is the chosen technology for implementing B-ISDN (Broadband integrated Services Digital Network). ATM provides different typs of service categories such as CBR (constant bit rate), VBR (variable bit rate) and ABR (available bit rate) classes of data transport.

The VBR service in ATM can be used to transport data traffic with very stringent real-time requirements or where timely delivery is important.There are two subclasses of VBR, first one is real-time VBR, which is used where time requirements are very stringent such as video conferencing. Other subclass is used where timely delivery is a must but some jitters can be tolerated such as multimedia email.

ATM switch maintain queue of packets (or cells) and based on schemes used, their performance changes. There are many variables that calculate the performance of a switch such as throughput, cell loss etc.

In most schemes, threshold is used to manage the buffe. There are different threshold methods, such as dynamic threshold, static threshold, push-out etc. In our project, we have compared the performance of all the schemes using dynamic and static threshold. We also purposed a new concept to calculate the threshold. This new concept is 'Fuzzy logic'.

Fuzzy logic has emerged as an indispensable tool for configuring human friendly machines and speech recognizable systems such as nursing, home robots and for developing artificial intelligent tools which support man in production control, medical diagnosis, general decision making, controlling of subway systems and complex industrial processes, expert systems.

Fuzzy logic is the latest area in which tremendous research is going on in the field of networking. Analytical explanations and simulation results are presented in our project. From the results it is concluded that fuzzy approach for the calculation of threshold, show more desirable results as compared to other types of thresholds.

INTRODUCTION

Asynchronous Transfer Mode (ATM) Concept

ATM is the culmination of all the developments in switching and transmission in the last twenty years. This includes the advent of packet switching and the change from coaxial to optical. ATM is fundamentally a packet switching technology, not a circuit switching technology. The transfer mode is called asynchronous because it is not synchronous i.e. not tied to a master clock, as most long distance telephone lines are. ATM networks are connection oriented. Making a call requires first sending a message to set up the connection.

After that subsequent cell all follow the same path the destination. Cell delivery is not guaranteed, but there order is [14].

The most basic service building block is the ATM virtual circuit, which is an end-to-end connection that has defined end points and routes but does have bandwidth dedicated to it. Bandwidth is allocated on demand by the network as users have data to transmit. Virtual circuits have many advantages over circuit switching (Virtual circuits are explained latter in the report). The basic idea behind the ATM is to transmit all information in small fixed size packets called cells.

CCITT definition a transfer mode in which the information is organized into cells; it is asynchronous in the sense that the recurrence of cells containing information from a particular user is not necessarily periodic.

No error protection or flow control on a link-by-link basis because links are assumed to be high quality with low bit error rate.

Basic ATM Switching Properties

ATM switch should satisfy the following requirements for CBR and VBR traffic types [14]:

- Bounded delay(less than 1ms/node)
- Arbitrary small cell loss probability (less than 10-6 per nodc)
- Close to 100% throughput
- Above 150 Mbps per port
- Self routing and distributed control
- Modularity and scalability
- Multicast function

ATM switches should be non-blocking for reducing the cell loss probability. In general, two types of conflict can occur inside the switch.

- **Output Conflict**: When more than one cell destined for the same output port has arrived, a cell conflict occurs at the output port. This conflict can be solved by increasing the number of cells accepted simultaneously at the output port (i.e. by using output buffer at the output port).
- **Internal Conflict**: When cell with different destination request the same internal link, an internal cell conflict occurs.

Multicasting Schemes

Unicasting and Broadcasting

Unicasting means sending a message from a single source to a single destination. Whereas in broadcasting, a message is sent to all the destinations; like in television transmission the signals are broadcasted to all the destinations through the satellites.

Multicasting

Multicasting can be simply defined as the ability to send one message to one or more destinations in a single operation. This is different than using replicated unicast, which sends messages from one node to a group of nodes by sending to each node individually. This will incur one operation for each destination node and is non-atomic. A 1:N multicast allows one source to reach N destinations. An M:N multicast allows M sources to reach N destinations.

Why Multicasting ?

Many envisioned applications in asynchronous transfer mode (ATM) networks are multicast in nature and are expected to generate a significant portion of the total traffic. Examples of such applications are broadcast video-conferencing, multiparty telephony and work group applications. The ability to support multicast traffic is therefore a basic functionality that needs to be implemented in ATM switches. Mechanisms have to be provided in the switches to replicate cells arriving at an incoming multicast virtual connection (VC) and deliver them to multiple outgoing legs of that connection.

Requirements for ATM multicast

ATM imposes specific requirements [11] that must be considered for the design of the multicast services. The short, fixed length of the ATM cell requires an adaptation layer at the end points to transfer complete message and guarantee that intermediate switches do not interleave cells from different sources. The overhead of setup and tear-down for the connection based ATM protocol require an efficient mechanism for adding and removing users to a multicast group. The limited size of the VPI/VCI field prevents the use of source-based routing, as used by the existing IP multicast routing programs.

	A			B		C		D
Timing	Real time	None	real time	None	real time	None	real time	None
Bit rate	Constant		Variable		Constant		Variable	
Mode	Connection Oriented				Connectionless			

Fig. 1: Multicast Application Characteristics

Fig. 1 gives an indication of the requirement of those application types that would require multicasting protocols.

Connection oriented protocols can incur a high overhead when setting up and destroying links, therefore connectionless links are preferable. Some applications that require multicasting such as audio would prefer a constant bit rate where as video is less susceptible to the jitters. This is due to a human's high sensitivity to audio jitter. It can then be taken from the Fig. 2 that class D services are along the lines needed to implement on an ATM network.

Multicasting schemes for shared memory switch

Various way of supporting multicast operation with shared-memory architecture can be categorized under two different classes [12]:

- Replication-at-receiving (RAR) or copying Network scheme
- Replication-at-sending (RAS)

A brief description of each of the multicast classes is given below.

RAR schemes

In RAR scheme, a multicast cell arriving at the switch and destined to m destinations is first copied m timing Fig. 2. A copy of the cell is linked to each output queue to which the multicast cell is destined. All copies are stored in the buffer and then each copy is served independently.

The RAR scheme has been used in several existing shared memory switched because it is relatively simple to implement [3]. In fact, once a cell has been replicated each copy of the cell can be treated in the same way as a unicast cell. Consequently, both the control and the structure of the linked lists are basically the same as those used in a unicast switch.

RAS scheme

In RAS scheme the multicast cell is not replicate before storage in shared buffer, only single instance of cell is stored in the buffer. Cell is replicated at the output port.this is the shown in Fig. 3.

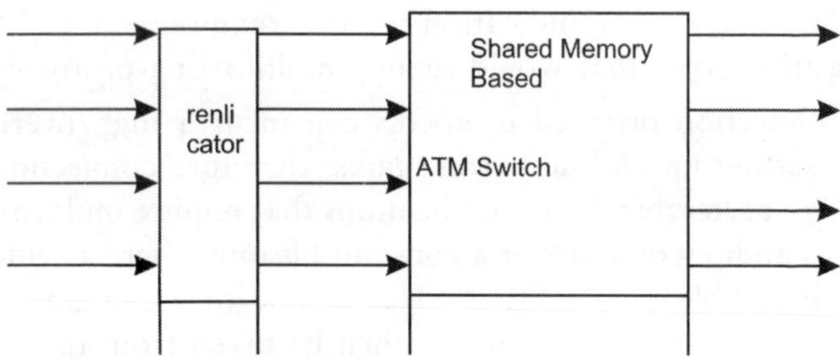

MWMR Multicast Scheme

Fig. 2: Shared Memory: Multicasting with copying n/w

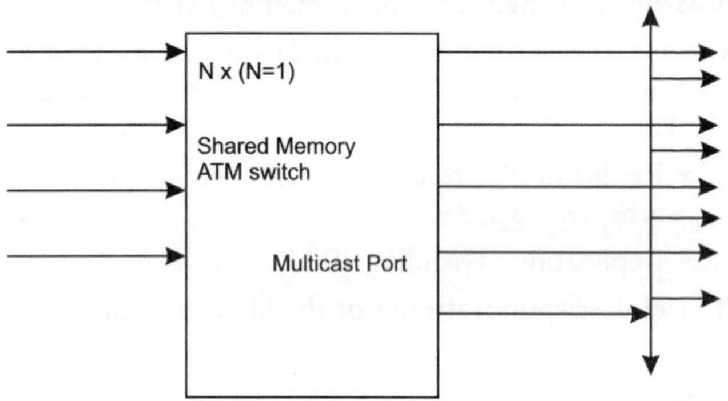

Fig. 3: SWSR Multicast Support employing a fanout bus For Replication

Multiple write multiple read (MWMR)

This is a straightforward solution to provide multicast support. The MWMR scheme applies to all those multicast schemes where an incoming multicast cell is replicated first, and then its multiple copies are used to write into and read out of the shared memory space for switching purpose. A multicast cell is replicated for all its multicast connections and switched to a predestined group of output ports with the help of a point-to-point routing network before being written to the shared memory space.

From a shared memory point of view, a multicast cell is replicated into multiple copies and stored in shared memory (multiple write); then multiple copies are eventually read out of the shared memory (multiple read) for their respective output port.

Single write single read (SWSR)

In this scheme, multicast cells form a separate logical queue within the shared memory space. A dedicated multicast output port is used to serve multicast cells in a first-in-first-out(FIFO) fashion in every cycle. In a given write cycle, upto N multicast cells or some combination of unicast and multicast cells can be written to the shared memory for switching purposes. During a given read cycle, upto N unicast cells and one multicast can be read out of the shared memory. If a multicast cell is read out of the shared memory, it is routed to the high-speed bus for its replication and transmission to its fanout destinations.

ATM Switches & Threshold Concepts

ATM switches

Many ATM cell switch designs have been described in the literature. Some of these have been implemented and tested. In the selection we will give a brief introduction to the principal of ATM cell switch design.

The general model for an ATM cell switch in Fig. 4. it has some number of input lines and some number of output lines, almost always the same number because the lines are bi-directional. ATM switches are generally synchronous in the sense that during a cycle, one cell is taken from each input line, if present, passed into the internal switching febric and eventually transmitted on the appropriate output line.

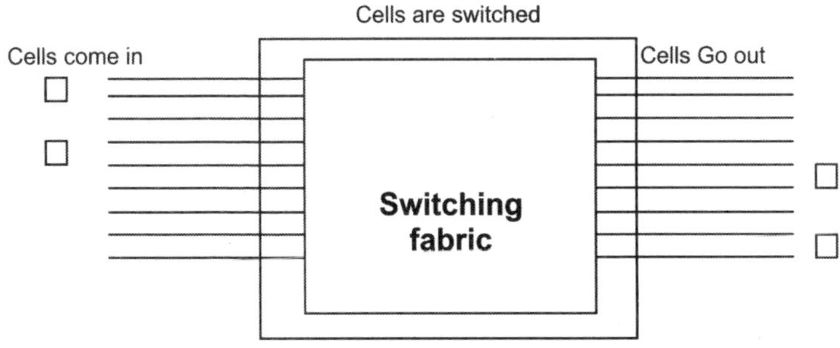

Fig. 4: A Generic ATM Switch

Switches may be pipelined, That is, it may take several cycles before an incoming cell appears on its output line. Cell arrive on the input lines asynchronously, so there is a master clock that makes the beginning of a cycle. Any cell fully arrived when the clock ticks is eligible for switching during that cycle. A cell not fully arrived has to wait until the next cycle.

Cells arrive at normally about 150 Mbps. This works out to slightly over 360, 000 cells/sec, which means that the cycle time of the switch has to be about 2.7μ sec. A commercial switch might have anywhere from 16 to 1024 input lines, which means that it must be prepared to accept and switching a batch of 16 to 1024 cells every 2.7μ sec. The fact that the cells are fixed length and short (53 bytes) makes it possible to build such switches. with longer variable length packets, high speed switching would be more complex. All ATM switches have to common goals:

1. Switch all cells with as low a discard rate as possible.
2. Never reorder the cells on a virtual circuit.

Goal one says that it is permitted to drop cells in emergencies, but that the loss rate should be as small as possible .A loss rate of 1 cell in 10 12 is probably acceptable. On a large switch, this loss rate is about 1or 2 cell per hour.

Goal two says that cells arriving on a virtual circuit in a certain order must also depart in that order, with no exception, ever.

Concept of Threshold

Most of the ATM switch architectures that have been proposed in the literature use some buffering to accommodate packets, whose service has been delayed due to contention for some resources within the switch.The location of these buffers and the queue lenth management scheme directly affect the performance of such a switch.We can apply threshold to increase the throughput. Threshold means placing restrictions on the amount of buffering a port can use. Some of the technioques are static threshold, and dynamic threshold [2]. In this thesis we propose a new scheme fuzzy approach to determine the threshold.

Static threshold

Static threshold (ST) scheme places limits on the maximum or minimum amount of buffering that should be available to any individual queue. In this method, an arriving cell is admitted only if the queue length at its destination output port is smaller then a given threshold.

Push out scheme

In this buffer management scheme, arriving cells are allowed to enter the buffer as long as there is space and when the buffer fills up, an incoming cell is allowed to enter by selectively overwriting another cell that is already in the buffer. In Push Out scheme [2] (PO) a cell that arrives to find the buffer full pushes out the cell at the head of the longest queue. While the incoming cell usurps at the physical space of the discarded cell; the incoming cell does not take over the discarded cell's position in its logical output port queue.

Indeed, the pushing and pushed cells may belong to different output queues. Rather, the arriving cell joins its own logical queue.

Dynamic threshold scheme

Dynamic threshold (DT) fairly regulates the sharing of memory among different output queue. The approach is conceptually similar to bottleneck flow control and to the bandwidth balancing mechanism in distributed queue dual bus (DQDB) networks.

The key idea is that the output queue length threshold, at any instant of time, is proportional to the current amount of unused buffering in the switch. Cell arrivals for an output port are blocked whenever the output port's queue length equals or exceeds the current threshold value. The DT technique deliberately holds a small amount of buffer space in reserve, but distributes the remaining buffer space equally among the active output queues.

All queues with sufficient traffic to warrant threshold should obtain the same amount space, called the control threshold. The control threshold value is determined by monitoring the total amount of unused buffer space.

Let at time t, T(t) be the control threshold and let Qi(t) be the length of queue i. Let Q(t) be the sum of all of the queue lengths, that is the title occupancy of the shared memory and B is the total buffer space. An arriving cell for queue I will be blocked at time t if Qi (t)>= T(t). All cells going to this queue will be blocked until the queue length drains below the control threshold and/or the threshold rises above the queue length.The simplest scheme is to set the control threshold to a multiple of the unused buffer space.

$$T(t) = \alpha(B - Qi (t)) = \alpha (B-\Sigma Qi (t))$$

If α is the power of two (positive or negetive), then the threshold computation is extremely easy to implement. Only a shift register is required.

Fuzzy System

Concept of fuzzy logic

Fuzzy systems are defined with a strong mathematical basis. These systems are rule-based system. The heart of a fuzzy system is a rule base which consist of if-Then rules. The rule are statements in which some words are characterized by continuous membership functions. A fuzzy system is basically made of a fuzzifier, a defuzzifier an inference engine and a rule base as shown in Fig. 5. The role of the fuzzifier is to map the crisp input data value to fuzzy sets defined by their membership functions depending on the degree of "possibility" of the input data. The goal of the defuzzifier is to map the output fuzzy sets to a crisp output value. It combines the different fuzzy sets with different degrees of possibility to produce a single numerical value. The fuzzy inference engine defines how the system should infer through the rules in the rule base to determine the output fuzzy sets.

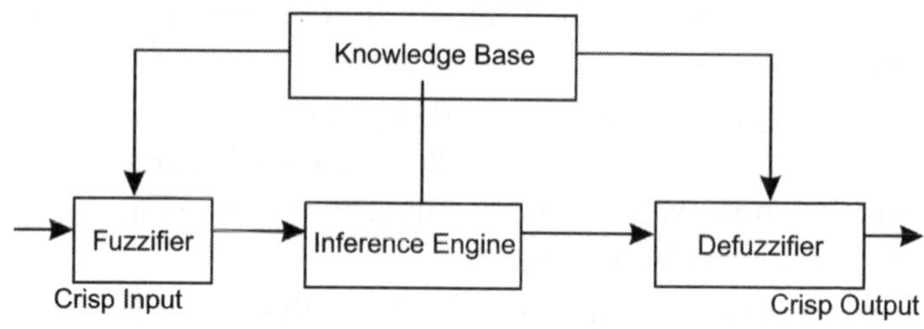

Fig. 5: Basic Fuzzy System

The fuzzy theory has emerged as a theory suited to represent uncertainity contained in the meaning of each word. Fuzzy logic has emerged as a indispensable tool [7] for configuring human friendly machines and speech recognizable systems such as nursing and home robots and for developing artificial intelligent tools [9] which support man in production control, medical diagnosis, general decision making, controlling of subway systems and complex industrial processes, expert systems.

Fuzzy logic was is basically a concept derived from the branch of mathematical theory of fuzzy sets. It is capable of expressing linguistic terms such as "may be false" or "sort of true". In general, fuzzy logic when applied to computers, allow them to emulate the human reasoning process, quantify imprecise information, make decisions based on vague and incomplete data yet by applying a "defuzzification" process, arrive at definite conclusions.

Our fuzzy approach

In our fuzzy approach, line occupancy as well as buffer occupancy is represented by triangular function as shown in Fig. 6.

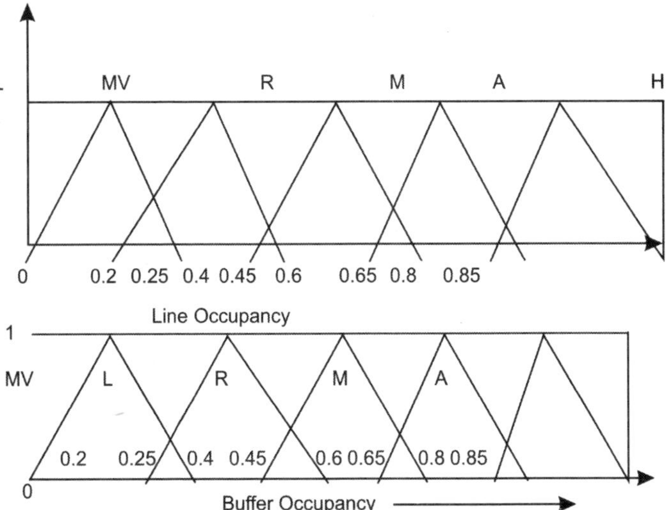

Fig. 6: L, B, M, A and H represent Low, Below, Medium, Above Medium and High membership sets respectively, MV represents membership value

Table 1: Look-Up Table

LO \ BO	L	B	M	A	H
L	L	B	B	M	A
B	B	B	M	M	H
M	B	M	M	A	H
A	M	A	A	A	H
H	A	H	H	H	H

From Fig. 6 the degree of membership, for particular set, associated with each valid buffer occupancy and line occupancy can be read. This quantification of membership is called fuzzification. Using these membership values and Table 1 corresponding sets of allocating space to be offerd, can be found out. This process is called rule-based inference. As an example, typical rule is when line occupancy is high and buffer occupancy is high, threshold value is high, i.e., allocation space will be high. Then by applying suitable defuzzication method, such as min-max or max-min defuzzification, the percentage allocation space to be offered at that particular line occupancy and at given buffer occupancy can be determined for defuzzification, with the set such as shown in Table 2, weighted average is used.

Table 2: Atypical Defuzzification Table

SET	L	B	M	A	H
I	0.2	0.4	0.6	0.8	1.0
II	0.4	0.5	0.7	0.9	1.0
III	0.5	0.6	0.8	0.9	1.0
IV	0.3	0.7	0.8	0.9	1.0

L: Low set, B:below medium set, M: Medium set,
A: above medium set, H: high set

RESULT AND CONCLUSION

Results

The results obtained after simulation are

Average Unicast Cell Delay

In all the three schemes, for the dynamic threshold (DT) the unicast cell delay increases rapidly after some load. This happens because as the load increases DT dynamically calculates threshold to buffer as much cells as possible. So naturally, the cells remain in the buffer for longer time and the delay increases.

But in the case of static threshold, cell delay increases linearly because the threshold is constant and only fixed amount of cells are stored, all the cells above the threshold are just discarded. So, cell delay in static and fuzzy is less than dynamic threshold scheme.

Average Multicast Cell Delay

In MWMR, multicast cell is treated same as unicast cell. So same reason holds for the average multicast cell delay as was for the unicast cell delay for all the three types of thresholds.

In SWSR-OM we have implemented multicast priority mode, so a multicast cell is given higher priority than the unicast cell. Hence, multicast cells are always allowed to set the output mask (OM) before the unicast cells, so more multicast cells can be accommodated in the queue that is why multicast cell delay increases rapidly at low loads. But as the load increases more and more cell loss occurs and the delay decreases.

In SWSR-OB, initially the multicast cell delay is negligible in all the three types of thresholds that we have applied, this happens because the multicast cells are just 10% of the total. So, initially all the multicast cells are accepted and transmitted.

Average Cell Loss

In the case of MWMR for dynamic threshold, as the load increases the DT adjusts the threshold dynamically and stores as much cells as possible. But after a certain limit it starts behaving like ST and hence cell loss increases rapidly.

In the case of SWSR-OM, as there is no buffer at the output ports so there is cell loss even at the low load which increases with the increase of load. For SWSR-OB, the reasons for the results are same as that of the MWMR scheme as there is buffer at the output port.

Throughput

The throughput increases almost linearly with the increase of load. The throughput for the static threshold is minimum and for dynamic threshold is highest because the cell loss in the case of DT is less as it dynamically changes the threshold.

Results for the Fuzzy System

The unicast cell delay and the multicast cell delay are lowest in the case of fuzzy approach. This a very strong point in favor of fuzzy approach because it fulfills the main reason for which ATM switches were made. As we all know, ATM switches were primarily made for handling real time data transmission for which delay should be minimum.

For fuzzy approach, the cell loss and throughput are in between the static threshold and the dynamic threshold. The results are better than the ST and can be improved further by using a different look-up-table.

Direction for Future Work

We have used ON-OFF traffic model for simulation, one can use any other model for simulation.

Initially, we used look-up-table 7.4(a) for the simulation purpose, the results were slightly improved. But when we used look-up-table 7.4(b) the results improved appreciably. So for future work, one can use different look-up-table based on experience and previous records to get better results. One can use artificial neural network for generating the inference engine to get the optimal look-up-table.

For the SWSR-OM scheme, the priority modes were not alternated, and only the multicast priority mode was used for evaluation purpose. So as an extension to this work one can perform simulation by alternating the priority modes between the multicast priority mode and the unicast priority mode at each output cycle to give a fair chance to both unicast and multicast cells to access their port.

Scholastic Study of Replication of Multimedia System in Distributed Environment

Rohit Chandra and *Vishal Srivastava*

ABSTRACT

Replicating data and services at multiple networked computers increase the service availability of distributed systems. This paper presents the design and implementation architecture of a replication mechanism for a distributed multimedia system medianode which is currently developed as an infrastructure to share multimedia-enhanced teaching materials among lecture groups. With the replication mechanism, medianode provides enhanced access to presentation materials in both connected and disconnected operation modes. The main contribution of this paper is the identification of new replication requirements in distributed media systems and a multicast-based update propagation mechanism by which not only the update events are signaled, but also the updated data are exchanged between replication managers.

INTRODUCTION

Replication is the maintenance of on-line copies of data and other resources. Replication of presentation materials and meta-data is an important key to providing high availability, fault tolerance and quality of service (QoS) in distributed multimedia systems. For example, when a user requires access (read/write) to a presentation material which comprises audio/video data and some resources which are not available in the local machine at this point of time, a local replication manager copies the required data from their original location and puts it into either one of the machines located nearby or the local machine without requiring any user interaction (user transparent). This function enhances the total performance of the distributed system, in this example, the presentation service system, by reducing the response delay that is often caused due to insufficient system resources at a given service time. Furthermore, because of the available replica in the local machine, the assurance that users can continue their presentation in a situation of network disconnection is significantly higher than without replica. The main contributions of this paper are:

(1) To identify the new replication requirements for multimedia systems in distributed environment.

(2) To build a replication mechanism for distributed multimedia systems.

To achieve these targets, we first study the characteristics of presentational media types which are handled in medianode system and extract new replica units and granularities which have neither been considered nor supported in existing replication mechanisms. Furthermore, we give a survey on existing replication mechanisms and identify their features and limitations. By prototyping our proposed replication mechanism in medianode, we prove its principle feasibility and identify further research issues such as how to combine the concept of quality of service (QoS) with replication mechanisms. The structure of the paper is as follows. In Section 2, we present our replication system model. After giving a short overview about medianode architecture, we define the scope of our replication mechanism in medianode and present the characteristics of presentational media types, for which we identify a need for new replica units and granularities. Section 3 presents the design and implementation architecture of our replication model. We describe the proposed replication maintenance mechanism, e.g. how and when replicas are created and how the updates are signalled and transported. In Section 4, we give an overview of related work. The merits and limitations of existing replication mechanisms are discussed and a comparison of our approach with previous work is given. We conclude the paper with a summary of our work and an outlook towards possible future extensions of our replication mechanism.

REPLICATION SYSTEM MODEL

Architectural Overview of Medianode

The medianode system architecture is intended for decentralized operation of a widely distributed system. Within this distributed system, each participating host is called a medianode and conceptually equal to all other participating nodes, i.e. a medianode is not considered a client or a server. Client or server tasks are taken on by medianode in the system depending on their resources and software modules.

The central element of a medianode is called its core. The core performs two primary tasks:-

(a) It dynamically loads code which implements the medianode's operations and instantiates objects

(b) The core implements the routing of requests between medianode's components (called bows) that are instantiated in a medianode.

Each dynamically loaded module implements a child class of medianode's root class, the bow class. Some bows implement basic operations that are necessary for the start of a medianode; these are not loaded dynamically but statically linked to the medianode binary and well known to the core. The bow class has three abstract subclasses which structure the operations of medianode in general. These subclasses are called Access Bow, Storage Bow and Verifier Bow.

Objects of the class Access Bow implement the visible activity of a medianode: e.g. an HTTP access bow implements means of requesting content from the medianode via the HTTP protocol, a Telnet access bow allows a user to connect to a medianode using the telnet application for basic information and management tasks. Storage Bows implement the functionality of distributed file systems and distributed databases. In medianode, such storage bows are always capable of operating in disconnected operation modes, i.e. they implement all functionality locally, keep all relevant data locally, and are able to react to requests to unreachable data. Verifier Bows are intended to check the availability and accessibility of data and services that have been requested by access bows or storage bows.

Scope of Our Replication System

By analyzing the service requirements distributed multimedia systems for the example of medianode, we identified a number of issues that the design of our replication system needs to address:

- High availability: The replication system in medianode should enable data/service access in both connected and disconnected operation modes. Users can keep multiple copies of their files on different medianodes that are distributed geographically across several universities.
- Consistency: Concurrent updates and system failures can lead to replicas not being consistent any more, i.e. stale state. The replication system should offer mechanisms for both resolving conflicts and keeping consistency between multiple replicas and their updates.
- Location and access transparency: Users do not need to know where presentation resources are physically located and how these resources are accessed.
- Cost efficient update transport: Due to the limitation of system and network resources, the replication system should use multicast-based transport mechanism for exchanging updates to reduce resource utilization.
- QoS support: The specific characteristics of presentational data, especially of multimedia data should be supported by the proposed replication mechanism. In medianode, we mainly focus on the replication service for accessing data in terms of 'inter-medianode', i.e. between medianodes, by providing replica maintenance in each medianode. Consequently, a replication manager can be implemented as one or a set of medianode's bow instances in each medianode. The replication managers communicate among each other to exchange update information through the whole medianodes. A replication service within a medianode, i.e., 'intra-medianode', is not considered for the first stage of our implementation. However, the

replication concept in this paper is straightforwardly applicable to the replication service for intramedianode scope.

Concept of Logically Centralized Database

For a technical realization of our proposed replication system, we use the concept of a so-called "logically centralized database (LCDB)" which especially enables the transparent access to presentation materials. Similar to the concept of location-independent identifiers in distributed database system, LCDB enables a mapping between logical and physical resources. So users do not need to know where presentation resources are located physically and how they are accessed. Requests from users, either for reading or writing any presentation materials, are first sent to the Access Bow of the local medianode that runs on the user's local machine. After successful check of the accessibility of the user and the availability of the requested resources, the corresponding storage bows send the target data to the users. Figure 1 illustrates the interface point, the bows building the LCDB and the interactions between the bows. Some additional remarks on LCDB are in order:

- According to the data types, all of the presentation contents and their meta-data are stored in corresponding storage bows.
- The 'front-end' of the storage bow API provides unique interfaces functions, independent of the data types: this is similar to the VFS (virtual file system) interface in UNIX systems.
- Replication has to be supported for most storage bows, although the number of replicas and the update frequency may differ between the individual bows.
- For the update propagation between replication managers, a multicast RPC (remote procedure call) communication mechanism is used.

Different Types of Presentation Data

Data organization comprises the storage of content data as well as meta information about this content data in a structured way. The typical data types which can be identified in medianode are the following:

- Presentation contents: this type of data comprises text, image, audio/video files and can be stored in file systems which should handle automatic data distribution and access, and also support the multimedia characteristics of this content type.
- Presentation description data, e.g. XML files.
- Meta-data of user, system, domain, and organization information. User's title, group, system platform, and university are examples for this meta-data category.
- Meta-data of system resource usage information such as memory usage, number of threads running within medianode process, number of loaded bows.
- Meta-data of user session and token information. Table 1 shows an overview of these data types with their characteristics.

Table 1: Data Categories and Their Characteristics in Medianode

target data	availability requirement	consistency requirement	persistency	update frequency	data size	QoS playback	global interest
presentation description	high	middle	yes	low	small (middle)	not required	yes
organizational data	high	high	yes	low	small	not required	yes
file/data description	high	middle	yes	middle	small	not required	yes
multimedia resources	high	middle	yes	middle	large	required	yes
system resources	middle (low)	middle	no	high	small	not required	not strong
user session taken	high	high	no	high	small	not required	no

Classification of Target Replicas

As argued in subsection 2.2, the main goal of replication is to increase the high availability of medianode's services and to decrease the response time for accesses to data located on other medianodes. To meet this goal, data which is characterized by a high availability requirement (see Table 1) should be replicated among the running medianodes.

We classify different types of target replicas according to their granularity (data size), requirement of QoS support, update frequency and whether their data type is 'persistent' or not ('volatile'). Indeed, there are three classes of replicas in medianode:

- Metareplicas (replicated metadata objects) that are persistent and of small size. An example would be a list medianodes (sites) which currently contain an up-to date copy of a certain file. This list itself is replicated to increase its availability and improve performance. A Metareplicas is a replica of this list.
- Softreplicas which are non-persistent and of small size. This kind of replicas can be used for reducing the number of messages exchanged between the local and remote medianodes, and thereby reducing the total service response time. i.e., if a local medianode knows about the available local system resources, then the local replication manager can copy the desired data into the local storage bow, and the service that is requested from users which requires exactly the data can be processed in a shorter response time. Information about the available system resource, user session and the validity of user tokens are replicas of this type.
- Truereplicas which are persistent and of large size. Content files of any media type, which also may be parts of presentation files, are True replicas. True replicas are the only replica type from the three types, to which the end users have access for direct manipulation (updating). On the other side, these are also the only replica type which requires the support of really high availability and QoS provision. All replicas which are created and maintained by our replication system are an identical copy of original media. Replicas with errors (non-identical copy) are not allowed to be created. Furthermore, we do not support any replication service for function calls, and elementary data types.

Design and Implementation Architecture

The replication mechanism

Basically, our replication system does not assume a client-server replication model, because there are no fixed clients and servers in the medianode architecture; every medianode may be client or server depending on its current operations. Peer-to-peer model with the following features is used for our replication system:

(a) Every replica manager keeps track of a local file table including replica information.

(b) Information whether and how many replicas are created is contained in the every file table. I.e. each local replica manager keeps track of which remote replica managers (medianode) are caching which replicas.

(c) Any access to the local replica for reading is allowed, and guaranteed that the local cached replica is valid until notified otherwise.

(d) If any update happens, the corresponding replica manager sends a multicast-based update signal to the replica managers which have the replica of the updated replica and therefore members of the multicast group.

(e) To prevent excessive usage of multicast addresses, the multicast IP addresses through which the replica managers communicate can be organized in small replica sub-groups. Examples for such sub-groups are file directories or a set of presentations about a same lecture topic.

Update distribution & transport mechanism

The update distribution mechanism in medianode differs between the three replica types and their managers. This is due to the fact that the three replica types have different levels of requirements on and characteristics of high availability, update frequency and consistency. Experience from [4] and [5] also shows that differentiating update distribution strategies makes sense for web and other distributed documents.

The medianode's replication system offers unique interface to the individual update signaling and transport protocols which are selectively and dynamically loaded and unloaded from the replica transport manager that is implemented as an instance of medianode's access bow. The possible update transport and signaling protocols are:

- RPC protocol as a simple update distribution protocol. This mechanism is mainly used at the first step of our simple and fast implementation.
- A multicast based RPC communication mechanism. In this case, the updates are propagated via multicast other replica managers which are members of the multicast group. RPC2 6, 9 is used for the first implementation. RPC2 offers the transmission of large files, such as the updated AV content files or diff-files, by using the Side Effect Descriptor. But, the RPC2 with Side Effect Descriptor does not guarantee any reliable transport of updates.
- LC-RTP based reliable multicast protocol [10]: It is originally developed as an extension of RTP protocol to support the reliable video streaming within the medianode project. We adopt LC-RTP and check the usability of the protocol, depending on the degree of reliability required for the individual groups of replicas.

Approaches for Resolving Update Conflicts

The possible conflicts that could appear during the shared use of presentational data and files are either-

(a) Update conflict when two or more replicas of an existing file are concurrently updated

(b) Naming conflict when two (or more) different files are given concurrently the same name

(c) update/delete conflict that occurs when one replica of a file is updated while another is deleted. In most existing replication systems, the conflict resolving problem for update conflicts was treated as a minor problem.

It was argued that most files do not get any conflicting updates; with the reason that only one person tends to update those [8]. Depending on the used replication model and policy, there are different approaches to resolving update conflicts, of which our replication system uses the following strategies 2, 6, 11, 13, and 15

- Swapping - to exchange the local peer's update with other peer's updates.
- Dominating - to ignore the updates of other peers and to keep the local tentative update as a final update.
- Merging - to integrate two or more updates and build one new update table.

Implementation Status

We have implemented a prototype of the proposed replication system model for Linux platform (Suse 7.0, Redhat 6.2). Implemented are the media (file) and its replica manager, update transport manager, replica service APIs which are Unix-like file operation functions such as open, create, read, write, close, and a Volatile storage bow which maintains user's session and token information. 15 gives a technically detailed description of our implementation.

Related Works

Several approaches to replication have already been proposed. The approaches differ for distributed file systems than those for Internet-based distributed web servers and those for transaction-based distributed DBMS. Well known replication systems in distributed file systems are Coda [6] and Roam [11] which keeps the file service semantics of Unix. Therefore, they make easy to develop applications based on them. They are based on either client-server model or peer-to-peer model and use often optimistic replication which can hide the effects of network latencies. Their replication units are mostly file system volumes which lead to a large size and relatively a low number of replicas.

There are some optimization works for these examples in terms of update protocol and replica unit. To keep the delay small and therefore maintain the sense of real-time interaction, it was desirable to use the unreliable transport protocol such as UDP. In the earlier phases, many approaches have used the unicast-based data exchanges by which the replication managers communicated with each other via 'one-to-one'. This has caused large delays and made the real-time interaction impossible. To overcome this problem, the multicast-based communication is used in some recent cases 8, 9, and 12. In the case Coda, the RPC2 protocol is used for multicast-based update exchange, which offers with Side Effect Descriptor the transmission of large files by using the Side Effect Descriptor.

For limiting the amount of storage used by a particular replica, Rumor and Roam developed the selective replication scheme 13. A particular user who only needs a few of the files in the volume, the user can control which files to store in his local replica with selective replication. A limitation or disadvantage of selective replication is the 'full back storing' mechanism: if a particular replica stores a particular file in a volume, all directories in the path of that file in the replicated volume must also be stored. Jet File 8 is a prototyped distributed file system which uses multicast communication and optimistic strategies for synchronization and distribution. The main merit of Jet File is its multicast-based callback mechanism by which the components of Jet File, such as file manager and versioning manager interact to exchange update information. However, the multicast callbacks in Jet File do not guarantee that they actually reach all of other replication peers, and the centralized versioning server which is responsible for serialization of all updates can lead to a overloaded system state. Furthermore, none of the existing replication systems does not support of the quality of service (QoS) characteristics of (file) data which they handle and replicate.

SUMMARY AND FUTURE WORK

In this paper, we presented a replication mechanism for distributed multimedia system medianode, and described the design and implementation architecture of the prototyped replication system. We first studied the characteristics of presentational media types which are handled in medianode, and extracted new replica units and granularities which have not been considered and not supported in existing replication mechanisms. We then built a replication mechanism for distributed multimedia systems based on the new requirements and the result of feature surveys. We are currently in the process of implementing the versioning and storage/transport load leveling mechanisms, which are integrated with the replication manager. With the forthcoming implementation we will be able to build medianode as a highly available, scalable and cooperative, distributed media server for multimedia-enhanced teaching. The next working steps are to design other replication services which provide service implementations such as:

- Predictive replication: To increase access availability and to reduce latency. Similar approaches are Hoarding 14, 16 and prefetched caching.
- QoS-aware replication for distributed multimedia systems, in which the decision whether a replica should be created from original file is made by checking the current usages of available system resources. An approach of combining replication, versioning and alternative media support is an good example for this replication model 17.

REFERENCES

1. The medianode project.
2. G. Coulouris, J. Dollimore and T. Kindberg. *Distributed Systems*, 3rd Ed., Addison-Wesley, 2001.
3. A. Eickler, A. Kemper and D. Kossman. Finding Data in the Neighborhood. In *Proc. of the 23rd VLDB Conference*, Athens, Greece, 1997.
4. P. Triantafillou and D.J. Taylor. Multiclass Replicated Data Management: Exploiting Replication to Improve Effciency. In *IEEE Trans. on Parallel and Distributed Systems*, pages 121-138, Vol. 5, No. 2, Feb. 1994.
5. G. Pierre, I. Kuz, M. van Steen and A.S. Tanenbaum. Differentiated Strategies for Replicating Web documents, In *Proc. of 5th International Workshop on Web Caching and Content Delivery*, Lisbon, May 2000.
6. M. Satyanarayanan, J.J. Kistler, P. Kumar, M.E. Okasaki, E.H. Siegel and D.C. Steer. Coda: A Highly Available File System for a Distributed Workstation Environment. In *IEEE Transaction on Computers*, 39(4), April 1990.

7. J. Yin, L. Alvisi, M. Dahlin and C. Lin. Volume Leases for Consistency in Large-Scale Systems. In *IEEE Transaction on Knowledge and Data Engineering*, 11(4), July1999

8. B. Groenvall, A. Westerlund and S. Pink. The Design of a Multicast-based Distributed File System. In *Proceedings of Third Symposium on Operating Systems Design and Implementation, (OSDI'99)*, New Orleans, Louisiana, pages 251-264. February, 1999

9. M. Satyanarayanan, and E.H. Siegel. Parallel Communication in a Large Distributed Environment. In *IEEE Trans. on Computers*, pages 328-348, Vol.39, No.3, March 1990.

10. M. Zink, A. Jones, C. Girwodz and R. Steinmetz. LC-RTP (Loss Collection RTP): Reliability for Video Caching in the Internet. In *Proceedings of ICPADS'00: Workshop*, pages 281-286. IEEE, July 2000.

11. D. Ratner, P. Reiher, and G. Popek. Roam: A Scalable replication System for Mobile Computing. In *Workshop on Mobile Databases and Distributed Systems (MDDS)*, September 1999

12. M. Mauve and V. Hilt. An Application Developer's Perspective on Reliable Multicast for Distributed Interactive Media. In *Computer Communication Review*, pages 28-38, 30(3), July 2000.

13. D.H. Ratner, Selective Replication: Fine grain control of replicated files. *Master's thesis, UCLA*, USA, 1995.

14. G.H Kuenning, Seer: Predictive File Hoarding for Disconnected Mobile Operation. *PhD. dissertation, UCLA-CSD-970015. UCLA*, USA, 1997

15. G. On and M. Liepert. Replication in medianode. *Technical Report TR-2000-03*, Darmstadt University of Technology, Germany, September 2000.

16. C. Griwodz, Wide-Area True Video-on-Demand by a Decentralized Cache-based Distribution Infrastructure. *PhD. dissertation*, Darmstadt University of Technology, Germany, April 2000.

17. J. Chung-I and M.A. Sirbu. *Distributed Network Storage with Quality-of-Service Guarantees.*

Multi-function "Smarter" Cards in Universities: Issues and Trends

Sanjeev Sharma and *Narendra Mohan*

ABSTRACT

As their application area and the number of applications supported increase, the benefits of card technologies (and, in particular, of smart cards) become more widely accepted. These benefits are especially relevant to University environment in which there are many uses for smart cards. Increasing numbers of universities around the world have some kind of "smart" student card, many of which are being developed to support multiple functions on a single card.

Card technologies such as magnetic cards and newer, "smarter" cards having a microprocessor chip are playing an increasingly important role in modern life. A single card has the potential to replace all the cards and documents currently found in your wallet - for example, your driver's licence, credit card(s), ATM cards, video rental cards, frequent flyer cards, staff identification cards, library cards, as well as the coins and currency notes.

This paper describes the issues associated with introducing smart cards to the Universities—particularly the benefits and success factors associated with introducing a multi-purpose, multi-function card.

INTRODUCTION

The types of cards currently available range from simple access cards, used to achieve computer access (or physical entry or passage), through to .wallets, stored value cards and universal prepayment cards(Fancher, 1997).more sophisticated cards which can be used as electronic purses.

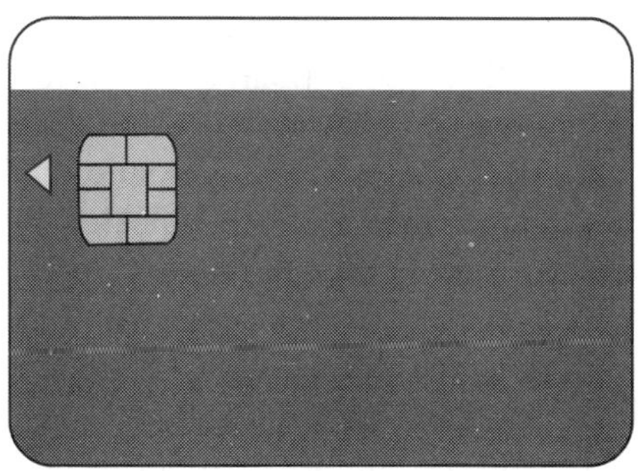

Fig. 1

A true smart card is an integrated circuit (IC) card with memory and a microcontroller, which makes it capable of making decisions next of kin, and instructions in case of emergency (Fancher, 1997). The Singaporean government commenced work on a national card scheme in 1991 which will allow them to completely withdraw currency notes and coins from circulation (see NUS, 1997). The potential a smart card solution offers for solving the problem of authenticating users and transactions over insecure networks means it is currently seen as the enabling technology which will support rapid growth in the use of electronic commerce over the internet.

Universities and the Proliferation of Cards

As the number of useful applications for smart cards has increased, so has the number of gaining access to security doors or bank accounts, telephone use, etc. Although the use of magnetic and smart cards in Universities has grown steadily over the past five years, there have so far been no successful implementations of multi-function smarter cards in university

Physically, a smart card is a plastic card of the same dimensions as today's credit cards, having a chip embedded within it. This chip has 100 times the storage capacity of the magnetic stripe found on the back of the average credit card, and allows up to 1 million write cycles. The placement of the chip is standardized, allowing the card to be used in existing terminals such as ATMs, as well as allowing readers to be built into vehicles such as vending machines or telephones.

Smart cards are increasingly being used around the world for such applications because of their ability to store and protect relatively large amounts of data: more than the information printed on a card, or contained in a barcode. In Germany, for instance, every citizen is being issued a health card identifying the holder's insurance provider and account number—and plans are in place to add medical information such as the name of the holder's doctor, blood type, allergies, medications, contact details for disparate applications developed. Multi-application cards are still quite rare, and the number of applications integrated has been slim. One domain which has been active in pursuing multi-application (or multi-function) cards is the University sector, because of the number of functions involved in managing student life. Students currently have to hold separate cards for functions such as: Photo ID, photocopying, storing meal vouchers,.

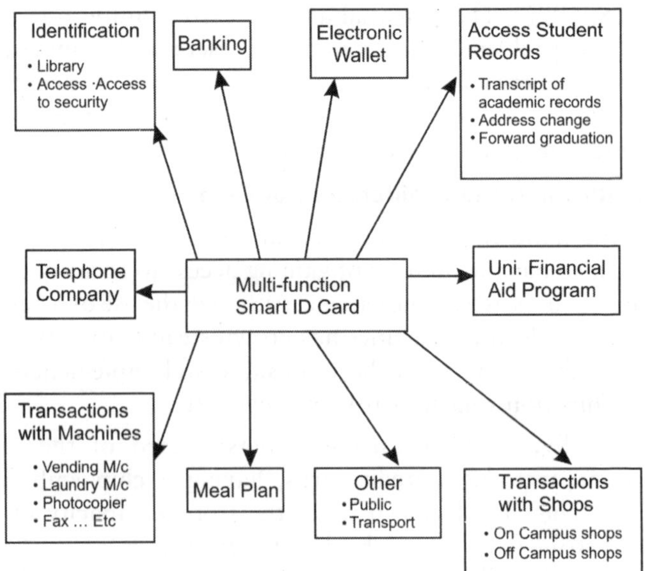

Figure 1: Functions of the Multi-purpose, Multi-function Smart ID Card

Issues Relevant to Multi-function "Smarter" Card in the University

Traditionally, smart cards have tended to handle a single application, rather than being linked to a number of applications. The variety of facilities and services available on a university campus which can be placed on a smart card, however, have made it a promising arena in which to introduce integrated systems. **We focused on issues associated with success of smart card systems in the universities.**

Although there have been numerous studies conducted on the implementation and application of smart cards, most have been focused on the areas of privacy, security and data storage on smart cards (eg Lokan, 1991; Farroukh and Hornung, 1995; Burke, 1996; Evans 1996; Smart Card Forum News, 1996; Smart Cards, 1997). These few topics have been examined across a variety of sectors: cases include access control and security in the health care sector (ISCIG, 1996, Farroukh and Hornung, 1995), internal passports for trainee pilots – for instance the airbus industry (TISCIG, 1997), in pedestrian area access control – for example the Singaporean armed forces, (TISCIG, 1997) and financial applications (Plunkett, 1966; Worthington, 1996; Arnavutian, 1997; Birch, 1997; Everett, 1997).

While these are unquestionably valuable and useful areas for study, we are interested in focusing certain issues which might affect the success of integrated, multiple-application systems. Rather than focus on user issues and the impact of smart cards as a technology, as most studies have done.

Benefits and Success Factors Associated with Introducing a Multi-Function "Smarter" Card

Versatility of cards

(The types of functions supported on the Chip, Magnetic Stripe or Contactless card). There are different types of ID cards in different universities, including magnetic stripe card, university smart card system. The university can also benefit from the following revenue opportunities with the bank:

- Interest on account balances.

- Royalty payment from the bank (Depending on the number of accounts).
- Revenue from ATM use.
- Commissions from point of sale.

Telephone – Phone Card Facilities

"Many of our students do not have their own phone or move frequently and the phone number changes."

Multiple Phone Service Selected Facilities (e.g. calling card, direct dial, voice mail): Extra Functionality

Through multi-function "smarter" cards some university ID cards can be linked with a telephone company, which provides many additional associated services such as Calling Card, Direct Dial, Voice mail. This impact of offering such functionality seemed worth.

Ability to Create/Support Separate Cost Centres

The cost centre concept is potentially an important feature in any project. A Department could keep different machines which are linked to the electronic purse feature such as photocopier, fax machine as cost centres.

User Data Entry/Modification

(Eg: Student record updates - Address Change, Forward Graduation Application). One aspect of implementing a multifunction "smarter" ID system would be to reduce administrative costs. If students can perform their minor data entry work, such as student record updates, address changes, and forward graduation applications, this will help to reduce enquires and data entry. Self service terminals may therefore result in better service to students.

Profitability of Card Scheme (e.g. subsidisation from banks/ phone companies necessary)

There are various ways of getting additional income for the university from a smart card system without charging students. These are smart card, contactless card, combination of above, multiple chip card. Different types of cards give different types of versatility to the user.

Limited Bank Access - Students Restricted to a Single Bank

The multifunction ID card systems identified can be linked either to a single bank or multiple banks. If the university is linked with a predefined single bank it may help the university to make additional income from the bank to cover expenses.

Unlimited Bank Access - Students can Access any Bank (maximising student choice)

If the system can be linked to multiple banks (i.e. there is no restriction on the banking feature), students have the opportunity to gain access to any bank or banks they wish. This issue was included to gather impressions as to whether maximizing student choice might be a success factor.

Closed System Scope - Students cannot use Card Outside Institution (maximum university control)

If a multifunction ID card system is implemented in a university without participation of third party organizations, such as banks, telephone companies and external vendors, the university has more control over the project.

Open System Scope–Students can use Card Outside Institution (More Flexibility to the User)

Conversely, if a system is implemented in a university which includes participating third party organizations such as the bank, telephone company and external vendors, the university has less control over the project but the project will give more flexibility to the user.

Profitable Relationship with Bank (University Commission)

It is seems that(by considering above factors) 80 per cent of their earnings are gained from commissions from the bank, so such relationships may be a success factor for a university. Opportunities include:

- Signing bonuses - (e.g : Number of purchases from the vending machine).
- Bank.
- Interest on account balances.

- Royalty payment from bank (Depending on number of accounts).
- Revenue from ATM use.
- Commissions from point of sale.
- Percentage from the Telephone company - Commission from long distance calls.
- Royalty payment from telecommunications company (Depending on number of links).
- Special edition card sales - $ 10.00, $ 25.00 and $ 50.00 cash on card.
- Expanded card base - Visitors, Alumni, Collectors.
- Id replacement cost.

Card Provides Pins for Wallet and Student Information (Privacy and Security Issues)

When we discuss multi-function smarter cards, privacy and security aspects of the stored data are a critical area. At the moment personal data such as a student's medical history is not typically stored in a smart ID card. But more sensitive information may be recorded if the system scope expands. Further more, there should be a secure place to store electronic cash. Some universities have provided PINs to protect electronic cash. One university in Canada protected the electronic purse only for transactions greater than $10. Some universities do not protect the electronic purse by using a PIN because of restrictions on the amount stored in the electronic purse.

Disaster Recovery Plan In Place

For various reasons computers and computer systems are subject to regular breakdowns. As a result of this there may be inconvenience to the university as well as to the user. Depending on the degree of inconvenience or problems caused, implementing a disaster recovery plan may be an essential feature of an on-line system. In case of failure, a proper disaster recovery plan will result in faster recovery.

CONCLUSION

Universities have been among the most active organizations implementing the potential of multi-function "smarter" card systems, because of the obvious match between the types and numbers of applications suited to smart cards. This paper has described the issues affecting multi-function "smarter" ID card applications in university environments. Smart cards clearly will bring convenience to students, much as credit and debit cards have done, and in many cases may reduce the need for paper money and small change. Contactless smart card technology is an excellent privacy enabling solution for the applications that need to protect personal information and ensure that. communication with contactless device is secure.

Now the technology offers hosting many applications from various industries on a single card which was bottleneck earlier. The real success of multi-function "smarter" cards in University is the need to have a single "smarter" card capable of multiple applications. Carrying multiple cards is very cumbersome and cannot solve the purpose of smart cards. Hence, it is very important that a single card should be able to handle multiple tasks like ID card, driving license, vehicle registration, and credit and debit cards.

REFERENCES

Kaplan, J. M. (1992), *Smart Cards: The Global Information Passport—Managing A Successful Smart Card Program*, International Thomson Computer Press.

Lindley, R. A. (1994), 'Key Strategies and Considerations for User Acceptance of Smart Card Based Systems'. Proceedings of the *Strategic Business Applications of Smart Card Conference- AIC Conference,* Sheraton Wentworth, Sydney, Australia, February 24-25, 1994.

Lindley, R.A. (1997), '*Smart Card Innovation*', Saim Pty Ltd, Australia.

Evans, R. (1996), 'Can the law cope with smart cards'. *Australian Lawyer,* 31(11) pp. 10-11.

Fancher, C.H. (1997) "In Your Pocket: Smartcards", *IEEE Spectrum,* 34(2), February, 47-53.

Helm, P.J. and Galloway, R. (1997), 'CAUDIT - Smart Card Evaluation Report', University of Sydney, December.

International Standards Organization (ISO) (1997), 'International Standards Organization (ISO) Home Page' [WWW document]. URL http://www.iso.ch. Accessed October 1997.

ISCIG. (1996), *International Smart Card Industry Guide*, Smart Card News Ltd, pp 69-73, ISBN 0 9524394.

Lonabocker, L. and Springfield, J. (1994), 'Reengineering for the 13th Generation'. Paper presented at the *1994 College and University Systems Exchange Annual Conference – CAUSE '94*, Orlando, Florida, USA, November 29 - December 2, 1994.

Lokan, J.C. (1991), 'The Design and Applications of Smart Cards'. *Australian Computer Journal*, 23(2) May 1991, pp. 159-146.

Smart Card Forum News (1996), 'Federal Reserve Board Proposes Application of Regulation E to Stored Value Cards', *Smart Card Forum News* 7(2), pp. 1-2.

Intelligent Multimedia Tutoring System for Effective Pedagogical Planning

14

D.S. Gangwar and *V.K. Deolia*

ABSTRACT

This paper investigates how multimedia frames and knowledge based intelligent tutoring system may be integrated to develop Knowledge Based Intelligent Multimedia Tutoring System (IMTS). Multimedia frames or m-frames are used as a framework by which semantic and syntactic information is represented within intelligent multimedia services model. Paper also covers architecture details of a typical IMTS and its development for interactive learning environment. As far as interactivity of the system is concerned it is controlled by the run time controller. IMTS user is an active learner and for considering a broad variety of learning style, learner control is variable within the range of navigation and strict system guidance. User interface of IMTS is based on fuzzy logic controller for representing pedagogical knowledge by artificial intelligence techniques such as neural networks and fuzzy logic.

INTRODUCTION

Role of a teacher is to make things interesting, interactive, and tangible for the learner. By making things simpler teacher helps learner in understanding basic principles and core concepts related to a particular domain. Once the threshold level is crossed by the student; he himself becomes competent to solve any of the real world problems, wherever his knowledge can be implemented. Intelligent Multimedia Tutoring Systems (IMTS) are educational systems that aim at providing one-to-one tuition of students [1]. The student interacts with the system by solving problems that are selected based on that student's ability. A domain model is used to store an understanding of the instructional domain, which is to interpret a student's solution and track their skills. Due to the large number of complex components comprising an IMTS, as shown in Fig. 1. Authoring Tools have been developed to aid their construction. This provides most of the intelligent components, yet the construction of the domain model remains notoriously difficult. IMTS have four major modules:

Domain Module

Student Module

Instructor Module

User Interface Module

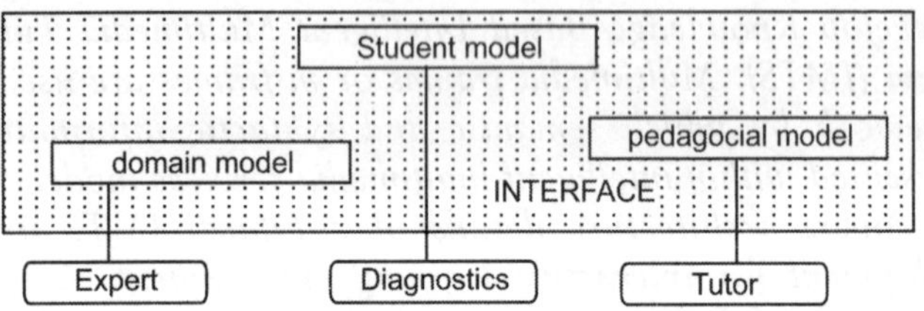

Fig. 1: Components of IMTS

This paper demonstrates knowledge acquisition techniques that can aid in the construction of new domain models. To achieve this goal effectively a detailed analysis of the domain model must be performed. The architecture of the IMTS and the knowledge representation has a strong influence on how efficiently the domain knowledge can be acquired. Therefore, goal of this discussion is to illustrate how the domain model, for use in IMTS Authoring Tools, can be designed to enable automated knowledge acquisition, higher speed system development, portability and the integration of independent domain models. The feedback from an IMTS is controlled by the pedagogical module, which implements the teaching strategies [5].

Present day learning technologies may help in developing trained novices rather expert in any particular discipline. The biggest drawback associated with learning aids being practiced by most of the educational activities is this that they do not provide control to the learner. This creates a difficult situation for learner to keep his interest alive in this process. At the same time rule based expert IMTS system offer a greater degree of freedom and even better communication and control over learning process.

Intelligent Multimedia Tutoring System

IMTS Authoring Tools are component-based to reduce the complexity of their implementation. The component diagram in Figure 2 shows each of the typical components for a Computer Based tutor. There are three components and three repositories. Each repository has no processing capability this is provided by the IMTS components. The courseware for an IMTS typically consists of problems and their ideal solutions. Many IMTS systems do not include instructional material. Domain model, which stores the domain knowledge required to make the IMTS intelligent. The constraint-based modeler is responsible for taking a Student Solution and interpreting its validity using the domain knowledge. Constraints are only one way to model the domain. IMTS Tutor that contains a Student Module has no facility for proving intelligent feedback for student solutions. These issues are taken care by pedagogical module, which is responsible taking decision for the teaching strategies.

A typical IMTS must have a domain model. The domain model stores the knowledge required to interpret the instructional material. This knowledge is formed from low-level rules or heuristics that describe the detail of domain concepts. This knowledge is represented in a language that is understood directly by the other components of the system. Specifically, its representation strongly influences the approach to student modeling and the pedagogical processing of the system. The domain model is not inherently intelligent.

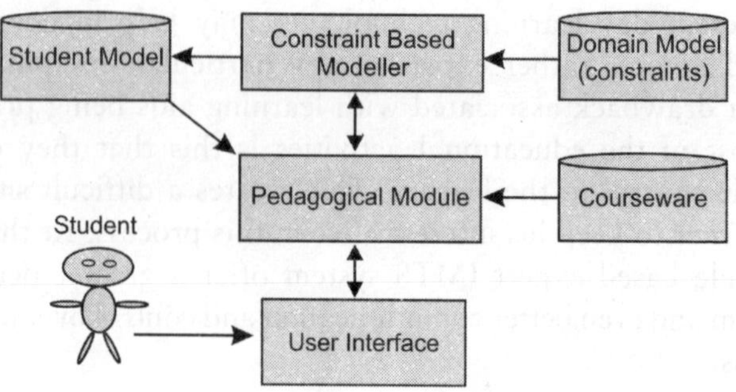

Fig. 2: Intelligent Multimedia Tutoring System

IMTS Authoring Tools

The goal of the IMTS Authoring Tool is to aid development by decreasing the effort and skill required, to aid the designer to consider the domain, to support good design principles and enable rapid prototyping [6]. T. Murry describes seven categories for the classification of IMTS Authoring Tools by type. These are:

- Curriculum Sequencing and Planning
- Tutoring Strategies
- Device Simulation and Equipment Training
- Domain Expert System
- Multiple Knowledge Types
- Special Purpose
- Intelligent/Adaptive Hypermedia.

Multimedia authoring tool provides the infrastructure and the intelligent components required to interpret the domain model. The domain model and courseware are effectively the only aspects that need to be constructed. The authoring interface for this includes a visual Ontology that allows the designer to construct a simple diagram to illustrate the structure of the domain. This aids the domain expert with their mental exploration of the system.

System Architecture

Since the architecture is intended to form an open system, tools for creating and editing media objects that are compatible with the architecture's GUI. From an author's point of view, media objects can be divided into several categories:

(Formatted) text

Graphics (based on vectors)

Pictures (based on pixels)

Animations

Audio sequences

Video sequences

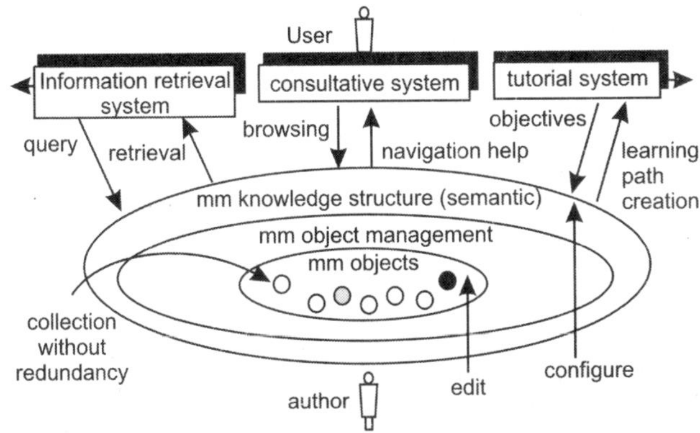

Fig. 3: IMTS Architecture

Technological advancements and dropping prices for multimedia systems are promoting pedagogical researchers to develop interactive learning environment. These systems provide a wide range of flexibility. From a methodological point of view, maximum domain independence is intended. The architecture provides authors and students with services for different areas of application, e.g., operator training and basics of operating systems. Figure (3) presents an overview of the system, both from an author's and a student's point of view. As seen from a student, multimedia objects constitute the smallest elements of information. Multimedia objects are built by combining media objects along local or time dimensions. A set of multimedia objects with minimal redundancy promises best conditions for high-level reusability. Increased reusability of multimedia learning contents is making IMTS a successful learning tool.

Knowledge Representation

An investigation of IMTS must begin with an understanding of what intelligence is and how it is presented in an IMTS. An IMTS has knowledge of an instructional domain and is able to provide feedback that reflects this. IMTS typically select a knowledge base that represents either declarative or procedural knowledge. Knowledge of the domain is not the only consideration. Constraints do not encapsulate the concepts of a domain. Concepts in this situation are considered to be the general ideas that the student must know to understand the domain. IMTS that represent domain concepts are able to determine how well a student is progressing in a specific area, and when to move to the next.

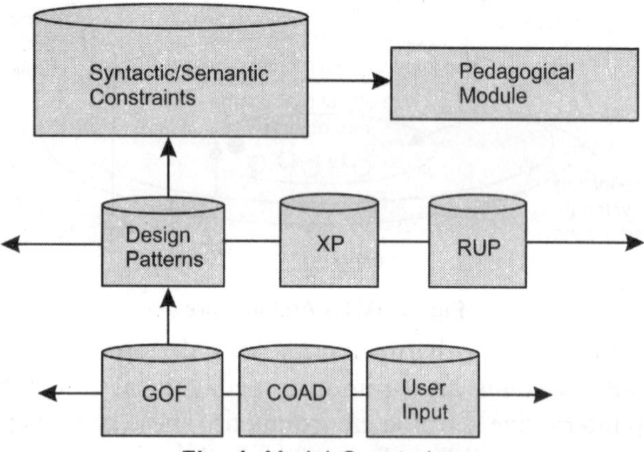

Fig. 4: Modal Constraints

The representation is a complex problem as it can affect every component within the IMTS. There are two ways to approach increasing the efficiency for knowledge representation in IMTS. The first is to investigate new domain modeling techniques that will allow for simpler generation of the domain. This also requires the consideration of how each of the IMTS components will use the new domain to process students interactions with the system. An initial investigation showed that the modular nature of constraints make them ideal for knowledge acquisition as each knowledge element is independent. It also indicated that this modularity could be extended to make the domain model platform independent.

Modal constraints are an addition suggested for domain modeling. Syntactic and semantic constraints are able to capture facts of domain concepts, and through the relevance condition the system is able to determine when it is appropriate to use them. With open-ended domains there are multiple solutions to a given problem. In this case the constraints are engineered to check dependencies that generate alternative solutions.

Modeling of constraints is achieved by allowing the constraints relevance condition to check against external variables. These variables are generated by the student model or specified by the student. As illustrated in Figure 4 the student would be able to select a modeling technique to attempt.

CONCLUSIONS

Learning may ultimately be its own reward. Technological advances in the field of computer sciences and artificial intelligence are also used in the teaching learning process. This paper describes domain and student knowledge representation in intelligent multimedia tutoring system. Main objective of this system is to improve the teaching-learning process in a specific domain. The knowledge is represented through semantic networks with frames and production rules. IMTS is a very appropriate tool for CAI (Computer Aided Instruction) beneficial for the students in the education curriculum. IMTS converts a student from a passive learner to an active learner by increasing user control for learning process as per needs of individual learner in interactive learning environment. As it is nicely said by Shri Aurobindo that "The first principle of true teaching is that nothing can be taught. The teacher is not an instructor or a taskmaster; he is a helper and a guide. His business is to suggest and not to impose. He does not actually train the pupils mind, he only shows him how to perfect his instruments of knowledge and helps and encourages him in the process. He does not impart knowledge to him; he shows him how to acquire knowledge for himself. He does not call forth the knowledge that is within; he only shows him where it lies and how it can be habituated to rise to the surface."

In support to his view, role of Intelligent Multimedia Tutoring System, having greater flexibility, adaptability and user control seems to be highly promising. In near future Computer Based

IMTS systems may play a pivotal role in teaching learning process. These systems can be more beneficial for the learner as they not only replace human tutor but also the drawbacks associated with human nature.

Acknowledgements

Authors express their gratitude towards Dr. Chandra Shekhar, Director CEERI Pilani; Prof. A.B. Bhattacharya, JPIIT NOIDA; Prof. Arun Kumar, MMMEC Gorakhpur; Prof. Jai Prakash GLAITM Mathura; Prof. B.B. Singh, MMMEC Gorakhpur; Prof. T.N. Sharma MNNIT Allahabad; Dr. I.K. Katiyan GIC Farrukhabad; Late Shri R.D. Gangwar SKIC Manjhana and one of our student Vivek Varshney, for their contribution in generation of a spark in my mind to think about IMTS and its role in teaching learning process. Authors would also like thank so many other persons havig different teaching methodology from above mentioned persons.

REFERENCES

1. Akpinar, Y., & Hartley, J.R. (1996). Designing interactive learning environments. *Journal of Computer-Assisted Learning*, 12(1), 33-46.
2. Buford J.F.K. (2004). *Multimedia Systems*. New Delhi: Pearson Education. 403-434.
3. Carbonell J.R.: AI in CAI: An Artificial-Intelligence Approach to Computer-Assisted Instruction, *IEEE Trans. Man-Machine Systems*, MMS-11(4), 1970, pp. 190-202.
4. Harry W. Agius, Marios C. Angelides, (1999). Developing Knowledge-Based Intelligent Multimedia Tutoring Systems Using Semantic Content-Based Modelling, *Artificial Intelligence Review*, Vol. 13 No. 1, pp. 55-83, Jan.
5. Milhem, W. D. (1996). Interactivity and computer-based instruction. *Journal of Educational Technology*, 24(3), 225-233.
6. Murray T, "Authoring Intelligent Tutoring Systems: An analysis of the state of the art," *Artificial Intelligence in Education*, Vol. 10, pp. 98-129, 1999.
7. Edutechwiki. (2005). *Artificial intelligence and education*. Available:. Last accessed 20 Jan 2008.

Requirements of Location Management in Wireless Networks: Efficiency and Scalability

Charul Bhatnagar and *Umesh Kumar Tiwari*

ABSTRACT

For all networks supporting mobility, some special functions are required for looking and checking up the current position of a mobile terminal, for providing the moving terminal not only with a permanent address for security features such as privacy, authentication and authorization but also to permit moving terminals to fully utilize the resources of the network. In a wireless network with millions of users, such as, mobile phone networks, the main function of location management is to make the network scalable and efficient. These functions include distributed servers for location storage, accounting and tracking of mobile terminals and authentication. The problems that come in the way of efficiency and scalability is that the performance of all operations should be practically independent of network size, number of current connections and load on the network. To maintain the overall performance of the network we must have to consider and address these problem domains. Here in this paper we are going to address and suggest a solution to these problems.

INTRODUCTION

Within a few years of evolution of the Internet, our way of working and living has changed dramatically. Both the individual users and business organizations can now reach people—whether they are other organizations, family, friends, merchants, businessman, customers, or suppliers-around the world instantly. Instead of using a desktop PC, we are running an Internet browser on an device that is portable, mobile, and wireless. With the click of a button or two from this unethered browser we can not only connect to the World Wide Web, but also access the same information that we can reach from our desktop.

Requirements and Characteristics of Wireless Network

Wireless network characteristics:

- Latency
- Bandwidth and run-time costs
- Error rates and unreliability

Wireless device constraints:

- Memory
- CPU power
- Battery life
- Variable device capabilities, possibly even changing dynamically
- Graphical User Interfaces (GUIs) and Non-Graphical User Interfaces
- Location in-dependence or dependence
- Security

Service requirements:

- Huge user base (Scalability)
- Management and Control
- Roaming

Methods Which may be Used in Location Management

Paging

In the attempt to locate recipients as quickly as possible, multiple methods of paging have been created. The most basic method used is Simultaneous Paging, where every user or host in the wireless location area is paged at the same time in order to find the user. Unless there are a relatively low number of users within the location area this will cause excessive amounts of paging. Although this method will find the user quicker than the following scheme of Sequential Paging, the costs make Simultaneous Paging rather inefficient.

An alternative scheme is Sequential Paging, where each user or host within a location area is paged in succession, with one common theory suggesting the polling of small user areas in order of decreasing user dwelling possibility. Unfortunately, this was found to have poor performance in some situations, as if the user was in an infrequently occupied location, not only might every user be paged, but a large delay could occur in network establishment. Additionally, this method requires accurate data gathering concerning common user locations, which necessitates more frequent location users and thereby increased costs.

Consequently, most real-world Sequential Paging methods simply poll the users nearest to the user area of the most recent location user, and then continue outward if the user is not immediately found. However, such a method will still be inefficient if the user's velocity is high or a location management scheme is used which specifies infrequent location users.

As an attempt to improve on previous models, another design called Intelligent Paging was introduced, this calculates specific paging areas to sequentially poll based upon a probability matrix. This method is essentially an optimized version of Sequential Paging.

However, this scheme has too much computational overhead incurred through updating and maintaining the matrix, and although perhaps optimal in theory, is effectively impossible for commercial wireless network implementation. Therefore, most current schemes use one of the first two methods presented. [Cowling04] While the best paging methods can significantly speed up the process of locating a user, significant improvements are possible by combining them with user mobility predictions.

User Mobility

For aid in effectively predicting the user's next location, user movement patterns are analyzed and mobility models are designed. Many such mobility models exist and can be used by networks in location management. The simplest of these models is *random-walk*, where user movements are assumed to be entirely random. While this is clearly going to lead to inaccurate predictions, it does require no knowledge of the individual user, and can be effective as a simulation tool. Frequently, random-walk is used to demonstrate the improvements a given scheme makes in comparison to this random method. A very general scheme, ignoring individual users but considering the network as a whole, is called *fluid-flow*. This method aggregates the movement patterns of users, and consequently can help optimize the network's utilization and design at a macroscopic level. However, fluid-flow provides no insight on a smaller scale, nor will it give any predictions as to specific user movements for any specific user. Markovian mobility models also exist, where user movements are predicted through past movements. At large computational cost, every inter-cell movement probability is defined for each user. An extension of the Markovian model, created at perhaps even greater cost, is the activity-based model. In this model, parameters such as time of day, current location, and predicted destination are also stored and evaluated to create movement probabilities. However, for all the resource expenditures required in implementing these methods, in a test of a simple activity-based scheme, unstable results were returned. An even more complex activity-based scheme might provide better results, but would not be implementable on a large scale due to its immense costs.

Problems in Location Management

[Cowling04] Research on all current models shows that none truly does a satisfactory job of predicting user movements, demonstrating the need for further research in this area. Consequently, [Cowling04] describes a possible enhancement as a scheme called Selective-prediction, where predictions are only made in regions where movements are easily foreseeable and a random prediction method is used elsewhere. To further this scheme, Cowling advocates a network where the base station (BS) learns the mobility characteristics of the region, in addition to the cell movement probabilities. This learning network provides the basis of a Markov model, with the full knowledge of movement probabilities and theoretically incurring low overhead. Additionally, the paper [Halepovic05] provides an in-depth analysis of sample user movement and network traffic. Empirical data gathered in these experiments reveals that the 10% most mobile users account for approximately two-thirds of the total number of connections within the network. Consequently, such users must be given appropriate consideration involving resource allocation. Over half of users appeared to be stationery, and most (but not all) such users generated much less cellular activity. Further tests within the paper reveal that a majority of users have a home or fix locations. This is a location, whether it is an actual home, office, or other place, from which a majority of their connections originate. This characteristic can be exploited by paging techniques and the customization possible in dynamic location management, as less updates may be necessary if a user is within their home area.

Proposed Solution

Dynamic location management

Dynamic Location Management is an advanced form of location management where the parameters of location management can be modified to best fit individual users and conditions. Theories have been and continually are being proposed regarding dynamic location users and location areas. Additionally, many are reexamining paging and mobility parameters based upon these developments. Many of these proposals in dynamic location management attempt to reduce computational overhead, paging costs, and the required number of location users. However, many of these proposals are excessively theoretical and complex, and are difficult to implement on a large scale.

Dynamic location update

Many dynamic location schemes exist, in order to improve upon excessively simple and wasteful static location user schemes. Additionally, these schemes are intended to be customizable, such that each user will have their own optimal location user standard, greatly reducing the overall number of location user updates.

One of these dynamic location management formats is **Threshold-Based**, where updates occur each time a parameter goes beyond a set threshold value. One possible threshold is time, where users update at constant time intervals. This saves user computation, but increases overhead significantly if the user does not move. This **Time-Based** scheme is very similar to the common static location user scheme, with the important difference of the time value being modifiable. Another threshold-based scheme requires a user update each time they traverse a certain number of connection.

This was found to work better than the time-based scheme, unless the users were constantly moving. In such a case, this method becomes quite similar to the static always-update scheme, where many unnecessary updates might occur.

Consequently, a preferable scheme was found, called distance-based. This called for an update only if the user moved a certain radial length of distance. However, this scheme is not perfect, as it requires the cellular device to keep track of such distances, which added much computational complexity. [Cowling04]

Another dynamic location user scheme is **Profile-based**. This functions by the network compiling a list of the most frequently accessed connections by the user, and only requiring a location user if the user moves outside of these common connections. As would be expected, this scheme is only effective if these predictions can be made accurately and without excessive overhead, but is otherwise inefficient. Additionally, this list must be relatively small, or else paging will become costly.

A more advanced scheme, built upon the efforts of previous methods, is called adaptive location user schemes. Adaptive location user schemes are very flexible and even may differ from each other; as such schemes are designed to take multiple parameters, such as velocity and mobility patterns, to determine the most efficient location areas. In such an example, having knowledge of a user's past movements combined with the users current speed and direction allows strong predictive power when determining a possible future location for paging.

CONCLUSION

Location users need not be as frequent, thereby reducing the overall location management costs. However, although these adaptive location management schemes are highly successful in terms of reducing location user costs, they are generally too difficult to implement for large networks, requiring excessive computational overhead.

REFERENCES

1. [Cowling04] James Cowling, "Dynamic Location Management in Heterogeneous Cellular Networks," MIT Thesis.
2. [Kyantakya04] K. Kyantakya and K. Jobmann, "Wireless Networks —Location Management in Cellular Networks.
3. The Wireless Application Protocol: Sandeep Singhal, Thomas Bridgman, Suryanarayana, Jari Alvinen, David Bevis: Low Price Edition
4. Mukesh Singhal, Niranjan G. Shivaratri: Advanced Concepts in Operating Systems; Tata McGraw-Hill Edition.
5. Mobile Communications: Jochen Schiller; Low Price Edition.

ARM: The Platform for Mobile Applications

16

Vijeta Verma and *Bhumika Gupta*

ABSTRACT

With the advent of new technologies and the blurring lines between mobile devices and computer hardware, applications are acquired to use. ARM (Advanced Risk Machine) architecture, which is a 32-bit, RISC processor architecture developed by ARM limited i.e. widely used in a number of embedded designs. The application discussed in the report is one such gem. ARM family provides most prolific 32-bit architecture, which are found in RISC CPUs. ARM CPUs are dominant in the mobile electronic market. The documentation has been done systematically and care has been taken to career all aspects ARM architecture, features of ARM architecture which includes important RISC features and ARM instruction set architecture which includes the application of 32-bit ARM and 16-bit thumb instruction. It also provides good support for Java acceleration (JaZell), security (Trust Zone), intelligent energy manager (IEM), SIMD, and NEON technologies. A worldwide community of ARM developers in semiconductor & product design companies includes software developers, system designers & hardware engineers now days, great emphasis on directly addressing the need to develop the system & software for an ARM-based system. This paper provides comprehensive description of the operation of the ARM core from a developers perspective with a clear emphasis's on software.

INTRODUCTION

The design of a general-purpose processor, in common with most engineering endeavors, requires the careful consideration of many trade-offs and compromises. We will start with the basic principles of processor instruction set and logic design and the techniques available to the designer to help achieve the design objectives.

We will start with the abstractions which are employed by computer hardware designers, of which the most important is the logic gate. The design of a simple processor is presented, from the instruction set, through a register transfer level description, down to logic gates.

The ideas behind the Reduced Instruction Set Computer (RISC) originated in processor research programmers at Stanford and Berkeley universities around 1980, though some of the central ideas can be traced back to earlier machines. In this chapter we look at the thinking that led to the RISC movement and consequently influenced the design of the ARM (Advanced Risk Machine) processor.

With the rapid development of markets for portable computer-based products, the power consumption of digital circuits is of increasing importance. At the end of the chapter we will look at the principles of low-power high-performance design.

Processor Architecture

A general-purpose processor is a finite-state automaton that executes instructions held in a memory. The state of the system is defined by the value held in the memory locations together with the values held in certain registers within the processor itself. Each instruction defines a particular way the total state should change and it also defines which instruction should be executed next.

The Stored-program Computer

The stored-program digital computer keeps its instructions and data in the same memory system, allowing the instructions to be treated as data when necessary. This enables the processor itself to generate instructions, which it can subsequently execute.

Although programs that do this at a fine granularity (self-modifying code) are generally considered bad form these days since they are very difficult to debug, use at a coarser granularity is fundamental to the way most computers operate. Whenever a computer loads in new program from disk (overwriting an old program) and then executes it the computer is employing this ability to change its own program.

The RISC Revolution

Into this world of increasingly complex instruction sets the Reduced Instruction Set Computer (RISC) was born. The RISC concept was major influence on the design of the ARM processor; indeed, RISC was the ARM's middle name. But before we look at either RISC or the ARM in more detail we need a bit more background on what processors. do and how they can be designed to do it quickly.

Table 1: Typical Dynamic Instruction Usage

Instruction type	Dynamic usage
Data movement	43%
Control flow	23%
Arithmetic operations	15%
Comparisons	13%
Logical operations	5%
Other	1%

FUNCTIONS OF PROCESSORS

It is a common misconception that computers spend their time computing, that is, carrying out arithmetic operations on user data. In practice they spend very little time 'computing' in this sense. Although they do a fair amount of arithmetic, most of this is with addresses in order to locate the relevant data items and program routines. Then, having found the user's data, most of the work is in moving it around rather than processing it in any transformational sense.

At the instruction set level, it is possible to measure the frequency of use of the various different instructions. It is very important to obtain dynamic measurements, that is, to measure the frequency of instructions that are executed, rather than the static frequency, which is just a count of the various instruction types in the binary image. These statistics were gathered running a print preview program on an ARM instruction emulator, but are broadly typical of what may be expected from other programs and instruction sets.

Pipelines

A processor executes an individual instruction in a sequence of steps. A typical sequence might be:

- Fetch the instruction from memory (fetch).
- Decode it to see what sort of instruction it is (dec).
- Access any operands that may be required from the register bank (reg).
- Combine the operands to form the result or a memory address (ALU).
- Access memory for a data operand, if necessary (mem).
- Write the result back to the register bank (res).

ARM Code Density and Thumb

The ARM processor design is based on RISC principles, but for various reasons suffers less from poor code density than most other RISCs. Its code density is still, however, not as good as some CISC processors. Where code density is of prime importance, ARM Limited has incorporated a novel mechanism, called the Thumb architecture, into some versions of the ARM processor. The Thumb instruction set is a 16-bit compressed form of the original 32-bit ARM instruction set, and employs dynamic decompression hardware in the instruction pipeline. Thumb code density is better than that achieved by most CISC processors.

Low Power Circuit Design

Various approaches to low-power design are listed below—

- Minimize the power supply voltage, V_{dd}.

  The quadratic contribution of the supply voltage to the power dissipation makes this obvious target. This is discussed further below.
- Minimize the circuit activity, A.

Techniques such as clock gating fall under this heading. Whenever a circuit function is not needed, activity should be eliminated.

- Minimize the number of gates.

  Simple circuits use less power than complex ones, all other things being equal, since the sum is over a smaller number of gate contributions.

- Minimize the clock frequency, f.

  Avoiding unnecessarily high clock rates is clearly desirable, but although a lower clock rate reduces the power consumption it also reduces performance, having a neutral effect on power-efficiency (measured, for example, in MIPS—Millions of Instructions Per Second —per watt). If, however, a reduced clock frequency allows operation at a reduced Vdd, this will be highly beneficial to the power-efficiency.

Low Power Strategies

To conclude this introduction to design techniques for low power consumption, here are some suggested strategies for low power applications.

- Minimize V_{dd}.

  Choose the lowest clock frequency that delivers the required performance, and then set the power supply voltage as low as is practical given the clock frequency and the requirements of the various system components. Be wary of reducing the supply voltage so far that leakage compromises standby power.

- Minimize off-chip activity.

  Off-chip capacitances are much higher than on-chip loads, so always minimize off-chip activity. Avoid allowing transients to drive off-chip loads and use caches to minimize accesses to off-chip memories.

- Minimize on-chip activity.

  Lower priority than minimizing off-chip activity, it is still important to avoid clocking unnecessary circuit functions (for example, by using gated clocks) and to employ sleep modes where possible.

- Exploit parallelism.

  Where the power supply voltage is a free variable parallelism can be exploited to improve power-efficiency. Duplicating a circuit allows the two circuits to sustain the same performance at half the clock frequency of the original circuit, which allows the required performance to be delivered with a lower supply voltage.

  Design for low power is an active research area and one where new ideas are being generated at a high rate. It is expected that a combination of process and design technology improvements will yield considerable further improvement in the power efficiency of high-speed digital circuits over the next decade.

ARM Architecture

The ARM processor is a Reduced Instruction Set Computer (RISC). The RISE concept, originated in processor research programmes at Stanford and Berkeley universities around 1980.

Now main emphasis is on how the RISC ideas helped shape the ARM processors. The ARM was originally developed at Acorn Computers Limited of Cambridge, England, between 1983 and 1985. It was the first RISE microprocessor developed for commercial use and has some significant difference from subsequent RISC architectures.

In 1990 ARM Limited was established as a separate company specifically to widen the exploitation of ARM technology, since when the ARM has been licensed to many semiconductor manufacturers around the world. It has become established as a market-leader for low-power and cost-sensitive embedded applications.

No processor is particularly useful without the support of hardware and software development tools. The ARM supported by a toolkit which includes an instruction set emulator for hardware modeling and software testing and benchmarking, an assembler, C and C++ compilers, a linker and a symbolic debugger.

The ACRON RISC Machine

The first ARM processor was developed at Acron Computers Limited of Cambridge, England, between October 1983 and April 1985. At that time, and until the formation of Advanced RISC Machines Limited (which later was renamed simply ARM Limited) in 1990, ARM stood for Acorn RISE Machine.

Acorn had developed a strong position in the UK personal computer market due to the success of the BBC (British Broadcasting Corporation) microcomputer. The BBC micro was a machine powered by the 8-bit 6502 microprocessor and rapidly became established at the dominant machine in UK schools following its introduction in January 1982 in support of a series of television programmes broadcast by the BBC. It also enjoyed enthusiastic support in the hobbyist market and found its C way into a number of research laboratories and higher education establishments.

Following the success of the BBC micro, Acorn's engineers looked at various microprocessors to build a successor machine around, but found all the commercial offerings lacking. The 16-bit CISC microprocessors that were available in 1983 were slower than standard memory parts. They also had instructions that took many dock cycles to complete (in some cases, many hundreds of clock cycles), giving them very long interrupt latencies. The BBC micro benefited greatly from the 6502's rapid interrupt response, so Acorn's designers were unwilling to accept a retrograde step in this aspect of the processor's performance.

The ARM, then was born through a serendipitous combination of factors; and became the core component in Acorn's product line. Later, after a judicious modification of the acronym expansion to Advanced RISE Machine, it lent its name to the company formed to broaden its market beyond Acorn's product range. Despite the change of name, the architecture still remains close to the original Acorn design.

Features used for ARM Architecture

The ARM architecture incorporated a number of features from the Berkeley RISE design, but a number of other features were rejected. Those that were used were:

- A load store architecture;
- Fixed-length 32-bit instructions;
- 3-address instruction formats.

The ARM Programmer's Model

A processor's instruction set defines the operations that the programmer can use to change the state of the system incorporating the processor. This state usually comprises the values of the data items in the processor's visible registers and the system's memory. Each instruction can be viewed as performing a defined transformation from the state before the instruction is executed to the state after it has completed. Although a processor will typically have many invisible registers involved in executing an instruction, the values of these registers before and after the instruction is executed are not significant; only the values in the visible registers have any significance. The visible registers in an ARM processor are shown.

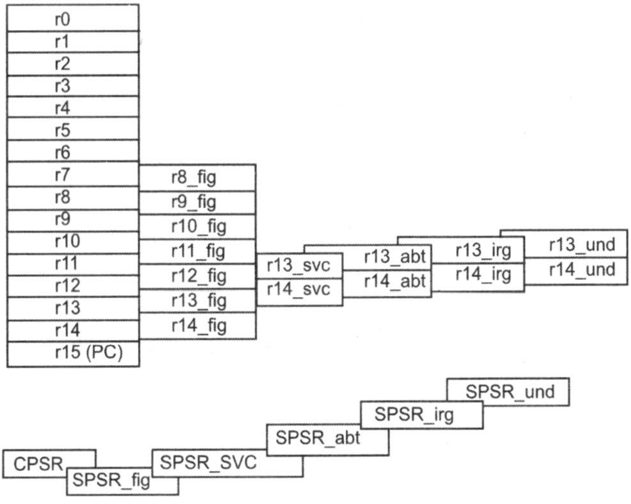

Fig. 1: ARM's visible registers

The Current Program Status Register (CPSR)

The CPSR is used in user-level programs to stare the condition code bits. These bits are used, far example, to record the result of a comparison operation and to control whether or not a conditional branch is taken. The user-level programmer need not usually be concerned with how this register is configured. The bits at the bottom of the register control the processor mode.

N: Negative; the last ALU operation which changed the flags produced a negative result (the tap bit of the 32-bit result was a one).

Z: Zero; the last ALU operation which changed the flags produced a zero result (every bit of the 32-bit result was zero).

C: Carry; the last ALU operation which changed the flags generated a carry-out, either as a result of an arithmetic operation in the ALU or from the shifter.

V: Overflow; the last arithmetic ALU operation which changed the flags generated an overflow into the sign bit.

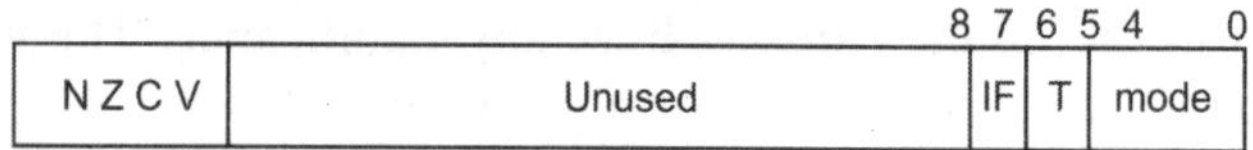

Fig. 2: ARM CPSR format

The Memory System

In addition to the processor register state, an ARM system has memory state. Memory may be viewed as a linear array-of-bytes-numbered from zero up to 232-1. Data items may be 8-bit bytes, 16-bit half-wards or 32-bit wards. Wards are always aligned an 4-byte boundaries (that is, the two least Significance address bits are zero) and half-words are aligned an even byte boundaries.

The memory organization is shown in this figure. This shows a small area of memory where each byte location a-unique number. A byte may occupy any of these locations, and a few examples are shown here. A word sized data item must occupy a group of four byte location starting at a byte address which is a multiple of four, and again the figure contains a couple of examples. Half words occupy two byte locations starting at an even byte address:

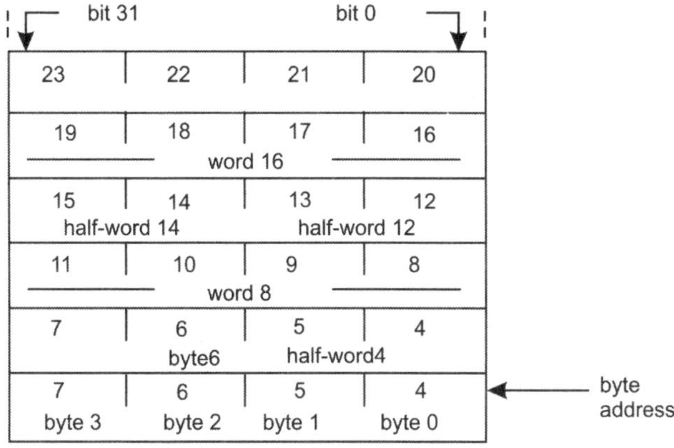

Fig. 3: ARM memory organization

Load-store Architecture

In common with most RISC processors, ARM employs a load-store architecture. This means that the instruction set will only process (add, subtract, and so on) values-which are in registers (or specified directly within the instruction itself), and will always place the results Distich processing into a register. The only Operations which apply to memory state are ones which copy memory values into registers (load instruction) or copy register values into memory (store instructions).

CISC processor typically allows a value from memory to be added to a value in a register, and sometimes allow a value in a register to be added to a value in memory. ARM does not support such 'memory-to-memory' operations.

The ARM Instruction Set

All ARM instruction is 32-bits (except the compressed 16-bit Thumb instructions) and is aligned on 4-byte boundaries in memory. The most notable features of the ARM instruction set are:

- The load-store architecture;
- 3-address data processing instructions (that is, the two source operand registers and the result register are all independently specified);

- Conditional execution of every instruction;
- The inclusion of very powerful load and store multiple register instructions;
- The ability to perform a general shift operation and a general ALU operation in a single instruction that executes in a single clock cycle;
- Open instruction set extension through the coprocessor instruction set, including adding new registers and data types to the programmer's model;
- A very dense 16-bit compressed representation of the instruction set in the thumb architecture.

To those readers familiar with modem RISC instruction sets, the ARM instruction set may appear to have rather more formats than other commercial RISC processors. While this is certainly the case and it does lead to more complex instruction decoding, it also leads to higher code density. For the small embedded systems that most ARM processors are used in, this code density advantage outweighs the small performance penalty incurred by the decode complexity. Thumb code extends this advantage to give ARM better code density than most CISC processors.

The Input/Output System

The ARM handles I/O (input/output) peripherals (such, as disk controllers, network interfaces, and so on) as memory-mapped devices with interrupt support: The internal registers in these devices appear as addressable locations within the, ARM's memory map and may be read and written using the same (load-store) instructions as any other memory locations.

The ARM Exceptions

The ARM architecture, supports a range of interrupts, traps and supervisor calls, all grouped wider the general heading of exceptions. The general way these are handled is the same in all, cases:

1. The current state is saved by copying the PC into r14_exc and the CPSR into SPSR_exc (where exc stands for the exception type).

2. The processor operating mode is changed to the appropriate exception mode.
3. The PC is forced to a value between 0016 and lC16, the particular value depending on the type of exception.

The ARM C Compiler

The ARM C compiler is compliant with the ANSI (American National Standards Institute) standard for C and is supported by the appropriate library of standard functions. It uses the ARM Procedure Call Standard for all externally available functions. It can be told to produce assembly source output instead of ARM object format, so the code can be inspected or even hand optimized, and then assembled subsequently. The compiler can also produce Thumb code.

The ARM Assembler

The ARM assembler is a full macro assembler which produces ARM object format output that can be linked with output from the C compiler.

Assembly source language is near machine-level, with most assembly instructions translating into single ARM (or Thumb) instruction.

Software Toolkit

ARM Limited supplies the complete set of tools described above, with some support utility programs and documentation, as the 'ARM Software Development Toolkit'. The Toolkit CD-ROM includes a PC version of the toolset that runs under most versions of the Windows operating system and includes full Windows-based project manager. The toolkit is updated as new versions of the ARM become available.

The ARM Project Manager is a graphical front-end for the tools described above. It supports the building of a single library or executable image from a list of files that make up a particular project. These files maybe:

- Source files (C, assembler, and so on);
- Library files;
- Object files;

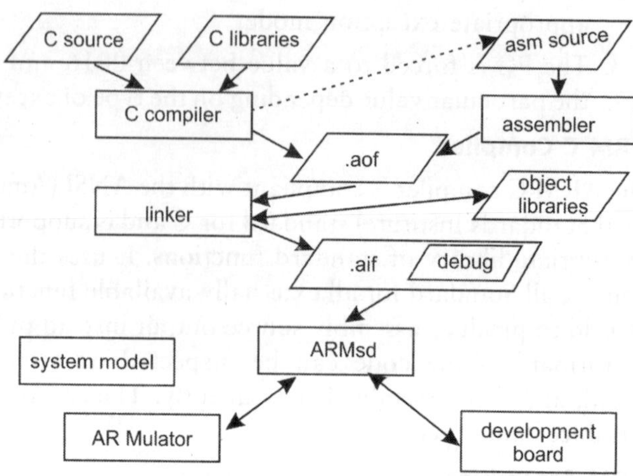

Fig. 4: The structure of ARM cross development toolkit

The source files may be edited within the Project Manager, a dependency list created and the output library or executable image built. There are many options which may be chosen for the build, such as:

- Whether the output should be optimized for code size or execution time.
- Whether the output should be in debug or release form.

(Code compiled for source-level debugging cannot be fully optimized since the mapping from the source to fully optimized output is too obscure for debugging purposes.)

Which ARM processor is the target (and, particularly, whether it supports the Thumb instruction set).

ARM Organization and Implementation

The organization of the ARM integer processor or core changed very little from the first 3 micron devices developed at Acorn Computers between 1983 and 1985 to the ARM6 and ARM7 developed by ARM Limited between 1990 and 1995, The 3-stage pipeline used by these processing was steadily tightened up and CMOS process technology reduced in feature size by almost an order of magnitude over this period, so the performance of the cores improved dramatically, but the basic principles of operation remained largely the same.

Since 1995 several new ARM cores have been introduced which deliver significantly higher performance through the use of 5-stage pipelines and separate instruction and data memories.

Stage Pipeline ARM Organization

The organization of an ARM with a 3-stage pipeline is illustrated in Figure 4. The principal components are:

- The register bank, which stores the processor state. It has two read ports and one write port which can each be used to access any register, plus an additional read port and an additional write port that give special access to r15, the program counter. (The additional write port on r15 allows it to be updated as the instruction fetch address is incremented and the read port allows instruction fetch to resume after a data address has been issued.)
- The barrel shifter, which can shift or rotate one operand by any number of bits.
- The ALU, which, performs the arithmetic and logic functions required by the instruction set.
- The address register and incrementer, which select and hold addresses and generate sequential addresses when required.
- The data registers, which hold data passing to and from memory.
- The instruction decoder and associated control logic.

In a single-cycle data processing instruction, two register operands are accessed, the value on the B bus is shifted and combined with the value on the A bus in the ALU, then the result is written back into the register bank. The program counter value is in the address register, from where it is fed into the incrementer, and then the incremented value is copied back into r15 in the register bank and also into the address register to be used as the address for the next instruction fetch.

ARM processors up to the ARM 7 employ a simple 3-stage pipeline with the following pipeline stages:

- Fetch: The instruction is fetched from memory and placed in the instruction pipeline.
- Decode: The instruction is decoded and the data path control signals prepared for the next cycle. In this stage the instruction 'owns' the decode logic but not the data path.
- Execute: The instruction 'owns' the data path; the register bank is read, an operand shifted, the ALU result generated and written back into a destination register.

When the processor is executing simple data processing instructions the pipeline enables one instruction to be completed every clock cycle. An individual instruction takes three clock cycles to complete, so it has three-cycle latency, but the throughput is one instruction per cycle. The 3-stage pipeline operation for single-cycle instructions is shown.

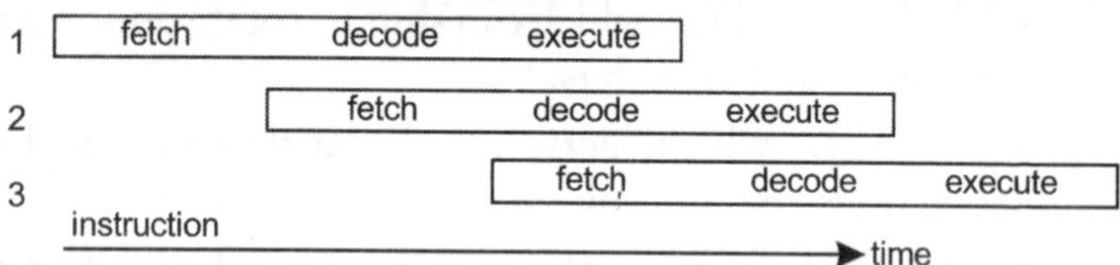

Fig. 5: ARM single-cycle instruction 3-stage pipeline operations

When a multi-cycle instruction is executed, the flow is less regular. This shows a sequence of single-cycle ADD instructions with a data store instruction, STR, occurring after the first ADD. The cycles that access main memory is shown with light shading so it can be seen that memory is used in every cycle. The data path is likewise used in every cycle, being involved in all the execute cycles, the address calculation and the data transfer. The decode logic is always generating the control signals for the data path to use in the next cycle, so in addition to the explicit decode cycles it is also generating the control for the data transfer during the address calculation cycle of the STR.

Thus, in this instruction sequence, all parts of the processor are active in every cycle and the memory is the limiting factor, defining the number of cycles the sequence must take. The simplest way to view breaks in the ARM pipeline is to observe that:

- All instructions occupy the data path for one or more adjacent cycles.
- For each cycle that an instruction occupies the data path, it occupies the decode logic in the immediately preceding cycle.

During the first data path cycle each instruction issues a fetch for the next instruction but one.

Branch instructions flush and refill the instruction pipeline.

The BARREL Shifter

The ARM architecture supports instructions which perform a shift operation in series with an ALU operation. The shifter performance is therefore critical since the lift time contributes directly to the data path cycle time.

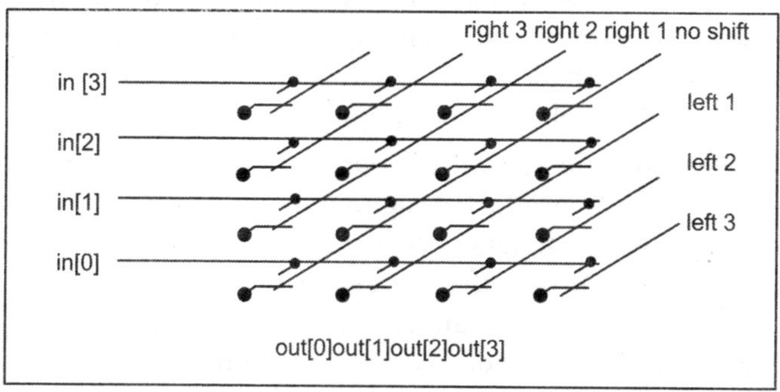

Fig. 6: The Cross-bar switch barrel shifter principle

In order to minimize the delay through the shifter a cross-bar switch matrix is used to steer each input to the appropriate output (The ARM processors use a 32×32 matrix).

The shifting functions are implemented by wiring switches along diagonals to a common control input:

For a left or right shift function, one diagonal is turned on. This connects all the input bits to their respective outputs where they are used. (Not all are used, since some bits 'fall off the end'.) In the ARM the barrel shifter operates in negative logic where a 'I' is represented as a potential near ground and a '0' by a potential near the supply. Recharging sets all the outputs to a logic '0', so those outputs that are not connected to any input during a particular switching operation remain at '0' giving the zero filling required by the shift semantics.

- For a rotate right function, the right shift diagonal is enabled together with the complementary left shift diagonal. For example, on the 4-bit matrix rotate right one bit is implemented using the 'right I' and the 'left 3' (3 = 4 - I) diagonals:
- Arithmetic shift right uses sign-extension rather than zero-fill for the unconnected output bits, S.
- Separate logic is used to decode the shift amount and discharge those outputs appropriately.

CONCLUSION

The ARM processor is a Reduced Instruction Set Computer (RISC) over the last ten years, the ARM architecture has become one of the most pervasive architecture in the world, with more than 1 billion ARM-based processors embedded in product ranging form cell phones to automotive braking system.

A worldwide community of ARM developers in semiconductor & product design companies includes software developers, system designers & hardware engineers. Nowadays, great emphasis on directly addressing the need to develop the system & software for an ARM-based system. This paper provides comprehensive description of the operation of the ARM core from a developers perspective with a clear emphasis's on software.

It demonstrates processor design, ARM architecture, ARM organization, implementation, pipelining and ARM instruction set. It covers both the ARM and Thumb instruction sets, outlines destinations among the version of the ARM architecture and also looks forward to the future of the ARM architecture.

REFERENCES

1. The Definitive Guide to the ARM Cortex-M3 by Joseph Yiu.
2. Low Power Methodology Manual by Michael Keating (Synopsys), David Flynn (ARM), Robert Aitken (ARM), Alan Gibbons (Synopsys) & Kaijian Shi (Synopsys).
3. ARM System Developer's Guide (Korean version) Hardbound ISBN:89-5550-839-5, 788 pages, publication date: 2005. In Korean language by Clabsys Co., Ltd. Published by SciTech Media., Inc.
4. ARM Architecture Reference Manual Second Edition, edited by David Seal: Addison-Wesley.
5. ARM System-on-chip Architecture In English language, by Steve Furber Second Edition published by Addison Wesley.
6. ARM System Developer's Guide Hardbound ISBN-10: 1558608745, ISBN-13: 978-1558608740, 704 pages, publication date: 2004 Imprint: Morgan Kauffman.

Caching and Replication in Mobile Data Management

17

Manoj Yadav, Mohd. Zuaib and
Diwakar Bhardwaj

ABSTRACT

Mobile data management has been an active area of research for the past fifteen years. Besides dealing with mobility itself, issues central in data management for mobile computing include low bandwidth, intermittent network connectivity and scarcity of resources with emphasis on power management. In this article, we focus on how caching and replication in mobile data management address these challenges. We consider two antagonistic criteria, that of ensuring quality of data in terms of consistency and coherency and that of achieving quality of service in terms of response time and availability.

INTRODUCTION

Mobile computing refers to computing using devices that are not attached to a specific location, but instead their position (network or geographical) changes. Mobile computing can be traced back to file systems and the need for disconnected operations in the end of the 80s. With the rapid growth in mobile technologies and the cost effectiveness in deploying wireless networks in the 90s, the goal of mobile computing was to support of AAA (anytime, anywhere and any-form) access to data by users from their portable computers and mobile phones, devices with small displays and limited resources. This led to research in mobile data management including transaction processing, query processing and data dissemination [22]. A key characteristic of all these research efforts was the great emphasis on the mobile computing challenges, including:

- *Intermittent Connectivity*. This refers to the fact that computation must proceed despite short or long periods of network unavailability.
- *Scarcity of Resources*. Due to the small sizes of portable devices, there are implicit restrictions.
- *Mobility*. The implications of mobility are varying. First, mobility introduces a number of technical challenges at the networking layer. It also offers a number of opportunities at the higher layers for explicitly using location information either at the semantic level (for instance, for providing personalization) or at the performance level (for instance, for data prefetching). Finally, it amplifies heterogeneity. In general, one can distinguish between single-hop and multi-hop underlying infrastructures. In *singlehop* infrastructures, each mobile device communicates with a stationary host, which corresponds to its point

Bulletin of the IEEE Computer Society Technical Committee on Data Engineering of attachment to the network. The rest of the routing is the responsibility of a stationary infrastructure, e.g. the Internet. On the other hand, in *multi-hop* wireless communication, an ad-hoc wireless network is formed in which, wireless hosts participate in routing messages among each other. In both infrastructures, the hosts between the source (or sources) that holds the data and the requester of data (or data sink) form a dissemination tree. The hosts (mobile or stationary) that form the dissemination tree may store data and take part in the computation towards achieving *in network* processing (e.g. aggregation).

Locally caching or replicating data at the wireless host or at the intermediate nodes of the dissemination tree are important for improving system performance and availability.

Caching and replication generally attempt to guarantee that most data requests are for data that is being held in main memory or local storage, negating the need to perform I/O, or a remote data retrieval. Hence, the use of appropriate caching/ replication schemes have been traditionally used to improve performance and reduce service time. In mobile environments the performance considerations go beyond simple speedups and data retrieval delays. In this article, we examine how caching and replication has been utilized in mobile data management and more specifically in the first infrastructure where data are cached at the mobile device in order to avoid excessive energy consumption and to cope with intermittent connectivity. In this paper, our focus is on consistency, that is, how to ensure the correctness of operations on cached data. In Section 2, we provide a brief taxonomy of related correctness criteria. While traditionally, cached data are read-only, in mobile computing, some restricted form of cache updates is supported especially in case of disconnections. We call this form of caching that allows cache updates at the client, *two-tier caching* and discuss it in detail in Section 3. In Section 4, we present issues related to disseminating updates from the rest of the network to the mobile device. Finally, Section 5 concludes the paper.

Consistency Levels

We consider the case in which a mobile computing device (such as a portable computer or cellular phone) is connected to the rest of the network typically through a wireless link. Wireless communication has a double impact on the mobile device since the limited bandwidth of wireless links increases the response times for accessing remote data from a mobile host and transmitting as well as receiving of data are high energy consumption operations. The principal goal is to store appropriate pieces of data locally at the mobile device so that it can operate on its own data, thus reducing the need for communication that consumes both energy and bandwidth. At some point, operations performed at the mobile device must be synchronized with operations performed at other sites. The complexity of this synchronization depends greatly on whether updates are allowed at the mobile device. The main reason for allowing such updates is to sustain network disconnections. When there are no local updates, the important issue is disseminating updates from the rest of the network to the mobile device. Synchronization depends on the level at which correctness is sought. This can be roughly categorized as replica-level correctness and transaction-level correctness. At the *replica level*, correctness or coherency requirements are expressed per item in terms of the allowable divergence among the values of the copies of each item. There are many ways to characterize the divergence among copies of an item. For example, with *quasi copies* [3], the coherency or freshness requirements between a cached copy of an item and its primary at theserver are specified by limiting (a) the number of updates (versions) between them, (b) their distance in time, or (c) the difference between their values. At the *transaction level*, the strictest form of correctness is achieved through global serializability that requires the execution of all transactions running at mobile and stationary hosts to be equivalent to some serial execution of the same transactions. In case of replication, one copy serializability provides equivalence with a serial execution on a one-copy database. One-copy serializability does not allow any divergence among copies.

There is a large number of correctness criteria proposed besides serializability. A practical such criterion 2 is snapshot isolation [5]. With snapshot isolation, a transaction is allowed to read data from any database snapshot at a time earlier than its start time. Central are also criteria that treat read-only transactions, i.e. transactions with no update operations, differently. Consistency of read-only transactions is achieved by ensuring that transactions read a database instance that does not violate any integrity constraints (as for example with snapshot isolation), while freshness of read-only transactions refers to the freshness of the values read [11]. Finally, *relaxed-currency serializability* allows update transactions to read out-of-date values as long as they satisfy some freshness constraints specified by the users [6]. There are two basic ways of propagating updates. Eager replication synchronizes all copies of an item within a single transaction, whereas with lazy replication, transactions for keeping replica coherent run as separate, independent database transactions after the original transaction. One-copy serializability as well as other forms of correctness can be achieved either through eager or lazy update propagation.

Two-tier Caching

In this section, we assume that data can be updated at the mobile device. The main motivation is support for disconnected operation. *Disconnected operation* refers to the autonomous operation of a mobile client, when network connectivity becomes unavailable for instance, due to physical constraints, or undesirable, for example, for reducing power consumption. Preloading or prefetching data to sustain a forthcoming disconnection is often termed *hoarding*. The content of data to be prefetched may be determined (a) automatically by the system by utilizing implicit information, most often based on the past history of data references, or (b) by instructions given explicitly by the users, as in *profile-driven data prefetching* [7], where a simple profile language is introduced for specifying the items to be prefetched along with their relative importance. Additional information such as a set of allowable operations or a characterization of the required data quality may also be cached along with data. For example, in the *Promotion infrastructure* [28, 15], the unit of caching and replication is a *compact*, an object that encapsulates the cached data, operations for accessing the cached data, state information (such as the number of accesses to the object), consistency rules that must be followed to guarantee consistency, and obligations (such as deadlines).

To allow concurrent operation at both the mobile client and other sites during disconnection, optimistic approaches to consistency control are typically deployed. Optimistic consistency maintenance protocols allow data to be accessed concurrently at multiple sites without a priori synchronization between the sites, potentially resulting in short term inconsistencies. Such protocols trade-off quality of data for improving quality of service.

Optimistic replication has been extensively studied as a means for consistency maintenance in distributed systems (for example, see [23] for a thorough recent survey). In this paper, we present some representative examples of optimistic protocols in the context of mobile computing. Consistent operation during disconnected operation has been also extensively addressed in the context of *network partitioning*. In this context, a network failure partitions the sites of a distributed database system into disconnected clusters. Various approaches have been proposed and are excellently reviewed in [8]. In general, protocols in network partition follow peer-to-peer models where transactions executed in any partition are of equal importance, whereas the related protocols in mobile computing most often consider transactions at the mobile host as second-class, for instance, by considering their updates as tentative. Furthermore, disconnections in mobile computing are common and some of them may be considered foreseeable. Disconnections correspond to the extreme case of total lack of connectivity. Other connectivity constraints, such as weak or intermittent connectivity also affect the protocols for enforcing consistency. In general, weak connectivity is handled by appropriately revising those operations whose deployment involves the network. For instance, the frequency of propagation to the server of updates performed at the local data may depend on connectivity conditions. In early research in mobile computing, a general concern has been whether issues such connectivity or mobility should be transparent or hidden from the users. In this respect, adapting the levels of transaction or replica correctness to the system conditions such as the availability of connectivity or the quality of the network connection and providing applications with less than strict notions of correctness can be seen as making such conditions visible to the users. This is also achieved by explicitly extending queries with quality of data specifications, for example, for constraining the divergence between copies. Some common characteristics of protocols for consistency in two-tier caching are:

- the propagation of updates performed at the mobile site follow in general lazy protocols.

- reads are allowed at the local data, while updates of local data are tentative in the sense that they need to be further validated before commitment.
- for integrating operations at the mobile hosts with transactions at other sites, in the case of replica level consistency, copies of an item are reconciled following some conflict resolution protocol. At the transaction-level, local transactions are validated against some application or system level criterion. If the criterion is met, the transaction is committed. Otherwise, the execution of the transaction is either aborted, reconciled or compensated. Such actions may have cascaded effects on other tentatively committed transactions that have seen the results of the transaction. Next, we present a number of consistency protocols that have been proposed for mobile computing.

Isolation-Only Transactions in Coda

Coda [24] is one of the first file systems designed to support disconnections and weak connectivity. Coda introduced isolation-only transactions (IOTs) [14] in file systems. An IOT is a sequence of file access operations. A transaction T is called a *first-class transaction*, if it does not have any partitioned file access, i.e. the mobile host maintains a connection for every file it has accessed. Otherwise, T is called a *second-class transaction*. Whereas the result of a first-class transaction is immediately committed, a second-class transaction remains in the pending state till connectivity is restored. The result of a second-class transaction is held within the local cache and visible only to subsequent accesses on the same host. Second-class transactions are guaranteed to be locally serializable among themselves. A first-class transaction is guaranteed to be serializable with all transactions that were previously resolved or committed at the fixed host. Upon reconnection, a second-class transaction T is validated against one of the following two serialization constraints. The first is global serializability, which means that if a pending transaction's local result were written to the fixed host as is, it would be serializable with all previously committed or resolved transactions. The second is a stronger consistency criterion called global certifiability (GC) which requires a pending transaction be globally serializable not only with, but also after all previously committed or resolved transactions.

Two-tier Replication

With *two-tier replication* [12], replicated data have two versions at mobile nodes: master and tentative versions. A master version records the most recent value received while the site was connected. A tentative version records local updates. There are two types of transactions analogous to second- and first-class IOTs: tentative and base transactions. A *tentative transaction* works on local tentative data and produces tentative data. A *base transaction* works only on master data and produce master data. Base transactions involve only connected sites. Upon reconnection, tentative transactions are reprocessed as base transactions. If they fail to meet some application-specific acceptance criteria, they are aborted.

Two-layer Transactions

With two-layer transactions [17], transactions that run solely at the mobile host are called *weak*, while the rest are called *strict*. A distinction is drawn between weak copies and strict copies. In contrast to strict copies, weak copies are only tentatively committed and hold possibly obsolete values. Weak transactions update weak copies, while strict transactions access strict copies located at any site. Weak copies are integrated with strict copies either when connectivity improves or when an application-defined freshness limit to the allowable deviation among weak and strict copies is passed. Before reconciliation, the results of weak transactions are visible only to weak transactions at the same site. Strict transactions are slower than weak 4 transactions, since they involve the wireless link but guarantee permanence of updates and currency of reads. During disconnection, applications can only use weak transactions. In this case, weak transactions have similar semantics with second-class IOTs [14] and tentative transactions [12]. Adaptability is achieved by restricting the number of strict transactions depending on the available connectivity and by adjusting the application-defined degree of divergence among copies.

Bayou [16, 26, 27] is built on a peer-to-peer architecture with a number of replicated servers weakly connected to each other. Bayou does not support full-fledged transactions. A user application can read-any and write-any available copy. Writes are propagated to other servers during pair-wise contracts called *antientropy* sessions. When a write is accepted by a Bayou server, it is initially deemed tentative. As in two-tier replication [12], each server maintains two views of the database: a copy that only reflects committed data and another full copy that also reflects the tentative writes currently known to the server. Eventually, each write is committed using a primary-commit schema. That is, one server designated as the primary takes responsibility for committing updates. Because servers may receive writes from clients and other servers in different orders, servers may need to undo the effects of some previous tentative execution of a write operation and re-apply it. The Bayou system provides dependency checks for automatic conflict detection and merge procedures for resolution. Instead of transactions, Bayou supports *sessions*. A session is an abstraction for a sequence of read and write operations performed during the execution of an application. *Session guarantees* are enforced to avoid inconsistencies when accessing copies at different servers; for example, a session guarantee may be that read operations reflect previous writes or that writes are propagated after writes that logically precede them. Different degrees of connectivity are supported by individually selectable session guarantees, choices of committed or tentative data, and by placing an age parameter on reads. Arbitrary disconnections among Bayou's servers are also supported since Bayou relies only on pair-wise communication. Thus, groups of servers may be disconnected from the rest of the system yet remain connected to each other.

Update Dissemination

In this section, we consider data at the mobile device to be read-only, as in traditional client-server caching [9]. In this case, the main issue is developing efficient protocols for disseminating server updates to mobile clients. Most such cache invalidation protocols developed for mobile computing focus on the case in which a large number of clients is attached to a single server.

Often, the server is equipped with an efficient broadcast facility that allows it to propagate updates to all of its clients. Different assumptions are made on whether the server maintains or not any information about which clients it is serving, what are the contents of their cache, and when their cache was last validated. Servers that hold such information are called *stateful*, while servers that do not are called *stateless*. Another issue pertinent to mobile computing is again handling disconnections, in particular, ensuring that cache invalidation are received by clients despite any temporary network unavailability. Update propagation may be either synchronous or asynchronous. In *synchronous* methods, the server broadcasts an invalidation report periodically. A client must listen for the report first to decide whether its cache is valid or not. Thus, each client is confident for the validity of its cache only as of the last invalidation report. This adds some latency to query processing, since to answer a query, a client has to wait for the next invalidation report. In case of disconnections, synchronous methods surpass asynchronous in that clients need only periodically tune in to read the invalidation report instead of continuously listening to the broadcast. However, if the client remains inactive longer than the period of the broadcast, the entire cache must be discarded, unless special checking is deployed. Invalidation protocols vary in the type of information they convey to the clients. In case of replica level correctness, it suffices that single read operations access current data. In this case, invalidation may include just a list of the updated items or in addition to this, their updated values. Including the updated values may be wasteful of bandwidth especially when the corresponding items are cached at only a few clients. On the other 5 hand, if the values are not included, the client must either discard the item from its cache or communicate with the server to receive the updated value. The reports can provide information for individual items or aggregate information for sets of items. In case of transaction level correctness, invalidation reports must include additional information regarding server transactions.

The efficiency of an update dissemination protocol depends on the connectivity behavior of the mobile clients. In [4], clients that are often connected are called workaholic, while clients that are often disconnected are the sleepers. Three synchronous strategies for stateless servers are considered. In the broadcasting *timestamps* strategy (*TS*), the invalidation report contains the timestamps of the latest change for items that have had updates in the last *w* seconds. In the *amnestic terminals* strategy (*AT*), the server only broadcasts the identifiers of the items that changed since the last invalidation report. In the *signatures* strategy, signatures are broadcast. A signature is a checksum computed over the value of a number of items by applying data compression techniques similar to those used for file comparison. Each of these strategies is shown to be effective for different types of clients. Signatures are best for long sleepers, that is, when the period of disconnection is long and hard to predict. The *AT* method is best for workaholic. Finally, *TS* is shown to be advantageous when the rate of queries is greater than the rate of updates provided that the clients are not workaholics.

Another model of operation in the content of mobile databases is that of a broadcast or push model [1]. In this model, the server broadcasts (periodically) data to a set of mobile clients. Clients monitor the broadcast and retrieve the data items they need as they arrive. Data of interest may also be cached locally at the client. When clients read data from the broadcast, a number of different replica-level correctness models are reasonable [2]. For example, if clients do not cache data, the server always broadcasts the most recent values, and there is no backchannel for on-demand data delivery, then the *latest value* model is a model that arise naturally. In this model, clients read the most recent value of a data item. Methods for enforcing transaction-level correctness are presented in [19]. With the *invalidation* method, the server broadcasts an invalidation report with the data items that have been updated since the broadcast of the previous report. Transactions that read obsolete items are aborted. With the *serialization graph testing* (SGT) method, the server broadcasts control information related to conflicting operations. Clients use this information to ensure that their read-only transactions are serializable with the server transactions. With *multiversion broadcast* [18, 20], multiple versions of each item are broadcast, so that client transactions always read a consistent database snapshot. A eneral theory of correctness for broadcast databases as well as the fundamental properties underlying the techniques for enforcing it are given in [21]. Correctness characterizes the freshness of the values seen by the clients with regards to the values at the server as well as the temporal discrepancy among the values read by the same transaction. More recently, the concept of materialized views was extended in the context of mobile databases to operate in a fashion similar to data caches supporting local query processing [13]. As in traditional databases, materialized views in mobile databases provide a means to present different portions of the databases based on users' perspectives and, similar to data warehouses, materialized views provide a mean to support personalized information gathering from multiple data sources. Personalization is expressed in the form of view maintenance options for recomputation and incremental maintenance. They offer a finer grain of control and balance between data availability and currency, the amount of wireless communication and the cost of maintaining consistency. In order to better characterize these personalization, in [13] *recomputational consistency* was introduced and the *materialized view consistency* [30] was enhanced with new levels which correspond to specific view currency customizations.

Summary

In this short article, we presented issues related to cache consistency in mobile computing. The methods presented can be considered as extensions of traditional client-server caching, where the client is a mobile device[6]. The main motivation for this form of caching is improving availability especially in the case of network disconnections.

Caching also improves performance through reducing the communication overhead in terms of both data access delays and energy consumption. An interesting extension of the current methods is hierarchical caching for the emerging infrastructures of multi-hop wireless networks. Besides the challenges due to mobility, hierarchical caching introduces new complications such as the multiple levels of intervening caches can that create adverse workloads for the caching schemes used at different levels. A hierarchical caching scheme must have the ability to adapt itself, thereby acting synergistically and cooperatively with other caching schemes on mobile peers [10]. Finally, mobile computing is often related to wireless computing and to computation involving small devices, including sensors or RFID tags. In the case of sensors, their limited power restricts the amount of processing and communication that sensors can perform before they become inactive. Thereby, an interesting question related to hierarchical caching is how caching at different sensors can help in the conservation of their energy, thereby prolonging the lifetime of a sensor network and improving the quality of the data [25, 29].

REFERENCES

1. S. Acharya, M.J. Franklin and A.B. Zdonik. Balancing push and pull for data broadcast. In *SIGMOD Conference*, pp. 183–194, 1997.
2. S. Acharya, M.J. Franklin, and S.B. Zdonik. Disseminating updates on broadcast disks. In *VLDB*, pp. 354–365, 1996.
3. R. Alonso, D. Barbara and H. Garcia-Molina. Data Caching Issues in an Information Retrieval System. *ACM Transactions on Database Systems (TODS)*, 15(3):359–384, September 1990
4. D.Barbar´a and T. Imielinski. Sleepers and workaholics: Caching strategies in mobile environments. *VLDBJ*, 4(4):567–602, 1995.
5. H. Berenson, P. Bernstein, J. Gray, J. Melton, E. O'Neil., and P. O'Neil. A Critique of ANSI SQL Isolation Levels. In *Proceedings of the ACM SIGMOD Conference*, pp. 1–10, 1995.
6. P. A. Bernstein, A. Fekete, H. Guo, R. Ramakrishnan, and P. Tamma. Relaxed-currency serializability for middle-tier caching and replication. In *SIGMOD Conference*, pp. 599–610, 2006.
7. M. Cherniack, E. F. Galvez, M. J. Franklin, and S. B. Zdonik. Profile-Driven Cache Management. In *Proceedings of the ICDE Conference*, pp. 645–656, 2003.
8. S.B. Davidson, H. Garcia-Molina and D. Skeen. Consistency in Partitioned Networks. *ACM Computing Surveys*, 17(3):341–370, September 1985.
9. M.J. Franklin, M.J. Carey and M. Livny. Transactional client-server cache consistency: Alternatives and performance. *ACM Trans. Database Syst.*, 22(3):315– 363, 1997.
10. P.K. Chrysanthis, G. Santhanakrishnan and A. Amer. Towards universal mobile caching. In *Proc. of the 4th ACM Int'l Workshop on Data Engineering for Wireless and Mobile Access*, June 2005.

11. H. Garcia-Molina and G. Wiederhold. Read-Only Transactions in a Distributed Database. *ACM Transactions on Database Systems*, 7(2):209–234, June 1982.

12. J. Gray, P. Helland, P. O'Neil and D. Shasha. The Dangers of Replication and a Solution. In *Proceedings of the ACM SIGMOD Conference*, pp. 173–182, Montreal, Canada, 1996-97.

13. S. Weissman Lauzac and P. K. Chrysanthis. Personalizing Information Gathering for Mobile Database Clients. In *Proceedings of the ACM Annual Symposium on Applied Computing*, pp. 49–56, 2002.

14. Q. Lu and M. Satyanarayanan. Improving Data Consistency in Mobile Computing Using Isolation-Only Transactions. In *Proceedings of the Fifth Workshop on Hot Topics in Operating Systems*, Orcas Island, Washington, May 1995.

15. S. Mazumdar and P.K. Chrysanthis. Localization of Integrity Constraints in Mobile Databases and Specification in PRO-MOTION. *ACM Mobile Networks*, 9(5):481–490, October 2004

16. K. Petersen, M. Spreitzer, D.B. Terry, M. Theimer, and A. J. Demers. Flexible update propagation for weakly consistent replication. In *SOSP*, pp. 288–301, 1997.

17. E. Pitoura and B. Bhargava. Data Consistency in Intermittently Connected Distributed Systems. *IEEE Transactions on Knowledge and Data Engineering*.

18. E. Pitoura and P.K. Chrysanthis. Exploiting versions for handling updates in broadcast disks. In *VLDB*, pp. 114–125, 1999.

19. E. Pitoura and P.K. Chrysanthis. Scalable processing of read-only transactions in broadcast push. In *ICDCS*, pp. 432–439, 1999.

20. E. Pitoura and P.K. Chrysanthis. Multiversion data broadcast. *IEEE Trans. Computers*, 51(10):1224–1230, 2002.

21. E. Pitoura, P.K. Chrysanthis, and K. Ramamritham. Characterizing the temporal and semantic coherency of broadcast-based data dissemination. In *ICDT*, pp. 410–424, 2003.

22. E. Pitoura and G. Samaras. *Data Management for Mobile Computing*. Kluwer Academic Publishers, 1998.

23. Y. Saito and M. Shapiro. Optimistic Replication. *ACM Computing Surveys*, 37(1):42–81, March 2005.

24. M. Satyanarayanan. The evolution of coda. *ACM Trans. Comput. Syst.*, 20(2):85–124, 2002.

25. M.A. Sharaf, J. Beaver, A. Labrinidis and P.K. Chrysanthis. Balancing energy efficiency and quality of aggregate data in sensor networks. pages 13(4):384-403, December 2004.

26. D. Terry, A. Demers, K. Petersen, M. Spreitzer, M. Theimer, and B.Welch. Session Guarantees for Weakly Consistent Replicated Data. In *Proceedings of the International Conference on Parallel and Distributed Information Systems*, pp. 140–149, September 1994.
27. D.B. Terry, M.M. Theimer, K. Petersen, A.J. Demers, M.J. Spreitzer and C.H. Hauser. Managing Update Conflicts in Bayou, a Weakly Connected Replicated Storage System. In *Proceedings of the 15th ACM Symposium on Operating Systems Principles*, December 1995.
28. G. Walborn and P.K. Chrysanthis. PRO-MOTION: Support for Mobile Database Access. *Personal and Ubiquitous Computing*, 1(3), September 1997.
29. D. Zeinalipour-Yazti, P. Andreou, P.K. Chrysanthis and G. Samaras. Mint views: Materialized in-network top-k views in sensor networks. In *Proceedings of the 7th International Conference in Mobile Data Management*, pp. 182–189, May 2007.
30. Y. Zhuge, H. Garcia-Molina, and J. Wiene. Consistency Algorithms for Multi-Source Warehouse View Maintenance. *Distributed and Parallel Databases*, 4(4), 1997.

Modeling and Verification of a Next Generation Mobile Channel

18

Mohd. Israil and *M. Salim Beg*

ABSTRACT

While most of today's mobile radio applications operate on a narrowband channel, this paper investigates a wideband mobile radio channel for next generation systems. In this paper a number of different cases of mobile radio channels have been simulated. These channels have different number of reflected paths with different power distribution in the respective paths. Mobile channel has been generated in this paper using simply tapped delay line model. The verification of the channel model has been carried out in order to confirm that it is a valid representation of the real vehicular mobile radio channel. The statistical properties of the designed high-speed channel like mean, variance and fading rate are investigated analytically and compared with the theoretically obtained values. The signal is transmitted at a bit rate of 144 kbit/s and a carrier frequency of 1800 MHz in this work.

INTRODUCTION

In order to accommodate new multimedia and Internet application services involving the transmission of text, audio, and image over wideband mobile radio systems, the transmission bit rate over such mobile channels becomes extremely high. In this case, the time delay spread of the channel becomes appreciably large compared to the signal element duration. As the antenna height of a mobile terminal is usually very small, the antenna is expected to have very little 'clearance', so obstacles and reflecting surfaces in the vicinity of the antenna have a substantial influence on the characteristics of the propagation path. Moreover, the propagation characteristics change from place to place and, if the mobile unit moves, from time to time. Thus, the transmission path between the transmitter and the receiver can vary from simple direct line-of-sight (LOS) to one that is severely obstructed by buildings, foliage and the terrain. The radio waves reach at the receiver after refection from various objects. This type of radio wave propagation is called multipath propagation. Due to multipath propagation, radio waves arrive at the receiver from different directions with different time delays, and they combine vectorially at the receiver antenna to give a resultant signal which can be large or small depending upon whether the incoming waves combine constructively or destructively.

As the mobile station moves from one location to another, the phase relationship between the various incoming waves changes; hence there are substantial amplitude fluctuations and the signal is said to be subject to fading. Multipath fading may also arise due to the movement of the surrounding objects from which the reflection of signals are coming to the receivers. Fading can be flat or of the frequency selective type. In a flat fading channel, all the frequency components are affecting in similar manner [6]. In frequency selective, different frequency components of the signal fade differently. A further cause of fading is the obstruction of the radio signals by buildings and hills, and this is known as 'shadowing'. Although this may lead to sudden deep fades, as when a vehicle passes under a low bridge, the fading rate due to shadowing is typically very much less rapid than that caused by multipath propagation [1]. It is important to note that whenever the relative motion exists, there is a Doppler shift of the frequency components within the received signal.

International Mobile Telecommunications-2000 (IMT-2000), Universal Mobile Telecommunications System (UMTS), and other standards for the third generation digital cellular mobile system, are categorized as the wideband mobile systems. The transmission bit-rate in both cases will be in the order of a few hundreds of Kbits/s up to a maximum of a few Mbits/s. At this high bit-rate, the time delay spread of the channel will definitely be much bigger than the transmitted signal element duration. International Telecommunication Union (ITU) for example, has outlined the time delay spread test environment for its IMT-2000 mobile radio system. The worst case of the time delay spread can span as much as 20 μs in its duration. At this much of time delay spread, the effect of frequency-selective fading will be dominant in IMT-2000 and hence gives rise to significant intersymbol interference in the received signal.

Apart from IMT-2000 and UMTS, Pahlavan and Levesque [2] have given two recommended wideband propagation models for mobile systems that are currently in operation. The models are for the Global System for Mobile communications (GSM) and the Joint Technical Committee (JTC) for Personal Communications System (PCS) air interface standards. As for the frequency spectrum, the wideband system will require much higher spectral space compared to the narrowband system. To cater for bandwidth of this order, the World Administrative of Radio Conference 1992 (WARC '92) has allocated the high-end UHF frequency spectrums for IMT-2000. A total of 230 MHz spectrum is reserved at 1885-2025 MHz and 2110-2200 MHz bands, which also included in the spectrums are, the 1980-2010 MHz and 2170-2200 MHz bands for satellite applications [1].

Channel Model

In digital communications, a mobile system is referred to as wideband if the time delay spread (τ_{sp}) of the channel, i.e. reciprocal of the coherence bandwidth, is much higher than the transmitted signal-element duration (T_s) i.e. reciprocal of the data rate [5, 6]. On the other hand, in the narrowband system, the time delay spread of the channel is lower than the transmitted signal-element duration.

$$\tau_{sp} >> T_s \qquad \text{(Wideband System)}$$
$$\tau_{sp} \leq T_s \qquad \text{(Narrowband System)}$$

In wideband mobile radio systems, frequency-selective fading effect due to the multipath is more concerned to the modem designer. This multipath propagation or frequency-selective fading effect is insignificant or non-existent in the narrowband system.

International Telecommunication Union-Radio Sector (ITU-R) has outlined the multipath propagation profile for its wideband IMT-2000 mobile radio system [1]. The model is in the form of channel impulse response, based on a tapped-delay line model. It is characterised by the number of taps, the time delay relative to the first tap, the average power relative to the strongest tap, and the Doppler spectrum for each tap. The relative time delay is allowed to have a variation ± 3% of from the given value so that the channel's sampling rate can be matched to some multiples of the transmission rates. The terrestrial test environments for IMT-2000 are categorised into 3 different environments namely indoor, outdoor pedestrian, and outdoor vehicular. This paper addresses itself to a data rate of 144 Kbits/s which has been standardized for users in fast moving vehicles over large areas (outdoor vehicular) [8].

The Multipath propagation profile in this paper is considering for the outdoor vehicular channel generated by the TDL model has been verified by checking the mean variance of the parameters used for the channel as given in the tables. Channel CH11 is the two path fading channel where ISI in the signal is equal to the power of the signal, which can be called as worst case channel. In the channel CH11 the power distribution between the paths is [50% : 50%]. And the channel CH12 is the two path fading channel with power distribution between the paths is [80% : 20%]. The mean and variance of the channels are given in Table 1 and Table 2. Table 1, shows the theoretical and simulated means and variance of the channel CH11 whereas Table 2 showing the wideband mobile radio channel is also subjected to the frequency (Doppler) spread just as in the case of the narrowband channel. Pahlavan and Levesque [5] have provided the Doppler shift range for the outdoor-terrestrial test environments. The fading channel model used in this present paper is based on the one developed by Clark & Jayasinghe [10]. With some appropriate modifications, this narrowband model can be further extended to represent the wideband channel in the IMT-2000 mobile systems.

The channel model is illustrated in Figure 1 where the input signal is fed to a tapped delay line. The delay signals at each of the taps are modulated in amplitude as well as in phase by complex-valued baseband random function $Q_1(t)$ in such a way that each of these represents a Rayleigh fading path. The number of taps is equal to the number of reflected signals reaching the receiver via different paths. Each tap gain function is independent of the other, which means that each of the reflected signals arrives via an independently fading path. The delayed and modulated signals are summed with additive noise, which has a Gaussian probability density (AWGN).

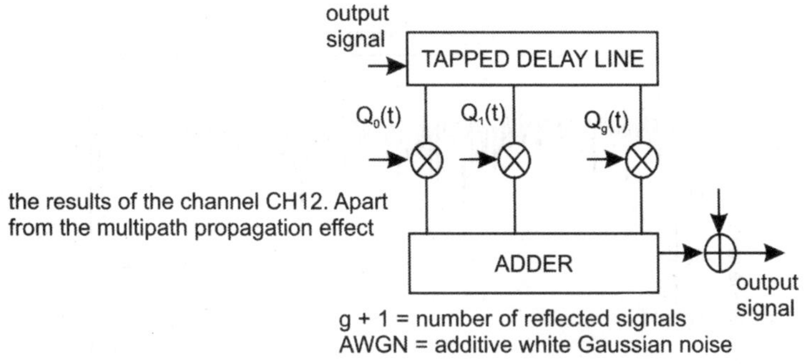

Fig. 1: Tapped delay line model of the channel

Each Rayleigh fading path is modeled as shown in Figure 2 where $q_1(t)$ and $q_2(t)$ are two statistically independent real-valued Gaussian random waveforms, each with zero mean and the same power spectral density which is taken to be Gaussian. The two processes $q_1(t)$ and $q_2(t)$ are themselves generated by passing white Gaussian noise with zero mean through two separate but identical filters. In this work, Bessel filters have been used as it can be seen in the Figure 2. Figure 3 shows the fluctuations in the amplitude of the signal due to the change in phase and ISI.

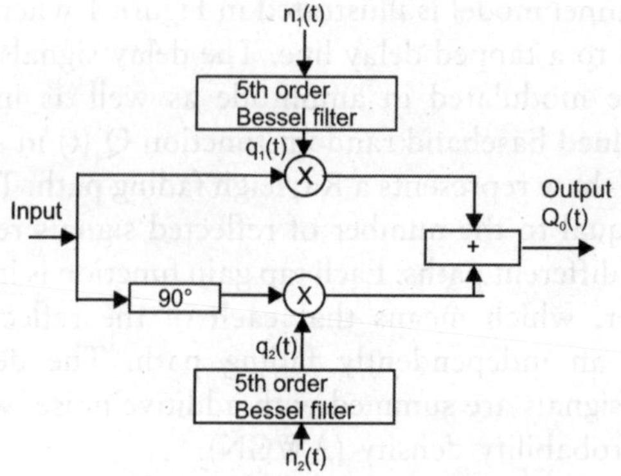

Fig. 2: Generation of Rayleigh fading path

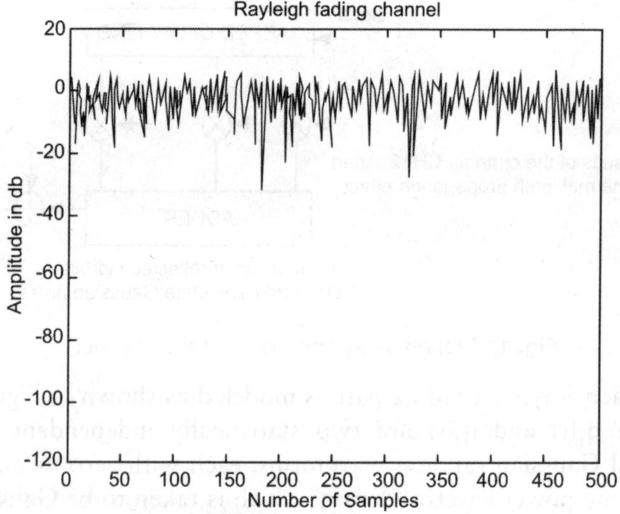

Fig. 3: Envelope of the fading channel

Verification of the Channel

In order to confirm the validity of the simulated channel, a number of tests have been carried out. The frequency spread used in this work and hence in the design of the 5-pole Bessel filter is $f_{sp} = 125\ Hz$

This is representative of outdoor mobile radio vehicular environment. The filter is sampled at a sampling frequency of 4800 Hz. The frequency response of the 5-pole Bessel filter has already been compared with the theoretical Gaussian spectrum given by equation (1) and they are found to agree reasonably well [11].

The Rayleigh distribution is obtained by the complex addition of two independent Gaussian variables (in this case $q_1(t)$ and $q_2(t)$) with zero mean and variance σ_N^2. Theoretically, the Rayleigh p.d.f. (probability density function) is represented as [12],

$$f_R(r) = \frac{r}{\sigma_N^2} \exp\left(\frac{r^2}{2\sigma_N^2}\right), \quad r \geq 0, \sigma_N > 0 \tag{1}$$

σ_N^2 = variance of each $q_1(t)$

Its mean and variance is respectively,

$$E[r] = \sigma_N \sqrt{\pi/2}, \quad VAR[r] = (2 - \pi/2)\sigma_N^2 \tag{2}$$

The Rayleigh c.d.f. (cumulative distribution function) is represented as,

$$F_R(r) = 1 - \exp\left(\frac{r^2}{2\sigma_N^2}\right), \quad \text{r} \geq 0, \ \sigma_N > 0 \tag{3}$$

The median of any distribution is defined as the point at which the value of the c.d.f. is 0.5. Therefore, the median r_m for a Rayleigh distribution can be obtained by the equation

$$0.5 = 1 - \exp\left(\frac{{r_m}^2}{2\sigma_N^2}\right) \tag{4}$$

therefore

$$r_m = \sigma_N \sqrt{2 \ln 2} \tag{5}$$

For a one-path Rayleigh fading channel model σ_N^2 = 0.5, which gives r_m = 0.832 or – 1.5975 dB.

Using equations (2) and (3), the fading rate f_e in terms of number of fades per second is given by

$f_e = f_{sp} / 1.356$

Therefore with f_{sp} of 125 Hz, the theoretical fading rate is given by

f_{sp} = 125/1.356 = 92.19 fades/sec

The fading rate of a channel in terms of number of fades per second depends only on the frequency spread used in the Bessel filter for the generation of that channel. It does not depend on the sampling rate used in the Bessel filter or on the interpolation factor, if any, used in the channel generation.

Table 1: Simulation Results of Two-Path Rayleigh Channel (CH11)

Parameter	Theoretical Value	Practical value
Mean of Rayleigh Path 1	0.6267	0.6230
Mean of Rayleigh Path 2	0.6267	0.6230
Variance of Rayleigh Path 1	0.1073	0.1127
Variance of Rayleigh Path 2	0.1073	0.1127
Mean of q1	0	-0.0014
Mean of q2	0	0.0023
Mean of q3	0	0.0014
Mean of q4	0	0.0023
Variance of q1	0.25	0.25
Variance of q2	0.25	0.25
Variance of q3	0.25	0.25
Variance of q4	0.25	0.25

Table 2: Simulation Results of Two-Path Rayleigh Channel (CH12)

Parameter	Theoretical Value	Practical value
Mean of Rayleigh Path 1	0.7927	0.8043
Mean of Rayleigh Path 2	0.3965	0.3912
Variance of Rayleigh Path 1	0.1717	0.1954
Variance of Rayleigh Path 2	0.0429	0.0472
Mean of q1	0	0.0860
Mean of q2	0	0.0073
Mean of q3	0	0.0062
Mean of q4	0	0.0160
Variance of q1	0.4	0.4000
Variance of q2	0.4	0.4352
Variance of q3	0.1	0.1000
Variance of q4	0.1	0.1000

CONCLUSION

A next generation mobile channel model has been presented in the paper. The channel has been generated and verified that it is a valid representation of real outdoor mobile radio channels. Statistical properties of the channel models have been investigated thoroughly as part of the verification processes. Although the channel model presented is very consistent with real mobile channels, it does show a slight deviation between the theoretical and the simulated values. This is due to the statistical nature of random variables in computer simulations. The simulation results show a plot and results of a slow fading channel encountered in wideband vehicular environment.

REFERENCES

1. M.H. Callendar, "Future Public Land Mobile Telecommunication Systems," IEEE Personal Communications, Vol. 1, No. 4, pp. 18-22, 4th Quarter 1994.
2. G.J. Foschini and J. Salz, "Digital Communications over Fading Channels", The Bell System Technical journal, Vol. 62, Feb. 1983 Number 2, part 1, pp. 429-456.
3. Adolf J. Giger and Willium T. Barnet, "Effects of Multipath propagation on Digital Radio", IEEE Transaction on Communications, Vol. COM-29, No. 9, September 1981, pp. 1345-1352.
4. T.A. Sexton and K. Pahlavan, "Channel modeling and adaptive equalization of indoor radio channels", IEEE Journal Selected Areas in Communications, Vol. 7, January 1989, pp. 114-121.
5. K. Pahlavan, S.J. Howard and T.A. Sexton, "Decision feedback equalization of the indoor radio channel" IEEE Trans. on Communication, Vol. COM-41, 1993, pp. 164-170.
6. M. Bhat and M. Salim Beg, "Computer simulation and modeling of high speed data transmission over mobile radio links", Journal of Institution of Engineers (I), Vol. 77, Sept. 1996, pp. 20-23.
7. T.S. Rappaport, Wireless Communications, Principles and Practice, Prentice Hall, New Jersey, 1996.
8. M. Salim Beg and Mohd Nazri Muhayiddin, "Receiver Signal Processing for Next Generation Wideband Digital Cellular System," Proceeding of International Wireless and Telecommunication Symposium (IWTS 98), Shah Alam, Malaysia, pp. 400-403, May 11-15, 1998.
9. M. Salim Beg, S.C. Tan and Hazemi Hamidi, "Performance Assessment of some Adaptive Equalizers in Mobile Radio Environments", Proc. Int. Symposium. on Wireless Personal Multimedia Communications, pp. 761-766, Bangkok, Thailand, Nov. 2000.

10. A.P. Clark and S.G. Jayasinghe, "Channel Estimation for Land Mobile Radio Systems", IEE Proceedings Part F, Vol. 134, N. 4, pp. 383-393, July 1987.
11. M.Salim Beg, "Novel Detection Techniques for data transmission over a fading channel" Ph.D. thesis, Loughborough University, UK, 1990.
12. M. Salim Beg and Mohd. Israil, "Adaptive Equalization for Indoor Fading Channel", Proceeding of National Conference on Emerging Trends in Communication and Computing (ETCC-07), 27-28 July 2007, NIT Hamirpur, pp. 382-385.

OFDM and Its Interferences

19

Surabhi and *Rajni*

ABSTRACT

OFDM is a signaling scheme that divides a digital signal across 1,000 or more signal carriers simultaneously. The capability to work around interfering signals is one of the most lucrative of a technology that threatens CDMA technology. This talent is pushing the technology forward in Europe. In densely populated areas where buildings, trucks, people and geographic projections can scatter the path of a signal. Broadcasters as well as high-speed data providers are anxious to eliminate multi-path fading effects. It's a wonderful technology that transmits larger amounts of data and provides greater security for data. This is very attractive to a hostile communications environment, as it shows resistance to multipath interference. It has strong benefits. Recent tests of Wi-LAN and W-OFDM technology has declared that a data rate of 30 Mbps can be achieved while traveling at 70 mph speeds. Mobile Industries are expecting a data rate of 10 Mbps is from 4G systems with OFDM. It is very important to analyse various interferences to capture more and more customers.

INTRODUCTION

OFDM is a digital transmission technique that uses a large number of carriers spaced apart at slightly different frequencies. Although frequency division multiplexing (FDM) implies multiple data streams, orthogonal FDM carries only one data stream broken up into multiple signals. Hundreds or thousands of carriers, known as "subcarriers", are used for a single data channel. It was first promoted in the early 1990s for wireless

LANs. OFDM is used in many wireless & mobile applications including Wi-Fi, digital radio and TV broadcasting in Europe and Japan and ultra-wideband (UWB). It is also used in land-based ADSL.

For a given overall data rate, increasing the number of carriers reduce the data rate that each individual carrier must convey, and hence (for a given modulation system) lengthens the symbol period. This means that the intersymbol interference affects a smaller percentage of each symbol as the number of carriers increase and hence the symbol period increases. For example, on the picture is shown a 8 bit long part of a data sequence. For a single carrier system, the responses of individual bits are overlapping, thus creating ISI. Multicarrier system is robust against these physical effects.

Data is transferred in a parallel way, Instead of transmitting in serial way. Only a small amount of the data is carried on each carrier, and by this lowering of the bit rate per carrier (not the total bit rate), the influence of ISI is significantly reduced. In principle, many modulation schemes could be used to modulate the data at a low bit rate onto each carrier.

The Importance of Orthogonality

The "orthogonal" part of the OFDM name indicates that there is a precise mathematical relationship between the frequencies of the carriers in the system. In a normal FDM system, the many carriers are spaced apart in such way that the signals can be received using conventional filters and demodulators. In such receivers, guard bands have to be introduced between the different carriers, and the introduction of these guard bands in the frequency domain results in a lowering of the spectrum efficiency. It is possible, however, to arrange the carriers in an OFDM signal so that the sidebands of the individual carriers overlap and the signals can still be received without adjacent carrier interference. In order to do this the carriers must be mathematically orthogonal. The receiver acts as a bank of demodulators, translating each carrier down to DC, the resulting signal then being integrated over a symbol period to

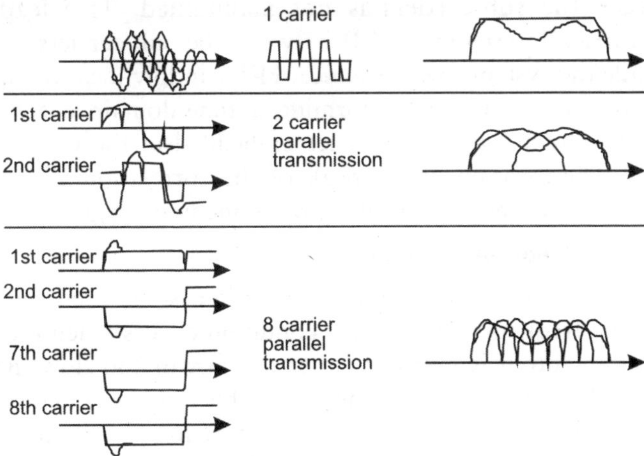

Fig. 1: The effect of adopting a multicarrier system.

recover the raw data. If the other carriers all beat down to frequencies which, in the time domain, have a whole number of cycles in the symbol period (t), then the integration process results in zero contribution from all these carriers. Thus the carriers are linearly independent (i.e. orthogonal) if the carrier spacing is a multiple of 1/t.

Mathematically, suppose we have a set of signals ψ, where ψ_p is the *p*-th element in the set.

The signals are orthogonal iff:

$$\int_a^b \Psi_p(t)\Psi_q^*(t)dt = \begin{Bmatrix} K \text{ for } p=q \\ O \text{ for } p\#q \end{Bmatrix} \qquad (1)$$

Where the * indicates the complex conjugate and interval [a, b] is a symbol period. A fairly simple mathematical proof exists, that the series *sin* (*mx*) for *m* = 1, 2,... is orthogonal over the interval –p to p. Much of transform theory makes the use of orthogonal series, although they are by no means the only example.

Impairments

There are various impairments encountered in the OFDM, discussed below. These impairememts introduces frequency offset in a practical system, and due to this freq. offset, orthogonality between the sub-carriers is not maintained. This leads to Intercarrier Interference (ICI) between the sub-carriers, which degrade the system's performance. FFT window location offsets are often corrected by performing a time-domain correlation with a known training sequence embedded in the transmitted signal. The location of the peak of the correlation allows the receiver to synchronize itself with the incoming signal.

Sampling frequency offset

Another potentially harmful situation is the presence of a sampling frequency offset. This condition occurs when the A/D converter output is sampled either too fast or too slow. Recall that F subscript S/2 is the highest available frequency in discrete-time where F subscript S is the sampling frequency. Sampling too fast essentially increases the value of F subscript S/2 and the result is a contracted (i.e. squashed) spectrum. Similarly, sampling too slow decreases the value of F subscript S/2 and results in an expanded spectrum. If the spectrum expands too much, aliasing of the spectrum can occur. Either type of sampling frequency offset results in IBI since the expansion or contraction of the spectrum prevents the received subcarriers from lining up with the FFT bin locations.

Uniform noise

Additive White Gaussian Noise (AWGN) is the most common impairment encountered in a communications system. In a wireless medium, the noise source is typically considered to be thermal noise that is Gaussian and uniform across the frequency range. Additional noise sources include atmospheric sources and solar radiation. In a contained media, such as a coaxial cable system, thermal noise will be present, but the system may also have other sources that can increase the noise in the system. The effect of AWGN on an OFDM system is similar to its effect on a single carrier system. The signal-to-noise ratio (SNR) is a function of the total signal power over the total noise power across the received channel. The uniform noise contributes to the SNR of each subcarrier in the OFDM system and the net result is equivalent to the effect on single channel systems.

Non-uniform noise

Noise in a communications channel can often be shaped, or "colored", by various effects. These effects can include transmit signal imperfections, transmission channel characteristics, or receiver frequency shaping. The implications of these effects for an OFDM system can be different compared to its single-carrier counterpart. The modulation of the OFDM system can be tailored for the noise characteristics. Another method involves sending the same data on several subcarriers, or sending data that can be considered lower priority. In extreme cases, the subcarriers can transmit no data, essentially turning them off.

Impulse noise

Impulse noise is a common impairment in a communications system arising from motors or lightning. Impulse noise is typically characterized as a short time-domain burst of energy. The burst may be repetitive or may be a single event. In either case, the frequency spectrum from this energy burst is wideband, typically much wider than the channel, but is present for only a short time period.

One of the most important concepts to understand about OFDM and its properties related to the FFT algorithm is how the algorithm changes the nature of the signal. In a single-carrier system, the symbol can be viewed as occupying all of the available frequency spectrum for the time duration of the symbol. A group of symbols then occupies all of the spectrum for the duration of the whole group, but in a time division arrangement.

OFDM, using the FFT, takes symbols and creates these groups directly and then transforms them. They are no longer time-domain multiplexed; they are now frequency-domain multiplexed. The OFDM symbol is now a collection of these source symbols, and this OFDM symbol now has a much longer duration. Each original symbol occupies only a small frequency region, but now occupies that region for the entire OFDM symbol duration. For impulses that are short in duration, the impulse energy masks a smaller percentage of time of each OFDM symbol compared to the single carrier case. Impulse noise can therefore have less of an effect on short duration noise.

Carrier interference

Single-carrier interference arises from other sources that may co-exist in the frequency range of interest. These can be generated by nearby circuits or other transmission sources. The single carrier system must handle this interference as a noise source for all information sent. The OFDM system can avoid the frequency region of interference by disabling or turning off the affected subcarriers. Narrowband modulated sources of interference can be considered similar to carrier interference in their impairment.

Phase noise

Noise can also be added to the signal through a frequency-conversion stage. The local oscillator used in the converter will inherently have some phase noise (uncertainty of actual frequency or phase of the signal) that will be transferred to the desired signal. Phase noise is shaped and is primarily concentrated near the carrier (or center frequency) of the signal.

Multipath effect

A major problem in most wireless systems is the presence of a multipath channel. In a multipath environment, the transmitted signal reflects off of several objects. As a result, multiple delayed versions of the transmitted signal arrive at the receiver. The multiple versions of the signal cause the received signal to be distorted. Many wired systems also have a similar problem where reflections occur due to impedance mismatches in the transmission line.

A multipath channel will cause two problems for an OFDM system. The first problem is intersymbol interference. This problem occurs when the received OFDM symbol is distorted by the previously transmitted OFDM symbol. The effect is similar to the intersymbol interference that occurs in a single-carrier system. However, in such systems, the interference is typically due to several other symbols instead of just the previous symbol; the symbol period in single carrier systems is typically much shorter than the time span of the channel, whereas the typical OFDM symbol period is much longer than the time span of the channel. The second problem is unique to multicarrier systems and is called Intrasymbol Interference. It is the result of interference amongst a given OFDM symbol's own subcarriers. The next sections illustrate how OFDM deals with these two types of interference.

Intersymbol interference

Assume that the time span of the channel is L subscript C samples long. Instead of a single carrier with a data rate of R symbols/second, an OFDM system has N subcarriers, each with a data rate of R/N symbols/second. Because the data rate is reduced by a factor of N, the OFDM symbol period is increased by a factor of N. By choosing an appropriate value for N, the length of the OFDM symbol becomes longer than the time span of the channel. Because of this configuration, the effect of intersymbol interference is the distortion of the first L subscript C samples of the received OFDM symbol. By noting that only the first few samples of the symbol are distorted, one can consider the use of a guard interval to remove the effect of intersymbol interference. The guard interval could be a section of all zero samples transmitted in front of each OFDM symbol. Since it does not contain any useful information, the guard interval would be discarded at the receiver. If the length of the guard interval is properly chosen such that it is longer than the time span of the channel, the OFDM symbol itself will not be distorted. Thus, by discarding the guard interval, the effects of intersymbol interference are thrown away as well.

Intrasymbol interference

The guard interval is not used in practical systems because it does not prevent an OFDM symbol from interfering with itself. This type of interference is called intrasymbol interference. The solution to the problem of intrasymbol interference involves a discrete-time property. Recall that in continuous-time, a convolution in time is equivalent to a multiplication in the frequency-domain. This property is true in discrete-time only if the signals are of infinite length or if at least one of the signals is periodic over the range of the convolution. It is not practical to have an infinite-length OFDM symbol; however, it is possible to make the OFDM symbol appear periodic. This periodic form is achieved by replacing the guard interval with something known as a cyclic prefix of length L subscript P samples. The cyclic prefix is a replica of the last L subscript P samples of the OFDM symbol where L subscript P > L subscript C. Since it contains redundant information, the cyclic prefix is discarded at the receiver. Like the case of the guard interval, this step removes the effects of intersymbol interference. Because of the way in which the cyclic prefix was formed, the cyclically-extended OFDM symbol now appears periodic when convolved with the channel. An important result is that the effect of the channel becomes multiplicative.

Non-ideal effects in an OFDM system

This section will examine the effects of non-idealities in an OFDM system. These effects will include impairments and receiver offsets. Because the fourier transform is a fundamental operation in OFDM, the effects of several offsets can be intuitively understood by applying fourier transform theory.

Local oscillator frequency offset

At start-up, the local oscillator (LO) frequency at the receiver is typically different from the LO frequency at the transmitter. A carrier tracking loop is used to adjust the receiver's LO frequency in order to match the transmitters LO frequency as closely as possible. The effect of having an LO frequency offset can be explained by Fourier Transform theory. The LO offset can be expressed mathematically by multiplying the received time-domain signalby a complex exponential whose frequency is equal to the LO offset amount. Recall from Fourier Transform theory that multiplication by a complex exponential in time is equivalent to a shift in frequency. The LO offset results in a frequency shift of the received signal spectrum. This shift causes a condition called "loss of orthogonality" to occur. The frequency shift causes the OFDM subcarriers to no longer be orthogonal. The orthogonality of the subcarriers is lost because the bins of the FFT will no longer line up with the peaks of the received signal's since pulses. The result is a distortion called inter-bin interference or IBI. IBI occurs when energy from one bin spills over into adjacent bins and this energy distorts the affected subcarriers. In Fourier Transform theory this effect is called DFT leakage. The left plot of figure shows the spectrum of a received OFDM signal with no LO offset. For the purpose of clarity, only one non-zero subcarrier was transmitted. Note that this subcarrier is not interfering with its adjacent subcarriers. The spectrum of the non-zero subcarrier actually extends over the entire range of the FFT, however, due to the orthogonal nature of the signal, the zero-crossings of the spectrum exactly line up with the other FFT bins. The right plot of figure shows the received spectrum of the same signal with one non-zero subcarrier, however, in this case there is an LO offset. This offset has resulted in a loss of orthogonality and the zero-crossings of the non-zero subcarrier's spectrum no longer line up with the FFT bins. The result is that energy from the non-zero subcarrier is spread out among all of the other subcarriers, with those subcarriers closest to the non-zero subcarrier receiving the most interference. This simple example was for the case of only one non-zero subcarrier. In a practical system, almost all of the subcarriers would be actively used for transmitting data. A given subcarrier would experience IBI due to energy from all of the other active subcarriers in the system. The central limit theorem states that the sum of a large number of random processes will result in a signal that has a Gaussian distribution. Because of this property, the IBI will manifest itself as additive Gaussian noise, thus lowering the effective SNR of the system. The effect of an LO frequency offset can be corrected by multiplying the signal by a correction factor. The correction factor would be a sinusoid with a frequency that is ideally equal to the amount of the LO frequency offset. Various carrier tracking algorithms exist that can adaptively determine the frequency that will correct for the offset.

LO phase offset

It is also possible to have an LO phase offset, separate from an LO frequency offset. The two offsets can occur in conjunction or one or the other can be present by itself. As the name suggests, an LO phase offset occurs when there is a difference between the phase of the LO output and the phase of the received signal. This effect can be represented mathematically by multiplying the time-domain signal by a complex exponential with a constant phase. The result is a constant phase rotation for all of the subcarriers in the frequency-domain. The constellation points for each subcarrier experience the same degree of rotation. If the phase rotation is small, the frequency-domain equalizer can correct this effect. Each filter coefficient in a frequency-domain equalizer multiplies its corresponding subcarrier by a complex gain (i.e. amplitude scaling and phase rotation). The equalizer's coefficients can be used to correct for a small phase rotation as long as the rotation doesn't cause the constellation points to rotate beyond the symbol decision regions. Larger phase rotations are corrected by a carrier tracking loop.

FFT window location offset

Another non-ideal effect that can occur in a real-world OFDM system is an FFT window location offset. An N-point FFT at the receiver processes data in blocks of N samples at a time. Ideally, the N samples taken in by the FFT will correspond to the N samples of a single transmitted OFDM symbol. In practice, a correlation is often used with a known preamble sequence located at the beginning of the transmission. This correlation operation aids the receiver in synchronizing itself with the received signal's OFDM symbol boundaries. However, inaccuracies still remain, and they manifest themselves as an offset in the FFT window location. The result is that the N samples sent to the FFT will not line up exactly with the corresponding OFDM symbol. If the offset is very large, part of the N samples will be from one OFDM symbol, and the rest of samples will be from another OFDM symbol. Such a situation would result in a severe distortion of the received subcarrier's constellations. Fortunately, such a large offset does not typically occur if a robust synchronization algorithm is used. More likely, an FFT window location offset of just a few samples will occur. The presence of the cyclic prefix gives enough headroom to enable a small offset to be present without taking samples from more than one OFDM symbol. However, even an offset of just one sample will cause some degree of distortion. Again, the effect can be understood from Fourier Transform theory. The offset can be viewed as a shift in time. As long as the FFT window location offset does not go beyond an OFDM symbol boundary, this shift in time is equivalent to a linearly-increasing phase rotation in the frequency-domain constellations. Constellations on subcarriers corresponding to low frequencies will be rotated slightly, whereas constellations on higher-frequency subcarriers will experience a larger rotation. The amount of rotation increases linearly as the subcarrier's FFT bin location increases.

CONCLUSION

OFDM has given an opportunity for service providers get high revenue with same infrastructure. It allows service providers to capture to as many customers in a service area as possible with resisting multipath interference efficiently.

REFERENCES

1. J.A.C. Bingham, May 1990, "Multicarrier Modulation for Data Transmission: An idea whose time has come," IEEE Communications Magazine, Vol. 28, No. 5, pp. 5-14.
2. J.M. Cioffi, Nov. 1991, "A Multicarrier Primer, in ANSI T1E1.4 Committee Contribution", No. 91-157, Boca Raton, FL.
3. S.B. Weinstein, P.M. Ebert, October 1971, " Data Transmission by Frequency-Division Multiplexing Using the Discrete Fourier Transform", IEEE Transactions on Communication Technology, Vol. COM-19, No. 5, pp. 628-634.
4. Stott, Summer 1998,"The Effects of Phase Noise in COFDM", EBU Technical. P. Shelswell, 1996/8, "The COFDM Modulation System: The Heart of Digital Audio Broadcasting", BBC Research and Development Report, BBC RD.

Segmentation of Satellite Images Using Mean Shift Algorithm for Coastal Boundary Extraction

Musheer Ahmad, Rashid Ali and *M. Qasim Rafiq*

ABSTRACT

The identification of coastline is critical for safe navigation, coastal resource management and coastal environmental protection. Image segmentation is one of the primary steps in image analysis for object identification. A variety of segmentation algorithms have been developed in the last few decades, but some of them are not suitable in the case of specific applications, especially in satellite images which, often, contain different textured regions or varying background and are often subjected to environmental effects. In this work, an image segmentation technique called Mean Shift is adopted and implemented to specifically extract the coastal boundaries from satellite images. Coastal boundaries are identified as the boundaries between the sea and landmass regions. Experimentally, we show that the algorithm is very much suitable for coastline extraction from satellite images.

INTRODUCTION

The study and the extraction of the different elements that compose an image constitute a fundamental task in the image analysis. Image analysis, usually, refers to a process of images provided by a computer in order to find the objects within the image. Image segmentation is one of the most critical tasks in automatic image analysis.

It consists of subdividing an image into its constituent homogeneous parts as well as extracting them. Some of the image segmentation techniques can also be applied to extract the features from the satellite images like coastlines. A coastline is the line of contact between land and a water surface. The delineation and extraction of coastlines and water bodies, e.g. rivers and lakes, is important and useful for various application fields such as oceanography, cartography, coastline erosion monitoring, coastal resource management, flood prediction, and the evaluation of water resources. Tracing the coastline manually is easy along relatively simple stretches of coast but it is impractical where the coastline becomes very complex. Automatic techniques are required to extract the waterline for large areas to update coastline maps and to evaluate the alterations due to natural and anthropic events. The identification of the coastline in remotely sensed images can be looked at as a boundary detection problem. In this paper, we perform the segmentation of satellite images to extract the meaningful features like boundaries of the water bodies. For the purpose of the segmentation of satellite images, we use a simple nonparametric procedure called mean shift algorithm. The paper is organized as follows. In Section II, we discuss the related work performed in the area. In Section III, we discuss the need and details of satellite image processing. We also discuss the basics of image segmentation and the image segmentation using mean shift algorithm. We present our results in Section IV. Finally we conclude in Section V.

Related Work

A lot of research studies have been done to extract and delineate water bodies from the satellite images. A technique for coastline extraction from remotely sensed images using texture analysis is described in [1]. A method for coastline detection in SAR (Synthetic Aperture Radar) images using texture analysis in textural or geometrical multi-resolution is suggested in [2]. A morphological segmentation based automated approach which consists of the combination of spectral and spatial information for coastline extraction has been suggested in [3]. A neural network classifier was used by Zhu [4] upon multi-temporal Landsat images to classify the changes of coastline in different periods. Here, we discuss a novel method for the coastline extraction from satellite images that uses mean shift algorithm.

Satellite Image Processing

In today's world of advanced technology where most satellite images are recorded in digital format. The development and application of various remote sensing platforms result in the production of huge amounts of satellite image data. In order to take advantage and make good use of satellite images data, we must be able to extract meaningful information from the imagery. Indeed, interpretation and analysis of satellite imagery involves the identification and/or measurement of various targets in an image in order to extract useful information about them. Targets in satellite images may be any feature or object which can be observed in an image, and have the following characteristics [5]:

- Targets may be a point, line, or area feature, means that they can have any form, a bus in a parking lot or a plane on a runway, a bridge or roadway, a large expanse of water or a field.
- The target must be distinguishable; it must contrast with other features around it in the image.

To extract the coastlines from satellite images, we have to perform pre-processing of the satellite image, image transformation, image segmentation, coastal boundary identification and its extraction. Image segmentation is one of the key steps in this satellite image processing.

Image Segmentation

The segmentation of an image can be defined as its partition into different regions (image objects), each characterized by certain properties. From the mathematical point of view, a segmentation of an image f is a partition of its domain D_f into n disjoint nonempty sets $X_1, X_2,..., X_n$ called segments such that the union of all segments equals D_f. The goal of image segmentation is to cluster pixels into salient image regions, i.e. regions corresponding to individual surfaces, objects, or natural parts of objects. Applications range from industrial quality control to medicine, robot navigation, geophysical exploration, remote sensing, and military applications. In all these areas, the quality of the final result depends largely on the quality of the segmentation. Segmentation could be used for object recognition, boundary estimation within motion or stereo systems, objects location in satellite images (water bodies, coasts, landmarks, roads, forests, etc.). Many image segmentation techniques have been developed and different classification schemes for these techniques have been proposed [6]. Some of these techniques are not suitable for satellite images which contain different textured regions or varying background and are often subjected to environmental effects.

Mean Shift Algorithm

Mean shift is a simple, nonparametric technique for estimation of the density gradient was proposed in 1975 by Fukunaga and Hostetler [7]. The idea was recently generalized by Cheng [8]. The Mean Shift Procedure [9] is described as below.

1. Decide the radius of the search window.
2. Decide the initial location of the search window.
3. Evaluate the mean shift vector and shift the search window by that amount in the direction of this vector.
4. Repeat till convergence, convergence is declared when the magnitude of the shift becomes less than 0.1.

Comaniciu and Meer have utilized it for feature space analysis [9, 10]. Feature space analysis is the procedure of recovering the centers of the high-density regions also called as modes.

Mean shift procedure exploits the property that image pixels that share similar properties tend to flock together forming segments within the image. When these pixels are mapped to a feature space, they flock together forming clusters with a densely populated center. The distribution of pixels within a cluster is random. This random distribution can be treated as a probability density function. In mean shift algorithm, the probability density function in turn is estimated using a multivariate kernel density function [10].

When used for image segmentation, the image data is first mapped into the feature space like LUV, resulting in a cluster pattern. The clusters correspond to significant features in the image, like dominant colors. Using the mean shift procedure, we can locate these clusters in the image to use for segmentation. The clusters are located by applying a search window in the feature space, which shifts towards cluster center. The magnitude and direction of the shift in feature space are based on the difference of the center of the window and the local mean value inside the window. When the magnitude of the shift becomes small (according to a threshold) the center of the search window is declared as a cluster center and the algorithm is said to have converged for one cluster. This procedure is repeated until all significant clusters have been extracted. The number of shifts needed to locate a cluster center in feature space depends on where the search begins. Search started in a high density region, reduces the number of shifts to reach the convergence. To find the best starting location for the search window, several randomly chosen locations in feature space are considered and the one with the highest density is selected.

The outline of a general procedure for feature space analysis is given below.

Feature Space Analysis [9]

1. Transform the image domain into the LUV feature space.
2. Define an adequate number of search windows at random locations in the feature space.
3. Find the high-density region centers by applying the mean shift algorithm to each window.
4. Validate the extracted centers with image domain constraints to provide the feature palette.
5. Allocate, using image domain information, the entire feature vectors to the feature palette.

The delineation of the clusters is the natural outcome of the mean shift segmentation process. After convergence, the data points visited by all the mean shift procedures converging to that mode, automatically delineates a cluster of arbitrary shape.

Experiment and Results

For experimentation purpose, we obtained the real satellite images from the database of the satellite images hosted by Intute—the best Web resource for education and research [11]. Intute hosts more than 2,000 satellite images covering many world regions; images include phenomena such as wildfires, coastal waters, mountain ranges, rivers, landmarks, cities. Images courtesy of a range of sources including: NASA Image Exchange, Visible Earth, ISS EarthKAM, and The Gateway to Astronaut Photography of Earth.

We selected the images that contained the landscapes along with water bodies. We implemented the procedure discussed in the preceding section for feature space analysis and apply it to the selected satellite images. The satellite image is first segmented into homogeneous regions using mean shift algorithm. In our case, the target area feature is the water body which is easily distinguishable with other features around it in the image. Then, the major water body is identified to extract the boundary of the water body from the segmented image.

The results for a set of four satellite images are shown in the Figures 1 to 4. The original satellite images are shown in Figures 1(a) to 4(a). The corresponding segmented images for each of the four satellite images are shown in Figures 1(b) to 4(b) respectively. The segmented images clearly depict that the water body is segmented as nearly one cluster. We can see in the segmentation results that the major water body is segmented from the landmass successfully. The coastline is basically at the boundary between the major water body and the landmass. The boundaries of the segments are captured and the coastline is extracted as the boundary between the water body and the landmass. The coastlines extracted from the four given satellite images are shown in Figures 1(c) to 4(c) respectively. The sharp and clear coastlines visible in these figures clearly point out that the results obtained are satisfactory.

Fig. 1(a): Original Image: Boston harbour

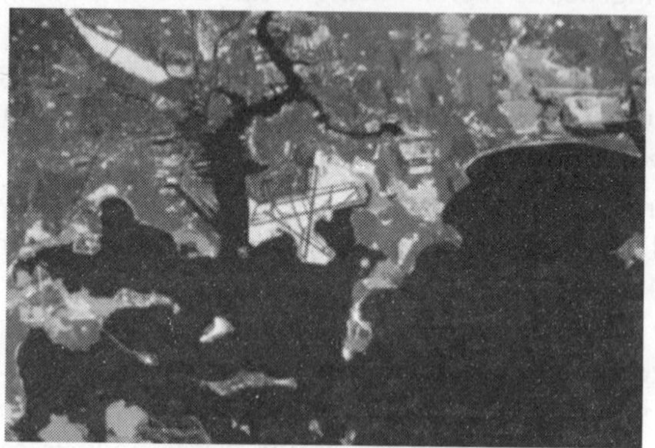

Fig. 1(b): Segmented Image

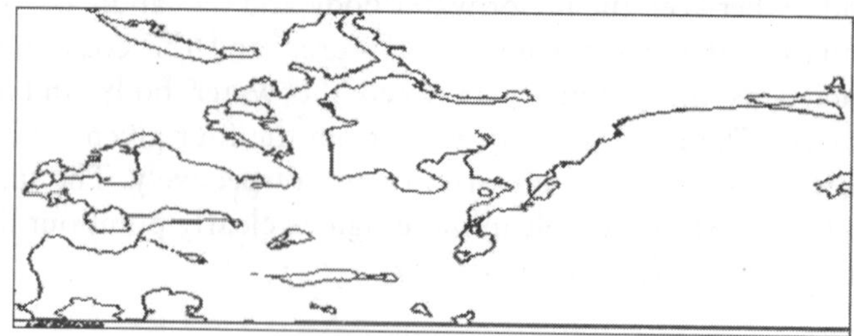

Fig. 1(c): Extracted Coastline

Fig. 2(a): Original Image: Lake Mead

Fig. 2(b): Segmented Images

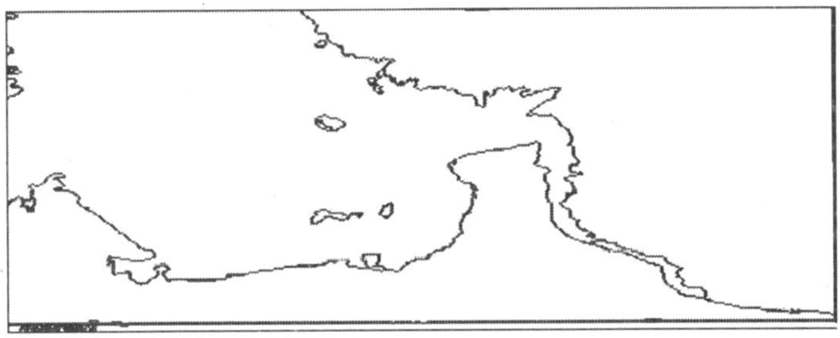

Fig. 2(c): Extracted Coastlines

Fig. 3(a): Original Image: Tokyo, Haneda

Fig. 3(b): Segmented Images

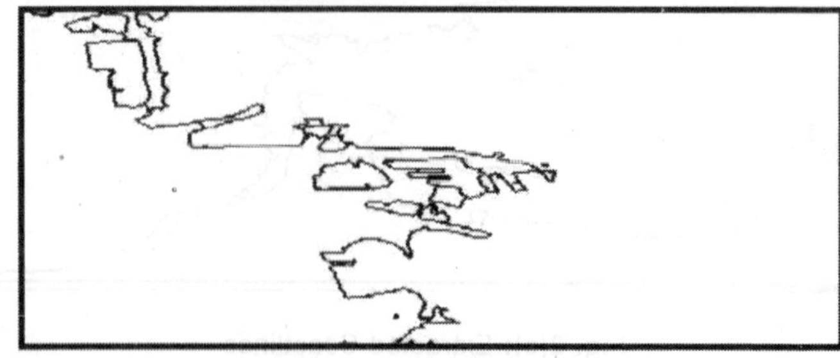

Fig. 3(c): Extracted Coastlines

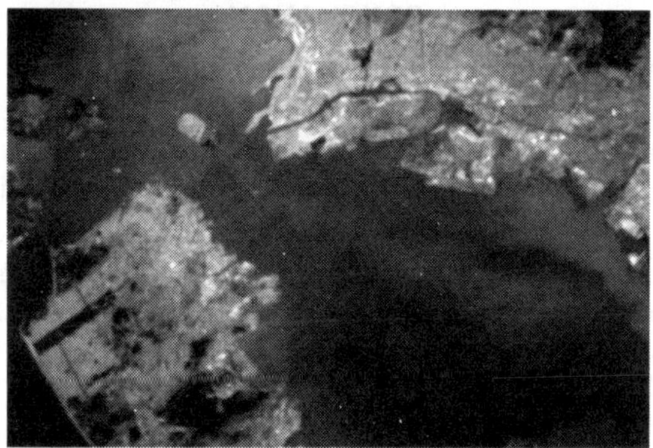

Fig. 4(a): Original Image: San Francisco

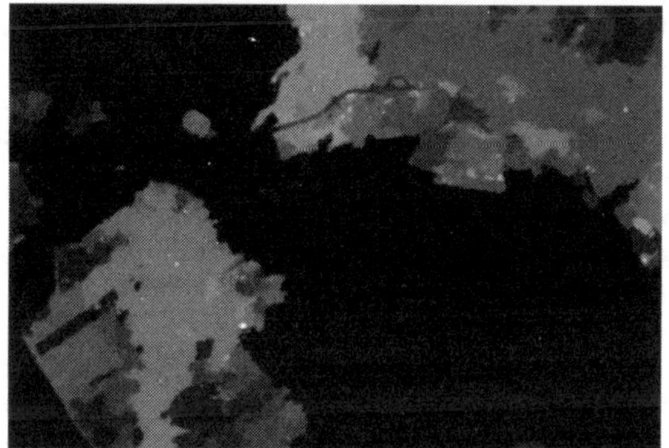

Fig. 4(b): Segmented Images

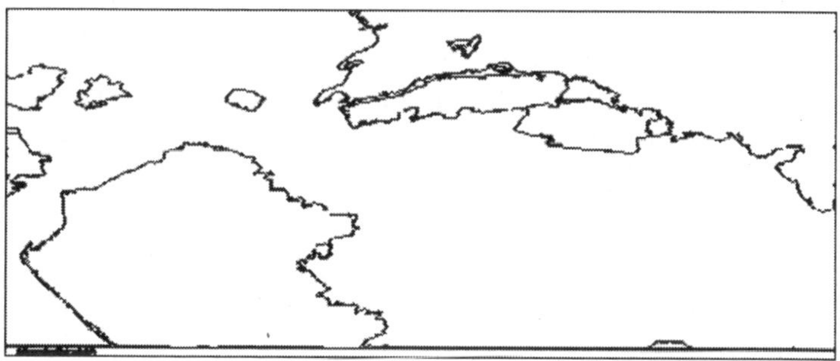

Fig. 4(c): Extracted Coastlines

CONCLUSION

In this paper, we discussed the segmentation of satellite images using mean shift algorithm to extract the coastal boundaries of the major water bodies. We experimented with a set of real satellite images hosted by Intute. The results of the process yield very much clear figures of the coastlines. Therefore, we conclude that mean shift procedure is a very much suitable segmentation technique for the coastline extraction from the satellite images. The algorithm can also be used for extracting other features from the different sets of satellite images satisfactorily.

REFERENCES

1. G. Bo, S. Delleplane and R. De Laurentiis, "Coastline extraction in remotely sensed images by means of texture features analysis". *International Geosciences and Remote Sensing Symposium, 2001, IGARSS '01*, Vol. 3, pp. 1493-1495, Sydney, NSW, Australia, 2001.
2. V.P. Onana, J.M. Ngono, H. Trebossen, J.P. Rudant and E. Tonye, "Coastline detection in SAR images using texture analysis in textural or geometrical multi-resolution". *International Geosciences and Remote Sensing Symposium, 2001. IGARSS '01*, Vol. 3, pp. 1549-1551, Sydney, NSW, Australia.
3. S. Bagli and P. Soille, "Morphological automatic extraction of coastline from pan-european landsat tm images". In *Proceedings of the Fifth International Symposium on GIS and Computer Cartography for Coastal Zone Management*, Vol. 3, pp. 58-59, Genova, 2003.
4. X. Zhu, "Remote sensing monitoring of coastline change in pearl river estuary". *22nd Asian Conference on Remote Sensing*, pp. 19-22, November, Singapore, 2001.
5. A. Rekik, M. Zribi, A.B. Hamida and M. Benjelloun. "Review of satellite image segmentation for an optimal fusion system based on the edge of region approaches". *IJCSNS International Journal of Computer Science and Network Security*, Vol. 7 No. 10, October 2007.
6. R.M. Haralick, L.G. Shapiro, "Survey, image segmentation techniques, Computer Vision, Graphics and Image Processing", Vol. 29, pp. 100-132, 1995.
7. K. Fukunaga, "Introduction to Statistical Pattern Recognition", Second Ed., Boston: Academic Press, 1990.

8. Y. Cheng, "Mean shift, mode seeking, and clustering", *IEEE Transaction on Pattern Analysis and Machine Intelligence.*, Vol. 17, pp. 790-799, 1995.
9. D. Comaniciu and P. Meer, "Robust Analysis of Feature Spaces: Color Image Segmentation". *In Proceedings of the 1997 Conference on Computer Vision and Pattern Recognition (CVPR'97)*, pp. 750-755, Washington, DC, USA, June 1997. IEEE Computer Society.
10. D. Comaniciu and P. Meer, "Mean shift: A robust approach toward feature space analysis". *IEEE Transactions on Pattern Analysis Machine Intelligence (PAMI '02)*, Vol. 24, issue 5, pp. 603-619, May 2002.
11. Intute—the best Web resource for education and research—World Guide —Satellite Images.

Identity Based Strong Bi-Designated Verifier (t, n) Threshold Proxy Signature Scheme

21

Sunder Lal and *Vandani Verma*

ABSTRACT

Proxy signature schemes have been invented to delegate signing rights. The paper proposes a new concept of Identify Based Strong Bi-Designated Verifier threshold proxy signature (ID-SBDVTPS) schemes. Such scheme enables an original signer to delegate the signature authority to a proxy group of 'n' members s.t. 't' or more than 't' proxy signers can cooperatively sign messages on behalf of the original signer and the signatures can only be verified by the two designated verifiers and they cannot convince anyone else of this fact.

INTRODUCTION

Certificate based cryptography allows the user to use an arbitrary string, unrelated to his identity, as his public key, when another user wants to use this public key, she must obtain an authorized certificate that contains this public key. This creates the certificate management problem. To address this problem, Shamir [12] introduced the concept of ID based cryptography in 1984. In ID-based public key cryptography (ID-PKC) user's public key is derived from certain aspects of his identity (e-mail address, phone no., etc.) and a trusted third party called key generating center (KGC) generates secret key for the users. ID-PKC is good alternative for certificate based public key settings. Mambo et al. [10] introduced the concept of proxy signatures in 1996. In a proxy signature scheme, an original signer delegates his signing capability to another user called proxy signer. Proxy signer signs message on behalf of the original signer, however proxy signatures are different from the original signatures. In the same year, Jakobsson et al. [2] proposed the concept of designated verifier signatures (DVS). In DVS schemes, only the designated verifier can check the validity of the signatures and cannot convince any third party about the validity of the signatures. Saeednia et al. [11] introduced the feature of strongness in DVS in 2003. Strong Designated Verifier Signature (SDVS) scheme forces the verification. Since then several SDVS [5, 6, 9, 13] schemes have been proposed. In 2003, Y. Desmedt [1] raised the problem of generating the designated verifier. However, the first bi-designated verifier signature scheme on bilinear maps was proposed by Laguillaumie et al. [8] in 2004. Lal et al. [7] proposed the ID-based strong bi-designated verifier signature scheme. Zhang [14] and Kim et al. [4] independently constructed the 1st threshold proxy signature scheme. In a (t, n) threshold proxy signature scheme, the original signer delegates his signing power to a group of n proxy signers such that t or more proxy signers can generate proxy signatures corporately, but any (t–1) or fewer proxy signers cannot create a valid proxy signature. The First ID based threshold proxy signature scheme is proposed by Xu et al. [15] in 2004. and the first ID-based designated verifier threshold proxy signature scheme is proposed by Juan et al. [3] in 2007. In such schemes, the designated verifier can only verify the threshold proxy signatures. The paper presents the extension of Juan et al. [3] scheme to bi-designated verifier. In our proposed scheme, any of the two designated verifiers can check the validity of the threshold proxy signatures but they cannot convince any third party about the validity of the signature. Anyone of them can check the validity of the signatures even if they don't know each other identity. Our scheme is useful in the situations where the signature verifier does not want to rely on a single person for the trueness of the signatures.

The rest of the paper is organized as follows—the next section contains some preliminaries about the formal definition of bilinear pairings and Gap Diffie Hellman group. In section 3 we present our ID-SBDVTPS scheme. In section 4 we analyze its security and end with concluding remarks in section 5.

Definitions

Bilinear pairings

Let G_1 be a cyclic additive group generated by P, whose order is a large prime number q and G_2 be a cyclic multiplicative group with the same order q. Let e: $G_1 \times G_1 \rightarrow G_2$ be a map with the following properties:

Bilinearity

$e(aP, bQ) = e(P, Q)^{ab} \forall P, Q \in G_1$ and $a, b \in Z_q^*$.

Non-degeneracy

$\exists P, Q \in G_1$, such that $e(P, Q) \# 1$, the identity of G_2.

Computability

There is an efficient algorithm to compute $e(P, Q) \forall P, Q \in G_1$.

Such pairings may be obtained by suitable modification in the Weil-pairing or the Tate-pairing on an elliptic curve defined over a finite field.

Computational problems

Decisional Diffie-Hellman Problem (DDHP)

Given P, aP, bP, cP in G_1, decide whether $c = ab \bmod q$.

Computational Diffie-Hellman Problem (CDHP)

Given P, aP, bP, compute abP

Bilinear Diffie-Hellman Problem (BDHP)

Given P, aP, bP, cP compute $e(P, P)^{abc}$.

Gap Diffie-Hellman Problem (GDHP)

A class of problems, where DDHP can be solved in polynomial time but no probabilistic algorithm exists that can solve CDHP in polynomial time.

Identity Based Strong Bi-Designated Verifier (t, n) Threshold Proxy Signature Scheme

Our scheme is the extension of Juan et al. [3] scheme. The single designated verifier is extended to bi-designated verifier to form our ID-SBDVTPS scheme. In our scheme, we have assumed Alice as the original signer, PS = $\{P_1, P_2, \ldots P_n\}$ as the group of 'n' proxy signers and Bob and Cindy as the two designated verifiers. The scheme is divided into six stages: setup, key-generation, secret-share generation, proxy-share generation, proxy-signature generation and proxy signature verification.

Setup

Assume K is a security parameter, G_1 is a GDH group prime order $q>2^k$ generated by P and e: $G_1 \times G_1 \rightarrow G_2$ is a bilinear map. KGC chooses a master key $s \in Z_q{}^*$ and set $P_{pub} = sP$. Chooses two cryptographic hash functions $H_1 : \{0,1\}^* \rightarrow Z_q{}^*$, $H_2 : \{0,1\}^* \times G_1 \rightarrow Z_q{}^*$ and $H_3 : \{0,1\}^* \times G_1 \times G_2 \rightarrow Z_q{}^*$. The system parameters $(q, G_1, G_2, e, P, P_{pub}, H_1, H_2, H_3)$ are made public and 's' is kept secret with KGC.

Key generation

- Given a users identity ID, compute public key $Q_{ID} = H_1(ID)$ and the associated secret key $S_{ID} = s^{-1}Q_{ID}.P$.

Secret share generation

- The proxy group applies a (t, n) verifiable secret sharing scheme to generate secret shares for all the proxy signers in PS as follows:
  - Each $P_i \in PS = \{P_1, P_2, \ldots P_n\}$ randomly chooses a (t–1) degree polynomial

    $f_i(x) = \sum_{l=1}^{t-1} a_{il}\, x^l + a_{io}$ with random coefficients $a_{il} \in Z_q{}^*$ and publishes $A_{il} = a_{il} P$, $l = 0, 1, 2, \ldots t-1$. P_i sends $f_i(j)$ to P_j via a secure channel for j # i.
  - On receiving $f_i(j)$, P_j can validate it by checking the equality $f_i(j)P = \sum_{k=0}^{t-1} j^k A_{ik}$, If it holds, each P_i computes his secret share $r_i = \sum_{k=1}^{n} f_k(i)$ and publishes $U_i = r_iP$.

Proxy share generation

- Every proxy signer $P_i \in PS$ gets their own proxy signing key share as follows:
  - The original signer Alice first randomly chooses $+r_w = Z_q^*$ and computes $U_w = r_w Q_{IDA} P$, $h_w = H_2(m_w, U_w)$, $V_w = (r_w + h_w)S_{IDA}$.
    The signature on m_w is $w = (U_w, V_w)$. Finally, Alice sends w and m_w to each $P_i \in PS$.
  - To verify a signature, the proxy signer P_i computes $h_w = H_2(m_w, U_w)$ and accepts the signature iff $e(P_{pub}, V_w) = e(P, U_w + h_w Q_{IDA}P)$ and rejects it otherwise. If the signature w is accepted, P_i computes $S_i = S_{IDi} + V_w$ as his own proxy secret.
  - P_i randomly chooses a (t – 1) degree polynomial $g_i(x) = \sum_{l=1}^{t-1} b_{il}x^l + S_i$ with random coefficients $b_{il} \in G_1$ and publishes $B_{il} = e(P, b_{il})$ for l = 1, 2, … t–1. B_{io} can be calculated by each proxy signer as $B_{io} = e(P, U_w + (Q_{IDPi} + h_w Q_{IDA})P)$. Furthermore, P_i sends $g_i(j)$ to P_j via a secure channel for i # j.
  - On receiving $g_j(i)$, P_i can validate it by checking the equality $e(P_{pub}, g_j(i)) = \prod_{k=0}^{t-1} B_{jk}^{i^k}$. Finally, P_i computes his proxy signing key share $SK_{Pi} = \sum_{k=0}^{t-1} g_k(i)$ and publishes $e(P_{pub}, SK_{Pi})$.

Proxy signature generation

- Let $D = \{P_1, P_2, \ldots P_t\}$ be the actual proxy signers who wants to sign message 'm' on behalf of the original signer Alice.
- Apply the Lagrange interpolation formula to compute $X = Q_{IDB}Q_{IDC}$, $g_{IDV} = e(XP, S_{IDi})$, $Y_i = g_{IDV}^{\gamma}$

$$Y = \prod_{i=0}^{t} Y_i^{\eta_i}, \eta_i = \prod_{j \neq i}^{j \in \{1,2,\ldots t\}} \frac{j}{j-i}, U = \sum_{i=1}^{t} \eta_i U_i$$

Let $H = H_3$ (m, U, Y). Each $P_i \in D$ computes $V_i = U_i + H\ SK_{Pi}$ and $\sigma_i = (U_i, V_i)$ be his own proxy signature share.

- On receiving σ_i, the designated clerk validates it by checking $e(P, V_i) = e(P, U_i)\ e(P, SK_{Pi})^H$. If it holds, then σ_i is the valid individual proxy signature on 'm'. If all the individual proxy signatures for 'm' are valid, then the clerk computes $V = \sum_{i=1}^{t} \eta_i V_i$. The proxy signature on 'm' is $\sigma = (m, V_w, m_w, U, V)$
- **Proxy signature verification:** To verify the proxy signature σ, the designated verifiers Bob (and Cindy) compute $Q_{IDC} = Q_{IDB}^{-1}$ X (Bob) $Y^* = e(S_{IDB}Q_{IDC}, U(\Sigma Q_{IDPi}))$ and accepts the signature iff $e(P_{pub}, V) = e(P_{pub}, U + nHV_w)\ e(P, (\Sigma Q_{IDPi})P)^H$.

Security analyses

In this section we analyze the security of the proposed ID-SBDVPS schemes.

Correctness

The following equation gives the correctness of the scheme for Bob

$$e(P_{pub}, V) = e(P_{pub}, \sum_{i=1}^{t} \eta_i\ V_i)$$

$$= e(P_{pub}, \sum_{i=1}^{t} \eta_i\ (U_i + H.SK_{Pi}))$$

$$= e(P_{pub}, \sum_{i=1}^{t} \eta_i\ U_i) e(P_{pub}, \sum_{i=1}^{t} \eta_i\ SK_{Pi})^H$$

$$= e(P_{pub}, U) e(P_{pub}, \sum_{i=1}^{t} \eta_i \sum_{k=1}^{n} g_k(i))^H$$

$$= e(P_{pub}, U) e(P_{pub}, (\sum S_{IDPi} + nV_w).H)$$

$$= e(P_{pub}, U) e(sP, s^{-1} \sum Q_{IDPi}\ P)^H e(P_{pub}, V_w)^{nH}$$

$$= e(P_{pub}, U) e(P, P)^{(\sum Q_{IDPi})H} e(P_{pub}, V_w)^{nH}$$

$$e(P_{pub}, V) = e(P_{pub}, U + nHV_w)\ e(P, (\Sigma Q_{IDPi})P)^H$$

Strongness

In the proposed scheme proxy signatures are generated in such a manner that only the two designated verifier Bob and Cindy can check the validity of the signatures using his secret key. Hence, our scheme provides the strongness property.

Proxy protected

Alice cannot generate a valid signature share on behalf of Pi, since he does not have any information about the secret key S_{IDPi} of each P_i. Hence, our scheme is proxy protected.

Secrecy

In our proposed scheme, the original signer Alice secret key cannot be derived from any information such as the shares of the proxy signing key, proxy signature etc. Even if 't' out of 'n' proxy signers collaborates to deliver the proxy share, they cannot calculate the Alice secret key. Hence, our scheme is secure.

CONCLUSION

In this paper, we have presented a new concept of Identity based strong bi-designated verifier (t, n) threshold proxy signature scheme. The scheme is applicable in the situations where receiver wants the signatures to be verified by two designated persons and no one other than these two designated persons can check the trueness of the signatures.

REFERENCES

1. Y. Desmedt. Verifier-Designated Signatures, Rump Session, Crypto '03 (2003).
2. M. Jakobsson, K. Sako, K.R. Impaliazzo. Designated verifier proofs and their applications. Eurocrypt 1996, LNCS #1070, Springer-Verlag, 1996, pp. 142-154.
3. X.L. Juan, X.Q. Liang, Z. Zheng. Identity based designated verifier threshold signature scheme, Journal of Computer Applications, pp. 1058-1061, Vol. 27 (05), 2007.
4. S. Kim, S. Park, D. Won. Proxy signatures revisited, Proc. Information and Communication Security (ICICS '97), LNCS#1334, Springer-Verlag, 1997, pp. 223-232.
5. K.P. Kumar, G. Shailaja, Ashutosh Saxena. Identity based strong designated verifier signature scheme. Cryptography eprint Archive Report 2006/134. Available at http://eprint.iacr.org/2006/134.pdf

6. Sunder Lal and Vandani Verma. Identity based strong designated verifier proxy signature scheme. Cryptography eprint Archive Report 2006/394. Available at http://eprint.iacr.org/2006/394.pdf
7. Sunder Lal and Vandani Verma. Some identity based strong bi-designated verifier signature scheme. Cryptography eprint Archive Report 2007/193. Available at http://eprint.iacr.org/2007/193.pdf
8. F. Laguillaumie and D. Vergnaud. Multi-Designated Verifiers Signatures. ICICS 2004, LNCS #3269 Springer-Verlag, 2004, pp. 495-507.
9. R. Lu and Z. Cao. Designated verifier proxy scheme with message recovery. Applied Mathematics and Computation, 169(2), 2005, pp. 1237-1246.
10. M. Mambo, K. Usuda and E. Okamoto. Proxy signatures, revisited, In Proc. Of ICICS'97, LNCS 1334, Springer-Verlag, 1997, pp. 223-232.
11. S. Saeednia, S. Kreme and O. Markotwich. An efficient strong designated verifier signature scheme. ICICS 2003, LNCS #2971, Springer-Verlag, 2003, pp. 40-54.
12. A. Shamir. ID based cryptosystems and signature scheme. Crypto '84, LNCS #196, Springer-Verlag, 1984, pp. 47-53.
13. G. Wang. Designated verifier proxy signature for e-commerce. IEEE International Conferences on Multimedia and Expo (ICME 2004) CD-ROM, ISBN- 0-7803-8604-3, Taipei, Taiwan, 2004, pp. 27-30.
14. J. Xu, Z. Zheng and D. Feng. ID Based Threshold Proxy Signature Cryptography eprint Archive Report 2004/250. Available at http://eprint.iacr.org/2004/250.pdf

Networking of Home Appliances to Assist the Persons with Movement Disabilities

22

Mohd. Rihan, M. Sarfaraz Alam and *M. Salim Beg*

ABSTRACT

The invasion of telecommunication into all aspects of our daily life has created a new meaning for the word network. In fact, network concept has now begun to move from the workplace to the home. All the home appliances are being networked to provide complete home automation and such a network of home appliances is called as home automation network. Home automation network can highly enhance comfort and security around the home. Apart from improving the user experience, the technology can be very helpful for people with physical disabilities.

The houses, equipped with a network of various appliances, are being considered as a good alternative for helping older persons and persons with disabilities to live good independent life. Numerous intelligent devices, embedded into the home network, can provide the resident with both movement assistance and 24-hour health monitoring. Modern home network systems tend to be not only physically versatile in functionality but also emotionally human-friendly, i.e. they may be able to perform their functions without disturbing the user and without causing him/her any pain, inconvenience, or movement restriction, instead possibly providing him/her with comfort and pleasure. In the present work a home network, consisting of five appliances is implemented, by using a telephone as the central controller.

INTRODUCTION

The home automation network is a network of all appliances in a home environment and it is a technology which allows the devices and systems to be controlled automatically. The degree to which this control is exercised is variable, being a function of the cost and the type of building into which the technology is to be installed.

At the advent of 1990s, the average house started to have interaction with many electrical devices. There were regular electric appliances such as refrigerator, electronic appliances such as television, communication appliances such as telephone, and information appliances such as computer. The functioning of all these appliances required dedicated wiring system. So a normal residential environment had various wiring systems including power wiring, telephone wiring, and cable TV wiring. Some homes also had additional wiring for home security and PC local area network etc. All these systems used different types of communication media and carried different types of signals completely independent of each other. At the same time due to great advancements in IC technology the computing costs experienced a sharp decline and miniaturization process gained momentum making dedicated microprocessor a common part of home appliances which resulted in enhanced intelligence level of home appliances. But this intelligence had not been utilized to its true potential as these appliances operated in complete isolation from each other. Under this scenario the need of a unified "home network" was felt keeping in mind various advantages it will offer such as (i) ease of use as an appliance can be controlled from different locations, (ii) sharing of information, and (iii) minimum wiring confusion and low cost. Such a home having a network of all household electrical appliances is aptly called as "Smart Home"[1, 2].

Section 2 and 3 of the paper describes the structure, working of home automation network and its role in improving the life of disabled people. In section 4 implementation details of telephone based controller are given. Result, conclusion and scope for future work are discussed in section 5.

Structure and Working of Home Automation Network

The key to control of appliances, in an automated home lies, in the ability of the products to communicate. The nature of these devices in a home network is very similar to that of other networks such as a computer network. Each switch or module has a unique "address". When a control signal is broadcast through the network, all of the modules in the network can hear the commands, but only those to which the signal is addressed will respond to it. In general the components of a typical home automation network are divided into following categories.

Sensors

Sensors monitor and measure activities in the surroundings. Examples are movement and heat sensors, humidity sensors, thermometers and smoke detectors.

Actuators

Actuators perform physical actions. Examples are door, window, and garage door openers, curtain, and awning engines, automatic light switches and relays.

Controllers

Controllers make choices based on programmed rules and occurrences. Controllers are microprocessors often built-in with sensors and actuators. They receive and process values from the sensor or other controllers. For instance the controller of a thermometer can be programmed to submit a message to switch off the electric heating when the temperature exceeds the desired value.

Network/Data Bus

The network is the transmitter of the signals in the system. The most used transmitters are signal cable (twisted pair), power line cable, radio signals (RF) and to some extent IR or optical fibres. All modern home automation systems have a bus-based network. In a bus-based network all the units in the system may read all the messages. The messages include the address of the one or several units who are to receive the message. The system unit or units recognizing their own address react to the content of the message. A unit can receive a message individually or as member of a group. Hence, in one case a message can be submitted for one lamp to light, and in another case a message for all lamps to light.

Central Unit

The function of central unit is the re-programming, maintenance of the network and to incorporate changes in the system. A personal computer is most commonly used as the central unit. In residential homes the programming and re-programming of the system must be simple and intuitive. A good user interface, documentation of the system and training of the staff are important factors for the system to be used in an efficient way.

Interface

The interface between the home network and the user is vital to ensure that the home control system is easy to understand and operate. The normal switches and dials used in the conventional home is the simplest form of interface for controlling appliances of the smart home. If a dedicated bus system or a wireless network is used, conventional switches may need to be replaced with ones that are specific to that form of communication. If infrared receivers are linked into the communication network and the appliances then infra red remote control units, similar to those used for consumer electronics products, can also be used as an interface with devices on the network. Telephones, Computers can also be used as controlling devices in the smart home. Computer screens allow large, easy to recognize visual representations of the home and can be used to send messages to, and receive messages from, the smart home. In some smart home Internet based control is also provided by adding a web server to the home. The addition of the web server would allow a visual representation of the home to be created as a web page and accessed from a web browser. This could be used to control the home either from inside or from outside over a local area network (LAN) [3].

Home Automation for Disabled Persons

The home networks, as explained in the previous section, include devices that have automatic functions and systems that can be remotely controlled by the user. The primary goal of this technology was to enhance the user experience inside the home. However, the home automation technology also presents a bright perspective for people with physical disabilities and older peoples also. Therefore a large number of projects are underway around the world to explore this aspect of home automation technology. Such houses are being designed keeping in mind the requirements of various types of disabled people, e.g. people with movement disabilities, with hearing impairment, and low vision etc.

The primary objective in the design of a home automation network for people with movement disabilities is the complete centralized control of all home appliances and installing devices for assistance in mobility and manipulation. Some of the devices to be installed in such homes are automatic kitchen equipment, light and door controllers, indoor temperature controllers, water temperature controllers, and home security devices. Typical electromechanical devices for assisting movement disabled persons are powered wheelchairs, specialized lifting devices for transfer of the user between wheelchair and bed, walking and lifting aids, etc.

Apart from the above mentioned conventional devices for movement assistance, specialized robotic systems may also be developed, which can be classified into three categories; desktop robots, wheelchair robots, and mobile robots, according to their usage [4].

Telephone Based Controller

In the design of automated home for persons with movement disabilities, the primary objective is centralized control of home appliances. Such control can be achieved using various options and telephone is one of them. In the present work, a telephone based controller is implemented for centralized control of five home appliances.

The function of this controller is to control the power supplied to the appliance via telephone line. The users can control some preliminary operations of their home appliances. These operations may include turning ON/OFF of air conditioner, the light fixtures, the heating system as well as the security system. It would be convenient and comfortable for the people to live in such an automated home. In this system the telephone numbers are sent by audio tones. When a button is pressed on the telephone set keypad, a tone is generated which is the resultant of two audio frequencies, and can be expressed as follows:

$$f(t) = A_0\sin(2*\Pi*f_a*t) + B_0\sin(2*\Pi*f_b*t)$$

Where f_a and f_b are two different audio frequencies with A and B as their peak amplitudes and f as the resultant DTMF signal. f_a belongs to the low frequency group and f_b belongs to the high frequency group.

The block diagram of controller is shown in Figure 1. It consists of two main parts:

Signal Decoding Unit

Device Switching Unit

Signal Decoding Unit

This is the main unit of the controller. It consists of a DTMF to BCD decoder IC CM-8870, 4 to 16 line decoder IC 74LS154 and Hex inverter IC 74LS04.The DTMF to BCD decoder IC CM8870 takes a valid tone signal from the telephone line. Then the tone signal is converted in to 4 bit BCD number output obtained at pins from 11 to 14. This output is fed to the 4-16 line decoder IC 74LS154. This IC takes the BCD number and decodes. According to that BCD number it selects the active low output line from 1 to 16 which is decimal equivalent of the BCD number present at its input pins. Since the output of this IC is low, the output is inverted to get logic high output. This inversion is carried out by hex inverter IC 74LS04. This IC inverts the data on its input terminal and gives the output.

Device Switching Unit

This unit consists of the D Flip Flop and the relay which is connected to the appliance. The high output of the hex inverter is given to the clock input of the flip flop. When key '1' is pressed, Q, the output of D-Flip Flop goes high. The output of the D flip-flop is applied to the base of the transistor. When the base voltage of the transistor is above 0.7 V, the emitter-base

(EB) junction of the transistor is forward biased as a result, transistor goes to saturation region; it is nothing but the switching ON of the transistor. This in turn switches on the relay. By this the device is switched ON. To switch OFF the device key '2' is pressed and the D flip flop receives a low level potential, resets input and Q goes low. As a result of this the device turns OFF [5, 6].

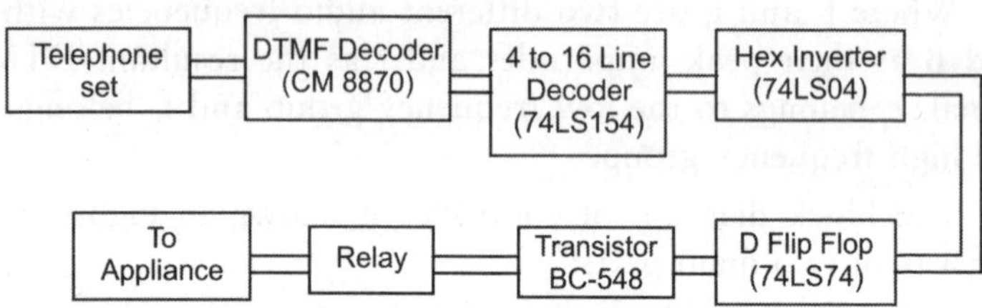

Fig. 1: Block Diagram of the Controller

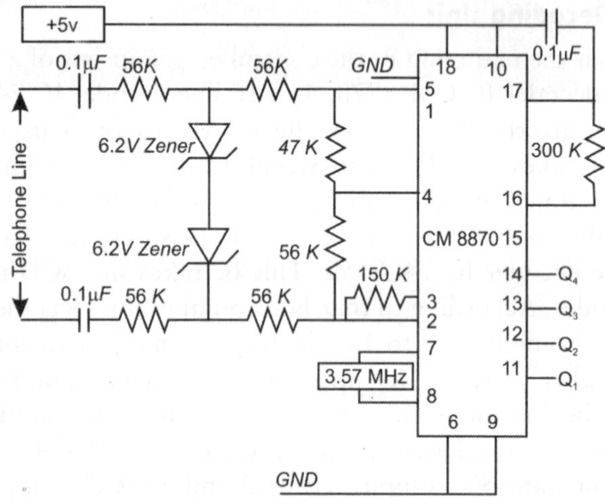

Fig. 2: Complete DTMF Decoder Circuit

CONCLUSION & SCOPE FOR FUTURE WORK

The concept of home automation network presents a powerful solution for a number of persons in the society who are plagued with movement disabilities. The technology can make their life much more pleasant and easier. In this work this aspect is explored by successfully implementing a telephone based controller for centralized control of home appliances. The home automation technology, especially in Indian context, is in the infancy stage and deserves to be pursued rigorously. With the advent of new technologies like MEMS, Mechatronics, and Nano technology, it is certain that miniaturization of the devices will further enhance the power of home automation technology.

REFERENCES

1. Mohd. Rihan, M. Salim Beg, Narayan Gehlot; "Developments in Home Automation and Networking", Proc. National Conference on "Computing for Nation Development", Bharati Vidyapeeth Institute of Computer & Management, New Delhi, 23-24 February, 2007, pp. 61-64.
2. Mohd. Rihan; "Control of Appliances in Automated Homes", M. Tech. Dissertation, Electrical Engg. Deptt., AMU, Aligarh, 2005 (Supervisor: M. Salim Beg).
3. Mohd. Rihan, M. Salim Beg, A. K. Gupta; "Control of Appliances in Automated Homes", National Conference on Cyber Security, Data Mining and ICT for the society, 18-19 January 2006, G. G. University, Bilaspur.
4. Dimitar H. Stefanov, Zeungnam Bien, Won-Chul Bang, "The Smart House for Older Persons and Persons With Physical Disabilities: Structure, Technology Arrangements, and Perspectives, IEEE Transactions on Neural 2004.

   Systems and Rehabilitation Engineering, Vol. 12, No. 2, June
5. Mohd. Ashar, Mohd. Imran Athar, Mohd. Farrukh Rehman, "Telephone Based Control of Electrical Appliances", B. Tech. Project, Electrical Engg. Deptt., AMU, Aligarh, 2007 (Supervisor: Mohd. Rihan).
6. Mohd. Rihan, M. Salim Beg, M. Ashar, M. Imran, M.F. Rehman, "Telephone Based Control of Electrical Appliances in a Smart Home".

   Ismail Coskun and Hamid Ardam, "A remote controller for home and office appliances by telephone" , IEEE transaction on Consumer Electronics, July 1998.

Role of Morphological Filter for Compressed Medical Image

Syed Abdaheer M. Ekram Khan and *Ravi Kumar*

ABSTRACT

A great promise of telemedicine has been to help the isolated or scattered populations to gain access to health services. In industrialized countries, telemedicine has proven to be a good tool for enabling access to knowledge and allowing information exchange, and showing that it is possible to bring good quality healthcare to isolated communities. High quality images can be used in biomedical technology to diagnose the diseases. These images are usually over 1MB of size and each can take more than 20 minutes to transmit over a standard phone line. Therefore, there is a need to compress these images without sacrificing their quality before they are transmitted to specialist hospitals for expert diagnosis, otherwise the transmission time can be long and costly. The modern compression schemes such as SPIHT and JPEG 2000 provide a very high compression rate but with considerable loss of quality. Due to high compression, the images have been indulged by ringing artifacts. In this paper we proposed the post processing techniques with the help of morphological filters to reduce the ringing artifacts and therefore to improve the quality of medical images at the receiver side. Simulation results demonstrate the effectiveness of these filters in removing the ringing artifacts.

INTRODUCTION

With the revolution of electronic and computer technologies, various data's (images) are digitized and transmitted for further processing effectively. Medical imaging has had a great impact on the diagnosis of diseases and surgical planning and it carries a lot of information about the patient. However, the limit of network bandwidth and storage capacity makes compression a necessary procedure to store and transmit the above said medical image data through electronic media, while the medical image compression ratio is limited with respect to the diagnostic acceptability [1, 3, 5, 6]. Digital medical images have played a vital role in the diagnosis. The CT and MRI images, a popular medical image modality, have distinguishing feature that need to be preserved when compressing.

The new still image compression standard JPEG 2000 [14] is a wavelet-based image coding algorithm which provides better quality than SPIHT (Set partitioning in Hierarchical Trees) [18] at low bit-rate and generally performs better. Images coded at medium bit-rate suffer from loss of detail and sharpness, as well as various coding artifacts. Ringing, one of the coding artifacts appear as small ripples around the edge of the image. To achieve sufficient image quality for medium bit-rate using wavelet-based image coders, post-processing efficiently improves compression results. Additionally, post-processing considers original image, meaning it can preserve image fidelity.

Recent publications from Yang and Galatsanos [22] described about iterative image restoration method, which is based on projection onto convex sets (POCS), to remove blocking and ringing artifacts [19, 20]. It was designed primarily for DCT based coder and therefore, not suitable for being a post-processor of JPEG 2000 [14]. The de-ringing algorithm proposed by Shen and Kuo [21], which is also described in JPEG 2000 VM 7.0, is considered a suitable post-processor for JPEG 2000

The de-ringing algorithm replaces each pixel value with a function of the values of neighboring pixels that are within a specified window. To avoid conflict with the above goal, that is smooth shade regions and sharp edges, the de-ringing algorithm uses a number of adaptive noise reduction algorithms. Essentially, the de-ringing algorithm attempts to detect edges in the image in a different way to preserve them. Shen and Kuo also introduced the idea of image ringing artifact reduction through nonlinear filtering by using different kinds of potential functions. Clearly, modeling the compression noise in the space domain is a difficult problem, particularly for ringing artifacts. Although characterizing the exact probabilistic model of the ringing artifacts is difficult, a threshold based on subject visual quality can be assumed to bind the amplitudes of these artifacts. The disadvantage is that most edges and ringing artifacts will be removed. Rest of the paper is organized as follows: Section II describes basic concept and idea about the proposed post processing method (Quad tree decomposition and Morphological filters). In Section III, describes the simulation result and comparison of the JPEG 2000 compressed image. Section IV comprises the conclusion.

The Proposed Post Processing Method

The fidelity of the reconstructed images gets lower value in terms of PSNR, due to the presence of quantizer [8] in compression block. Hence our proposed scheme enhances the fidelity as well as suppresses the unwanted ringing artifacts which occurred during compression process at medium bit rate. The proposed post-processing algorithm consists of quad-tree decomposition, and of morphology based filtering [7,10, 13], as described in the following subsections.

Quad Tree Decomposition Method

Since the ringing artifacts appear mostly in edge and texture areas, a criterion is needed for identifying smooth or textured regions on an image. This work adopts the quad-tree partition scheme, which is efficient and block-based, to pre-process the compressed image. The purpose of this scheme is to enable the post-processing method to focus on the local feature of the compressed image to promote global image quality. Initially, a threshold is required to classify block smoothness and set a minimum block size to stop the partition. To mark block smoothness, we calculate the absolute difference between the maximum and minimum gray value in a block. If this absolute difference exceeds the pre-defined threshold, the block is divided into four half-sized sub-blocks. Partition processing is repeated in each block until the smoothness meets the defined criterion or the block size equals the previously defined minimum size. Following quad-tree partition, the image is divided into different sized blocks according to its features. In large blocks, namely 8 × 8 or larger, the gray-scale value of the block is almost the same. The main concern of this study is that the features of small blocks, that is, 4 × 4 and 2 × 2, may contain important information for natural images, such as edge, texture, and ringing artifacts. Applying a morphology based filter [7] to these small blocks would reduce ringing around the edge while maintaining and reconstructing edge detail.

Morphology Based Filtering

After partitioning the ringing artified medical image from low bit rate compression process, it will pass through the morphological based filter section for getting enhancement of such image quality. The most helpful SE and morphology operation is evaluated by means of the absolute difference between the filtered image block and the original image block. The most helpful type of morphological operation [10] means that the absolute difference between filtered image block and the original image decreased more than other types. In the gray scale morphology, we define the gray scale dilation as an operation that selects the largest pixel value from the mask window (the same dimension as the SE) provided that the corresponding element in the SE window is 1. Similarly, the gray scale erosion is defined as an operation that selects the smallest pixel value from the mask window provided that the corresponding element in the SE window is 1. Various Morphological operators for gray scale image are as follows:

The set processing morphological erosion dilation and opening and closing are defined by:

Erosion: $X\Re\overline{N} = \{Z : N_Z \subseteq X\} = \bigcap_{Y\in N} X_{-Y}$

Dilation: $XD\overline{N} = \{Z : N_Z \cap X\} = \bigcup_{Y\in N} X_{-Y}$

Opening: $f_N(Z) = \left[(f\Re N)\overline{D}N\right](Z)$

Closing: $f^N(Z) = \left[(f\overline{D}N)\Re N\right](Z)$

where the set X is a binary signal or image to be filtered, the set N is called the structuring element of the morphological filter.

The symbols ℜ and D denote Minkowski subtraction and Minkowski addition, respectively. The opening and closing operations are also complementary, and when applied in sequence, they form the doubly compound morphological operators open-close (OC) and close-open (CO) as follows.

Open-Closing: OC $(f; N) = (fN)\, N$; Close-Opening: CO $(f; N) = (f^{N})\, N$

Experimental Results

In this section, we will demonstrate some simulation results of our post-processing algorithm. We make some experiments on the 256 × 256 gray scale MRI images with 8 bits per pixel. The MRI image is compressed by JPEG 2000 [14] at bit-rate from 0.2 and 0.25. Due to high compression rate it may produce some ringing artifacts in the image. For removing this alising based problem we have developed an algorithm based on morphological filters. In this we use 8 types of morphological filter [15] with predefined structuring element. The PSNR ratio of compressed image and filtered image are also displayed in Table 1. The relation between quality factor and compression ratio for the various quality factors are shown in Fig. 2. By the help of this graphical result we can analyze the quality of the image with compression rate. We also show some filtered images in the proposed method. For a clear view, we only show the most complicated quarters of the whole images, i.e. we truncate the images to figures of 256 by 256.

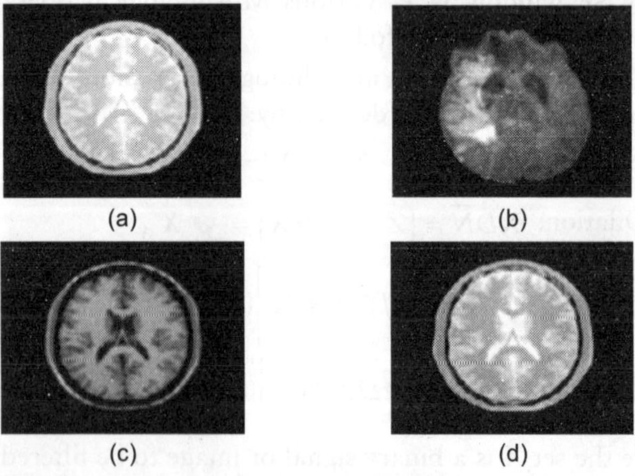

Fig. 1: Images of proposed method (a) Original Image, (b) Image with Ringing artifacts, (c) Dilated Image, (d) Eroded Image

The image shown in Fig. 1(a) is an original MRI image, which is compressed with JPEG 2000 coder at 0.23 bpp and the decoded images is shown in Fig. 1(b). It can be seen that this image suffers with ringing artifacts.

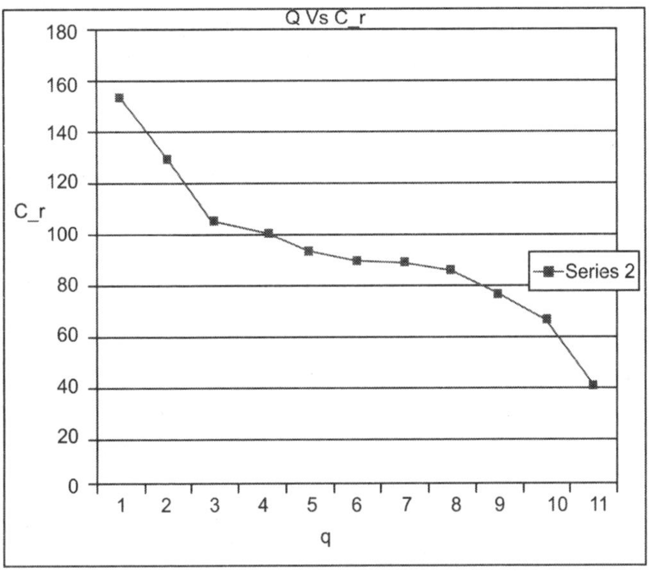

Fig. 2: Compression Vs Quality Factor

This image is post processed using dilation and erosion based morphological filters. The processed images are shown in Fig. 1(c) and (d) respectively. It can be observed from these figures that morphological filters can successfully reduce the ringing artifacts and hence result in the improved video quality. Further, it is observed that erosion operation is performed better than the dilation operation.

From Fig. 2 we can easily determine the important role of compression ratio and its effect with the quality of image. With the help of this data we can easily conclude the need and necessity of post processing method. We have also evaluated and compared the performances of dilation and erosion operation with different structuring elements. The results are listed in Table 1. As the result shows that the MRI image can be compressed at near low bit-rate [0.233 bpp] meanwhile preserve the important detail by using the post-processing algorithm.

Table 1: PSNR Ratio Improvement of Various Morphological Filter Operations

Sl.No.	Structuring Element	PSNR of the Ringing Image	PSNR of the Dilated Ringing Image (I1)	PSNR of the Eroded Image of I1
1.	Matrix element [010;111;110]	28.45	35.45	42.99
2.	Arbitrary (eye (3))	28.45	35.55	42.55
3.	Rectangle [2 3]	28.45	35.89	42.97
4.	Square, 2	28.45	36.86	45.97

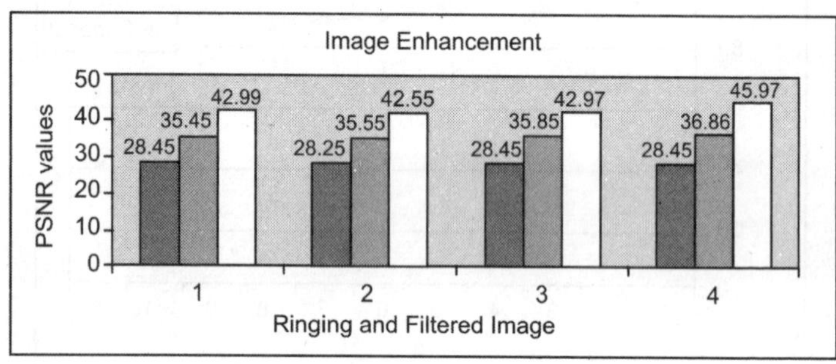

Fig. 3: Performance Evaluation of Morphological Filter

From above graphical analysis we can easily predict the role of morphological filter in post processing techniques. In this experiment the PSNR values are improved by applying various morphological operators and also it suggest the suitable morphological filter operation for ringing artified image. This analysis shows that it will form the corner stone for making easy transmission of medical images through the communication channels.

CONCLUSION

Wavelet based JPEG 2000 [14] compression technique leads to better solution over other compression techniques. These techniques give the basic solution for band width and time delay related problems. However the medical images have some distinguishing features that need more attention to perform compression procedure. As the compression ratio above 20:1, the compressed images develop the ringing artifacts, which impacted the diagnostic acceptability. In this work we developed a post processing algorithm which defines the necessary action against the ringing artifacts. By adopting this idea as a basic one for implementing the real time telemedicine techniques by the way we can help the society, who are living in very rural backward areas.

REFERENCES

1. A.K. Jain, "Image data Compression: A review," in Proc. IEEE, Vol. 69, pp. 349-389, 1981.
2. R. C. Gonzalez and R.E. Woods, Digital Image Processing, Addision-Wesley, Reading, MA, 1992.
3. S. Wong, L. Zaremba, D. Gooden, and H.K. Huang, "Radio logic Image Compression - a review," Proc. IEEE, Vol. 83, No. 2, pp. 194-219, 1995.
4. Y.G. Wu and S.C. Tai, "Medical Image Compression by Discrete Cosine Transform Spectral Similarity Strategy," IEEE Trans. Information Technology in Biomedicine, Vol. 5, No. 3, pp. 236-243, September 2001.
5. P.C. Cosman, R.M. Gray, and R.A. Olshen, "Evaluating quality of compressed medical images: SNR, subjective rating, and diagnostic accuracy," Proceedings of the IEEE, Vol. 82, No. 6, June 1994, pp. 919-932.
6. J.S. Taur, and C.W. Tao, "Medical Image Compression using Principal Component Analysis," International Conference on Image Processing, Vol. 1, 1996, pp. 903-906
7. J. Serra, Image Analysis and Mathematical Morphology, Academic Press, New York, 1982.
8. T. Senoo and B. Girod, "Vector quantization for entropy coding image sub bands," IEEE Transactions on Image Processing, 1(4):526-533, Oct. 1992.
9. A. Gersho and R.M. Gray, Vector Quantization and Signal Compression, Kluwer Academic Press, 1992.
10. Egger, W. Li, and M. Kunt, "Very Low Bit Rate Image Compression Using an Adaptive Morphological Sub band Decomposition", to be published in Proceedings of the IEEE, Special Issue on Advances in Image and Video Compression, Early 1995.
11. Eikelboom RH, et al., 2000, "Methods and limits of digital image compression of retinal images for telemedicine", Invest. Ophthal. Vis. Sci., In Press.

12. Tan WH, Bister M. Uncommitted morphological merging of watershed segments. International Conference on Image Processing (ICIP), 2003.
13. Al-OTUM, H. M. Morphological Operators for Colour Image Processing based on Mahalanobis Distance Measure, Opt. Eng.J. 42 No. 9 (Sep. 2003).
14. C. Christopoulos, A. Skodras, and T. Ebrahimi, "The JPEG 2000 Still Image Coding System: An Overview," *IEEE Transactions on Consumer Electronics*, Vol. 46, No. 4, pp. 1103-1127, November 2000.
15. R. Wootton, "The possible use of telemedicine in developing countries," J. Telemedicine and Tele Care, Vol. 3, pp. 23-26, 1998.
16. D. Wright D, "Telemedicine and developing countries: A report of Study Group 2 of the ITU Development Sector," *J. Telemedicine and Telecare*, London, Vol. 4, Suppl. 2, pp. 1-85, 1997.
17. M. Antonini, N. Barlaud, P. Mathieu and I. Daubechies, "Image coding using wavelet transform", IEEE Trans. Image Processing, Vol. 1, pp. 205-220, 1992.
18. A. Said and W.A. Pearlman, "A new, fast, and efficient image codec based on set partitioning in hierarchical trees," IEEE Trans. Circuits and System for Video Technology, Vol. 6, No. 3, pp. 243-250, Jun. 1996.
19. Tariq Bakir and Stanley J. Reeves, "A filter design method for minimizing ringing in a region of Interest in MR Spectroscopic images", IEEE trans. Medical Imaging, Vol. 9, No. 6, pp. 585-600, Jun. 2000.
20. Shen-Chuan Tai, Yen-Yu Chen, and Shin-Feng SHeu, "Design a Morphological deranging Filter of Ultra Sound Images," GVIP 05 conference, 19-21 December 2005, CICC, Cairo, Egypt.
21. S.O. Aase and T.A. Ramstad, "Ringing reduction in low bit rate image sub band coding using projection onto a space of paraboloids," Signal Processing: Image Communication, 1993.
22. Y. Yang and N.P. Galatsanos, "Removal of compression artifacts using projections onto convex sets and line process modeling," IEEE Trans. Image Processing, Vol. 6, pp. 1345-1357, Oct. 1997.

High Speed Ethernet Technologies for Telemedicine and E-Health

Salma Shaheen and *Mohd. Ajmal Kafeel*

ABSTRACT

In view of the rapidly escalating costs of good medical care, there is a strong need to improve the efficiency of healthcare systems. This necessitates use of ultra-modern technologies relating to ICT (Information and Communications Technologies) today. The resulting field of Telemedicine and e-health has thus assumed huge importance and is the subject of study in this paper. Related developments have led to emergence of new fields such as Telecardiology, Teledermatology, Telepathology, Teleradiology, Teleopthalmology, Telenursing, Telepsychiatry, and Telesurgery. An effective Telemedicine and/or E-health system needs a good communication infrastructure for an efficient exchange of text, audio, image, and video data between various electronic devices including computers. In view of the large bandwidth requirements of channels for transferring above-mentioned kinds of multimedia data, a high speed Local Area Network (LAN) infrastructure technology is required to be used within the hospital premises. The most popular LAN technology is the Ethernet which has a lion's share in the huge LAN market. This paper presents a critical analysis of some of the recent developments and new Ethernet-related products that are now available for deployment, and would be particularly useful for Telemedicine applications.

INTRODUCTION

Telemedicine (from the Greek tele, "at a distance" and the Latin medicus, or physician), is literally "medicine practiced from a distance". Telemedicine is the use of information and communication technology to provide diagnostic and therapeutic health care services, expertise and medical information to individuals who are at some distance from the health care provider [1]. The electronic tools used in telemedicine include:

(1) low-tech tools, which includes telephones, facsimile machine, video cameras, and monitors.

(2) High tech tools, which includes computers, digital imagery, and internet.

Telemedicine can be implemented either online (real time transmission) where the consulting professional participates in the examination of the patient while diagnostic information is collected and transmitted, or offline (store and forward transmission), where the consulting professional reviews data asynchronous with its collection [2]. Telecommunication devices serially moves information (voice, image, numeric data, characters) in the form of electromagnetic signals from transmitter to receiver via a medium, which can be a guided (twisted-pair cable, coaxial and fiber optic cables) or unguided (wireless). But with all networked information systems there is a limitation on available bandwidth which is determined by Shannon formula: $C=B \log_2 (1+S/N)$

Where: C is the capacity of the channel in bps.

B is the bandwidth of the channel.

S/N is signal to noise ration in dBs.

Two major developments have facilitated the telemedicine trend. High-speed T1 and Ethernet lines enable the transfer of large quantities of information rapidly, dramatically expanding the types of studies that are available for telemedicine. It's no longer just single-frame X-rays that can be transferred; it's now almost any medical imaging study, in near or actual real time can be transferred without much delay or much distortion.

Telemedicine Applications

In 1974 NASA contracted with SCI Systems of Houston to conduct a study to determine the minimal television system requirements for Tele-diagnosis. The experiment was conducted with the help of a simulated telemedicine system. First, high-quality videotape was made of actual medical examination conducted by a nurse under the direction of a physician watching on closed-circuit television. This was the baseline for the study. Next, these videotapes were electronically degraded to simulate television systems of less than broadcast quality. Finally, the baseline and degraded video Statistical significance between the means of the standard monochrome system and the lesser quality systems did not occur until the resolution was reduced below 200 lines or until the frame rate was reduced below 10 frames/second. There was no significant difference in the overall diagnostic results as the pictorial information was altered. There was no significant difference in remote treatment designations as a function of TV system type that would cause detriment to patients. The supplementary study of radiographic film televised transmission (25 cases) showed that no diagnostic differences occurred between the TV evaluations and the direct film evaluations for TV resolutions above 200 lines if special optical lenses and scanning techniques were utilized.

Any of the existing transmission telecommunication technologies can be used to deliver medical information as long as the transmission speed/bandwidth is sufficient for the quality required. In practice, e-health data can be transferred in different forms, ranging from a high quality, two-way, full-motion video link to sound and still images. For instance the bandwith demands for the audio signals are:

Voice normal 64kbps (16-32kbps)

Hi-fi 1.4Mbps (192kbps)

Video requirements for remote medical diagnosis:

Video images are categorized into three types and each demands its own transmission rate:

(1) Black and white — Unit size: 307 KB/frames, 640 × 480@ 8 bits.

Examination: 30 frames/sec, 8.8 MB/sec

(2) Color partial bandwidth (Pseudo color)	Unit size: 614KB/frame, 640 × 480@16bits. Examination: 30 frames/sec, 8.8 MB/sec
(3) Color full bandwidth (true color)	Unit size: 921 KB/frame, 640 × 480@24 bits. Examination: 30 frames/sec, 26.3 MB/sec

There are types of still images, which require different rate of transmission:

(1) Chest X-ray digitized	Unit size: 4 bytes/film, 2K × 2K@8 bits. Examination: 4-10 films/study, 16-40 MBs
(2) Magnetic resonance study	Unit size: 64 KB/frame, 256 × 256@8 bits. Examination: 40 frame/study, 2.5 MB
(3) Computed tomography	Unit size: 256 KB/frame, 512 × 512 @ 8 bits. Examination: 40 frame/study, 10 MB/study
(4) Pathology slide	Unit size: 12 MB/film, 2K × 2K@ 24 bits. Examination: 4-6 slides/study, 72 MBs

Bandwidth required for clinical equipment varies for each equipment:

(1) Pulse oxymeter - 9.6KBps
(2) Electrocardiogram - 57.6KBps
(3) Blood pressure monitor - 57.6KBps
(4) Electronic stethoscope - 57.6KBps
(5) Spirometer - 14.4KBps
(6) Glucometer - 1.2 KBps

Thus, voice and low resolution images need lower bandwidth (1KBps-100KBps). High definition images, CD, audio, videoconferencing and VCR quality video require higher bandwidth (100KBps - 10MBps). Multimedia file transfer broadcast video HDTV and visualization requires bandwidth up to even 1GBps.

Telepathology

Involves rendering diagnostic opinions on specimens at remote locations using a computer and telecommunication technologies. Many biopsy specimens require analysis by sub specialists with expertise in specific areas of pathology. Specialist consultations are routine in modern pathology. The use of video technology to examine and consult on microscopic slides has been validated.

Two principle paradigms:

Remote dynamic screening by robotic video microscopy.

Remote diagnosis from selected still video microscope images.

The former requires high-speed telecommunication skills and is more appealing. The latter involves a significant reduction in data and dependent on fields selected on remote locations. This communication will describe a currently functioning system which uses ordinary home and office personal computers (PC's), ordinary modems, simple everyday popular software, without any additional capital expenditures except for:

- A small video camera mounted atop the lab's microscope.
- An ordinary color television having "video-in" and "video-out" jacks.
- A small and simple device called a digitizer, which plugs into the lab computer's parallel port and receives the video signal from the television.

It shows all the steps that have to be done for remote pathology is to place the slide under the microscope and make sure that the area of interest is in good focus as seen on the television monitor. The lab technician can be guided by the remote pathologist to select the appropriate region of interest by virtue of a "persistence-scope" image seen by the remote pathologist real time as the technician scans around and zooms in manually communicating with the pathologist on a voice telephone line separate from the modem line. The lab microscope must have a standard "C-mount" interface, enabling smooth interfacing with a wide variety of high resolution, low cost, video cameras. The video camera mounted atop the microscope via the c-mount is adjusted so the optimal focus of the image as seen by the tech directly peering into the micro-scope, is in synchronization with the optimal focus of the image as seen via the television, but the technician must use the television as his guide as the pathologist digitizes the image. An S-video connector would be a nice option although standard RCA-type connectors on the camera and television and digitizer produce acceptable images. The television monitor can be any TV which has a "video-in" input jack (either RCA or S-video), as well as a "video-out" jack, which we see on all VCR's and many televisions. "Video-in" connects to the video camera and "video-out" connects with the digitizer. If one looks in back of a home television, these jacks are often standard on the television, and always on the VCR. The digitizer can be either internal in the lab computer or external, usually plugging into the computer's parallel port. The other end of the digitizer connects with the "video-out" jack of the television. Like the TV and video camera, it can have either RCA jacks or the higher resolution S-video jacks, or both options. The digitizer comes with free software easily installed into Windows. Any lab PC or IBM-clone host computer with, at least, VGA graphics, will be sufficient for host digitizing and remote viewing. The faster the processor, co-processor, and clock the better. The more RAM (8 megabytes minimum suggested) the better. The only absolute requirement is that the display color be 256, or 8-bit. Anything lower would result in poor quality images and anything higher would result in the networking software not installing or working properly. The networking software must be installed into both the lab (host) and home (remote) computers, each computers display set for 256 colors upon installing and using. Networking hardware, such as Ethernet cards, is not needed as the networking will be possible entirely by virtue of MODEMS connections to each other. Networking software enables easy transfer of image files from the host to the remote. The remote computer may be similar to the host computer in configuration, except the remote computer does not need a digitizer or digitizing software, but it does need good image viewing software. Commonly used image viewing software are Lview, PSP, Cshow, or MS Imager. If the transferred images are uncompressed and in 24-bit format such as a BMP, TIFF, or PCX, they may look only slightly better than compressed 24-bit images, or JPEG images, but the uncompressed image may take 15 minutes to transfer while the compressed JPEG image may take 15 seconds! Therefore, compressed (JPEG or JFIF) images are the industry standard for images which are to be transferred. The EYES of the remote pathologist interpret the image and a valuable opinion is rendered. The technical/legal/ethical questions of how good do the images have to be before an accurate, guilt-free, diagnosis can be rendered, are solely in the beholder's same eyes.

Teledermatology

It involves various activities such as talking with the patient to elicit a history, visual pattern recognition, surgical treatment and pre- & postoperative management. Teledermatology can serve as a good model for other telemedicine specialties. In particular, a key element in making a dermatological diagnosis as shown in Figure 1, is visual inspection of the skin, which can be readily transmitted via telemedicine techniques. The majority of dermatologists practice in or around urban areas, which leaves rural areas with fewer specialists.

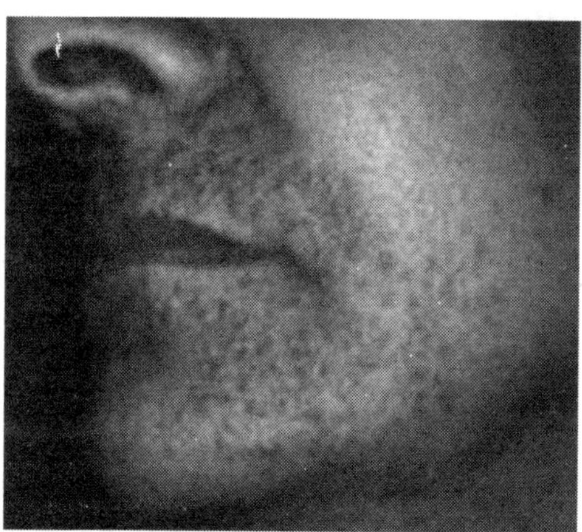

Fig. 1: A case of dermatological diagnosis

Teledermatology can be a means of delivering specialist care to these out of reach patients. Teledermatology programs use a combination of live-interactive video (IATV) and store-and-forward (S&F) technology. Teledermatology uses the capabilities of special peripherals connected to the Telehealth Station. The process involves transmitting images of the skin for expert interpretation and diagnosis. During a videoconference, the Patient Camera can transmit a view of areas of the body, and can zoom in on affected areas, displaying these images at the remote site as shown in Figure 3. To save dermatology images as files, the Health station can take a 'snapshot' for future consults, second opinions or comparisons [6].

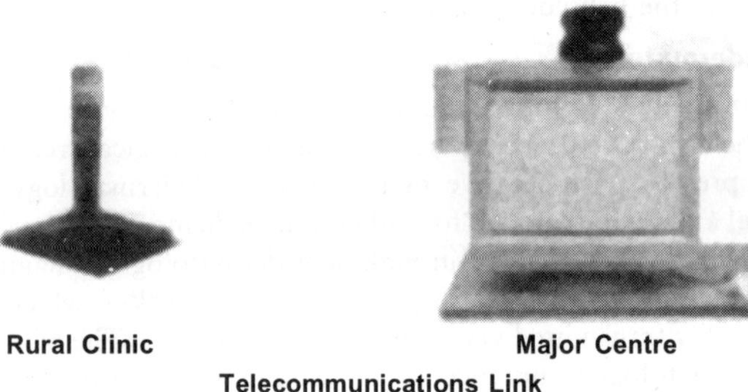

Fig. 2: Schematic diagram of Teledermatology

Telepsychiatry

Telepsychiatry allows an existing mental health service to expand its services into a larger geographic area. Its simple beauty is that it's really a video conferencing session with a twist. The twist being the practitioner can have controlled the camera at both ends of the session so he/she can see everything in the patient's environment. The patient can even walk around the room and the doctor can follow throughout the videoconference.

"The benefits described by the early pioneers have been huge that is better coordination of treatment plans between specialists and community-based physicians during hospitalization and after the patient returns home, and Ongoing contact between hospitalized individuals and family members who may be located at great distances from the treatment facility" (U.S. Mental Health Telemedicine, July 1998).

In the demonstration graphic as shown in Figure 3 the doctor can see the patient on the screen and can see him/herself in the top right hand corner of the screen. The doctor can also control the camera zoom on the remote camera. If desired, control of camera zoom can be at the remote location and controlled by administrative staff [7].

Fig. 3: Demo for Telepsychiatry

In view of the large bandwidth requirements of channels for transferring above mentioned kind of multimedia data, a high speed LAN infrastructure is required to be used with in hospital premises. The most popular LAN technology is the Ethernet which has a lion's share in the huge LAN market.

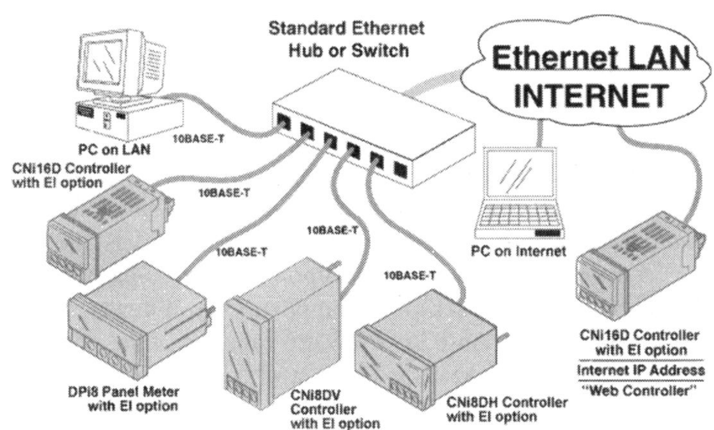

Fig. 4: Ethernet LAN

Fast Ethernet is used widely at this point and provides customers with 100 Mbps performance, a ten-fold increase. Fast EtherChannel is a Cisco value-added feature that provides bandwidth up to 800 Mbps. There is now a standard for Gigabit Ethernet as well and Cisco provides Gigabit Ethernet solutions with 1000 Mbps performance.

Fig. 5: Fast EtherChannel

Fast EtherChannel provides a solution for network managers who require higher bandwidth between servers, routers, and switches than Fast Ethernet technology can currently provide. Fast EtherChannel is the grouping of multiple Fast Ethernet interfaces into one logical transmission path providing parallel bandwidth between switches, servers, and Cisco routers. Fast EtherChannel provides bandwidth aggregation by combining parallel 100-Mbps Ethernet links (200-Mbps full-duplex) to provide flexible, incremental bandwidth between network devices. For example, network managers can deploy Fast EtherChannel consisting of pairs of full-duplex Fast Ethernet to provide 400+ Mbps between the wiring closet and the data center, while in the data center bandwidths of up to 800 Mbps can be provided between servers and the network backbone to provide large amounts of scalable incremental bandwidth. Cisco's Fast EtherChannel technology builds upon standards-based 802.3 full-duplex Fast Ethernet. It is supported by industry leaders such as Adaptec, Compaq, Hewlett-Packard, Intel, Micron, Silicon Graphics, Sun Microsystems, and Xircom and is scalable to Gigabit Ethernet in the future. In some cases like mentioned above multimedia file transfer video HDTV and visualization require bandwidth upto even in excess of 1 Gbps, fast EtherChannel technology may not be enough. Gigabit networking is important to accommodate these evolving needs. Gigabit

Ethernet builds on the Ethernet protocol but increases speed tenfold over Fast Ethernet, to 1000 Mbps, or 1 Gbps. It promises to be a dominant player in high-speed LAN backbones and server connectivity. Because Gigabit Ethernet significantly leverages on Ethernet, network managers will be able to leverage their existing knowledge base to manage and maintain Gigabit networks. The Gigabit Ethernet spec addresses three forms of transmission media though not all are available yet:

- 1000BaseLX: Long-wave (LW) laser over single-mode and multimode fiber
- 1000BaseSX: Short-wave (SW) laser over multimode fiber
- 1000BaseCX: Transmission over balanced shielded 150-ohm 2-pair STP copper cable
- 1000BaseT: Category 5 UTP copper wiring Gigabit Ethernet allows Ethernet to scale from 10 Mbps at the desktop, to 100 Mbps to the workgroup, to 1000 Mbps in the data center. By leveraging the current Ethernet standards as well as the installed base of Ethernet and Fast Ethernet switches and routers, network managers do not need to retrain and relearn a new technology to provide support for Gigabit Ethernet.

CONCLUSION

The choice of technology to be implemented not only depends on the nature of information to be transmitted and the time frame over which it must be sent to achieve the desired clinical goals but also that offer reduced operating costs, reduced maintenance costs, consistent performance and operational features throughout their extended network. Ethernet LAN technology is the one that gaining popularity and providing the above mentioned application implementations.

REFERENCES

Anthoula, P. Anagnostaki, Sotiris Pavlopoulos, Efthivoulos Kyriakou, and Dimitris Koutsouris. A Novel Codification Scheme Based on the "VITAL" and "DICOM" Standards for Telemedicine Applications. IEEE Trans. Biomed. Eng 2002; 49(12): 1399-1411.

Bansal, A. "Mobile E-Health for developing countries".

2. Doolittle, G.C and Cook D (1999). Defining the needs of a telemedicine service. Introduction to Telemedicine (Wootton R, and Craig J, eds.) Royal Society of Medicine Press, London, England: 79-92.
3. Epping-Jordan, J., Bengoa R, Kawar R, Sabate E. The challenge of chronic conditions: WHO responds. BMJ 2001; 323:947-8.
4. Forkner-Dunn, J. Internet-based Patient Self-care: The Next Generation of Health Care Delivery. J Med Internet Res 2003; 5(2): e8. URL: http://www.jmir.org/2003/2/e8/
5. Gerber, B.S., Eiser AR. The patient-physician relationship in the Internet age: future prospects and the research agenda. J Med Internet Res 2001 Apr-Jun; 3(2): e15.
6. Girzadas, J., Given, R. Distinguish Yourself With E-health. Healthcare Informatics March 2003.URL: http://www.healthcare-informatics.com/issues/2003/03_03/mar.htm
7. Grimson, J, Grimson W, Hasselbring, W. The SI challenge in health care. Commun. ACM 2000; 43(6): 49-55.
8. Kane, B., Sands DZ. Guidelines for the clinical use of electronic mail with patients. J Amer Med Inform Assoc. 1998; 5(1): 104-111.
9. Kedar, I., Ternullo JL, Weinrib CE, Kelleher KM, Bennett HB, Kvedar JC. Internet based consultations to transfer knowledge for patients requiring specialized care: retrospective case review. BMJ 2003; 326:696-9.
10. McKimm, J., Jollie C, Cantillon P. Web based learning. BMJ 2003; 326:870-873.
11. Payton, F., Brennan, P. How a community health information network is really used. Commun. ACM 1999; 42(12): 85-89.

    Roine, R., A. Ohinmaa, and D. Hailey, "Assessing telemedicine: a systematic review of the literature," CMAJ, Vol. 165, pp. 765-771, 2001.
12. Shannon, G., Nesbitt T, Bakalar R, Kratochwill E, Kvedar J, Vargas L. Organizational models of telemedicine and regional telemedicine networks. Telemed J E Health 2002; 8(1): 61-70.
13. Wootton, R. Telemedicine and developing countries-successful implementation will require a shared approach. J Telemed Telecare 2001; 7(suppl 1): 1-6.
14. World Health Organization. Innovative care for chronic conditions: building blocks for action. Geneva: WHO, 2002.

Analysis of Near Far Problem in Spread Spectrum System

25

Amit Rathi, Bramha Prasad Pandey, Rakesh Kumar, Arun Kumar Verma and *Abhay Chaturvedi*

ABSTRACT

The term spread spectrum (SS) has been widely used in military and commercial communication systems. A spread spectrum system requires significantly more radio frequency (RF) bandwidth compared to conventional modulation techniques. Spread spectrum is a technique where a information signal is modulated two times in such a way as to generate an wide bandwidth signal that does not significantly interfere with other signal. In this paper, a technical analysis of near far problem in spread spectrum is presented and simulation results shows that FHSS is less susceptible to near far problem than DSSS.

INTRODUCTION

Spread spectrum system is type of modulation technique in which modulated signal bandwidth is much greater than the base band signal bandwidth. In this technique the energy generated at one or more discrete frequencies is intentionally spreaded in time or frequency domain. Spread spectrum offers various advantages that cannot be obtained by conventional modulation techniques but the performance of spread spectrum system is degraded by near far problem. In this paper the performance of two types of spread spectrum systems, i.e. direct sequence spread spectrum (DSSS) and frequency hopped spread spectrum (FHSS) on the basis of near far problem is analyzed and results shows that FHSS system is less affected by near far problem compared to DSSS.

Spread Spectrum System

In spread spectrum system, spectral spreading is done at the transmitter by a pseudo noise code. The pseudo noise code used in spread spectrum system is the periodic sequence of 1s and 0s with certain autocorrelation and cross correlation properties. This same code is used at the receiver to despread the signal to recover the information signal.

Spread spectrum system can be broadly categorized in two types, i.e. direct sequence spread spectrum (DSSS) and frequency hopped spread spectrum (FHSS).

Direct sequence spread spectrum

Direct sequence spread spectrum systems are so called because they use a locally generated pseudo-noise code or sequence to encode the digital data to be transmitted. Data for transmission is simply modulo-2 added or XORed with the faster pseudo noise sequence. This combination of the data and the high speed PN sequence is then used to directly modulate an RF carrier. The ratio of the code rate to the information rate determines the extent of spreading and is also called the processing gain.

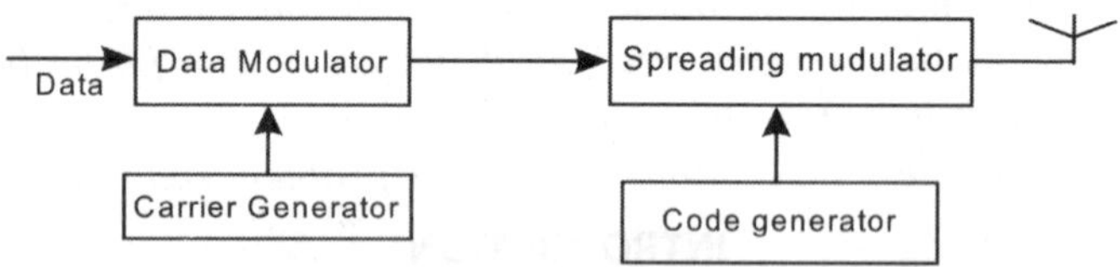

Fig. 1: Block Diagram of DS-SS Signal transmitter

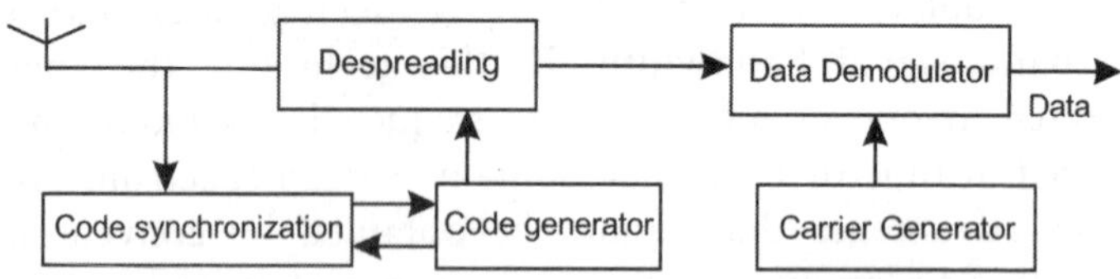

Fig. 2: Block Diagram of DS-SS Signal Receiver

Assume f is the frequency of the message data signal, with corresponding time period $T=1/f$ and the PN code has a frequency f_c with corresponding time period, $T_C=1/f_c$.

Let the data signal is represented by $d(t)$ and let the PN sequence is represented $n(t)$, so the transmitted signal is

$s(t) = d(t)\, n(t)$.

The PN code has very high autocorrelation properties and very low cross correlation properties, so, when the modulated data signal is correlated (multiplied) with the PN code sequence at the receiver, the received signal is given by.

$s(t)n(t)=d(t)n(t)n(t)=d(t)$ as $n(t)n(t) = 1$

Now, when the signal is correlated with the PN code sequence, the data signal that is part of $y(t)$ is de-spread (demodulated) exactly to produce $d(t)$. But i (t) and n (t) spreads after correlation with PN code sequence at the receiver.

Frequency hopped spread spectrum system

Frequency hopped spread spectrum is the second main type of spread spectrum system. In FH-SS, the modulating data signal is not spread over the whole large bandwidth; but the large bandwidth is separated into N sub-frequency bands, and the signal "hops" from one band to the next in a pseudorandom method. The center frequency of the signal varies from one hop to the next, changing from one sub-frequency band to another.

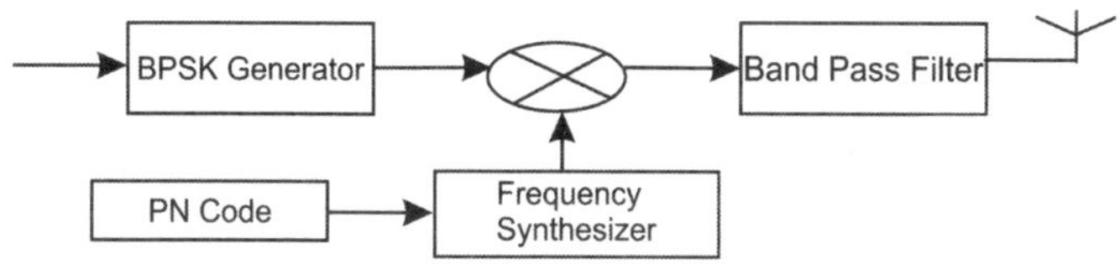

Fig. 3: Block Diagram of FH-SS Signal transmitter

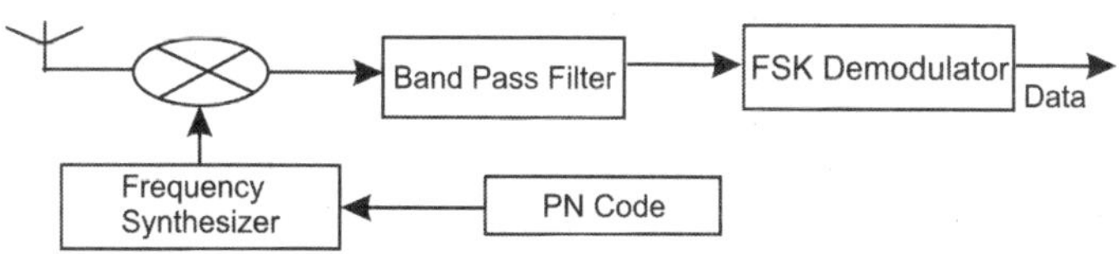

Fig. 4: Block Diagram of FH-SS Signal Receiver

Near-Far Problem in Spread Spectrum

The near-far problem is a situation that is common in wireless communication systems (in particular, spread spectrum). The near-far problem can also be called the *hearability problem*. The problem is that there exist a receiver and two transmitters (one close to the receiver; the other far away). If both transmitters transmit simultaneously and at equal powers, the receiver will receive more power from the nearer transmitter due to the inverse square law. This makes farther located transmitter more difficult, if not impossible, to "understand." Since one transmission's signal is the other's noise, the signal-to-noise ratio (SNR) for the farther transmitter is much lower. If the nearer transmitter transmits a signal that is orders of magnitude higher than the farther transmitter then the SNR for the farther transmitter may be below the delectability level and the farther transmitter may just as well not transmit. This effectively jams the communication channel.

The DSSS system suffer from near-far problem as if streanth of unwanted signal is strong due to the proximity of its transmitter to receiver and the streanth of desired signal is weak due to the remoteness of its transmitter from the receiver, the unwanted signal may be drawn out the desired signal. Where as FHSS is more immune to near far problem then than DSSS. In FHSS signals do not use same frequency simultaneously hence the relative power of co channel signals in FHSS is not so critical as in DSSS.

In spread spectrum systems, this is commonly solved by dynamic output power adjustment of the transmitters. That is, the closer transmitters use less power so that the SNR for all transmitters at the receiver is roughly the same. This sometimes can have a noticeable impact on battery life, which can be dramatically different depending on distance from the base station. In high-noise situations, however, closer transmitters may boost their output power, which forces distant transmitters to boost their output to maintain a good SNR. Other transmitters react to the rising noise floor by increasing their output. This process continues, and eventually distant transmitters lose their ability to maintain a usable SNR and drop from the network. This process is called power control runaway. This principle may be used to explain why an area with low signal is perfectly usable when the cell isn't heavily loaded, but when load is higher, service quality degrades significantly, sometimes to the point of unusability.

RESULTS AND CONCLUSION

Analysis of the near far problem in spread spectrum system is done in Matlab 7.0.4. Simlulation of DSSS and FHSS system is done and the output of received signals are compared in the two cases, first when the received signal is recived from a nearer position and in the second case when the received signal is received from the farther position. Output from the two cases are compared for both the two types of spread spectrum system, i.e. direct sequence spread spectrum (DSSS) and frequency hopped spread spectrum (FHSS). Figures 5 and 6 show the simulation results for DSSS and FHSS systems respectively.

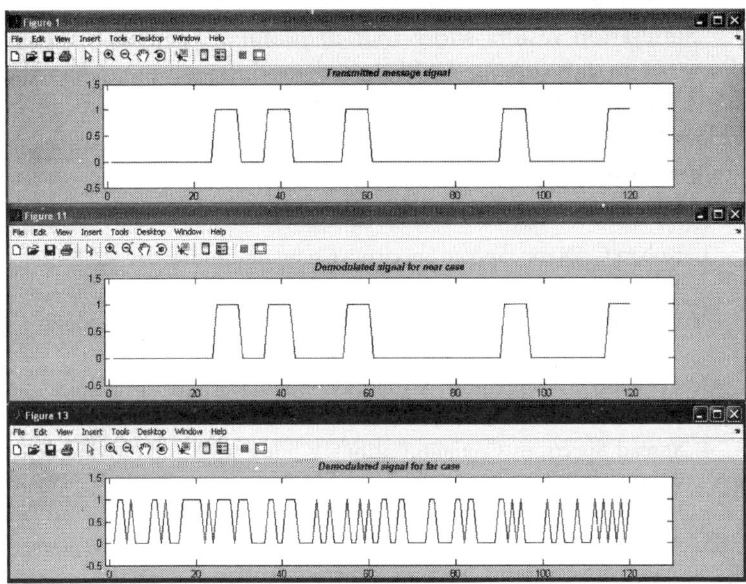

Fig. 5: Results for DSSS systems in near case and far case

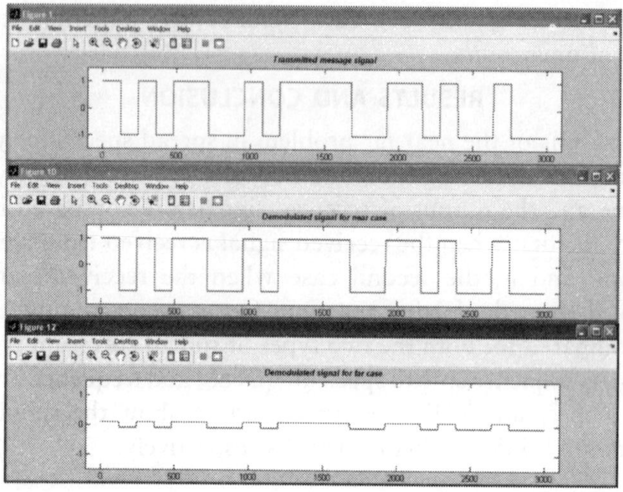

Fig. 6: Results for FHSS systems in near and far case

Simulation results show that demodulated signal becomes distorted in far case in DSSS but demodulated signal has the same shape (undistorted) having the attenuated amplitude in FHSS. So conclusion is that FHSS suffers less in near far problem compared to DSSS.

REFERENCES

1. Robert C. Dixon. Spread Spectrum Communications, Second Edition, John Wiley and Sons, New York, 1984.
2. Dr. Kamilo Feher. Wireless Digital Communications, Modulation and Spread Spectrum applications, U.S. addition.
3. Theodore S. Rappaport, Wireless Communications—principles and practices, 2nd edition.
4. Spread Spectrum Communications Volume 1, 2 and 3. Marvin K. Simon, Jim K. Omura, Robert A Scholtz and Barry K. Levitt. Computer Science Press. ISBN 0-88175-017-7 (Set).
5. Appendix 4 - Multiplication of Direct Sequence Signals. Spread Spectrum Systems Second Edition Robert C. Dixon. Wiley Interscience.
6. A.W. Houghton, C.D. Reeve, "Detection of spreadspectrum signals using the time-domain filtered cross spectral density", IEE Proceedings - Radar, Sonar and Navigation, December 1995, Vol. 142, No. 6, pp. 286-292.

7. T.S.D. Tsui, T.G. Clarkson. "Spread Spectrum Communication Techniques," Electronics and Communication Engineering Journal, February 1994.
8. P. Johansson, "Rasmus—A spread spectrum and modulation evaluation system", Report FOA-R- -00-01439-504- - SE, Defence Research Establishment, Sweden 2000.
9. A.G. Piersol, "Time delay estimation using phase data", IEEE Transaction on Acoustics, Speech, Signal Processing, June 1981, Vol. 29, No.3, pt. 2, pp. 471-477.
10. Laurence B. Milstein, Donal L. Schilling. "The Effect of Frequency-Selective Fading on a Noncoherent FH-FSK System Operating with partial Band Tone Interference," IEEE Transactions on Communications, Vol. COM-30, May 1982, pp. 904-912.

On the Scalability of Ad Hoc Networks: A Traffic Analysis at the Center of a Network

26

Sumit Agrawal, Chhavi Kaushik and *Diwakar Bhardwaj*

ABSTRACT

We investigate the inherent scalability problem of ad hoc networks originated from the nature of multi-hop networks. First; the expected packet traffic at the center of a network is analyzed. The result shows that the expected packet traffic at the center of a network is linearly related with the network size, that is, the expected packet traffic at the center of a network is O(k), where k is the radius of a network. From the result, the upper bound of the diameter of a network D = 2k, that guarantees the network is scalable, is obtained. The upper bound is given by C/r/—1, where C is the channel capacity available to each node and r is the packet arrival rate at each node.

INTRODUCTION

An ad hoc network is an autonomous system of nodes connected by wireless links, where the communications between nodes are often achieved by multi-hop links. With the increased interest in the mobile communications in the wireless communication community and the promise of convenient infrastructure-free communication of ad hoc networks, the development of *large-scale* ad hoc networks has drawn a lot of attention and the scalability of ad hoc networks has been the subject of extensive research. Because of the multi-hop nature of ad hoc networks, the scalability of ad hoc networks inherent scalability problem is originated from the nature of multi-hop networks. In our is directly related to the routing protocol.

For in this paper, we investigate the inherent scalability problem of ad hoc networks. This analysis, we recognize that the center of the example, a mobile ad hoc network can be made more scalable by reducing the overhead of the number of nodes in the network [5]. Thus, for a network with large number of nodes, much of the traffic carried by the nodes are relayed traffic and the proportion of the actual useful throughput diminishes as N growsrouting protocol [2]. A comparison study of the scalability of various routing protocols by Santiv´a˜nez et al. is available in [3]. Huang and Lai showed that the scalability of an ad hoc network is also affected by the underlying physical layer [4]. While the routing protocol is a prominent factor of the scalability of ad hoc networks, the scalability is subject to the fundamental limitation imposed by the multi-hop nature of ad hoc networks. Even with an ideal routing protocol that can handle constantly changing topology of the mobile nodes in the network, the network will not scale indefinitely due to the physical constraint such as the bandwidth of the channel. In a multi-hop network environment, the problems caused by the physical constraint will be exacerbated as the network size grows. In a typical route the number of hops is of order N, where N is the network is the "hot spot" of the network in the sense that most of the relayed traffic goes through the center of the network. Thus, we first analyze the expected packet traffic at the center of a network, where the expected packet traffic includes the relayed packets. We find that the expected packet traffic at the center of the network is O(k), where k is the radius of the network in the number of hops. From this result, the upper bound of the diameter of a network D = 2k is obtained to guarantee the network is scalable.

The paper is organized as follows. In Section II, the analysis model of the network is described. In Section III, the scalability of the network is investigated; in Section III-A, the expected packet traffic at the center of a network is analyzed, and it is used to obtain the upper bound of the network size in Section III-B. Section IV concludes the paper.

Analysis Model of the Network

In this paper, we investigate the inherent scalability problem of ad hoc networks which is originated from the nature of multi-hop networks. This is accomplished by analyzing the relationship between the expected packet traffic at the center of a network and the network size. For the analysis, we make the following assumptions on the network.

(1) *Uniform geometric distribution of the nodes*: We consider a network structured in honey comb shape as shown in Fig. 1. The transmission power of a node should be high enough to reach the neighbor nodes while causing minimal interference at other nodes. Thus, we assume that each node has 6 neighboring nodes (except for the nodes at the boundary), where a neighbor node means a node with a single-hop wireless link.

(2) *Stationary nodes*: Nodes in the network are assumed to be stationary. Even though the topology may constantly change in ad hoc networks, by freezing the topology of the network, we can analyze the expected packet traffic at each node of the *snapshot* of the network, and it will make the analysis much easier. Furthermore, in most mobility scenarios, the relative movement of the nodes to the packet transit time is insignifcant [6].

(3) *Identical node property*: We assume that all nodes in the network will act equally in terms of the demand on the physical resources, and of the needs to communicate with one another. Thus, it is assumed that all nodes generate packets at the same rate.

(4) *Uniform distribution of destination*: It is assumed that the distribution of the destination nodes is uniform over the entire network of interest. Here, "uniform" means that the probability of transmitting a packet from a source node to any of other N-1 nodes is the same as 1/N-1.

(5) *Shortest path*: We assume each packet is relayed through the shortest path available. If there are more than one

paths of the same length to the destination, the probability of each path being chosen is identical.

In this paper, it is assumed that the nodes are stationary. Grossglauser and Tse showed that the mobility of nodes increases the capacity of the wireless ad hoc networks [7]. They used a quite unique routing strategy with loose delay constraints which has only two hops from a source node to a destination node. However, their routing strategy depends heavily on the movement of the nodes and the long time delay limits the applicability of the result in many situations.

The Scalability of a Network

A. Packet Traffic at the Center of a Network

A network model we consider is illustrated in Fig. 1. The size of the network is given by the radius k, and the radius is defined as the number of hops from the center node to the boundary node. The number of nodes N and the radius k have the following relationship:

$$N = 1+(1+2+\cdots+k)\cdot 6 = 1+3k(k+1) \quad (1)$$

The expected packet traffic at the center node *n*0 can be calculated by exploiting the symmetry of the network. First, we calculate the expected packet traffic generated by the nodes in the shaded areas *B* and *C* that pass or destined to *n*0, then it is multiplied by 6 to obtain the total amount of the expected packet traffic at *n*0. Note that, because of the shortest path assumption, the packets generated by nodes in *B may* pass *n*0 only when the packets' destination nodes are in *D*. Similarly, packets generated by nodes in *C may* pass *n*0 only when the destination nodes are in *E*. Let *ns* and *nd* represent the source and the destination nodes, respectively. Then, assuming a uniform distribution of destination nodes, that is the probability of a packet from a source node *ns* is transmitted to a destination node *nd* is 1/(N -1) for all nodes *nd* is not equal to *ns*, the expected packet traffic at node *n*0, PT*n*0 , can be calculated as follows:

$$PT_{no} = \{\sum_{n_s \in B}\sum_{n_d \in D}\frac{p_{no(n_s,n_d).r}}{N-1} + \sum_{n_s \in C}\sum_{n_d \in E}\frac{p_{no(n_s,n_d).r}}{N-1}\}\times 6 \quad (2)$$

where r is the number of packets a node generates in a unit time (the packet arrival rate), and *pn*0 (*ns*, *nd*) is the probability that *ns* will send a packet to *nd* through *n*0.

Define

$$B \rightarrow D = \sum_{n_s \in B} \sum_{n_d \in D} p_{no}(n_s, n_d)$$

$$C \rightarrow E = \sum_{n_s \in C} \sum_{n_d \in E} p_{no}(n_s, n_d)$$

Then, (2) can be written as

$$PT_{no} = \{(B \rightarrow D) + (C \rightarrow E)\} \times \frac{6r}{N-1}$$
$$= \{(B \rightarrow E) + (B \rightarrow F) + (C \rightarrow E)$$
$$+(B' \rightarrow E) - (B' \rightarrow E)\} \times \frac{6r}{N-1} \quad (3)$$

Since *B*, *C*, and *B'* are mutually exclusive areas, (3) can be reduced as follows:

$$PT_{no} = \{[(B \cup C \cup B') \rightarrow E] - [(B' \rightarrow E) - (B \rightarrow F)]\} \times \frac{6r}{N-1}$$

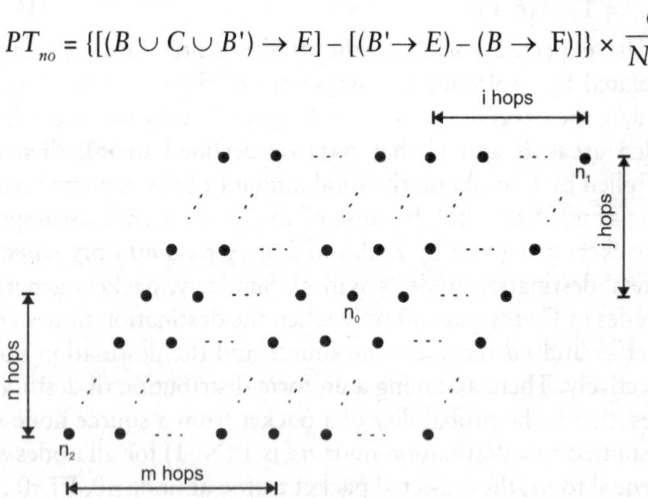

Fig. 2: The paths from the source node (n_1) to the destination node (n_2).

Since $B \cup C \cup B' = A$ and

$$B' \to E = B \to E;$$
$$B \to E = B \to F',$$

We have

$$PT_{no} = \{[(A \to E) - [CB \to E) - (B \to F)]\}\frac{6r}{N-1}$$
$$= \{(A \to E) - (B \to G)\} \times \frac{6r}{N-1} \quad (4)$$

Thus, the expected packet traffic at n_0 can be expressed as follows:

$$PT_{no} = \{\sum_{n_s \in A}\sum_{n_d \in E}\frac{p_{no(n_s,n_d).r}}{N-1} + \sum_{n_s \in B}\sum_{n_d \in G}\frac{p_{no(n_s,n_d).r}}{N-1}\} \times 6 \quad (5)$$

The probability *pn0 (ns, nd)* can be calculated from the shortest path with equal probability assumption (see assumption 5) in Section II. Consider Fig. 2, where the number of hops from *n*1 to *n*0 is *i* + *j*, and the number of hops from *n*0 to *n*2 is *m*+*n*. Then, the probability f(*i*, *j*, *m*, *n*) that a packet from *n*1 to *n*2 will pass *n*0 is calculated by

$$f(i,j,m,n) = \frac{{}_{i+j}C_i \cdot {}_{m+n}C_n}{{}_{i+j+m+n}C_{i+m}} \quad (6)$$

Note that *i+j+m+nCi+m* is the total number of the shortest paths from *n*1 to *n*2, and *i+jCi* · *m+nCn* is the number of the shortest paths from *n*1 to that include node *n*0. Let *ni*, be a node whose location is indicated by the indices *i* and *j* as shown in the Fig. 3. Then, for *i*, *j* > 0 and *m*, *n* >= 0, it can be shown that

$$p_{no}(n_{i,j}, n_{-m,-n}) = f(i,j,m,n) \quad (7)$$

By substituting (1) and (7) into (5), PT*n*0 can be written as

$$PT_{no} = \frac{2r}{k(k+1)}(\sum_{i=0}^{k}\sum_{j=0}^{k-i}\sum_{m=0}^{k}\sum_{n=0}^{k-m} f(i,j,m,n)$$

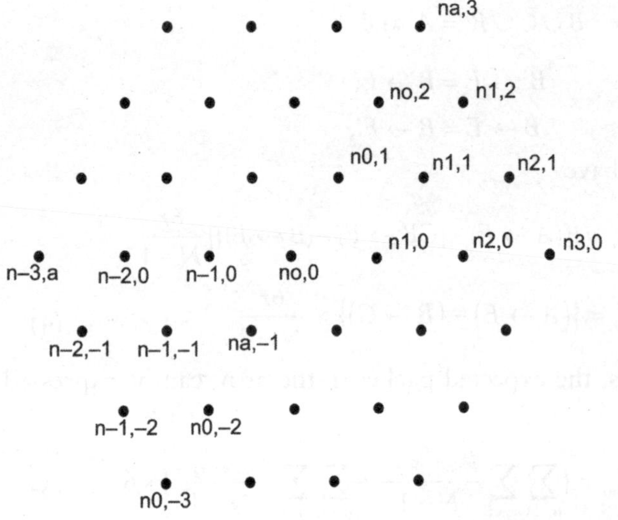

Fig. 3: A netwrok model with node indices (k = 3).

$$-\sum_{m=0}^{k}\sum_{n=0}^{k-m} f(0,0,m,n)) - 2r \tag{8}$$

From (6), the term with the double summation in (8) can be readily calculated as follows:

$$\sum_{m=0}^{k}\sum_{n=0}^{k-m} f(0,0,m,n) = \sum_{m=0}^{k}\sum_{n=0}^{k-m} \frac{m!n!}{(m+n)!}\frac{(m+n)!}{m!n!}$$
$$= (k+1)(\frac{k}{2}+1) \tag{9}$$

The term with the quadruple summation is also reduced to a simple form as follow:

$$\sum_{i=0}^{k}\sum_{j=0}^{k-i}\sum_{m=0}^{k}\sum_{n=0}^{k-m} f(i,j,m,n)$$
$$= \sum_{i=0}^{k}\sum_{j=0}^{k-i}\sum_{m=0}^{k}\sum_{n=0}^{k-m} \frac{(i+j)!(m+n)!(i+m)!(j+n)!}{(i+j+m+n)!i!j!m!n!} \tag{10}$$
$$= (k+1)^3$$

Equation (10) can be easily verified by substituting a positive integer into k. We leave (10) as a conjecture without proof. Finally, substituting (9) and (10) into (8), we have

$$PT_{no} = (2k+1) \times r \tag{11}$$

which is an unexpectedly simple form. Equation (11) indicates that the expected packet traffic at the center of a network is linearly related to the radius k of the network. Note that PT*n*0 is O(k) as opposed to the number of nodes N which is O(k2).

B. The Upper Bound of a Network Size

Let C be the channel capacity available to each node, that is the maximum achievable throughput determined by the physical layer and medium access control layer. If the expected packet traffic at a node is greater than C, the node is not able to handle the traffic load. Thus, to make a network scalable, we must guarantee that PT*n*0 is smaller than C. That is, from (11),

$$(2k+1) \times r = PT_{no} < C \tag{12}$$

Let $D = 2k$ be the diameter of a network, then (12) can be written as

$$D < \frac{C}{r} - 1 \tag{13}$$

Equation (13) gives an upper bound of the diameter of a scalable ad hoc network with an ideal shortest path routing protocol. Note that the upper bound is inversely proportional to *r*; the network is more scalable when the packet arrival rate is small.

C. Discussion

In the analysis, *r* represents the packet arrival rate at each node and we do not take into account the overhead caused by the control packets of the routing protocol. The amount of the routing overhead depends not only on the mobility of the nodes but also on the network size. As the network size grows, the routing overhead is expected to grow. Consequently, PT*n*0 may be larger than that given in (11). As shown in (1), the number of node N is O(k2) as same as in the most of networks. Even though our result in (11) and (13) are obtained under assumption of symmetric topology of the network, the results are also applicable to general networks. Thus, we can presume that the expected packet traffic at the center of the network will be O(k).

CONCLUSION

An ad hoc network is an autonomous system of nodes connected by wireless links, where the communications between nodes are often achieved by multi-hop links. In this paper, we have investigated the inherent scalability problem of ad hoc networks which is originated from the nature of multihop networks. The scalability of ad hoc networks depends not only on the routing protocol, but also on the traffic patterns, physical layer and medium access control layer. In the analysis, we recognized that the center of the network is the "hot spot" of the network in the sense that most of the relayed traffic goes through the center of the network. Thus, the expected packet traffic at the center of a network was first analyzed and the ideal shortest path routing protocol was used. The result shows that the expected packet traffic at the center of a network is linearly related with the radius of a network k, that is, the expected packet traffic at the center of a network is O(k). From the result, the upper bound of the diameter of a network $D = 2k$ is obtained to guarantee the network scalable. The upper bound is given by C/r - 1, where C is the channel capacity available to each node and r is the packet arrival rate at each node.

REFERENCES

1. IRTF RRG ad hoc Network Scaling Research Subgroup, http://www.flarion.com/ans-research/.
2. C. Santiv´a˜nez, R. Ramanathan, and I. Stavrakakis, "Making link-state routing scale for ad hoc networks," in *Proceedings the 2001 ACM International Symposium on Mobile Ad Hoc Networking & Computing,MobiHOC'2001*, Long Beach, California, October 2001.
3. C. Santiv´a˜nez, B. McDonald, I. Stavrakakis, and R. Ramanathan, "On the scalability of ad hoc routing protocols," in *Proceedings of IEEE Infocom'02*, New York, June 2002.
4. Lifei Huang and Ten-Hwang Lai, "On the scalability of IEEE 802.11 ad hoc networks," *in Proceedings of the Third ACM International Symposium on Mobile Ad Hoc Networking and Computing (MobiHoc 2002)*, Lausanne, Switzerland, June 2002.
5. Piyush Gupta and P.R. Kumar, "The capacity of wireless networks," *IEEE Transactions on Information Theory*, Vol. 46, No. 2, pp. 388-404, March 2000.

6. J. Li, C. Blake, D.S.J. De Couto, H.I. Lee, and R. Morris, "Capacity of ad hoc wireless networks," in *Proceedings of the 7th ACM International Conference on Mobile Computing and Networking*, Rome, Italy, July 2001, pp. 61-69.
7. Matthias Grossglauser and David Tse, "Mobility increases the capacity of ad-hoc wireless networks," in *Proceedings of IEEE infocom 2001*, Anchorage, Alaska, April 2001.

An Architectural Framework for Video Retrieval based on Key Frame Extraction

27

Pallavi Sinha, Udayan Ghose and *Anurag Jain*

ABSTRACT

As a result of decreased costs for storage devices, increased network bandwidth, and improved compression techniques, digital videos are more accessible than ever. To help users find and retrieve relevant video effectively and to facilitate new and better ways of entertainment, advanced technologies must be developed for indexing, filtering, searching, and mining the vast amount of videos now available on the web. To achieve more efficient video indexing and access, we analyze and find out the key frames/candidate signature from the video shots. The video shot segmentation and representative frame selection strategy are first utilized to parse the continuous video streams into physical units. Video shot grouping, group merging, and scene clustering schemes are then proposed to organize the video shots into a hierarchical structure using clustered scenes, groups and shots, in increasing granularity from top to bottom. Then video processing techniques are integrated to mine event information, such as dialog, soccer videos of user choice and clinical operation, for the detected scenes. This paper will propose an architectural framework for key frame analysis. This paper will also provide highlights on the problems of existing data mining tools when applied to video databases.

INTRODUCTION

As a result of decreased costs for storage devices, increased network bandwidth, and improved compression techniques, digitalvideos are more accessible than ever. To help users find and retrieve relevant video more effectively and to facilitate new and better ways of entertainment, advanced technologies must be developed for indexing, filtering, searching, and mining the vast amount of video now available on the web. While numerous papers have appeared on data mining, few deal with video data mining directly [1]. We can now use various video-processing techniques to segment video sequence into shots, region-of-interest (ROI), etc. for database management or retrieval; however, the mining of knowledge from video data is still in its infancy. To facilitate the mining process, these questions must first be answered:

1. What is the objective of video data mining?
2. Can general data mining techniques be used on video data directly?
3. If not, what requirements would allow general mining techniques to be applied to video data? [1]

Simply stated, the objective of video data mining is the organizing of video data for knowledge exploring or mining, where the knowledge can be explained as special patterns (e.g. events, clusters, classification, etc.), which may be unknown before the processing.

Various Issues of Using Data Mining Tools on Video Databases

Many successful data mining techniques have been developed through academic research and industry, hence, an intuitive solution for video data mining is to use these strategies on video data directly; Unfortunately, due to the inherent complexity of the video data, existing data mining tools suffer from the following problems when applied to video databases:

Video database modeling

Most traditional data mining techniques work on the relational database, where the relationship between data items is explicitly specified. However, video documents are obviously not a relational dataset, and although we may now retrieve video frames (and even physical shots) with satisfactory results, acquiring the relational relationships among video frames (or shots) is still an open problem. Consequently, traditional data mining techniques cannot be utilized in video data mining directly; a distinct database model must first be addressed [1-2].

Database model problem

Data mining techniques work on the relational database. Unfortunately, video documents are generally unstructured in semantics and cannot be represented easily via the relational data model. A good video database model is necessary and critical to support more efficient video database management and mining.

Video data organizing

Existing video retrieval systems first partition videos into a set of access units such as shots, or regions, and then follow the paradigm of representing video content via a set of feature attributes (i.e. metadata) such as color, shape, motion etc. Thus, video mining can be achieved by applying the data mining techniques to the metadata directly. Unfortunately, there is a semantic gap between low-level visual features and high-level semantic concepts. The capability of bridging the semantic gap is the first requirement for existing mining tools to be used in video mining. To achieve this goal, some video mining strategies use closed-caption or speech recognition techniques; however, for videos that have no closed-caption or low audio signal quality (such videos represent a majority of the videos from our daily lives) these approaches are invalid [1,3]. On the other hand, most schemes use low-level features and various indexing strategies, e.g. Decision tree, R-tree, etc. for video content management. The results generated with these approaches may consist of thousands of internal nodes, which are consequently very difficult to comprehend and interpret. Moreover, the constructed tree structures do not make sense to database indexing and human perception. Detecting similar or unusual patterns is not the only objective for video mining. The current challenge is how to organize video data for effective mining. The capability of supporting more efficient video database indexing is the second requirement for existing mining tools to be applicable to video mining.

Security and privacy

As more and more techniques are developed to access video data, there is an urgent need for data protection. For example, one of the current challenges is to protect children from accessing inappropriate videos on the Internet. In addition, video data are often used in various environments with very different objectives. An effective video database management structure is needed to maintain data integrity and security. User-adaptive database access control is becoming an important topic in the areas of networks, database, national security, and social studies. Multilevel security is needed for access control of various video database applications. The capability of supporting a secure and organized video access is the third requirement for the existing mining tools to be applied to video data mining [4].

Video content structure mining

In general, most videos from daily life can be represented using a hierarchy of five levels (video, scene, group, shot and frame). To clarify our objective, we first present the definition of video content structure.

Definition 1: The video content structure is defined as a hierarchy of clustered scenes, video scenes, video groups and video shots (whose definitions are given below), increasing in granularity from top to bottom. Although there exist videos with very little content structure (such as sports videos, surveillance videos etc.), a content structure can be found in most videos from our daily lives.

Definition 2: In this paper, the video shot, video group, video scene, clustered scene, key frames and feature database are defined as follows:

- *A video shot*: is the simplest element in videos and films; it records the frames resulting from a single continuous running of the camera, from the moment it is turned on to the moment it is turned off. [6]
- *A video group*: is an intermediate entity between the physical shots and semantic scenes; examples of groups consist of temporally or spatially related video shots.

- *A video scene*: is a collection of semantically related and temporally adjacent groups depicting and conveying a high-level concept or story.
- *A clustered scene*: is a collection of visually similar video scenes that may be shown in various places in the video. [4]
- *Key Frame/candidate frame database*: The key frames obtained from the video shots are stored in the database. The keyframes, which are coming, are compared with the sample key frames in the database. If the particular key frame is satisfying the minimum criteria to be selected as a key frame then the frame is selected as a key frame. For this the minimum criteria will be support and confidence. [5]
- *Feature Database*: the feature database is useful for the store and retrieval of the particular feature of videos. These features are useful for the comparison purpose. Feature extraction includes two parts: **Temporal** and **Motion**. [4] These features are extracted from video shots and still image features, such as color, texture and shape, are extracted from key frames. These feature data are organized automatically using clustering methods, and its key frames can represent a video stream hierarchically. The features are extracted from the key frames and the features are matched with the features from other key frames and if matched then that particular video is identified and displayed.

An Architectural Framework for Video Retrieval

Video data mining is nowadays very important aspect for the detection and retrieval of special pattern, relation between them. This paper helps in designing a framework to find out the key frame/candidate signature from the video shot.

Core video is divided into the video shots. There are many shot detection techniques available which can be used for division of the core video. There are techniques, which are useful for detection of the shot 16 times faster.

Taking core video and divide the video into the number of frames with the help of the Mat lab. The features are extracted from the frame. There are many features, which is considered for the future use. Histogram, threshold, levels, color cube analysis, etc. are some features. This framework first extracts low-level feature, which will help in analysis.

This framework takes candidate frame as input from user. The user can select as many frames as a key frames. Now these key frames are stored into the temporary folder for storage. All the selected candidate images are stored here. Then two key frames are selected and difference image is calculated. Each candidate signature or key frame is then analyzed and all the features are extracted.

First key frame is taken and all the features are extracted such as threshold, color cube, levels, decomposition, and histogram analysis. In the same manner features for all the key frames are analyzed and find out.

Now all the features extracted are stored into the database. When next similar or different type of video comes that time the features of that particular video and the features, which are stored in the database, are compared and matched. If features are matched up to some extent then the video is identified as a previous video and the respective clip is displayed otherwise no matching clip will be shown.

The framework or architecture for video retrieval from key frames is shown in Figure 1.

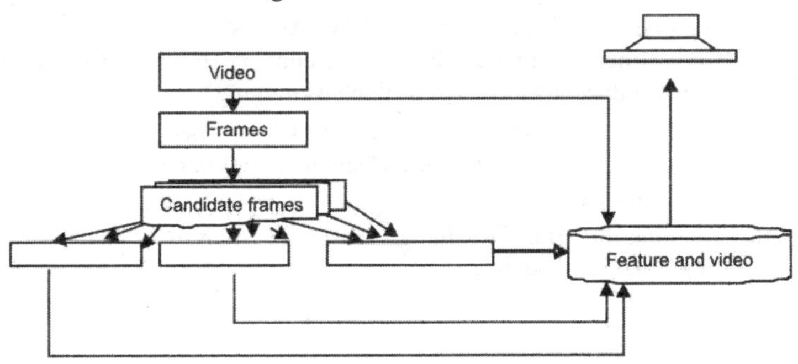

Fig. 1: Proposed architecture for Candidate frames analysis

CONCLUSIONS

In this paper, we have addressed the potential problems faced by various data mining tools when mining valuable information from video databases. These problems may be modeling video databases, organizing the video data for fast retrieval and problems related to security and privacy. Further we have discussed the definition of various terms to be used for designing the architectural framework for video retrieval from key frames extraction. Then in the last part of this paper we have designed the architectural framework for retrieval of video from key frame extraction for video mining of data. In this first we take the raw data of videos, which are then converted into frames, which will help in making the comparison between the key frames and the frame selected. Features of the frames are extracted and stored in the feature database, which ultimately leads to retrieval of valuable information of video data for video mining.

REFERENCES

1. Xingquan Zhu, Walid G. Aref, Jianping Fan, Ann C. Catlin and Ahmed K. Elmagarmid, "Medical Video mining for Efficient Database Indexing, Management and Access".
2. R. Agrawal, T. Imeielinski, and A. Swami, "Data mining: A performance perspective", *IEEE TKDE*, 5(6), 1993.
3. U. Fayyad and R. Uthurusamy, "Data mining and knowledge discovery in database", Communication of ACM, 39(11), 1996.
4. Xingquan Zhu, Jianping Fan, Walid G. Aref, Ahmed K. Elmagarmid, "ClassMiner: Mining medical video content structure and events towards efficient access and scalable skimming".
5. Shu-Ching Chen, Mei-Ling Shyu, Min Chen, Chengeui Zhang, "A decision Tree-based Multimodal Data Mining Framework for Soccer Goal Detection".
6. Di Zhong and Shih-Fu Chang, "Structure Analysis of sports video using Domain models".

Survey of Estimation of Network Reliability

28

Diwakar Bhardwaj and *Manu Pratap Singh*

ABSTRACT

Estimating the reliability of a computer network has been a subject of great interest. It is a well known fact that this problem is NP-hard. In this paper we present a survey on the various approaches of evaluating the network reliability. Remarkable work has been done for estimating the network reliability of a network with unreliable nodes or with unreliable edges or both at a time. There are combinatorial approach for Monte Carlo reliability estimation of a network, Tree cut and enumerate algorithm, Prepositional Directed Acyclic Graph (PDAG), algorithms using artificial neural network and some other using the concept of Graph Theory. The core of this paper is to discuss the features, characteristics as well as their comparative analysis of the different approaches.

INTRODUCTION TO THE PROBLEM

Reliability and cost are two important considerations when designing communications networks, especially backbone telecommunications networks, wide area networks, local area networks and data communications networks located in industrial facilities. If the nodes (stations, terminals or computer sites) of the network are fixed, the main design decisions are selection of the type and routing of links (cables or lines) of the network to ensure proper and reliable operation while meeting cost objectives. The following typically define the problem assumptions:

1. The location of each network node is given.

2. Nodes are perfectly reliable.
3. Link costs and reliabilities are fixed and known.
4. Each link is bi-directional.
5. There are no redundant links in the network.
6. Links are either operational or failed.
7. The failures of links are independent.
8. No repair is considered.

Mathematically, the design optimization problem can be expressed as:

Ñ1 N Minimize Z(x) =

□ □ cij xij

i □ 1 j □ i

s.t. R(x) □ Ro

where,

N number of nodes

(i,j) a link between nodes i and j

xij decision variable, e.g., xij□{0,1} for networks with identical link reliability

x a link topology of x12, ... , xij, ... , xN-1,N

R(x) reliability of x

Ro network reliability requirement

Z objective function cij cost of (i,j)

k is the number of choices for the links (assuming the links have the same number of choices).

For example, a ten node network (N = 10) with links of identical reliability (k = 2) has 3.5□1013 possible designs. A ten node network with five alternative link cost/reliability choices has 1035 possible designs. Clearly for networks of realistic size, a computationally expedient alternative to the exact network reliability calculation must be found to use during the design optimization procedure.

The network design problem is especially difficult when considering all-terminal network reliability (also called uniform or overall network reliability), defined as the probability that all nodes can communicate with all other nodes.

(This is equivalent to all-terminal stationary availability when a mission time is not implicitly assumed.) The difficulty arises because the exact calculation of all-terminal network reliability is NP-hard, that is, computational effort increases exponentially with network size [14]. One way to calculate the exact network reliability is to enumerate all possible minimal cut sets of a network as in [3]. Other similar approaches to exactly calculating network reliability are given in [2, 4, 22].These methods are not computationally practical for large networks since the fundamental step of enumeration of minimal cutsets is NP-hard [21]. Monte Carlo stochastic simulation methods can estimate network reliability very precisely [12, 27], however, simulation must be repeated numerous times to ensure a good estimate. Therefore, the simulation approach also incurs significant computational effort when estimating the reliability of the network, especially for highly reliable networks where failures are rare. In this paper we are discussing various approaches of estimating network reliability:

Monte Carlo Approach

Claim 1: Let N be a network with identical nodes and identical edges and with the k-connectivity criterion. Then its reliability may be expressed in the following form [1]:

$$R(n)=\sum_{\pi\in\Pi} f(\pi) \qquad (1)$$

Where

$$f(\pi)=\sum_{i=r(\pi)}^{n}\frac{1}{i!(n-i)}p_v^i q_v^{n-i}\sum_{j=s(\pi)}^{m}\frac{1}{j!(m-j)!}p_e^j q_j^{m-j} \qquad (2)$$

Where p_v and p_e are the node and edge for up probabilities, respectively.

Claim 2: Let N be a network with identical and unreliable nodes and with identical and unreliable edges. Suppose that the criterion is the residual connectedness. Then there are the following bounds for network reliability [1]:

$$\text{Rlow}(n) = \sum_{\pi\in\Pi} \text{flow}(\pi) \le R(N) \le \text{Rup}(N) \sum_{\pi\in\Pi} \text{fup}(\pi) \quad (3)$$

$$\text{Where flow}(\pi) = \frac{1}{\text{r}(\pi)!\,(n - r(\pi))!}\,\frac{1}{s(\pi)!\,(m - S(\pi))!} \times$$

$$pr(\pi)q\;n - r(\pi) \text{ and}$$

$$\text{Fup}(\pi) = \sum_{i=r(\pi)}^{n} \frac{1}{i!(n-i)!}\,pi\;q\;n - i \sum_{j=s(\pi)}^{m} \frac{1}{j!(m-j)!} \quad (4)$$

Draw Back: Computations increases exponentially with size.

Neural Networks for Reliability Estimation

Learning occurs because the error between the ANN output and the target output is calculated and used to adjust the weighted synapses. This continues until errors are small enough or no more weight changes are occurring. The ANN is then trained and the weights are fixed. The trained ANN can be used for new inputs to perform function approximation or classification tasks. (intercepts) are calculated by minimizing squared error over the data set, ANN weights are determined by minimizing error over the data set. However, there are also important dissimilarities between statistics and ANN. ANN have many free parameters (i.e. weighted connections). An ANN with five inputs, an intermediate (hidden) layer of five neurons and a single output has 36 trainable weights, where a simple multiple linear regression would have six (five slopes and an intercept). ANN can accommodate redundant free parameters rather well, but there is significant danger in over fitting an ANN model [15]. An overfitted ANN would be strongly dependent on the data set (sample) used to build it, and may poorly reflect the underlying relationship (population). Therefore, thorough validation of ANN using data not used in training is essential.

An important property of ANN, under certain conditions, is that they are universal approximators [13, 16, 26]. This means that the bias associated with choosing a functional form, as is done in regression analysis when a linear relationship is selected, is minimized. This is a substantial advantage over traditional statistical prediction models, as the relationship between network topology and all-terminal reliability is highly non-linear with significant, but complex, interactions among the links.

In this approach, ANN are developed, or trained, based on the all-terminal reliability of a very small set of possible network topologies and link reliabilities for a given number of nodes. The resulting ANN is used to estimate network reliability as a function of the link reliabilities and the topology during the search for the optimal topology. In this way, estimates of the reliability of numerous topologies are available without costly calculation or simulation. A disadvantage of using ANN as a reliability evaluator is that the reliability prediction is only an estimate that may be subject to bias and/or variance depending on the adequacy of the ANN. A similar approach was used for design of series-parallel systems when considering cost and reliability [7], however it had less practical utility because reliability of series-parallel systems can be exactly calculated quite easily with closed form mathematical expressions.

Training and Validating the Neural Networks

A back propagation training algorithm [25] was selected because of its powerful approximation capacity and its applicability to both binary and continuous inputs. The number of

□ N (N ? 1) □

nodes in the network, and thus the number of possible links □

□ □ , for a given ANN was fixed.

2 □

Networks with Identical Link Reliability

Limiting the links chosen to be in a network topology to those with the same reliability (i.e., k=2) simplifies the problem of estimating network reliability because the number of possible topologies grows exponentially with an increase in k (see equation 1). In this case, if xij = 1, the link is chosen for the network topology and if xij = 0, no link is present. However, to make the ANN more applicable to a variety of design problems, five different values of link reliability were chosen to be included in a single ANN. For the problems studied, these link reliability values are 0.80, 0.85, 0.90, 0.95 and 0.99. To clarify, the ANN in this section would be appropriate for network design problems using any of these five link reliabilities, however, for a given design problem all links must have the same reliability. This is relaxed in the next section where networks with varying link reliabilities are considered.

The inputs to the ANN were:

1. The architecture of the network as indicated by a series of binary variables (xij).

   The length of the string of 0's and 1's is equal to N (N ? 1).
2. The link reliability (0.80, 0.85, 0.90, 0.95, 0.99).
3. The calculated upperbound using the method of [19, 20].

The upperbound calculation, while adding computational effort of O(N3), significantly improved the estimation precision of the ANN. Without the upper bound as an input, the errors of the ANN reported in section 4 were nearly doubled. Any upper bound could be used, such as that in [17], however the one chosen is rather unique in that it is applicable to networks with links with different reliability values, and it has been shown to more precise than other bounds that could accommodate links of different reliabilities [19, 20].

The output of the ANN was the estimated all-terminal network reliability. For the training and validation sets, the target network reliability was the exact value as calculated using the backtracking technique of [3]. This procedure essentially enumerates the cutsets and calculates the network unreliablity, (1-R(x)), as detailed below:

Step 0: (Initialization). Mark all links as free; create a stack that is initially empty.

Step 1: (Generate modified cutset)

(a) Find a set of free links that together with all inoperative links will form a network-cut.

(b) Mark all the links found in 1(a) inoperative and add them to the stack.

(c) The stack now represents a modified cutset; add its probability to a cumulative sum.

Step 2: (Backtrack)

(a) If the stack is empty, end.

(b) Take a link off the top of the stack.

(c) If the link is inoperative and if when made operative, a spanning tree of operative links exists, then mark it free and go to 2(a).

(d) If the link is inoperative and the condition tested in 2(c) does not hold, then mark it operative, put it back on the stack and go to Step 1.

(e) If the link is operative, then mark it free and go to 2(a).

A node size of ten was chosen to investigate the approach of this paper. A set of 750 network topologies were randomly generated (ensuring each network formed at least a spanning tree, i.e., $R(x) > 0$) with 150 observations of each link reliability. Remembering that the total number of network designs that could be handled by this ANN is 5 □ 245 or 1.7 □ 1014, 750 is an exceedingly small sample indeed. The upperbound of each network topology and the exact network reliability were calculated to use as an input and as the target output, respectively. After preliminary experiments, a network architecture of 47 inputs (45 possible arcs, the link reliability and the network upperbound), 47 hidden neurons in one hidden layer and a single output was used. Because most actual network topology designs will be highly reliable, it is important that the reliability estimation be precise when R(x) □ 0.90. If the first ANN (just described) estimated a reliability of 0.90 or greater, the network topology, the link reliability and the upperbound were input to the second, specialized ANN, as shown in Figure 1. This ANN was trained on 250 randomly generated topologies (using the same five link reliabilities) that had actual all-terminal reliabilities of 0.90 or greater. As in the general ANN, there were equal number (50) observations of each link reliability in the data set. Also as in the general ANN, a five-fold grouped cross validation procedure was used for ANN training and validation. The ANN architecture was the same as the first network. Using the network reliability estimate from the first ANN as an additional input to the specialized ANN was tried, but this did not improve predictive performance of the specialized ANN.

Networks with Varying Link Reliability

Allowing links of different reliability within a single network topology is an important real world consideration. It does greatly expand the number of possible network topologies, complicating both the network design problem and the estimation of all-terminal network reliability. Using the same set of five link reliabilities from section 3.1, networks with mixes of these were randomly generated (using equal probability on each link type). For these networks, k = 6 (i.e., one of the five reliability values or 0, which indicates the link is not present in the network topology). To clarify, the ANN in this section would be appropriate for network design problems using any of these five link reliabilities in any combination. The binary topology inputs of section 3.1 are no longer applicable. Instead, the reliability value of each link is input (0, 0.80, 0.85, 0.90, 0.95, 0.99) and the input of the single link reliability from section 3.1 is eliminated, leaving 46 inputs for a ten node network.

The inputs to the ANN were:

1. The architecture of the network as indicated by a series of real valued variables(xij). The length of the string is equal to N (N ? 1) .
2. The calculated upperbound using the method of [19, 20] of the network.

As in section 3.1, 750 randomly generated network topologies were used for training and validating the ANN and the exact all-terminal network reliability using backtracking [3] was used as the target. The ANN architecture used 46 hidden neurons in a single hidden layer and a single output. Also, as in section 3.1, the strategy of a general ANN for all network topologies and a specialized ANN for highly reliable (□ 0.90) networks was used. The specialized networks were trained and validated using a set of 250 randomly generated topologies. Again, there were 46 inputs to the neural network, a single output and 46 hidden neurons in one hidden layer.

COMPUTATIONAL RESULTS

Networks with Identical Link Reliability

Tables 1 and 2 give the five-fold results in root mean squared error (RMSE) for the general ANN and the specialized ANN, respectively, for networks with identical link reliability (those described in section 3.1). It can be seen that the ANN estimations always improve upon the upperbound estimates, sometimes significantly. Furthermore, the errors of the specialized ANN are much less than that of the general ANN, allowing a more precise network reliability estimation for those topologies that are likely to be considered the best. Figure 2 shows an example of one of the five-fold validations comparing the estimation of the ANN on the test set with the actual reliability while Figure 3 shows the same for the specialized ANN. It can be seen that the predictions of the ANN are unbiased and are quite precise. Where the general ANN is less precise (at R(x) □ 0.90), the specialized ANN does a much better job. The mean absolute error (MAE) of the application general ANN is 0.036 and the MAE of the application specialized ANN is 0.007. Of course, these errors may be positive or negative since an ANN is an unbiased estimator while the upperbound errors will always be positive.

A statistical analysis of the estimations of the ANN and the upperbound with the exact network reliability showed that the ANN was statistically closer to the exact value. Specifically, an ANOVA for the general ANN over the 750 test observations was significant with a p value of < 0.0000. A Tukey test for mean differences at □ = 0.05 resulted in the exact reliability from backtracking and the ANN in the same statistical group while the upperbound formed a second group. A paired t test between the exact value and the ANN had a p value of 0.0183 with a mean difference of –0.0041 while a paired t test between the exact value and the upperbound had a p value of < 0.0000 and a mean difference of –0.0515. For the specialized ANN using the 250 test observations, the ANOVA had a p value of 0.0019 and the ANN and the exact values were again in one statistical group using the Tukey test at □ = 0.05, while the upperbound formed a second group.

The paired t test between the exact reliability and the ANN estimation had a p value of 0.0527 with a mean difference of –0.0012 while the paired t test between the exact value and the upperbound had a p value of < 0.0000 with a mean difference of –0.0082.

Networks with Varying Link Reliability

This problem is much harder than that described in the preceding section, however the ANN prediction performed well. Table 3 gives the results over the five-fold cross validation for the general purpose ANN while Table 4 gives the same results for the specialized ANN. It can be seen that the RMS error of the ANN is still significantly less than that of the upperbound. A graphic view shows that the ANN estimate is unbiased while the upperbound estimate is biased upwards, of course (Figure 4). Figures 5 and 6 show the absolute error of the ANN versus the error of the upperbound for the first fold of the test set for the general and specialized ANN, respectively. It can be easily seen that while the upperbound sometimes performs better than the ANN, the maximum errors of the ANN are much less. That is, the worst cases of the ANN are much better estimates than the worst cases of the upperbound. This has practical importance since a large error may badly mislead the optimization search where small errors will not. Therefore, the ANN can engender a more reliable search than the upperbound. As in the preceding section, a statistical analysis of the estimations of the ANN and the upperbound with the exact network reliability showed that the ANN was statistically closer to the exact value. The ANOVA for the general ANN over the 750 test observations was significant with a p value of < 0.0000. A Tukey test for mean differences at □ = 0.05 grouped the exact reliability from backtracking and the ANN together while the upperbound formed a separate group. A paired t test between the exact value and the ANN had a p value of 0.0195 with a mean difference of –0.0054 while a paired t test between the exact value and the upperbound had a p value of < 0.0000 and a mean difference of –0.0511. For the specialized ANN using the 250 test observations, the ANOVA had a p value of 0.0032 and the ANN and the exact values were again in one statistical group using the Tukey test at □ = 0.05, while the upperbound formed another. The paired t test between the exact value and the ANN had a p value of 0.6682 (not statistically different) with a mean difference of –0.00027 while the paired t test between the exact value and the upperbound had a p value of < 0.0000 with a mean difference of –0.00746.

Conclusions and Discussion

The ANN approach to estimating all-terminal reliability worked well. Using an extremely small fraction of the possible network topologies for a ten node problem, a general ANN and a specialized ANN were trained and validated. Subsequent use of the ANN during network design optimization will be basically computationally "free". The recommended approach is to use the ANN estimation during the optimization for all topologies considered and then exactly calculate 1 the network reliability on only the optimal topology, or the few best topologies. In this way, almost all of the computational effort of reliability calculation is eliminated while maintaining a workable design optimization method.

It is likely that confining the ANN for networks with identical link reliability to only a single link reliability would further improve its precision, however this would reduce flexibility during the design phase. Another alteration is to not randomly generate the network topologies for training and validation, but use a design of experiments to obtain a balance of topologies with different number of links, node degrees, reliabilities, etc. As a further extension, this methodology may work using function approximation methods other than neural networks, such as regression or spline fitting. Finally, this approach of substituting a computationally expedient approximation for the exact objective function calculation in iterative optimization can be feasible and effective for many problems. The important issues are to develop an approximation that is precise enough, especially in the search space regions of greatest interest, and saves sufficient computational effort to make the sacrifice of the exact objective function calculation worthwhile or, alternatively, estimate it accurately with Monte Carlo simulation.

Network Topology, Link Reliability and Reliability Upper Bound

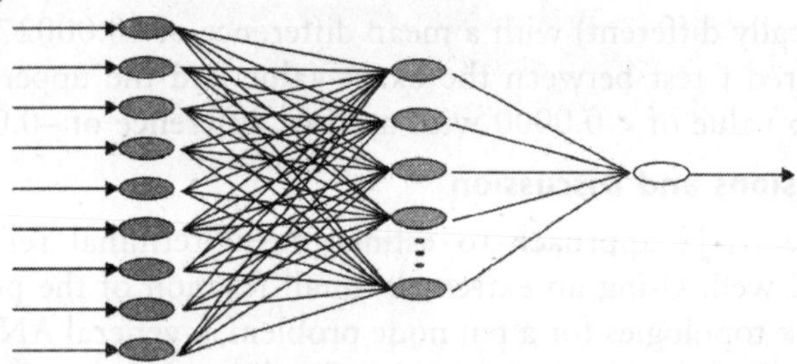

General ANN Estimate of Network Reliability If estimate □ 0.90
Network Topology, Link Reliability and Reliability Upper Bound

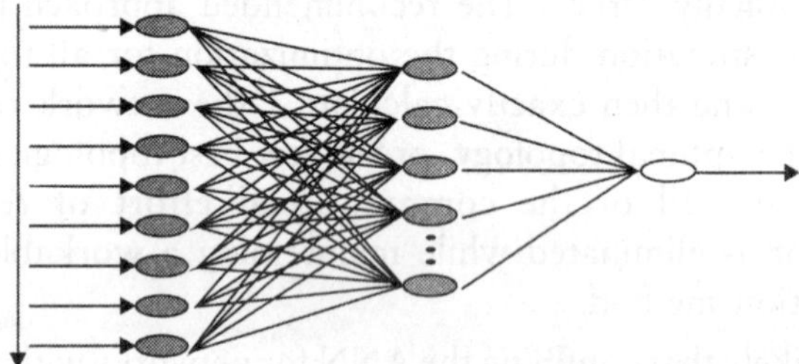

Estimate of Network Reliability Specialized ANN

Fig. 1: The Hierarchy of a General ANN and a Specialized ANN

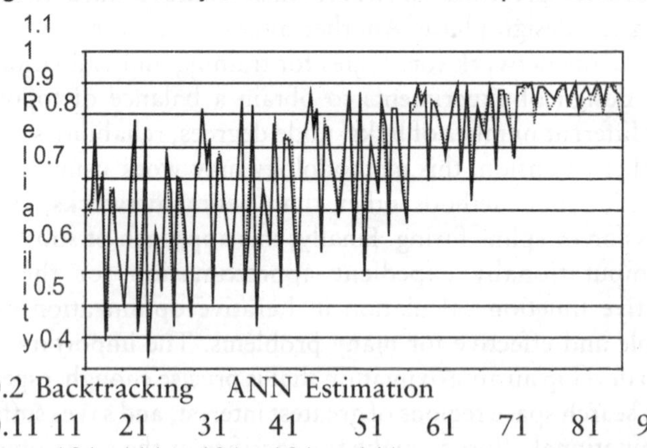

Network Topology (Test Set)

Fig. 2: General Neural Network Estimation of Reliability versus Actual (Backtracking) Reliability on the Fifth Test Fold for Networks with Identical Link Reliability.

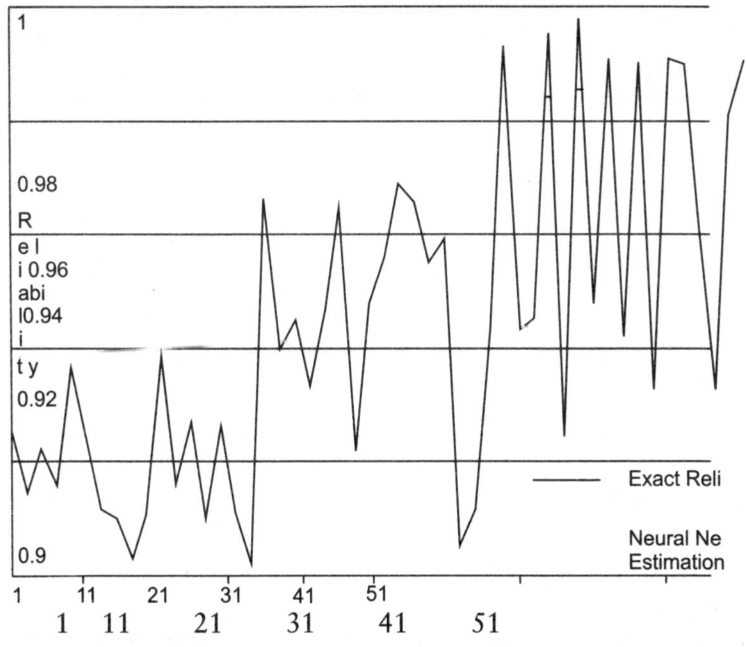

Fig. 3: Specialized Neural Network Estimation of Reliability versus Actual Reliability on the First Test Fold for Networks with Identical Link Reliability.

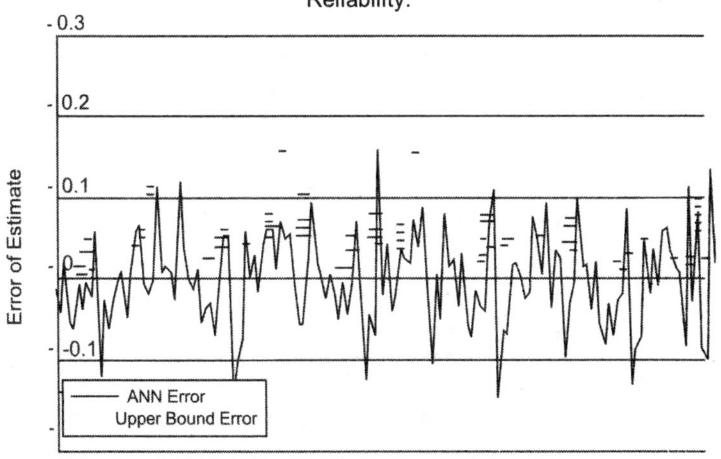

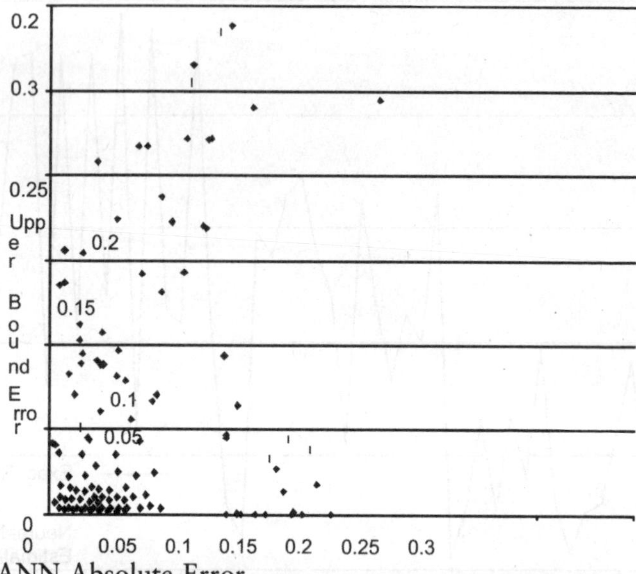

Fig. 4: General Neural Network Absolute Estimation Error (x axis) versus Upper Bound Error (y axis) on the First Test Fold for Networks with Varying Link Reliability.

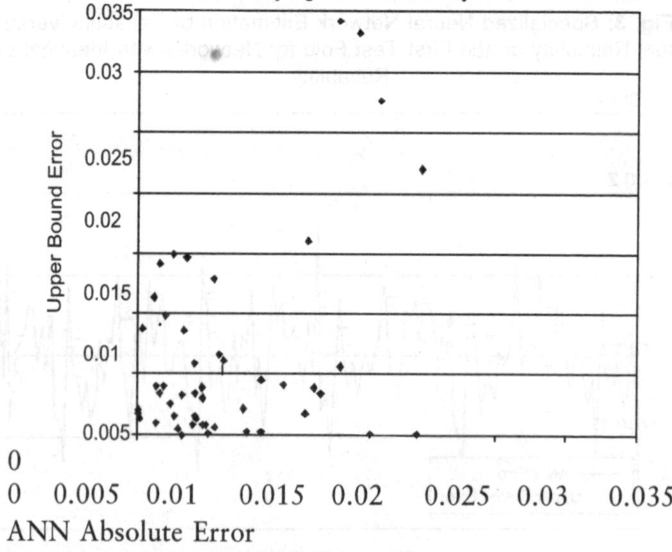

Fig. 5: Specialized Neural Network Absolute Estimation Error (x axis) versus Upper Bound Error (y axis) on the First Test Fold for Networks with Varying Link Reliability.

Table 1: Errors for the General Neural Network with Identical Link Reliability

Fold	RMSE Training	RMSE Testing	RMSE Upperbound
Set1	0.03672	0.04260	0.08875
Set2	0.03073	0.05004	0.08954
Set3	0.03444	0.03067	0.07158
Set4	0.03123	0.05666	0.07312
Set5	0.03173	0.05131	0.08800
Average	0.03297	0.04626	0.08220

Table 2: Errors for the Specialized Neural Network with Identical Link Reliability

Fold	RMSE Training	RMSE Testing	RMSE Upperbound
Set1	0.00664	0.00688	0.01232
Set2	0.00583	0.01271	0.01371
Set3	0.00630	0.00892	0.00908
Set4	0.00629	0.00795	0.00927
Set5	0.00555	0.01125	0.01598
Average	0.00612	0.00954	0.01207

Table 3: Errors for the General Neural Network with Varying Link Reliability

Fold	RMSE Training	RMSE Testing	RMSE Upperbound
Set1	0.04562	0.05869	0.08880
Set2	0.04332	0.07042	0.10325
Set3	0.04813	0.04758	0.06856
Set4	0.04562	0.06454	0.07523
Set5	0.04249	0.07177	0.09908
Average	0.04504	0.06260	0.08698

Table 4: Errors for the Specialized Neural Network with Varying Link Reliability

Fold	RMSE Training	RMSE Testing	RMSE Upperbound
Set1	0.00817	0.00823	0.01031
Set2	0.00726	0.01211	0.01376
Set3	0.00781	0.00927	0.01401
Set4	0.00792	0.00902	0.01127
Set5	0.00763	0.01037	0.01451
Average	0.00776	0.00980	0.01277

Reliability Estimation Using Neural Optimization Approaches

We consider the network as a neuron model for the units of feedback network, where theoutput of each unit is fed to all the other units with weights w_{ij}, for all *i* and *j*. The output function of each of the units is binary (either 0 or 1) so that

$$<s^i> = f(x^i) = \mathrm{sgn}(x^i), \quad (1)$$

and

$$\sum_{x^i=j=1}^{N} w_{ij} < s_j > -\theta_i \quad (2)$$

Where θ_i is the threshold for the unit *i*. We have assume $\theta_i = 0$ for all *i*.

We have considered asynchronously updation of unit of a state, where a unit is selected at random and its new state is computed. Another unit is selected at random and its state is updated using the current state of the network and this updation continues until no further change in the state takes place for all units. That is, the state at time (*t*+1) is same as the state at time *t* for all units. That is

$$<s^i(t+1)> = <s^i(t), \qquad \text{for all } i \quad (3)$$

A stochastic network will evolve differently each time it is run, in the sense that the trajectory of the state of the network becomes a sample function of random process. So, there will never be a static stable state but a dynamic equilibrium for a stochastic network, if the ensemble average state of the network does not change with time. The ensemble average means that for several (infinitely large) runs of the network the average value of the state (<*s*>) of the network are computed. The average of the state is given in term s of the average value (<s^i>) of the output of each unit (*i*) of the network. That is,

$$\langle s^i \rangle = \int s_i p(s_1, s_2, \ldots\ldots, s_i, \ldots\ldots, s_N)\, ds_1 ds_2 \ldots ds_i \ldots ds_N \qquad (4)$$

Where $p(s) = p(..s^1, s^2, \ldots, s^1 \ldots, s^N)$ is the joint probability density function of the component of the state vectors.

The probability distribution of states should be stationary or independent of time for a network sate to be in a stochastic equilibrium. If stationarity of the probability distribution of state is achieved at a given temperature, then network is in thermal equilibrium [11].

To speed up the process of simulated annealing, the mean-field annealing approximation is used [18], in which the stochastic update of the binary units is replaced by deterministic analog state [19]. In mean-field approximation the fluctuating value activation values of each unit is replaced by its average value.. That is x is replaced by <x^i>.

$$\langle x^i \rangle = \left\langle \sum_j w_{ij}\, s_j \right\rangle = \sum_j w_{ij} \langle s_j \rangle \qquad (5)$$

Where <s^i> represents the expectation or average of the random quantities.

Similarly, the average of the state of the ith unit is given by

$$\langle s^i \rangle = \tanh\left(x^i / T\right), \qquad (6)$$

From eq. (5) and (6), we have

$$\langle s^i \rangle = \left(\frac{1}{T} \sum_j w_{ij} \langle s_j \rangle \right) \tanh \qquad (7)$$

The mean-field approximation for the eq. (3) can be given as

$$< s^i(t+1) > = \tanh\left(\sum_{j=1}^{N} w_{ij} < s_j(t) > \right), i = 1, 2, \ldots\ldots, N \; (8)$$

Using above approach we propose an energy function (E) to evaluate the reliability of the network, as follows:

Where <s^i> is the expectation of the ith unit and P(s^i) is the probability of the output of the ith unit in the network.

On updation of kth unit in the network, the change in energy can be given as

$$E_1^{old} = -\frac{1}{2}\sum_i\sum_j w_{ij}\langle s_i\rangle^{old}\langle s_j\rangle^{old} + \sum_i\langle s_i\rangle^{old}\theta_i - \frac{1}{2}\sum_i\sum_k w_{ik}\langle s_i\rangle^{old}\langle s_k\rangle^{old} - \frac{1}{2}\sum_j\sum_k w_{jk}\langle s_j\rangle^{old}\langle s_k\rangle^{old} + \sum_k\langle s_k\rangle^{old}\theta_k \quad (10)$$

$$E_1^{new} = -\frac{1}{2}\sum_i\sum_j w_{ij}\langle s_j\rangle^{new}\langle s_j\rangle^{new} + \sum_i\langle s_i\rangle^{new}\theta_i - \frac{1}{2}\sum_i\sum_k w_{ik}\langle s_i\rangle^{new}\langle s_k\rangle^{new} - \frac{1}{2}\sum_j\sum_k w_{jk}\langle s_j\rangle^{new}\langle s_k\rangle^{new} + \sum_k\langle s_k\rangle^{new}\theta_k \quad (11)$$

$$\Delta E_1 = E_1^{new} - E_1^{old} \quad (12)$$

$$= -\langle\Delta s_k\rangle\left(\sum w_{ik}\langle s_i\rangle - \theta_i\right) \quad (13)$$

As $\theta_i = 0$ for all i in our case, so

$$\Delta E_1 = -\langle\Delta s_k\rangle\left(\sum w_{ik}\langle s_i\rangle\right) \quad (14)$$

Where $\langle\Delta s_k\rangle$ can be given as

$$\langle\Delta s_k\rangle = P(s^i = 1|x^i) - P(s^i = 0|x^i)$$

or $$= P(s^i = 0|x\ ) - P(s^i = 1|x^i) \quad (15)$$

Where as the change in energy due to second term can be given as

$$E_2^{old} = -\frac{1}{2}\sum_i P(s_i)^{old}P(s_j)^{old}w_{ij} - \frac{1}{2}\sum_i P(s_i)^{old}P(s_k)^{old}w_{ik} -$$

$$\frac{1}{2}\sum_j P\left(s_j\right)^{old} P\left(s_k\right)^{old} w_{jk} \tag{16}$$

$$E_2^{new} = -\frac{1}{2}\sum_i P(s_i)^{new} P(s_j)^{new} w_{ij} - \frac{1}{2}\sum_i P(s_i)^{new} P(s_k)^{new} w_{ik} -$$

$$\frac{1}{2}\sum_j P\left(s_j\right)^{new} P\left(s_k\right)^{new} w_{jk} \tag{17}$$

$$\Delta E_2 = E_2^{new} - E_2^{old} \tag{18}$$

$$= -\Delta P\left(s_k\right)\left[\sum w_{ik} P\left(s_i\right)\right] \tag{19}$$

Total change in energy, from eq. (14) and (19)

$$\Delta E = \Delta E_1 + \Delta E_2 \tag{20}$$

This energy function will be minimum, if the term $<\Delta s_k>$ and $\Delta P(s_k)$ are positive i.e. for $< \Delta s_k >$ to be positive, we should have

$$P(s^i = 1|x^i) - P(s^i = 0|x^i) > P(s^i = 0|x^i)$$

Or

$$P(s^i = 0|x^i) - P(s^i = 1|x\ ) > P(s^i = 1|x^i)$$

and $\Delta P\left(s_k\right)$ to be positive, we should have

$$P(s^i = 1|x^i) - P(s^i = 0|x^i) > P(s^i = 0|x^i)$$

Where $P(s^i = 1|x^i) = \dfrac{1}{1 + \exp\left(-x_i - \theta\right)/T}$

CONCLUSION

It has been proved that evolutionary approaches are much better than the traditional approaches. Estimating Network reliability using neural network approaches are much efficient as compared to combinatorial approaches because the computational efforts grows exponentially with size in combinatorial approaches.

REFERENCES

1. K.K. Aggarwal, Y.C. Chopra and J.S. Bajwa, "Topological layout of links for optimising the overall reliability in a computer communication system," Microelectronics and Reliability, Vol. 22, 1982, pp. 347-351.

2. K.K. Aggarwal and S. Rai, "Reliability evaluation in computer-communication networks," IEEE Transactions on Reliability, Vol. R-30, 1981 Apr, pp. 32-35.
3. M. Ball and R.M. Van Slyke, "Backtracking algorithms for network reliability analysis," Annals of Discrete Mathematics, Vol. 1, 1977, pp. 49-64.
4. J.K. Cavers, "Cutset manipulations for communication network reliability estimation," IEEE Transactions on Communications, Vol. Com-23, 1975 Jun, pp. 569-575.
5. B. Cheng and D.M. Titterington, "Neural networks: A review from a statistical perspective," Statistical Science, Vol. 9, 1994, pp. 2-54.
6. Y.C. Chopra, B.S. Sohi, R.K. Tiwari and K.K. Aggarwal, "Network topology for maximizing the terminal reliability in a computer communication network," Microelectronics & Reliability, Vol. 24, 1984, pp. 911-913.
7. D.W. Coit and A.E. Smith, "Solving the redundancy allocation problem using a combined neural network/genetic algorithm approach," Computers and Operations Research, Vol. 23, 1996, pp. 515-526.
8. D.L. Deeter and A.E. Smith, "Heuristic optimization of network design considering all-terminal reliability," Proceedings of the Reliability and Maintainability Symposium, 1997, pp. 194-199.
9. D.L. Deeter and A.E. Smith, "Economic design of reliable networks," IIE Transactions, Vol. 30, 1998, in print.
10. B. Dengiz, F. Altiparmak and A.E. Smith, "Efficient optimization of all-terminal reliable networks using an evolutionary approach," IEEE Transactions on Reliability, Vol. 46, 1997, pp. 18-26.
11. B. Dengiz, F. Altiparmak and A.E. Smith, "Local search genetic algorithm for optimal design of reliable networks," IEEE Transactions on Evolutionary Computation, Vol. 1, 1997, pp. 179-188.
12. G.S. Fishman, "A Monte Carlo sampling plan for estimating network reliability," Operations Research, Vol. 34, 1986, pp. 581-594.
13. K. Funahashi, "On the approximate realization of continuous mappings by neural networks," Neural Networks, Vol. 2, 1989, pp. 183-192.
14. M.R. Garey and D. S. Johnson, Computers and Intractability: A Guide to the Theory of NP- Completeness, W.H. Freeman and Co., San Francisco, 1979.
15. S. Geman, E. Bienenstock and R. Doursat, "Neural networks and the bias/variance dilemma," Neural Computation, Vol. 4, 1992, pp. 1-58.

16. K. Hornik, M. Stinchcombe and H. White, "Multilayer feedforward networks are universal approximators," Neural Networks, Vol. 2, 1989, pp. 359-366.

17. R.H. Jan, "Design of reliable networks," Computers and Operations Research, Vol. 20, 1993, pp. 25-34.

18. R.H. Jan, F.J. Hwang and S.T. Chen, "Topological optimization of a communication network subject to a reliability constraint," IEEE Transactions on Reliability, Vol. 42, 1993, pp. 63-70.

19. A. Konak and A.E. Smith, "A general upperbound for all-terminal network reliability and its uses," Proceedings of the Industrial Engineering Research Conference, Banff, Canada, May 1998, CD Rom format.

20. A. Konak and A.E. Smith, "An improved general upperbound for all-terminal network reliability," in revision at IIE Transactions.

21. J.S. Provan and M.O. Ball, "The complexity of counting cuts and of computing the probability that a graph is connected," SIAM Journal of Computing, Vol. 12, 1983 Nov., pp. 777-788.

22. S. Rai, "A cutset approach to reliability evaluation in communication networks," IEEE Transactions on Reliability, Vol. R-31, 1982 Dec, pp. 428-431.

23. J.M. Twomey and A.E. Smith, "Bias and variance of validation methods for function approximation neural networks under conditions of sparse data," IEEE Transactions on Systems, Man, and Cybernetics, Part C, Vol. 28, August 1998, pp. 417-430.

24. A.N. Venetsanopoulos and I. Singh, "Topological optimization of communication networks subject to reliability constraints," Problem of Control and Information Theory, Vol. 15, 1986, pp. 63-78.

25. Paul J. Werbos, Beyond Regression: New Tools for Prediction and Analysis in the Behavioral Sciences, unpublished Ph.D. Thesis, Harvard University, 1974.

26. H. White, "Connectionist nonparametric regression: Multilayer feedforward networks can learn arbitrary mappings," Neural Networks, Vol. 3, 1990, pp. 535-549.

27. M.S. Yeh, J.S. Lin and W.C. Yeh, "A new Monte Carlo method for estimating network reliability," Proceedings of the 16th International Conference on Computers & Industrial Engineering, 1994, pp. 723-726.

28. Y. Shpungin [2006], Combinatorial approach to reliability evaluation of network with Unreliable nodes and Unreliable edges, International journal of Computer Science Vol. 1 Number 3.

29. Kin-Ping Hui [2005], "Network Reliability Estimation", Ph.D. dissertation, Faculty of Engineering, Computer and Mathematical Science, University of Adelaide.
30. M Lomonsov, Y. Shpungin [1999], "Combinatorics of reliability Monte Carlo",, Random Structure and Algorithms, No. 4, pp. 329-343.
31. C.J. Colburn, "The Combinatorics of Network Reliability , Oxford University Press.
32. F.T. Boesch [1988], "A survey and introduction to network reliability theory", IEEE, University of Amslerdam.
33. Chat Srivaree-Ratana and Alice E. Smith, "Estimating all terminal network reliability Using Neural Network".

Possible Optimization Approaches of Network Search Algorithm in GSM+UMTS Environment

29

Tathagato Mukhopadhyay and *Balaram Bhattacharyya*

ABSTRACT

3GPP has defined several frequency bands for deployment of GSM and UMTS across the globe. GSM and UMTS cells operating in different frequency bands can co-exist in the same geographical area. Each mobile User Equipment (UE) is capable of supporting a subset of frequency bands defined in the standards. At power-on, UE needs to search for cells belonging to its preferred operator. Several other triggers are there to perform similar search. Without prior knowledge on carrier frequencies, searching for available UMTS cells in a geographical area involves significant amount of processing load. However, appropriately designed storage and retrieval mechanism of possible carrier information may reduce it substantially. Reduced processing is particularly useful for roaming UE's to improve average standby time. This paper describes some techniques of storing and usage of carrier frequency information during cell search.

INTRODUCTION

Third-Generation Partnership Project (3GPP) has defined 10 frequency bands for deployment of Universal Mobile Terrestrial System – Frequency Division Duplex (UMTS-FDD) across the globe. Each frequency band contains a range of carrier frequencies for each of uplink and downlink. Bandwidth of each UMTS-FDD carrier is 5MHz. Thus, if the central frequency of a UMTS FDD carrier is F_c, spectral limit of the carrier is between F_c-2.5 MHz to F_c+2.5 MHz. Each standardized frequency band for UMTS-FDD system uniquely defines the following parameters:

A lower bound (F_L) in MHz,

An upper bound (F_H) in MHz,

UMTS Assigned Radio Frequency Carrier Number (UARFCN) mapping. Central frequencies of UMTS FDD carriers can be aligned to a 200 KHz raster within the range. Each frequency value aligned to a 200 KHz raster within F_L and F_H is mapped to an unique number between 0 – 65535. These numbers are known by UARFCN numbers. There can be upto $(F_H - F_L)*5$ different UARFCN numbers within a frequency band. Mapping scheme between frequency values in MHz and UARFCN numbers vary between different frequency bands.

Special carrier frequencies (optional). Certain frequency bands define a set of special central frequencies aligned to 100 KHz raster. Each of these special carrier frequencies are mapped to one unique UARFCN number.

An UMTS UE stores the above parameters for each frequency band supported by it, and it is not necessary for each UE to support all 10 frequency bands. However, UE may support different UMTS frequency band combinations. Most of the UE's supporting UMTS support GSM-GPRS also. In a typical present day deployment scenario, an operator is allocated a spectrum pair of 5, 10 or 15 MHz within a frequency band, and normally the operators prefer to deploy a combination of GSM and UMTS cells in a geographical area. There can be at most 1 UMTS carrier frequency within a 5 MHz spectrum, and 2 and 3 within 10 MHz and 15 MHz spectrums respectively.

In a particular area, when an UE is powered on, or it is roaming from one network coverage area to the another, it needs to search for cells belonging to its preferred operator. The entire network system belonging to a mobile operator in a large geographical area (a state or metro city in India, for example) is identified by an unique Public Land Mobile Network Identity (PLMN Id). Each PLMN Id contains 3 BCD digits of Mobile Country Code (MCC) and 2 to 3 digits of Mobile Network Code (MNC). In Release 6 and Release 7 UMTS networks, a cell might belong to one or more PLMN's. Broadcast channel of each cell carries PLMN Id's of each PLMN to which the cell belongs. PLMN-id's corresponding to one or more cellular operators are stored in the Universal Subscriber Identity Module (USIM) in each UE. USIMs are enhanced version of SIM-cards used in GSM mobiles. A preference order of PLMNs in the USIM is maintained depending on subscription profile, service profile, charging information etc. UE needs to attempt to find a PLMN according to that priority order. If UE finds a suitable cell belonging to a preferred PLMN, it needs to perform a registration procedure with the PLMN through control plane signalling. So, UE needs to perform the following steps to find out if there is coverage of a preferred operator in a geographical area:

1. Search for possible FDD carriers. In absence of any prior information, UE needs to scan all supported FDD frequency bands one by one. Within each band, for each downlink UARFCN, UE needs to check if the corresponding frequency value is the centre frequency of a potential FDD carrier. For example, for UMTS frequency band 1, F_L = 2110 MHz, F_H = 2170 MHz, UARFCN_Low = 10550, UARFCN_High = 10850. There are 300 UARFCN values within frequency band 1. So, UE needs to perform a check for potential FDD carriers 300 times within frequency band 1.
2. Once a potential FDD carrier is found, UE needs to search for cells on the carrier. There can be more than one neighbouring cells on a single UMTS FDD carrier.
3. Once the set of cells is found, UE needs to listen to the broadcast information of each cell to find out the PLMN id of the cell.
4. If the UE supports multiple frequency bands, the above three steps need to be performed for each supported band.

The above steps are highly processing intensive for UMTS. So, if this search is to be performed several times a day due to various triggers, average standby time for UE comes down. Also, the user experiences annoying delay between switching on the mobile and getting the service availability indication. The amount of processing and processing delay may come down significantly, if some intelligent techniques are used to limit the region of search to some chosen frequency values or ranges.

Brief Review of Prior Work

In 3GPP, since the beginning of radio subsystem standardization, there has been several discussions on this topic. It is largely suggested that UE should store some data on possible UMTS carrier frequency values based on previous searches or measurements on a non-volatile storage (Universal subscriber identity module (USIM) or some non-volatile memory area (NVM)) to be used across power-on cycles. A provision has been made in the specification of Radio Resource Control (RRC) protocol to optionally include carrier frequency information into certain downlink messages. However, no specific scheme of storage and retrieval of carrier frequency information has been standardised by 3GPP. Thus, UE implementers are free to choose an appropriate optimised technique based on their memory and processing capabilities.

Problem statement: This paper intends to determine possible approaches of optimizing network search for UE by localising the frequency and cell search region depending on different triggers.

Method

Some network search triggers and possible optimizations

As per standard, an UE needs to search for PLMNs in the following scenarios:

1. *During power-on, search for last-registered PLMN*: When the UE is powered-on, it needs to search for the PLMN with which it was registered before being powered down. Once registered to a particular PLMN, UE gets to know about neighbouring cell information through several control plane signalling. If UE can collate and store this information in a non-volatile storage (USIM or NVM) before power-off, the same can be accessed by UE during next power-on. Best way to store the carrier frequency and frequency band

information is by storing corresponding UARFCN numbers.

2. *During power-on, last registered PLMN not found*: This possibility arises if the user has moved from the coverge area of previous PLMN to a new area (for example in India, the user has moved from one state to the other one keeping his mobile switched off). UE needs to search for the PLMNs listed in PLMN list in USIM. If the UE retains the observed carrier frequency and band information obtained from earlier roaming instances, limited search on those stored carrier frequencies can be successful. Scan on entire range can be resorted to only after detecting failure of stored information search. During scan of entire supported frequency bands, priority can be given to those frequency bands which were previously found to be part of chosen PLMNs.
3. *Recovering from coverage loss*: When registered to a PLMN, UE needs to continuously monitor signal strength from serving as well as neighbouring cells of the same PLMN to perform cell reselection. Neighbour cell list is signalled to UE in different control-plane signalling mechanism. UE detects coverage loss if the serving cell and all cells in neighbour list is weak or undetectable. In the first few seconds of coverage loss, UE is supposed to monitor if any cell of the registered PLMN is found again. After that phase, UE needs to look for suitable cells of other PLMNs. During the first phase, it is highly unlikely for the UE to move into an area of the same PLMN where the set of carriers are completely different. So it is enough to limit cell search on carriers found just before detecting out of coverage. For the next phase, stored information search may enable UE to get coverage of a new PLMN faster. In case stored information scan fails, UE needs to start scanning entire range of supported frequency bands.
4. *Manual mode PLMN selection*: In this case, UE has to perform a complete scan. Certain optimizations of

intelligently skipping certain frequency range during complete scan can reduce the amount of processing by a large extent.

5. *Periodic search for higher priority PLMNs*: When UE is under coverage of some PLMN, it periodically needs to search if a higher priority PLMN (as per the PLMN list in USIM) is available. In this case, limited scan based on stored information may result in finding a higher priority PLMN quickly. UE has to fall-back on entire-range scan if limited scan fails.

Handling Carrier Frequency Information

When an UE is under coverage of a cell belonging to a PLMN, it needs to listen to the broadcast channel of the cell. Information regarding neighbouring UMTS and GSM cells, their carrier frequency and band information, and respective PLMN id's are broadcasted in each cell's broadcast channel. The neighbouring cell information signalled to UE through Radio Resource Control (RRC) protocol has at most 3 UMTS carriers and upto 32 GSM carriers. UE gets newer neighbouring cell information as it moves from one cell to the other. When a call is established or is ongoing, network signals some neighbouring cell and frequency information to the UE from time to time as part of Radio Resource Control (RRC) protocol. If the UE keeps collating the carrier frequency and frequency band values from all the neighbouring cell information it receives, a data storage of possible carrier frequency values can be formed.

It is not possible for UE to maintain all the carrier frequencies seen by it in the past due to memory constraint. Certain entries need to be purged for creating new entries in a way similar to a caching mechanism.

In USIM, there is an element named EFnetpar to store UARFCN and GSM carrier frequencies and band information. This element is of variable length which can store upto 8 UARFCNs for UMTS-FDD carriers and upto 32 GSM carrier information. EFnetpar is meant to be used to store the latest carrier frequency information of only the last registered PLMN. Carrier information of other PLMNs in an area should be stored into a non-volatile memory area which can be maintained across power-off cycle.

The suggested data structure for stored carrier information is an array of elements containing the following logical parameters:

- PLMN id,
- timestamp : A time-stamp of the storage time, so that purging old entries can be done based on an oldest-entry-first purging mechanism,
- number of successful search : A counter which indicates the number of times the PLMN has been found from the carrier list in the current element. In case old entries need to be purged, priority is given on lower value of 'number of successful search' for purging,
- number of FDD carrier frequencies,
- UARFCN values for UMTS-FDD cells,
- number of GSM carriers,
- ARFCN values and GSM frequency band informations.

Corresponding to one PLMN id, a storage of carrier frequency values can be built up in the following way:

1. Create a new element and store the PLMN id. If there is not enough memory available, one element is purged out of the storage. Choice of the element should be made based on oldest timestamp and lowest number of successful search.
2. Initialise one UARFCN list corresponding to the PLMN id,
3. Put the carrier information from the current neighbouring cell list into the UARFCN list,
4. As and when UE receives a new neighbour cell information through RRC protocol, add new frequency values into UARFCN list. Continue addition until at least one UARFCN corresponding to UMTS-FDD carrier remains common between the UARFCN list and signalled neighbour cell list.
5. If no UARFCN is common in step (4), start from step (1) to make a new entry.

Two or more elements in the list may have the same PLMN id. Entries containing the same PLMN id collectively maintains disjoint frequency profile set seen by the UE. All the entries together store the mobility profile of the UE seen in different times.

During limited scan based on stored information for a chosen PLMN id, entries with lowest elapsed time is picked, and cell search on the list of carriers is performed. If no cells of chosen PLMN are found on any of the listed UMTS-FDD carriers, the UARFCN value is removed from the list. If all UARFCN values are removed from the list, the entry is deleted. If cells on at least one listed carrier is found to be part of chosen PLMN, its 'number of successful search' entry is incremented by 1.

During roaming, if services are rejected during registration in a particular PLMN, all elements regarding that PLMN is purged.

Optimization during blind scan

Following points are to be taken into account for reducing the frequency search range during scan of all supported frequency bands.

a. *Minimum frequency spacing*: As each UMTS FDD carrier is of 5 MHz bandwidth, the minimum spacing between two UMTS FDD carrier central frequencies is approximately 5 MHz (may be around 4.5 MHz in extremely congested areas). Certain UMTS FDD frequency bands overlap with GSM frequency bands. In such cases, one GSM carrier frequency and the UMTS FDD carrier central frequency should have approximately 2.5 MHz spacing at the minimum.

b. *Skip frequencies in unwanted range*: If in the present search cycle, an UMTS-FDD carrier with UARFCN = u is found to be part of a different PLMN, the range of frequencies from u to u + 25 (there are 25 possible UARFCN values for a 5 MHz bandwidth) can be skipped as no other UMTS carrier can have central frequency within that range. Once a GSM carrier is found in frequency f_gsm, no UMTS FDD carrier can have central frequency between f_gsm and f_gsm+2.5 MHz. This range can be skipped from range scan.

c. *Narrowing frequency range scan through neighbor cell info*: If an UMTS-FDD cell is found to be part of a different PLMN than the preferred one, UE may listen to its broadcast channel to get the neighbouring cell information and their respective PLMN ids. If none of the UMTS-FDD or GSM carriers in the neighbour list belong to preferred PLMN, frequency ranges around those carriers can be skipped from search. If the range scan is performed to check for available PLMNs in an area, these carrier information can be stored in the frequency list storage mentioned above.

Algorithm for optimising the number of successful searches vis-a-vis memory requirement will play a crucial role towards better performance with low battery consumption for mobile operations under roaming condition.

REFERENCES

1. 3GPP TS 23.122v7.9.0 : 3rd Generation Partnership Project, Technical Specification Group Core Network and Terminals; Non-Access-Stratum (NAS) functions related to Mobile Station (MS) in idle mode (Release 7).
2. 3GPP TS 24.008v7.8.0 : 3rd Generation Partnership Project; Technical Specification Group Core Network and Terminals; Mobile radio interface Layer 3 specification; Core network protocols; Stage 3 (Release 7).
3. 3GPP TS 25.101v7.8.0 : 3rd Generation Partnership Project; Technical Specification Group Radio Access Network; User Equipment (UE) radio transmission and reception (FDD) (Release 7).
4. 3GPP TS 25.214v7.5.0 : 3rd Generation Partnership Project; Technical Specification Group Radio Access Network; Physical layer procedures (FDD) (Release 7).
5. 3GPP TS 25.304v7.2.0 : 3rd Generation Partnership Project; Technical Specification Group Radio Access Network; User Equipment (UE) procedures in idle mode and procedures for cell reselection in connected mode (Release 7).
6. 3GPP TS 25.331 : 3rd Generation Partnership Project; Technical Specification Group Radio Access Network; Radio Resource Control (RRC) protocol (Release 7).

Load Balancing Using Application Server Approach

30

Gagan Garg, Pallavi Chaudhary and *Ashish Sharma*

ABSTRACT

Load balancing refers to increasing the capacity of a server from beyond a single server. For a website it aims at maximizing the response. Presence of World Wide Web has brought a challenge of bulk requests in front of experts. The study aims at meeting the required performance efficiency. For a web cluster, the load is intelligently distributed to achieve best performance and efficient balancing of systems. The system remains transparent to the client who is benefited by the design as response is quite faster.

INTRODUCTION

With the explosive popularity of the internet and the World Wide Web (WWW), there is a rapidly growing need to provide unprecedented access to globally distributed data sources through the internet. Web accessibility will be an essential component of the services that future digital libraries should provide for clients. This need has created a strong demand for database access capability through the internet [1], and high performance scalable web servers [2,3]. As most popular web sites are experiencing overload from an, increasing number of users accessing the sites at the same time, it is desired that scalable web servers should adapt to the changing access characteristics and should be capable of handling a large number of concurrent requests simultaneously, with reasonable response times and minimal request drop rates. A collection of web documents may be viewed as a directed graph, where each document is a node and each hyperlink (or image reference) is a directed link from one node to another. If there is a way to distribute this graph amongst many server computers in such a way that the load is evenly distributed despite the dynamically changing web access patterns, then the problem of load balancing, one of the most important issues of creating a distributed web server has been solved. Our solution will take this graph-based approach and will be based on the hypothesis that most web sites only have a few well-known entry points (www.washingtonpost.com) from which users start navigating through the site's documents. The proposed solution is to dynamically modify the web documents to change their hyperlink connectivity, and thereby distributing the document graph adaptively amongst several servers. The dynamic modifications will be performed automatically by the web servers and will require no user intervention. All the well-known entry points will be maintained at the home servers where the web documents originate, while less known internal documents may be migrated to alternate server computers which we call co-op servers for load balancing purposes. The home servers and co-op servers can serve collectively as a distributed cooperative web server (DCWS) for the need of web request processing with great flexibility and scalability. Load balancing (also known as *high availability switch over*) is a mechanism where the server load is distributed to different nodes within the server cluster, based on a load balancing policy. Rather than execute an application on a single server, the system executes application code on a dynamically selected server. When a client requests a service, one (or more) of the cooperating servers is chosen to execute the request. Load balancers act as single points of entry into the cluster and as traffic directors to individual web or application servers.

If there is only one web server responding to all the incoming HTTP requests for your website, the capacity of the web server may not be able to handle high volumes of incoming traffic once the website becomes popular. The website's pages will load slowly as some of the users will have to wait until the web server is free to process their requests. The increase in traffic and connections to your website can lead to a point where upgrading the server hardware will no longer be cost effective.

In order to achieve web server scalability, more servers need to be added to distribute the load among the group of servers, which is also known as a *server cluster*. The load distribution among these servers is known as load balancing. Load balancing applies to all types of servers (application server, database server), however, we will be devoting this section for load balancing of web servers (HTTP server) only.

Two popular methods of load balancing in a cluster are *DNS round robin and hardware load balancing*. DNS round robin provides a single logical name, returning any IP address of the nodes in the cluster. This option is inexpensive, simple, and easy to set up, but it doesn't provide any server affinity or high availability. In contrast, hardware load balancing solves the limitations of DNS round robin through virtual IP addressing. Here, the load balancer shows a single IP address for the cluster, which maps the addresses of each machine in the cluster. The load balancer receives each request and rewrites headers to point to other machines in the cluster. If we remove any machine in the cluster, the changes take effect immediately. The advantages of hardware load balancing are server affinity and high availability; the disadvantages are that it's very expensive and complex to set up.

There are many different algorithms to define the load distribution policy, ranging from a simple round robin algorithm to more sophisticated algorithms used to perform the load balancing. Some of the commonly used algorithms are:

- Round-robin
- Random
- Weight-based
- Minimum load
- Last access time
- Programmatic parameter-based (where the load balancer can choose a server based upon method input arguments)

Load-balancing algorithms affect statistical variance, speed, and simplicity. For example, the weight-based algorithm has a longer computational time than the other algorithms.

Background and Related Work

Various load balancing techniques based on domain name service (DNS) have been proposed in the literature. The NCSA scalable web server is built on a cluster of identically configured servers, and uses round-robin DNS scheduling and Andrew file system (AFS) for load sharing among the servers [2.4]. The IBM scalable web server is built on an SP-2 parallel system, which is essentially a cluster of identical RS6000 workstations. The IBM web server uses a TCP router instead of DNS scheduling for improved load balancing [11], but its use is limited to tightly coupled systems such as SP-2.

The presence of heterogeneous web servers not only increases the complexity of the DNS scheduling, but also makes a simple round-robin scheduling not directly applicable. Numerous variations of the round-robin DNS scheduling have been proposed for heterogeneous web servers and non-uniform client distribution. Two-tier round-robin DNS scheduling divides clients into two classes normal and hot to handle non-uniform distribution of client requests [5]. Probabilistic and deterministic algorithms based on adaptive TTL (time-to-live) approach have been proposed [6]. Lower TTL values are assigned when the DNS chooses a less capable server or an address mapping request comes from a hot client. Another solution proposed in [7] attempts to develop a distributed scheduling heuristic based on a multi-variant cost function (CPU, disk and network utilization), which helps make the decision on task migration. Two techniques are used for load balancing: DNS rotation and HTTP URL redirection. DNS rotation is used for initial load distribution, and HTTP, URL redirection is used to dynamically adjust network load based on server utilization. A potential problem with DNS rotation is the development of “hot spots”, which lead to serious load imbalances. A detailed study of the techniques for an online digital library was reported in [8].

Dynamic server selection [9] is proposed as a client-based solution, in which clients automatically determine the best server for a given file without a prior knowledge of server performance. The technique relies on replication of web documents by proxy servers. It is assumed that a list of proxy servers exists which contain a given document. A hybrid buffer management algorithm [3] has been proposed to balance intra-cluster network traffic and disk access by dynamically controlling the amount of data replication. A centralized round-robin router is used to route requests amongst multiple servers.

The Cisco Local Director Cisco systems [10] use a virtual server to handle incoming requests at a virtual IP address. The Local Director functions as an intelligent router, routing requests from the virtual IP address to physical servers at real IP addresses. It is intended to be a general purpose solution, capable of handling other services in addition to the web. No discussion is given in the white paper as to what extent the Local Director is a bottleneck of the system.

Fast Packet Interposing is a user-level technique developed in [11] and is used by the Magic Router to distribute load. The Magic Router is used to make a cluster of servers appear to have a single IP address without modifications to any servers. Fast Packet Interposing is used to modify network addresses within the data packets that pass through the Magic Router. Fault tolerance and Load Balancing are stressed by the paper. The Magic Router is expected to be a bottleneck as all packets must arrive through it as a central resource.

A technique called dynamic packet rewriting (DPR) [12] is used to distribute load. DPR attempts to route requests at the IP level, by manipulating the methods in which an IP address is mapped to a host. It is a distributed algorithm, and attempts to eliminate the bottleneck of a centralized solution, such as a centralized round-robin router. Each host acts as both a web server and a packet-level router for incoming requests. DNS rotation is used as an initial partitioning method to achieve a rough distribution.

VARIOUS APPROACHES

DNS Approach

How DNS load balancing works

When the request comes to the DNS server to resolve the domain name, it gives out one of the several canonical names in a rotated order. This redirects the request to one of the several servers in a server group. Once the BIND feature of DNS resolves the domain to one of the servers, subsequent requests from the same client are sent to the same server.

DNS load balancing implementation (Multiple CNAMES)

This approach works for BIND 4 name servers, where multiple CNAMES are not considered as a configuration error. Assuming there are 4 web servers in the cluster configured with IP addresses 123.45.67. [1-4], add all of them to the DNS with Address records (A Names) as below. The srv[1-4] can be set to any name you want, such as foo[1-4], but should match the next step.

```
srv1 IN A 123.45.67.1
srv2 IN A 123.45.67.2
srv3 IN A 123.45.67.3
srv4 IN A 123.45.67.4
```

Add the following canonical names to resolve www.domain.com to one of these servers.

```
www IN CNAME srv1.domain.tld.
IN CNAME srv2.domain.tld.
IN CNAME srv3.domain.tld.
IN CNAME srv4.domain.tld.
```

The DNS server will resolve the www.domain.com to one of the listed servers in a rotated manner. That will spread the requests over the group of servers.

Note: The requests sent to http://domain.com (without 'www') should be forwarded to http://www.domain.com in this case to work. For BIND 8 name servers, the above approach will throw an error for multiple CNAMES. This can be avoided by an explicit multiple CNAME configuration option as shown below.

DNS load balancing implementation (Multiple A Records)

This above approach with multiple CNAMES for one domain name is not a valid DNS server configuration for BIND 9 and above. In this case, multiple A records are used.

www.domain.tld. 60 IN A 123.45.67.1

www.domain.tld. 60 IN A 123.45.67.2

www.domain.tld. 60 IN A 123.45.67.3

www.domain.tld. 60 IN A 123.45.67.4

The TTL value should be kept to a low value, so that the DNS cache is refreshed faster.

Other considerations

The DNS based load balancing method shown above does not take care of various potential issues such as unavailable servers (if one server goes down), or DNS caching by other name servers. The DNS server does not have any knowledge of the server availability and will continue to point to an unavailable server. It can only differentiate by IP address, but not by server port. The IP address can also be cached by other nameservers, hence requests may not be sent to the load balancing DNS server.

Considering the functionality, the round robin DNS is not a load balancing mechanism but a load distribution option. Some of these drawbacks can be overcome by implementing an advanced version of the DNS load balancer using Perl scripts.

Some other variety of load balancing can be performed by using a proxy server, where one of the web servers, is solely used for re-routing of traffic to the other servers.

When you enter a URL in a browser (say, www.loadbalancedsite.com), the browser sends a request to the DNS asking it to return the IP address of the site. This is called the DNS lookup. After the Web browser gets the IP address for that site, it contacts the site using the IP address, and displays the page for you.

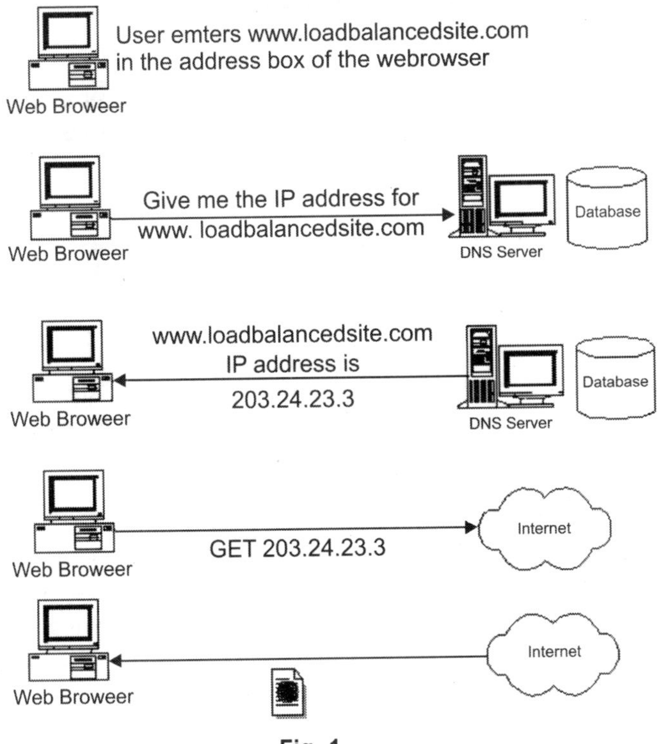

Fig. 1

The DNS server generally contains a single IP address mapped to a particular site name. In our fictional example, our site www.loadbalancedsite.com maps to the IP address 203.24.23.3To balance server loads using DNS, the DNS server maintains several different IP addresses for a site name. The multiple IP addresses represent the machines in the cluster, all of which map to the same single logical site name. Using our example, www.loadbalancedsite.com could be hosted on three machines in a cluster with the following IP addresses:

203.34.23.3

203.34.23.4

203.34.23.5

In this case, the DNS server contains the following mappings:

www.loadbalancedsite.com 203.34.23.3

www.loadbalancedsite.com 203.34.23.4

www.loadbalancedsite.com 203.34.23.5

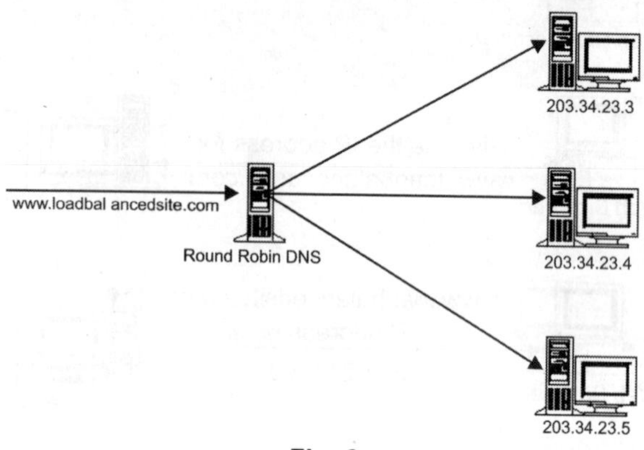

Fig. 2

When the first request arrives at the DNS server, it returns the IP address 203.34.23.3, the first machine. On the second request, it returns the second IP address: 203.34.23.4. and so on. On the fourth request, the first IP address is returned again.

Using the above DNS round robin, all of the requests to the particular site have been evenly distributed among all of the machines in the cluster. Therefore, with the DNS round robin method of load balancing, all of the nodes in the cluster are exposed to the net.

Advantages of DNS round robin

The main advantages of DNS round robin are that it's cheap and easy:

- **Inexpensive and easy to set up.** The system administrator only needs to make a few changes in the DNS server to support round robin, and many of the newer DNS servers already include support. It doesn't require any code change to the Web application; in fact, Web applications aren't aware of the load-balancing scheme in front of it.
- **Simplicity.** It does not require any networking experts to set up or debug the system in case a problem arises.

Disadvantages of DNS round robin

Two main disadvantages of this software-based method of load balancing are that it offers no real support for server affinity and doesn't support high availability.

- **No support for server affinity.** Server affinity is a load-balancing system's ability to manage a user's requests, either to a specific server or any server, depending on whether session information is maintained on the server or at an underlying, database level. Without server affinity, DNS round robin relies on one of three methods devised to maintain session control or user identity to requests coming in over HTTP, which is a stateless protocol.
- cookies
- hidden fields
- URL rewriting

When a user makes a first request, the Web server returns a text-based token uniquely identifying that user. Subsequent requests include this token using either cookies, URL rewriting, or hidden fields, allowing the server to appear to maintain a session between client and server. When a user establishes a session with one server, all subsequent requests usually go to the same server.

The problem is that the browser caches that server's IP address. Once the cache expires, the browser makes another request to the DNS server for the IP address associated with the domain name. If the DNS server returns a different IP address, that of another server in the cluster, the session information is lost.

- **No support for high availability.** Consider a cluster of n nodes. If a node goes down, then every nth request to the DNS server directs you to the dead node. An advanced router solves this problem by checking nodes at regular intervals, detecting failed nodes and removing them from the list, so no requests go to them. However, the problem still exists if the node is up but the Web application running on the node goes down.

Changes to the cluster take time to propagate through the rest of the Internet. One reason is that many large organizations —ISPs, corporations, agencies—cache their DNS requests to reduce network traffic and request time. When a user within these organizations makes a DNS request, it's checked against the cache's list of DNS names mapped to IP addresses. If it finds an entry, it returns the IP address to the user. If an entry is not found in its local cache, the ISP sends this DNS request to the DNS server and caches response.

When a cached entry expires, the ISP updates its local database by contacting other DNS servers. When your list of servers changes, it can take a while for the cached entries on other organizations' networks to expire and look for the updated list of servers. During that period, a client can still attempt to hit the downed server node, if that client's ISP still has an entry pointing to it. In such a case, some users of that ISP couldn't access your site on their first attempt, even if your cluster has redundant servers up and running.

This is a bigger problem when removing a node than when adding one. When you drop a node, a user may be trying to hit a non-existing server. When you add one, that server may just be under-utilized until its IP address propagates to all the DNS servers.

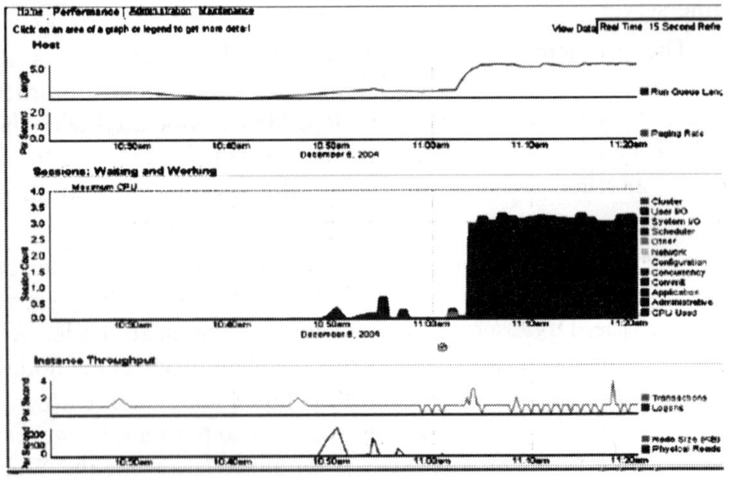

Fig. 3

Hardware Load Balancers

Hardware load balancers solve many of the problems faced by the round robin software solution through virtual IP addresses. The load balancer shows a single (virtual) IP address to the outside world, which maps to the addresses of each machine in the cluster. So, in a way, the load balancer exposes the IP address of the entire cluster to the world.

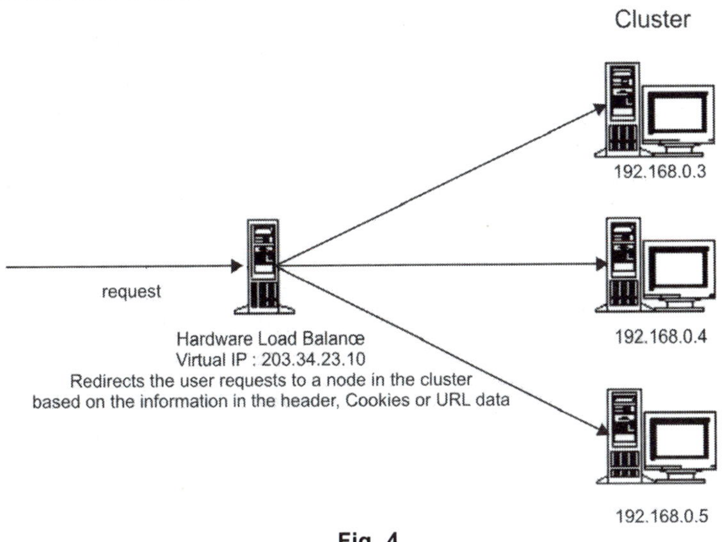

Fig. 4

When a request comes to the load balancer, it rewrites the request's header to point to other machines in the cluster. If a machine is removed from the cluster, the request doesn't run the risk of hitting a dead server, since all of the machines in the cluster appear to have the same IP address. This address remains the same even if a node in the cluster is down. Moreover, cached DNS entries around the Internet aren't a problem. When a response is returned, the client sees it coming from the hardware load balancer machine. In other words, the client is dealing with a single machine, the hardware load balancer.

Advantages of Hardware Load Balancers

- **Server affinity.** The hardware load balancer reads the cookies or URL readings on each request made by the client. Based on this information, it can rewrite the header information and send the request to the appropriate node in the cluster, where its session is maintained.

Hardware load balancers can provide server affinity in HTTP communication, but not through a secure channel, such as HTTPS. In a secure channel, the messages are SSL-encrypted, and this prevents the load balancer from reading the session information.

- **High Availability Through Failover.** Failover happens when one node in a cluster cannot process a request and redirects it to another. There are two types of failover:
  - **Request Level Failover**. When one node in a cluster cannot process a request (often because it's down), it passes it along to another node.
  - **Transparent Session Failover**. When an invocation fails, it's transparently routed to another node in the cluster to complete the execution.

  Hardware load balancers provide request-level failover; when the load balancer detects that a particular node has gone down, it redirects all subsequent requests to that dead node to another active node in the cluster. However, any session information on the dead node will be lost when requests are redirected to a new node.

  Transparent session failover requires execution knowledge for a single process in a node, since the hardware load balancer can only detect network-level problems, not errors. In the execution process of a single node, hardware load balancers do not provide transparent session failover. To achieve transparent session failover, the nodes in the cluster must collaborate among each other and have something like a shared memory area or a common database where all the session data is stored. Therefore, if a node in the cluster has a problem, a session can continue in another node.
- **Metrics.** Since all requests to a Web application must pass through the load-balancing system, the system can determine the number of active sessions, the number

of active sessions connected in any instance, response times, peak load times, the number of sessions during peak load, the number of sessions during minimum load, and more. All this audit information is used to fine tune the entire system for optimal performance.

Disadvantages of Hardware Load Balancers

The drawbacks to the hardware route are the costs, the complexity of setting up, and the vulnerability to a single point of failure. Since all requests pass through a single hardware load balancer, the failure of that piece of hardware sinks the entire site.

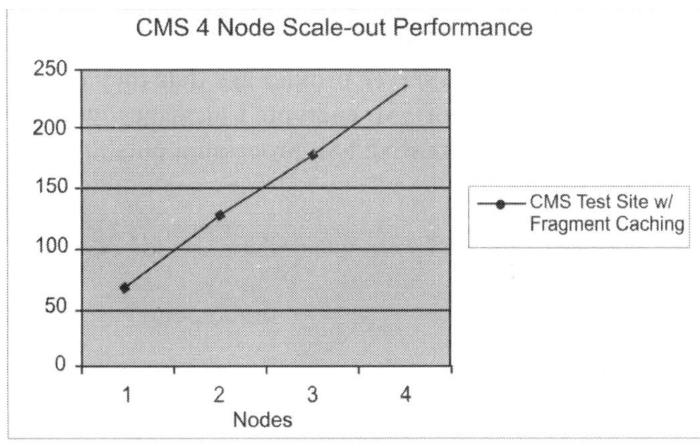

Fig. 5

Load Balancing HTTPS Requests

As mentioned above, it's difficult to load balance and maintain session information of requests that come in over HTTPS, as they're encrypted. The hardware load balancer cannot redirect requests based on the information in the header, cookies, or URL readings. There are two options to solve this problem:

Web Server Proxies

A Web server proxy that sits in front of a cluster of Web servers takes all requests and decrypts them. Then it redirects them to the appropriate node, based on header information in the header, cookies, and URL readings.

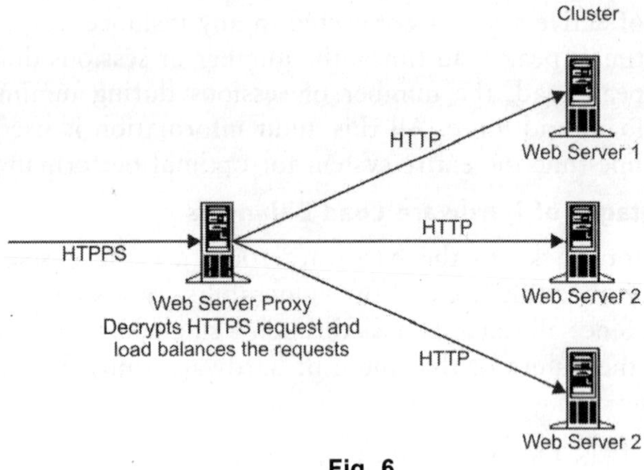

Fig. 6

The advantages of Web server proxies are that they offer a way to get server affinity for SSL-encrypted messages, without any extra hardware. But extensive SSL processing puts an extra load on the proxy.

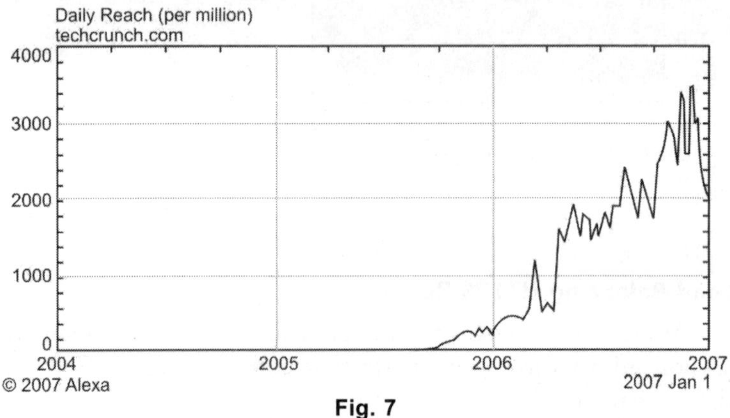

Fig. 7

Apache Tomcat

In many serving systems, Apache and Tomcat servers work together to handle all HTTP requests. Apache handles the request for static pages (including HTML, JPEG, and GIF files), while Tomcat handles requests for dynamic pages (JSPs or servlets). Tomcat servers can also handle static pages, but in combined systems, they're usually set up to handle dynamic requests.

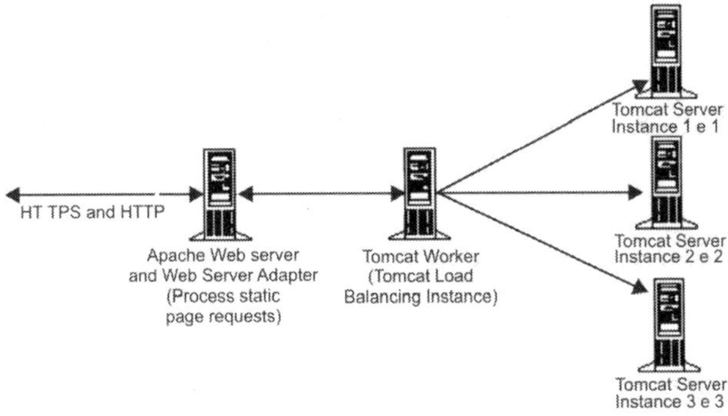

Fig. 8

You can also configure Apache and Tomcat to handle HTTPS requests and to balance loads. To achieve this, you run multiple instances of Tomcat servers on one or more machines. If all of the Tomcat servers are running on one machine, they should be configured to listen on different ports. To implement load balancing, you create a special type of Tomcat instance, called a Tomcat Worker.

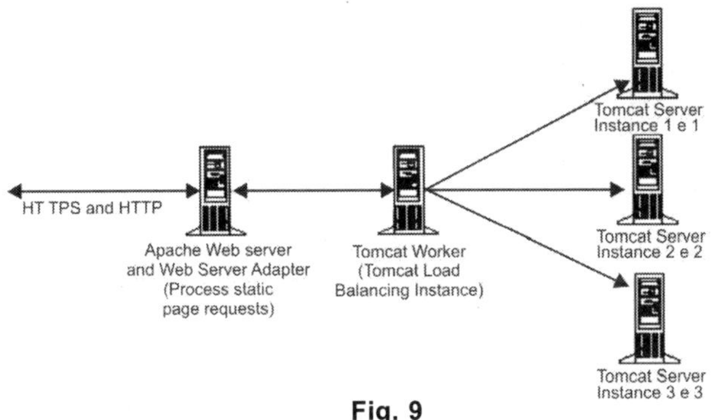

Fig. 9

As shown in the illustration, the Apache Web server receives HTTP and HTTPS requests from clients. If the request is HTTPS, the Apache Web server decrypts the request and sends it to a Web server adapter, which in turn sends the request to the Tomcat Worker, which contains a load-balancing algorithm. Similar to the Web server proxy, this algorithm balances the load among Tomcat instances.

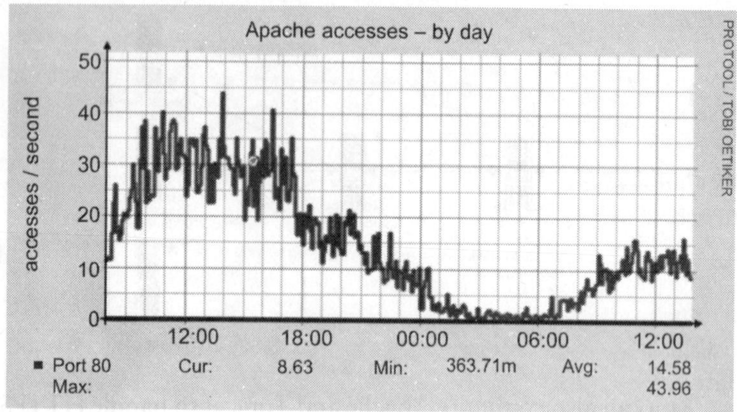

Fig. 10

Proposed System of Application Server

The proposed system of application server makes use of a script that acts an interface between the client request and the servers. The system overcomes the disadvantage of Round Robin approach of meeting a request with a dead end and of Hardware Load Balancers of central dependency and increased routing costs.

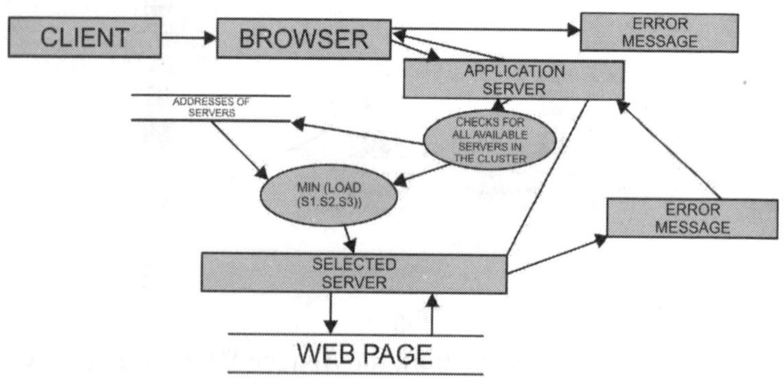

Fig. 11

The application server is nothing but an application governing the selection of appropriate server.

Detailed Working

A script termed as load balancing script is used instead of an entirely different physical system. The script is invoked each time a request for the website is made, by typing the corresponding URL on the browser. This script resides within the connecting http servlets that bind the cluster together and are responsible for server deployment. The invocation is immediate. The script firstly communicates with all the servers in the cluster to determine the working systems. Then out of the working servers the server with least load is selected. This is done on the basis of approach of counters. A counter variable is assigned to each server which determines its load at a specific instance of time. A distinct threshold is decided on the basis of requirement of the system. Each time a request is directed to a server, its counter variable is increased. Threshold value depends upon the total number of the servers and the exposure of the system. The script handles all the processes of session handling, request redirecting. Also in case of instant failure send directing method is invoked that helps in recovery of data. The ASA framework consists of a suite of load balancing policies and a collection of cooperative an script as shown in Figure 1. The suite of polices specify the strategies of load information gathering, the conditions for activating load balancing operations, and the metrics for server selection and job reallocation. It defines four *policies*:

1. *Information Gathering Policy* specifies the strategy for the collection of load information including the frequency and method of information gathering. The frequency is determined based on a tradeoff between the accuracy of load information and the overhead of information collection. Different schemes can be designed for this policy. Each server can dispatch its own mobile agent to collect load information. Or, the servers can share the information collected by a common mobile agent.
2. *Initiation Policy* determines who starts the load balancing process. The process can be initiated by an overloaded server (called *sender-initiated*) or by an under-loaded server (called *receiver-initiated*).
3. *Server Selection Policy* selects an appropriate server based on the load information to which the workload on an overloaded server can be reallocated. Different

strategies can be applied to the selection. For example, the find-best strategy selects the least loaded server among all servers and the find-first strategy selects the first server whose load is below a threshold.

4. *Job Transfer Policy* determines when job reallocation should be performed and which job(s) (i.e. client requests) should be reallocated. Job reallocation is activated by a threshold-based strategy. In a sender-initiated method, the job transfer is invoked when the workload on a server exceeds a threshold. In a receiver-initiated method, a server starts the process to fetch jobs from other servers when its workload is below a threshold. The threshold can be a pre-defined *static* value or a *dynamic* value that is assessed at runtime based on the load distribution among the servers. When job reallocation is required, the appropriate job(s) will be selected from the job queue on a server and transferred to another server.

Advantages of the System

- The cost of establishing the system is less in comparison to hardware Load Balancers as does not require different hardware for routing.
- The request will never meet a dead end.
- There is no extensive SSL processing, so there is no extra load like in Web Proxies.
- The design is not complex.
- Routing is not complex as requests are simply redirected.
- It's easy to detect the presence of faulty servers.

Disadvantages of the System

- There is no sharing of memory in the system being developed as it requires the installation of mirror discs.
- The system is restricted to lesser no of requests and servers due to lesser available resources at personal level.

Future Work

The developed system has good prospects in future as meets the utmost requirement.

Future works involve setting up a larger system for a registered and fully developed website. Better availability of resources is required to benefit from the system.

REFERENCES

1. Tam Nguyen and V. Srinivasan. Accessing relational databases from the World Wide Web. *In Proceedings of the 1996 ACM-SIGMOD Conference*, pages 529--540, Montreal, Canada, June 1996.
2. Eric Dean Katz, Michelle Butler, and Robert McGrath. A scalable HTTP server: The NCSA prototype. *Computer Networks and ISDN Systems*, 27:155--164, 1994.
3. Venkataraman, Shivakumar, Miron Livny, and Jeffrey F. Naughton. Memory management for scalable web data servers. *In the 13th Inter. Conference on Data Engineering*, pages 510--519, Birmingham, UK, April 1997.
4. Thomas T. Kwan, Robert E. McGrath, and Daniel A.Reed. Ncsa's world wide web server: Design and performance. *IEEE Computer*, 28(11):68--74, November 1995.
5. Michele Colajanmi, Philip S. Yu, and Daniel M. Dias. Scheduling algorithms for distributed web servers. *In Proceedings of the 17th International Conference on Distributed Computing Systems*, pages 169--176, Baltimore, MD, May 1997.
6. Michele Colajanmi and Philip S. Yu. Adaptive TTL schemes for load balancing of distributed web servers. *ACM Sigmetrics Performance Evaluation Review*, 25(2):36--42, September 1997.
7. Daniel Andresen, Tao Yang, and Oscar H. Ibarra. Toward a scalable distributed WWW server on workstation clusters. *Journal of Parallel and Distributed Computing*, 42:91--100, 1997.
8. D. Andresen, T. Yang, O. Egecioglu, O. Ibarra, and T. Smith. Scalability issues for high performance digital libraries on the world wide web. *In Proceedings of ADL'96 Forum on Research and Technology Advances in Digital Libraries*, pages 91--100, Washington D.C., May 1996.
9. Mark E. Crovella and Robert L. Carter. Dynamic server selection in the internet. *In the Third IEEE Workshop on the Architecture and Implementation of High Performance Communication Subsystems (HPCS'95)*, August 1995. Also available as TR-95-014, Boston University.

10. Cisco System. Scaling the internet web servers, November 1997. White Paper.
11. Eric Anderson, Dave Patterson, and Eric Brewer. The Magic Router: An application of fast packet interposing. Submitted for publication.
12. Azer Bestavros, Mark Crovella, Jun Liu, and David Martin. Distributed packet rewriting and its application to scalable server architectures. Technical Report TR-98-003, Boston University, Boston, MA

Use of FPGA for Future Software Defined Radio Systems

31

Pallavi Gupta and *M. Salim Beg*

ABSTRACT

Software-defined radio (SDR) is a new and a very useful technology that allows one radio platform to service multiple radio standards. Determining the digital hardware composition of a software radio is a key design step in its creation. The hardware design of course is much more complex for software radio than conventional radio because of its additional capabilities. As new radio standards are deployed and are used extensively with the already existing standards, the need for multiband multi–mode (MBMR) transceivers have increased. This paper describes how the evolving FPGA technology's unique combination of size, power efficiency and field programmability offers a transition of FPGAs from ASICs to embedded products. This work is based on a recently developed FPGA based SDR Design Bench. It is used here to demonstrate SDR capability to switch, under software control between two disparate modulation schemes.

INTRODUCTION

Software defined radio (SDR), or software radio, refers to wireless communication in which computer defines transmitter modulation and receiver also uses computer to determine the signal intelligence. The primary goal of SDR is to replace as many analog components and hardwired digital VLSI devices of the transceiver as possible with programmable devices [21]. The SDR forum stipulates that ideal SDR products must possess two fundamental features - Flexibility towards operational standards and independence from carrier frequencies [10]. The hardware flexibility provided by programmable logic is the key to deliver the performance required by SDR products. During last five years, FPGAs have made dramatic gains in several critical areas in order to accommodate DSP functions. The gate density of these devices has nicely followed Moore's law, doubling approximately every 18 months. Some recently announced devices are boasting of 10 million gates. Gate arrays are typically structured as logic cells equipped with memory and capable of performing math functions. These high-density logic cells are now available in a wide range of basic "cores" to support fast multipliers, block memory to handle FFT processing and distributed memory for FIR filters [17].

Key Hardware Elements

Real time software radios can be built using a variety of digital hardware consisting of ASIC, FPGA and DSPs. There are basically four key issues that define the digital hardware composition-

Flexibility: ability to handle variety of air interfaces and protocols even if they are yet to be defined.

Modularity: it allows easy replacement or upgrading of sub-systems to take advantage of new technology. Its important aspect is ramification of to software development.

Scalability: it allows radio to enhance its capability such as increasing the number of channels that a base station can handle.

Performance: it is closely tied to other three issues. The performance matrix like power consumption, relative cost and computational capabilities are traded for each other in overall design.

Broadly, there are three technical solutions to general hardware viz. (i) High speed DSPs, (ii) Multiple ASICs, (iii) Reconfigurable logic.

High Speed DSPs: High-speed instruction set processors are increasing in speed, decreasing in feature size and improving in low power operation. The Texas TMS320C5506 functions at

900 MIPS at lowest stand-by power of 0.12 mw. These can be repeatedly modified and upgraded using a high level language like C. The flexibility, however, sometimes comes at the cost of efficiency. Moreover, for certain applications more than one DSP is used to reduce the execution time and coordinating these multiple DSPs in single design is a challenging task for the programmer.

Multiple ASICs: Different ASICs are used for different bands and modes. This seems simple but it has serious inherent issues such as large silicon area, cost and power consumption. Moreover each implementation is typical combination of standards and is unable to handle additional upgrades in field.

Reconfigurable Logic: It allows the interconnection pattern to be loaded and changed after the device is manufactured. Silicon area is no longer a problem, and it provides a common platform, which can support any number of modes and bands and can be upgraded when in field [9,14].

FPGA in SDR

An FPGA is the ultimate field programmable device (FPD) technology in terms of user customization of the system. It allows the system architect to perform area-performance trade-offs and to therefore right size the functional components in the system.

With FPGA technology, the control of the silicon is put back into the hands of the system developer rather than the chip architect. In fact, one way to view FPGA is as a miniature silicon foundry with turnaround times of hours rather than months, as is the case with ASICs.

There are two basic categories of FPGAs on the market today: SRAM-based FPGAs and Antifuse-based FPGAs. In the first category, Xilinx and Altera are the leading manufacturers in terms of number of users, with the major competitor being AT&T. For antifuse-based products, Actel, Quicklogic and Cypress, and Xilinx offer competing products. The basic structure of Xilinx FPGAs is array-based, meaning that each chip comprises a two dimensional array of logic blocks that can be interconnected via horizontal and vertical routing channels. Xilinx introduced

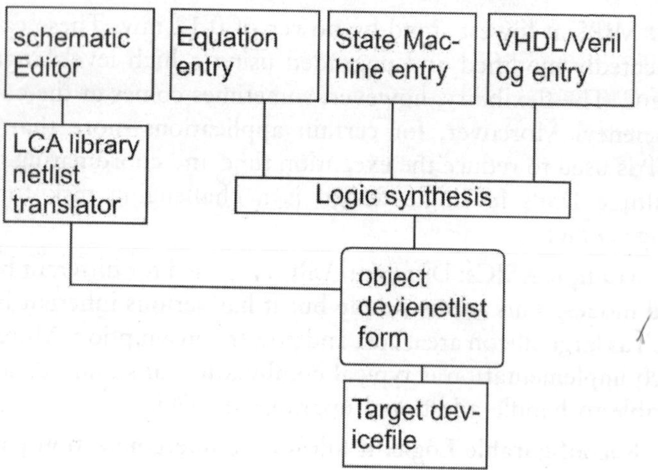

Fig. 1 The FPGA Design flow architecture

the first FPGA family, called the XC2000 series, in about 1985 and now offers three more generations: XC3000, XC4000, and XC5000. The XC4000 features a logic block (called a Configurable Logic Block (CLB) is based on look-up tables (LUTs). Circuit designers usually use hardware description languages such as VHDL or Verilog to program FPGA.

One of the driving objectives underlying SDR concepts is the desire to have a single hardware platform that has the capability to service a number of radio environments. This type of reconfigurability could be used in several ways. For example, from the perspective of a manufacturer developing infrastructure equipment or a network operator looking to build out a network, a soft radio system could be deployed in Europe and configured to support, say, UMTS or GSM standards, or that same system could be operated in the United States with a CDMA2000 radio personality profile. The one system could also be operated as a multimode radio in an environment where both wideband and narrowband CDMA communications are employed. Radio agility is important in situations where standards are fluid. Consider the evolution of the 3GPP standard and the length of time required for the standard to stabilize. It is also important during transition periods. For example, as we move from 2G to 3G mobile cellular systems multiple standards will need to coexist: Personal Digital Communication System (PCS) Global System for Mobile communications (GSM), IS-95, Personal Handy phone System (PHS), DECT, EDGE, GPRS, IMT-2000, CDMA2000 and so on.

Multistandard support will be a fact of life for the foreseeable future. Radio designers working with FPGA technology implement IF sampled receivers, channelizers of different varieties including classical digital down- and up-conversion architectures, FFT-based polyphase transforms, multistage multirate polyphase decimators and interpolators, adaptive interference cancellers for DSSS channels, multi-user detection and rake receivers (including acquisition and tracking). More recently, FPGAs have been used to construct space-time processors for advanced smart-antenna systems. FPGAs are extremely adept and flexible at implementing fast Fourier transforms, and this functionality has been used to construct orthogonal frequency-division multiplexing modulators and demodulators. When the 4G wireless network build-out takes place, multimode operation will be required to support third-generation wireless direct-sequence spread spectrum and OFDM systems. FPGA based soft radios can be viewed as a means to future-proof infrastructure investments by keeping radio hardware from becoming obsolete as new standards and techniques become available. There is another category, which can be programmed in the field i.e. high-speed digital signal processors. The comparison between the two is given in the Table 1.

Table 1 Comparison of DSP and FPGA[9,14]

Property	DSP	FPGA
Language	C,C++,assembly	VHDL/Verilog
Speed	Limited by clock speed of DSP chip	Fast for optimum design
Reconfigurability	Done by retrieving data stored at some memory location	Done by downloading different data

Power consumption	Depends on number of memory chips	Can be decreased by optimized programming
Parallelism	Generally sequential	Generally parallel
Implementation method	Repeated operation of MAC	Forming interconnections

Application and Testing

This Polarizone software radio system SDB05 is an ideal platform for implementing a wide range of applications. The design bench is programmable at the baseband and the RF section. By using the new FPGA design tools and IP Libraries for this highly configurable FPGA-based product, system designers can eliminate need for custom boards. Since FPGA "hardware" can be radically reconfigured with no new board design, the same products used in the current project can be easily retooled for future applications. In this paper FPGA based SDB05 is used as reconfigurable base band processing system with a flexibility to implement the software radio concept largely at the modulation technique to demonstrate its suitability as MBBR with reprogrammable hardware.

The SDB05 has a transmitter and a receiver, which follow the SDR design approach. At the transmitter, the base band processing is performed on a xilinx spartan3 / virtex2 processor. Digital up-conversion and the analog up-conversion are performed on the base-band signal to raise the frequency to 2.4 GHz. Suitable antennas are provided at the transmitting and receiving side. The received signals are down converted to base-band and the processing is done using a spartan3 / virtex2 platform. The base-band processor demodulates the received signal and the received data is then fed to appropriate subsystems for further processing and decoding.

The software used are –

- Xilinx ISE series 7.x
- Spartan 3 libraries and device files
- Chipscope pro softwarev7.xi

- HDL files for BPSK, QPSK and QAM modulation
- Software control interface for the RF frequency and power selection [13]

The authors have transmitted and received data using BPSK modulation /demodulation and QPSK modulation / demodulation on the same hardware by reprogramming only. The received signal plots for QAM modulation techniques are shown in figures 2 and 3. The transmitted signal plots for QAM modulation techniques are shown in figures 4 and 5. Similar results were received with BPSK modulation.

CONCLUSION

In this paper, the authors have elaborated fundamental features of FPGA as applied to SDR, technological motivations for development of reconfigurable MBMMR and its commercial application. The paper concludes that using FPGA is a successful approach for SDR systems. Numerous alternatives exist for digital signal processing hardware. The choice depends on many factors including speed, power consumption, product cost, non–recurring engineering cost, needed flexibility, and many other factors. The optimal dividing line in software radio design between the alternatives (DSP/FPGA/ASIC) will change with the evolution of technology, but the general design principle that speed, power consumption and flexibility must be traded off will always be true.

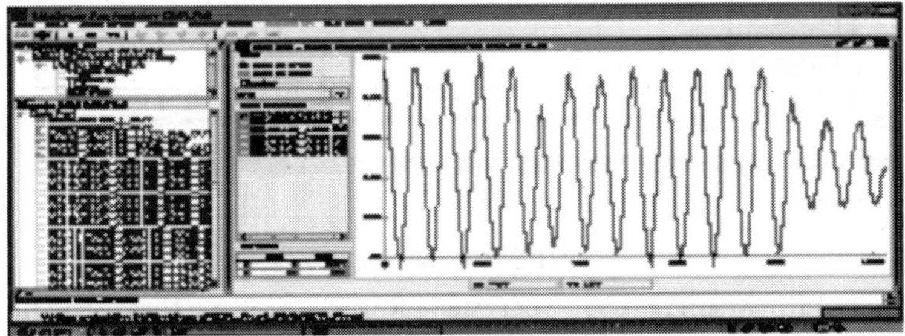

Fig. 2

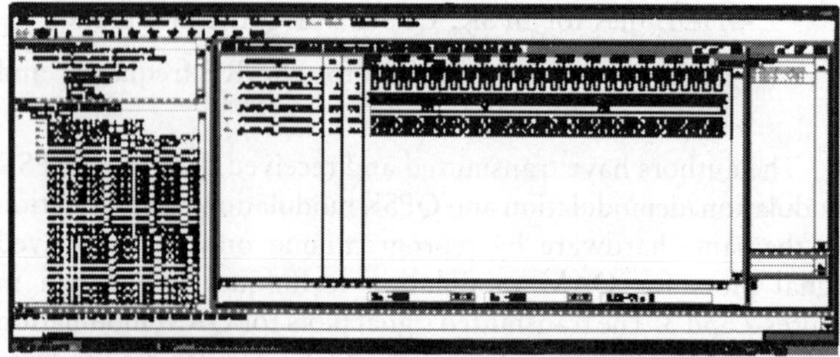

Fig. 3

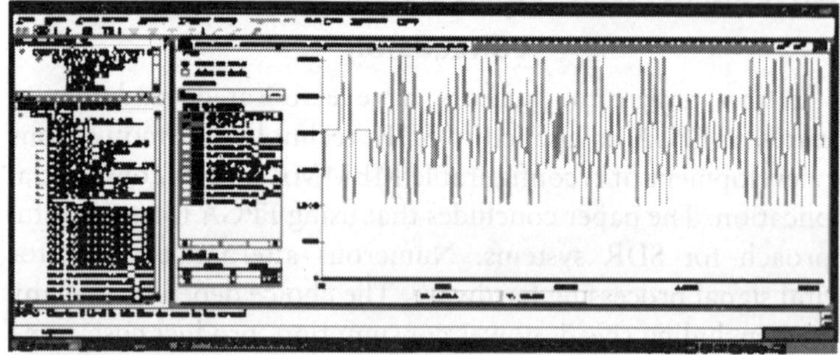

Fig. 4

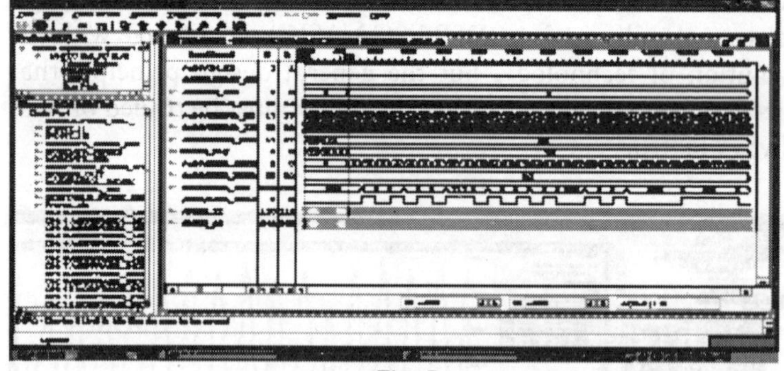

Fig. 5

REFERENCES

1. Joe Mitola, "The Software Radio Architecture", IEEE Communications Magazine, May1995, pp. 26-37.
2. Joe Mitola, "Software Radios: Survey, Critical Evaluation and Future Directions". Proceeding of the National Telesystems Conference, NY, IEEE Press, pp. 25-36, May 1992.

3. A. W Jeffery., "Analog-to-Digital converters and their applications in Radio Receivers", IEEE Communication Magazine, May 1995, pp. 39-45.
4. B. Rupert, "The DSP Bottleneck" IEEE Communication Magazine, May 1995, pp. 46-54..
5. M. Sadiku and C.Akujuobi, "Software Defined Radio- A brief overview" IEEE Potentials 2004.
6. Li Weidong Yao yan, "Software Radio: Technology & Implementation ICCT'98, October 1998, China.
7. J. H. Reed, "Software radio – A modern approach to Radio Engineering", 1st edition, Pearson Education.
8. Polarizone SDB04 Developer's Guide version 1.0, September 2005.
9. M. Cummings, "FPGA in Software Radio" IEEE communication Magazine 1999.
10. Graham Schelle, J Fifield, D. Ggrunwald "A Software Defined Radio Application utilizing modern FPGAs and NOC interconnects", IEEE Communication Magazine, pp. 177-182, 2007.
11. A. Stefano, G. Fiscelli, C. Ggiaconia "An FPGA based Software Defined Radio platform for the 2.4 GHz ISM Band", IEEE Communications Magazine, pp. 73-76, 2006.
12. C Dick, H Pedersen "Designing FPGA signal processing data paths for SDR", ESC China 2002, Conference proceedings, 2006.

Emerging Trends in Wireless Communication

32

Indu Agrawal

ABSTRACT

Wireless technologies are one of the major drivers of this era. These networks are largely invisible to consumers, yet powerful enough to transform their lives.

Wireless data services and systems represent a rapidly growing and increasingly important segment of the communications industry. This paper presents detailed study of this field, emphasizing three major elements: 1) technologies utilized in existing and currently planned wireless data services, 2) issues related to the performance of these systems, and 3) discernible trends in the continuing development of wireless data systems. While the wireless data industry is becoming increasingly diverse and fragmented, one can identify a few mainstreams which relate directly to users' requirement for data services. On one hand, there are requirements for relatively low-speed data services supporting mobile users over wide geographical areas, as provided by mobile data networks. On the other hand, there are requirements for high-speed data services in local areas, as provided by wireless LAN's. The system-level issues are somewhat different for these two categories of services, and this has led to different technology choices in the two domains, which will be discussed in the paper.

INTRODUCTION

In this era, all things are going to be very simple with the use of new technologies. So, in this context new technologies in the field of wireless communication come into mind. First, this field can be divided in two parts

(1) wireless data communication

(2) wireless telecommunication.

So, in this paper, wireless data communication field is being discussed. The world today is experiencing high growth in the field of information technology. Connectivity to internet, which today boasts to be the world's digital vault of information, happens to be a key role in this scenario and upcoming technology which has revolutionized the networking is WiMAX The WiMAX forum which is a non profit organization dedicated to promoting and certifying Networkers are looking at an array of choices of wireless technologies i.e. IEEE 802.11 technologies, Bluetooth, WiMAX according to their requirements. All these technologies will be described in a manner so that a user can opt suitable technology according to requirement.

IEEE 802.11 Technologies

802.11

In 1997, the Institute of Electrical and Electronics Engineers (IEEE) created the first WLAN standard. They called it *802.11* after the name of the group formed to oversee its development.

Unfortunately, 802.11 only supported a maximum network bandwidth of 1 and 2 Mbps—too slow for most applications. For this reason, ordinary 802.11 wireless products are no longer manufactured.

802.11b

IEEE expanded on the original 802.11 standard in July 1999, creating the *802.11b* specification. 802.11b supports bandwidth up to 5.5 to 11 Mbps, comparable to traditional *Ethernet*.

802.11b uses the same unregulated radio signaling frequency (2.4 GHz) as the original 802.11 standard. Vendors often prefer use of these frequencies because of low production costs.

- **Advantages of 802.11b** - lowest cost; signal range is good and not easily obstructed
- **Disadvantages of 802.11b** - slowest maximum speed; home appliances may interfere on the unregulated frequency band

802.11a

In fact, 802.11a was created at the same time. Due to its higher cost, 802.11a is usually found on business networks whereas 802.11b better serves the home market.

802.11a supports data rate up to 54 Mbps and signals in a regulated frequency spectrum around 5.725 GHz. This higher frequency compared to 802.11b shortens the range of 802.11a networks.

- **Advantages of 802.11a** - fast maximum speed; regulated frequencies prevent signal interference from other devices
- **Disadvantages of 802.11a** - highest cost; shorter range signal that is more easily obstructed

802.11g

In 2002 and 2003, WLAN products supporting a newer standard called 802.11g emerged on the market. 802.11g attempts to combine the best of both 802.11a and 802.11b. 802.11g supports bandwidth up to 54 Mbps, and it uses the 2.4 GHz frequency for greater range. 802.11g is backwards compatible with 802.11b, meaning that 802.11g access points will work with 802.11b wireless network adapters and vice versa.

- **Advantages of 802.11g** - fast maximum speed; signal range is good and not easily obstructed
- **Disadvantages of 802.11g** - costs more than 802.11b; appliances may interfere on the unregulated signal frequency

802.11n

The newest IEEE standard in the Wi-Fi category is 802.11n. It was designed to improve on 802.11g in the amount of bandwidth supported by utilizing multiple wireless signals and antennas (called MIMO technology) instead of one.

When this standard is finalized, 802.11n connections should support data rates of over 100 Mbps. 802.11n also offers somewhat better range over earlier Wi-Fi standards due to its increased signal intensity. 802.11n equipment will be backward compatible with 802.11g gear.

- **Advantages of 802.11n** - fastest maximum speed and best signal range; more resistant to signal interference from outside sources
- **Disadvantages of 802.11n** - standard is not yet finalized; costs more than 802.11g; the use of multiple signals may greatly interfere with nearby 802.11b/g based networks.

Architecture of 802.11

In the architecture, standard defined two kinds of service sets: (1) The Basic Service Set (BSS), (2) The Extended Service Set (ESS).

Basic Service Set (BSS): A BSS is made of stationary or mobile wireless stations and an optional central base station, known as the Access Point (AP) [5].

The BSS without an AP is called as 'ad-hoc' network architecture for devices within mutual communication range. Ad-hoc network generally uses a decentralized medium, i. e. each device is independent and competes for medium access. However ad-hoc network is called as infrastructure network when it has a centralized device i.e. access point [1], [5]

The Extended Service Set (ESS): In IEEE 802.11 standard when communicating devices belonging to different coverage areas, distribution services are needed to communicate through a wired network. Access Points are used to bridge with wired networks forming a WLAN [5]

IEEE 802.11 defines two MAC sublayers:

(i) **Distributed Coordination Function (DCF):** DCF uses CSMA/CA as the access method [5]

(ii) **Point Coordination Function** (PCF): PCF is an optional access method that can be implemented in an infrastructure network (not in an ad hoc network) and provides a contention-free service [1], [5].

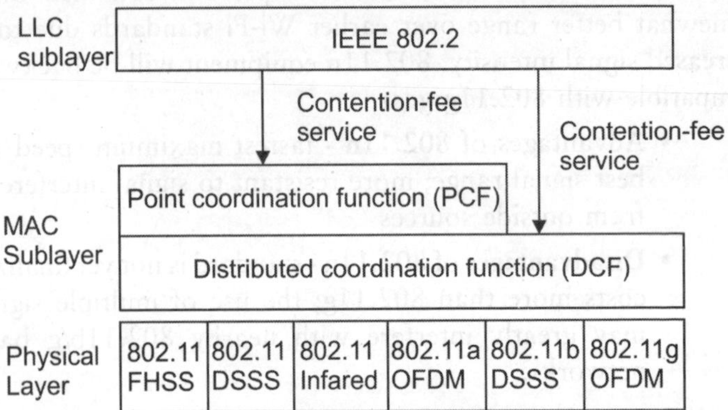

Bluetooth

Bluetooth, a standard and communications protocol, is an alternative wireless network technology that followed a different development path than the 802.11 family. Bluetooth supports a very short range (approximately 10 meters) and relatively low data rate (1 Mbps in practice) designed for low-power network devices like handhelds. The low manufacturing cost of Bluetooth hardware also appeals to industry vendors. You can readily find Bluetooth in the netowrking of PDAs or cell phones with PCs, but it is rarely used for general-purpose WLAN networking due to the range and speed considerations.

On the basis of power consumption, Bluetooth can be classified in three classes:

Class	Maximum Permitted Power mW(dBm)	Range (approximate)
Class 1	100 mW (20 dBm)	~100 meters
Class 2	2.5 mW (4 dBm)	~10 meters
Class 3	1 mW (0 dBm)	~1 meter

In the network of bluetooth, there is one master and several slaves. A master Bluetooth device can communicate with up to seven slave devices. This network group of up to eight devices is called a *piconet*. Bluetooth specification allows connecting two or more piconets together to form a *scatternet*, with some devices acting as a bridge by simultaneously playing the master role and the slave role in one piconet [1], [2].

A device like personal computer must have a Bluetooth adapter in order to be able to communicate with other. Bluetooth devices (such as mobile phones, mice and keyboards).

Bluetooth Layer

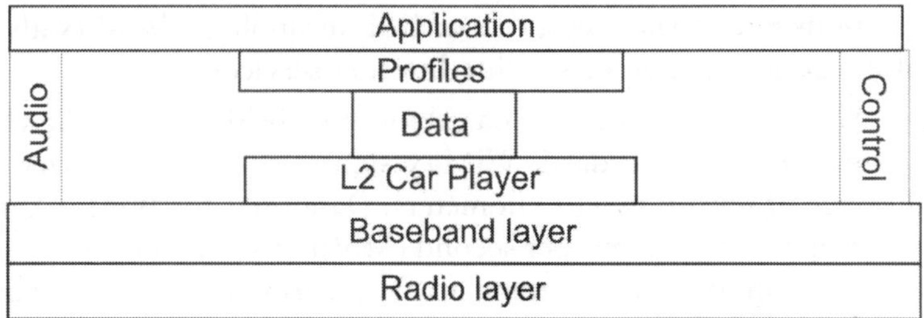

Radio layer is just like physical layer of internet model. Bluetooth uses frequency-hopping spread spectrum (FHSS) method in 2.4 GHz ISM band. Baseband layer is equivalent to the MAC sublayer in LANs. Bluetooth uses a form of TDMA that is called TDD-TDMA (time division duplex TDMA). This is a kind of half-duplex communication. There can be two types of communication: (1) Single-Secondary Communication, (2) Multiple-Secondary Communication. Two type of links can be created between a primary and a secondary: (1) Synchronous connection-oriented (SCO) links and (2) Asynchronous conntionless link (ACL). SCO link is used when avoiding latency is more important than integrity. ACL is used when data integrity is more important than avoiding latency. The Logical Link Control and Adaption Protocol, or L2CAP has specific duties: multiplexing, segmentation and reassembly, quality of service (QoS), and group management [5].

The specification is based on *frequency-hopping spread spectrum* technology, which improves resistance to radio frequency interference by avoiding the use of crowded frequencies in the hopping sequence.

- **Advantages of Bluetooth:** low cost, low power consumption.
- **Disadvantages of Bluetooth:** more prone to virus attack, rarely used for general-purpose WLAN networking due to the range and speed considerations.

WiMas

WiMax is the term which is used for a long-range wireless networking standard. WiMax technology has the potential to deliver high-speed Internet access to rural areas and other locations not serviced by cable or DSL technology. WiMax also offers an alternative to satellite Internet services.

WiMax technology is based on the IEEE 802.16 WAN communications standard. WiMax signals can function over a distance of several miles / kilometers. Data rates for WiMax can reach up to 75 megabits per second (Mb/s). A number of wireless signaling options exist ranging anywhere from the 2 GHz range up to 66 GHz [6].

A WiMax system has two major physical components, a WiMax tower of a range about 8000 square km and a receiver which is often a PCMCIA card inserted into the PC or laptop. The tower is connected to the internet using a standard wired high speed connection like T3. The user device connects to the WiMax tower through the microwave link. The WiMax can provide both a non line of sight communication as well as line of sight. A non line of sight communication uses a small antenna on the computer itself to connect to the WiMax antenna in a lower frequency range 2GHz to 11 GHz, which allows transmissions to be less, disrupted by physical obstruction. Line of sight communication uses a static dish antenna pointing straight to the WiMax antenna and is stable as well as stronger in a higher frequency range of 66 GHz providing less interference and more bandwidth. Similar to other types of Internet access, consumers will subscribe and pay a recurring fee to connect to the Internet via WiMax [4].

WiMax is developed by an industry consortium, overseen by a group called the WiMax Forum. The WiMax Forum certifies

WiMax equipment to ensure it meets the technology standards. WiMax is not a replacement for Wi-Fi hotspot and home networking technologies primarily for cost reasons.

WiMax is based on OFDMA technology. This is multi-carrier modulation scheme in which a single wideband transmission is replaced by many parallel narrowband transmissions.

Advantages of WiMax: last-mile connectivity in MANs, increased bandwidth for a variety of data-intensive applications with high data rates [3].

Disadvantages of WiMax: high bandwidth requirement, installation of this technology at user end is very costly [3].

Comparison:

Each wireless technology has its unique strengths and limitations and no single technology effectively meets the needs of all the applications. A comparison of various parameters of the above mentioned wireless technologies is shown below

Standard	Technique	Band	Rate (Mbps)
802.11	FHSS	2.4 GHz	1 and 2
	DSSS	2.4 GHz	1 and 2
		Infrared	1 and 2
802.11a	OFDM	5.725 GHz	6 to 54
802.11b	DSSS	2.4 GHz	6.5 to 11
802.11g	OFDM	2.4 GHz	22 and 54
Bluetooth	FHSS	2.4 GHz	1
WiMax	OFDM	2 to 66 GHz	75

CONCLUSION

Wireless technologies offer us a wide variety of options for data communication enabling a user to adopt any technology according to his requirement after analyzing comparison of the technologies. However, the insatiable nature of user will always lead to more TRENDS IN WIRELESS COMMUNICATION.

REFERENCES

1. Mane P.B., et all, "Wireless Protocol Standards and their Impact", icon ADELCO 2007.
2. Theodore S. Rappaport, et all, "Wireless Communication: past events and a future perspective", IEEE Communication May-2002
3. Deepak Pareek, "WiMax", published by John Wiley & Sons, Ltd.
4. Behrouz A Forouzan, "Data Comminication and Networking", 4th Edition, Tata McGraw Hill

Decision Making Techniques: Application Areas and Limitations

Ashish Sawhney, Sanjay Kumar and *Abid Haleem*

ABSTRACT

Decision making process as extensive significance in various areas of engg. and allied applications and efficient and effective use of resources can be done with its usage.

This paper deals with a various decision making techniques, their applications and limitations.

With the help of available literature some of the major decision making techniques has been identified. A brief on each technique has been provided . A table has been provided listing the major researches of these fourteen decision making techniques.

In a separate table major application of these decision making techniques have also been discussed. This paper may provide to the user of available decision making techniques at various levels and help in evolving a better application and subsequent decision.

INTRODUCTION

Decision making is a repetitive activity used to reach a conclusion which is best under the circumstances. We all make thousands of decisions every day, yet we don't feel any need to talk or discuss about decision making. Most people do not have an understanding of what decision-making is or involves yet they use various decision making techniques. What is decision-making? Decision making is the study of identifying and choosing alternatives based on the values and preferences of the decision-maker. Every decision making process produces a final choice.

Decision making is a psychological event. This means that although we don't see a decision, we can infer from observable behavior that a decision has been made. Decision making is the process of sufficiently reducing uncertainty and doubt about alternatives to allow a reasonable choice to be made from among them.The industrial engineering is concerned with bringing together and effective utilization of various resources to facilitate efficient production operation. Efficient utilization of resources means that input to the production such as people, material, information and equipments are used in right way so that they form an integrated combination to meet production and operation objectives. Industrial engineering is not restricted only to manufacturing activities. It includes service sector for meeting these specified criteria the decision made at each level must be very efficient and appropriate. Hence, the decision maker should be very efficient and should be able to make fast and efficient decisions at each level. For achieving this decision makers use many modern methods to face the competition and increase production and profits. (Shankar R, 2006).

Decision Making

Decision making is very useful in maintaining and increasing the production and productivity of the firm to meet the growing demand and increasing competition. The productivity depends upon many factors like machines used, automation, management, processes involved, work design, work environment, program, technology, manufacturing strategy and various external factors. To increase productivity all these factors are to be kept in mind and thus action plans be decided based upon these factors. Hence, decision making and decision makers play a very important role in increasing productivity of any firm and supply chain. (Triantaphyllou, E., 1994).

Thus the issue of improving group's and individual's abilities to solve problems and make decisions is very important in education, industry, and government. Hence, decision making has a very important role and should be a very efficient and effective procedure. (Huitt W, 1992). For this cause some standard steps are formulated, although it is purely the wish of the decision maker as to he should follow these steps or not. Each decision maker may follow seven steps to reach an efficient decision first being defining the problem. First of all the problem is identified for which a decision is to be made. After that planning for decision making. Planning allows decisions to be made in a much more comfortable and intelligent way. Planning even makes decisions easier by providing guidelines and goals for the decision. Planning allows the establishment of independent goals. Planning provides a standard of measurement. Planning converts values to action. Planning allows limited resources to be committed in an orderly way. After these steps various other steps are Gathering information, Identifying alternatives, Predicting future consequences, Compare alternatives, Select the best alternative. (Harris Robert, 1998)

As a means of understanding the significance of a decision so that decision maker can know how much time and resources to spend on it, three levels of decision have been used. We all see practically that some decisions are more important than others, whether in their immediate impact or long term significance. *Strategic decision making level*: Here a decision concerns general direction, long term goals, philosophies and values. These decisions are the least structured and most imaginative; they are the most risky and of the most uncertain outcome, partly because they reach so far into the future and partly because they are of such importance. Strategic decisions are the most important one and are of highest level. Example whether to purchase a small car or a bigger one to fulfill your family needs after your marriage will be a strategic decision. *Tactical decision making level*: Tactical decisions support strategic decisions. They tend to be medium range, medium significance, with moderate consequences. Example if you decided to purchase a big car, then saving the money and investing it will be a tactical decision. *Operational decision making level:* These are short term decisions, used to support tactical decisions. Their impact is immediate, short term, short range, and usually low cost. The consequences of a bad operational decision will be minimal, although a series of bad or sloppy operational decisions can cause harm. Example, if your tactical decision is to save money and invest it, then your operational decision is to search for an appropriate bank to invest and secure your money.

The ethical principles of decision making vary considerably. Some common choices of principles are where the most powerful person/group decides followed in Dictatorship or oligarchy, where everyone participates in a certain class of meta-decisions followed in Parliamentary democracy and where everyone participates in every decision followed in direct democracy, consensus decision making .

Decision Making Techniques

T-Chart. In one form, it can be a list of positive and negative attributes surrounding a particular choice. A T-Chart is an orderly, graphic representation of alternative features or points involved in a decision. Drawing up such a chart ensures that both the positive and negative aspects of each direction or decision will be taken into account.

Example: We want to make a decision which car to purchase with available alternatives suiting the decision maker. Alternatives are a petrol car or diesel car. Therefore, the T-Chart for petrol driven car (refer Table 1) may be (It can vary for every decision maker).

Table 1: T-Chart for Petrol Driven Vehicle

PROS	CONS
Better efficiency	Petrol is costlier
Low maintenance	Less life
Better pick up	More expensive

P.M.I. The T-Chart idea has been refined by Edward de Bono into a three part chart, which are PMI for plus, minus, and interesting. Here you first list all the pons or plus or good points of the idea, then all the cons or minus or bad points, and finally all the interesting points which can be consequences, areas of uncertainty, or attributes that you view as either good or bad at this point. The "interesting" category also allows exploration of the idea or choices outside the context of judgment you don't have to evaluate the attribute into a positive or negative category.

Buriden's Ass. Everybody faces a problem in decision making if there are two or more choices that are equally attractive. This result in consumption of more time required to make the decision. This is due to the fact that the decision maker gets confused in deciding which choice will be better. From an old fable of an ass placed between two equally nice bales of hay. The ass couldn't decide which bale to turn to because they were both so attractive, and so it starved to death from indecision .This method of decision making is used when two or more equally attractive alternatives are faced. The method is simply to list all the negative points or drawbacks about each decision. That is, when two or more alternatives seem very desirable, we become blinded to any drawbacks. The Buriden's Ass method simply focuses on the drawbacks. Example, your firm wants to increase your total cost to the company. It offers you these choices: (1) work less hours per week so that your per-hour pay rate will increase, (2) an increase in hourly pay, (3) a long paid vacation each year and continue to work at the same hourly pay. Now in this case each of the three choices comes out exactly the same in terms of economic values and is equally attractive.

Measured Criteria. In this technique, you list the criteria you want your decision to meet and assign points to each criterion based on its relative importance in the decision. Then, each alternative is given a certain number of points according to how fully it meets the criterion. For points, you can use a scale of 1 to 10, 1 to 100, or any other range that makes sense to your decision. Example, you want to decide which car to purchase out of three car named car1, car2 and car3.(refer Table 2)

Table 2: Example of Table Used in Measured Criteria Listing All Present Alternatives with their Weighted Values

	Possible Points	Car1	Car2	Car3
Speed	20	18	15	11
Comfort	10	9	7	8
Safety	20	17	13	19

So in this case we see that total points for car 1 are more than any other therefore car 1 will be the best choice.

PEST Analysis Method. PEST stands for Political, Economic, Social and Technological factors. Sometimes, PEST analysis is also called STEP analysis with same factors as PEST analysis. PEST is also extended to PESTELI model which consists of seven or even more factors, by adding Environmental, Legislative and Industry Analysis. STEEPLED is another interpretation which Political, Economic, Social, Technological, Ecological or Environmental, Ethical, Demographic and Legal. They all are used to assess the market for a business or organizational unit. The PEST analysis is a useful tool for understanding market growth or decline, and as such the position, potential and direction for a business. A PEST analysis is a business measurement tool. Table 3 shows various factors involved in the PEST analysis.

Table 3: Various Factors Involved In Pest Analysis

Political	Economic
• Ecological/environmental issues.	• Home economy situation
• Current legislation home market	• Home economy trends
• Future legislation	• Overseas economies and trends
• European/international legislation	• General taxation issues
• Regulatory bodies and processes	• Taxation specific to product /services
• Government policies	• Seasonality/weather issues
• Government term and change	• Market and trade cycles
• Trading policies	• Specific industry factors
• Funding, grants and initiatives	• Market routes and distribution trends
• Home market lobbying/pressure groups	• Customer/end-user drivers
• International pressure groups	• Interest and exchange rates
• Wars and conflict	• International trade/ monetary issues

Social	Technological
• Lifestyle trends	• Competing technology development
• Demographics	• Research funding
• Consumer attitudes and opinions	• Associated/dependent technologies
• Media views	• Replacement technology/ solutions
• Law changes affecting social factors	• Maturity of technology
• Brand, company, technology image	• Manufacturing maturity and capacity
• Consumer buying patterns	• Information and
• Fashion and role models	communications
• Major events and influences	• Consumer buying mechanisms /technology
• Buying access and trends	• Technology legislation
• Ethnic/religious factors	• Innovation potential
• Advertising and publicity	• Technology access, licensing, patents
• Ethical issues	• Intellectual property issues
	• Global communications

Porter's Five Forces. Porter's Five Forces model provides suggested points under each main heading, by which you can develop a broad and sophisticated analysis of competitive position, as might be used when creating strategy, plans, or making investment decisions about a business or organization. Michael Porter's famous Five Forces of Competitive Position model as shown in Figure 1 gives a simple perspective for analyzing the competitive strength and position of a business organization. Porter's five forces takes existing competitive rivalry between suppliers and elaborates strength of competition in the industry it helps in identifying:

Threat of new market entrants: The ease with which new competitors can enter the market if they see that you are making good profits and hence, increase the competition.

Bargaining power of buyers: The power of your customers to drive down your prices

Power of suppliers: The power of suppliers to drive up the prices of your inputs

Threat of substitute products: The extent to which different products and services can be used in place of your own.

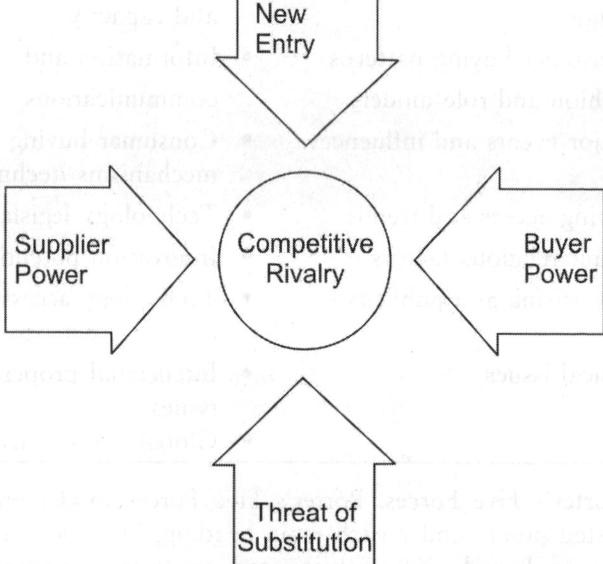

Fig. 1: Figure Showing Relation Between Various Porters' Factors.

This tool was created by Harvard Business School professor, Michael Porter, to analyze the attractiveness and likely-profitability of an industry. In this method after making such a table "+" sign is given to quantity in favor and "-"to a quantity against the decision maker. Thus, the decision maker gets an easy way to look over all the issues and decide accordingly.

Brainstorming Process. Brainstorming is a group *creativity technique* that was designed to generate a large number of ideas for the solution of a problem. Brainstorming with a group of people is a powerful technique. Brainstorming creates new ideas, solves problems, motivates and develops teams. Brainstorming motivates because it involves members of a team in bigger management issues, and it gets a team working together. However, brainstorming is not simply a random activity. A basic procedure of a brainstorming process is given in Figure 2

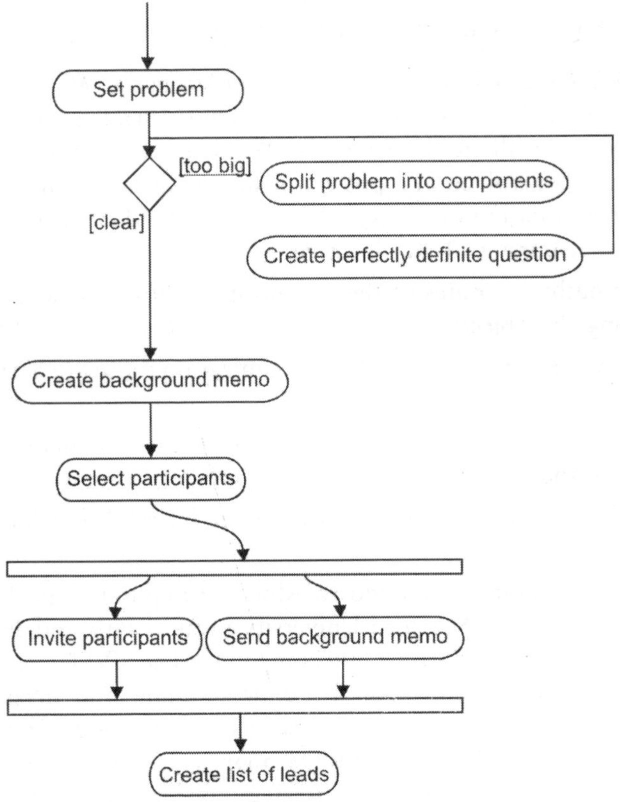

Fig. 2: Basic Procedure of Brainstorming Process

Brainstorming needs to be structured and it follows brainstorming rules.

Brainstorming process can be briefed stepwise as:

- Define and agree the objective.
- Select participants
- Brainstorm ideas and suggestions having agreed a time limit.
- Categorize/condense/combine/refine.
- Assess/analyze effects or results.
- Prioritize options/rank list as appropriate.
- Agree action and timescale.
- Control and monitor follow-up.

S.W.O.T. Analysis. SWOT stands for Strengths, Weaknesses, Opportunities and Threats. SWOT Analysis is a strategic planning tool used to evaluate the Strengths, Weaknesses, Opportunities, and Threats involved in a project or in a business venture or in any other situation of an organization or individual requiring a decision in pursuit of an objective.

Strength: attributes of the organization those are helpful to achieving the objective.

Weaknesses: attributes of the organization those are harmful to achieving the objective.

Opportunities: external conditions those are helpful to achieving the objective.

Threats: external conditions those are harmful to achieving the objective.

The technique is credited to Albert Humphrey, who led a research project at Stanford University in the 1960s and 1970s using data from the Fortune 500 companies. The SWOT analysis is an extremely useful tool for understanding and decision-making for all sorts of situations in business and organizations or at the personal level. The SWOT analysis headings provide a good framework for reviewing strategy, position and direction of a company or business proposition, or any other idea. A SWOT analysis measures a business unit, a proposition or idea. SWOT analysis can be used for all sorts of decision-making, and the SWOT template enables proactive thinking, rather than relying on habitual or instinctive reactions.

Analytic Hierarchy Process (AHP). AHP is a mathematical decision making technique that allows consideration of both qualitative and quantitative aspects of decisions, providing a useful mechanism for checking the consistency of the evaluation measures and alternatives suggested by the team thus reducing bias in decision making. It reduces complex decisions to a series of one-on-one comparisons, and then synthesizes the results. Compared to other techniques like ranking or rating techniques, the AHP uses the human ability to compare single properties of alternatives. It not only helps decision makers choose the best alternative, but also provides a clear rationale for the choice. Developed by Thomas Saaty in the 1970s, AHP provides a proven, effective means to deal with complex decision making and can assist with identifying and weighting selection criteria, analyzing the data collected for the criteria and expediting the decision-making process. Combined with meeting automation, organizations can minimize common pitfalls of team decision making process, such as lack of focus, planning, participation or ownership, which ultimately are costly distractions that can prevent teams from making the right choice.

The first step is for the team to decompose the goal into its constituent parts, progressing from the general to the specific. In its simplest form, this structure comprises a goal, criteria and alternative levels. Each set of alternatives would then be further divided into an appropriate level of detail, recognizing that the more criteria included, the less important each individual criterion may become.

Next, assign a relative weight to each one. Each criterion has a local (immediate) and global priority. The sum of all the criteria beneath a given parent criterion in each tier of the model must equal one. Its global priority shows its relative importance within the overall model.

Finally, after the criteria are weighted and the information is collected, put the information into the model. Scoring is on a relative basis, not an absolute basis, comparing one choice to another. Relative scores for each choice are computed within each leaf of the hierarchy. Scores are then synthesized through the model, yielding a composite score for each choice at every tier, as well as an overall score.

Buyer Decision Processes: Buyer decision processes are the decision making processes undertaken by consumers in regard to a potential market transaction before, during, and after the purchase of a product or service. More generally, decision making is the cognitive process of selecting a course of action from among multiple alternatives. Common examples include shopping, deciding what to eat. Decision making is said to be a psychological construct. This means that although we can never "see" a decision, we can infer from observable behavior that a decision has been made. Therefore, we conclude that a psychological event that we call "decision making" has occurred. It is a construction that imputes commitment to action. That is, based on observable actions, we assume that people have made a commitment to effect the action. In general there are three ways of analyzing consumer buying decisions. They are:

Economic models—These models are largely quantitative and are based on the assumptions of rationality and near perfect knowledge. The consumer is seen to maximize their utility. See consumer theory. Game theory can also be used in some circumstances.

Psychological models—These models concentrate on psychological and cognitive processes such as motivation and need reduction. They are qualitative rather than quantitative and build on sociological factors like cultural influences and family influences.

Consumer behavior models—These are practical models used by marketers. They typically blend both economic and psychological models.

Cost-Benefit Analysis. The process involves monetary calculations of initial and ongoing expenses vs. expected return. It is the process of weighing the total expected costs against the total expected benefits of one or more actions in order to choose the best or most profitable option. Constructing plausible measures of the costs and benefits of specific actions is often very difficult. In practice, analysts try to estimate costs and benefits either by using survey methods or by drawing inferences from market behavior. For example, a product manager may compare manufacturing and marketing expenses to projected sales for a proposed product, and only decide to produce it if he expects the revenues to eventually recoup the costs. Cost-benefit analysis attempts to put all relevant costs and benefits on a common temporal footing. A discount rate is chosen, which is then used to compute all relevant future costs and benefits in present-value terms. Most commonly, the discount rate used for present-value calculations is an interest rate taken from financial markets.

Force Field Analysis. Force field analysis is one of the most influential developments in the field of social science. Force field analysis provides a framework for looking at the factors (forces) that influence a situation, originally social situations. It looks at forces that are either driving movement toward a goal (helping forces) or blocking movement toward a goal (hindering forces). The principle, developed by Kurt Lewin, is a significant contribution to the fields of social science, psychology, social psychology, organizational development, process management, and change management. Lewin, a social psychologist, believed the "field" to be a Gestalt psychological environment existing in an individual's (or in the collective group) mind at a certain point in time that can be mathematically described in a *topological* constellation of constructs. The "field" is very dynamic, changing with time and experience. When fully constructed, an individual's "field" (Lewin used the term "life space") describes that person's motives, values, needs, moods, goals, anxieties, and ideals. Lewin believed that changes of an individual's "life space" depend upon that individual's internalization of external stimuli (from the physical and social world) into the "life space." Although Lewin did not use the word "experiential," (see *experiential learning*) he nonetheless believed that interaction (experience) of the "life space" with "external stimuli" (at what he calls the "boundary zone") were important for development (or regression). For Lewin, development (or regression) of an individual occurs when their "life space" has a "boundary zone" experience with external stimuli. Note, it is not merely the experience that causes change in the "life space," but the acceptance (internalization) of external stimuli. Lewin took these same principles and applied them to the analysis of group conflict, learning, adolescence, hatred, morale, German society, etc. This approach allowed him to break down common misconceptions of these social phenomena, and to determine their basic elemental constructs. He used theory, mathematics, and common sense to define a force field, and hence to determine the causes of human and group behavior.

Monte Carlo Simulation Method. Simulation is the use of quantities system model that has the designed characteristics of reality in order to produce the essence of actual operation by developing a series of organized experiments to predict the behavior of the process over a short period of time. Monte Carlo methods are a widely used class of computational algorithms for simulating the behavior of various physical and mathematical systems, and for other computations. They are distinguished from other simulation methods (such as molecular dynamics) by being stochastic, that is nondeterministic in some manner—usually by using random numbers (or, more often, pseudo-random numbers)—as opposed to deterministic algorithms. Because of the repetition of algorithms and the large number of calculations involved, Monte Carlo is a method suited to calculation using a computer, utilizing many techniques of simulation. A Monte Carlo algorithm is often a numerical Monte Carlo method used to find solutions to mathematical problems (which may have many variables) that cannot easily be solved, for many types of problems, its efficiency relative to other numerical methods increases as the dimension of the problem increases. Or it may be a method for solving other mathematical problems that relies on (pseudo-)random numbers.

Procedure of Monte Carlo simulation:

Decide the probability distribution of important variables for the stochastic process.

Calculate the cumulative probability for each variable in first step.

Decide an interval of random numbers for each variable.

Generate variable numbers.

Simulate a series of trials and determine simulated value of the actual random variables.

Six Thinking Hats. Six Thinking Hats is the title and subject of a book by Edward De Bono, published in 1985. De Bono considered human cognition and thought to be of several types, approaches, or orientations. He theorized that of these approaches, most people used only one or two of the approaches and that people developed thinking habits which in turn limited people to those approaches. De Bono believed that if the various approaches could be identified and a system of their use developed which could be taught, that people could be more productive in meetings and in collaborating within groups and teams by deliberately using the approaches. As a result of his investigations, De Bono was able to describe a process of deliberately adopting a particular approach to a problem as an implementation of Parallel Thinking™ as well as an aid to lateral thinking. Six different approaches are described, and each is symbolized by the act of putting on a colored hat, either actually or imaginatively. This, he suggests, can be done either by individuals working alone or in groups.

De Bono's six hats are:

- The White Hat calls for information known or needed. The facts, just the facts.
- The Yellow Hat symbolizes brightness and optimism. Under this hat you explore the positives and probe for value and benefit
- The Black Hat is judgment - the devil's advocate or why something may not work. Spot the difficulties and dangers; where things might go wrong. Probably, the most powerful and useful of the Hats but a problem if overused.
- The Red Hat signifies feelings, hunches and intuition. When using this hat you can express emotions and feelings and share fears, likes, dislikes, loves, and hates.

- The Green Hat focuses on creativity; the possibilities, alternatives, and new ideas. It's an opportunity to express new concepts and new perceptions.
- The Blue Hat is used to manage the thinking process. It's the control mechanism that ensures the Six Thinking Hats® guidelines are observed.

The main purposes of using Six Thinking Hats are:

- Focus and improve the thinking process.
- Encourage creative, parallel and lateral thinking.
- Improve communication.
- Speed up decision making.
- Avoid debate.

De Bono believed that the key to a successful use of the Six Think Hats methodology was the deliberate focusing of the discussion on a particular approach as needed during the meeting or collaboration session. For instance, a meeting may be called to review a particular problem and to develop a solution for the problem. The Six Thinking Hats method could then be used in a sequence to first of all explore the problem, and then develop a set of solutions, and to finally choose a solution through critical examination of the solution set. So, the meeting may start with everyone assuming the Blue hat to discuss how the meeting will be conducted and to develop the goals and objectives. The discussion may then move to Red hat thinking in order to collect opinions and reactions to the problem. This phase may also be used to develop constraints for the actual solution such as who will be affected by the problem and/or solutions. Next, the discussion may move to the Green hat in order to generate ideas and possible solutions. Next, the discussion may move between White hat thinking as part of developing information and Black hat thinking to develop criticisms of the solution set. Because everyone is focused on a particular approach at any one time, the group tends to be more collaborative than if one person is reacting emotionally (Red hat) while another person is trying to be objective (White hat) and still another person is being critical of the points which emerge from the discussion (Black hat). Table 4: shows various decision making techniques and their researchers name is also referred.

Table 4: Various Decision Making Techniques with Their Researchers References

SNo	Decision Making Technique	Researchers
1.	T Chart	Robert Harris, 1998.
2	PMI	Edward de Bono, 1992. Robert Harris, 1998.
3.	Buriden's Ass	D. Power Robert Harris, 1998.
4.	Measured Criteria	Robert Harris, 1998.
5.	PEST Analysis Method	Byars, L., 1991 Cooper, L., 2000
6.	Porter's Five Forces.	Porter, M., 1998. Thurlby B, 1998 Sanderson, S., 1998.
7.	Brainstorming Process	Osborn, A.F., 1963. Nijstad, B. A., Stroebe, W., Lodewijkx, H. F. M., 2003.
8.	S.W.O.T. Analysis.	De Witt, B. and Meyer, R., 1998 Adams, J., 2005.
9.	Analytic Hierarchy Process	McCaffrey, James. 2005
10.	Buyer Decision Processes	Nicosia, F., 1966. Simon, H., 1947.
11.	Cost-Benefit Analysis	Bent Flyvbjerg, Mette K., Skamris Holm, and Søren L. Buhl, 2002
12.	Force Field Analysis	Lewin K., 1943. Thomas, Joe, 1985.
13	Monte Carlo Simulation	Dr Shankar R, 2006
14.	Six Thinking Hats	Edward De Bono., 1985.

Applications of Decision Making Techniques

Some of the major applications of different decision making techniques were explored and have been shown below in a tabulated form in Table no 5.

Table 5: Applications of Various Decision Making Techniques

S.No.	Decision Making Technique	Application Areas
1.	T-Chart	This tool is applied in smaller decision making activities or as a part of a complex decision making activity. This tool is applied in early stages of decision making to make a clear picture that the decision maker should further advance his course of action or not.
2.	PMI	The main application of PMI tool is to check that it is going to improve the situation or not before you move straight to action on some course of action. This tool is a primary tool and hence is the most important one. This tool is very flexible and is used in almost every type of decision making activity.
3.	Buriden's Ass	This technique is especially useful for those decisions involving several alternatives and several criteria. This tool is used in those problems where two or more equally attractive situation come in front of the decision maker. Making This type of scenario can lead to indecision or a decision which is not timely.
4.	Measured Criteria	This technique is used when we have more than two options available which satisfy the set of criteria that the decision maker requires and the decision maker has to choose the best out of them.
5.	Pest Market Analysis Tool	The PEST analysis is a useful tool for understanding market growth or decline, and as such the position, potential and direction for a business.

		A PEST analysis is a business measurement tool. The PEST analysis headings are a framework for reviewing a situation and can be used to review a strategy or position, direction of a company, a marketing proposition, or idea. PEST is used in analysis for business and strategic planning, marketing planning, business and product development and research reports.
6.	Porter's Five Forces	The five forces concept provides entrepreneurs with an excellent tool to examine the profit potential in a particular industry. All these five forces combined determine the attractiveness of a market. It also provides necessary input for performing other analysis like swot analysis.
7.	Brainstorming Process	Brainstorming is used in improving the organization, performance, and developing the team. Brainstorming finds its application in organizations and market where creative problem solving is to be carried out within groups.
8.	S.W.O.T. Analysis	SWOT Analysis is a tool for auditing an organization, a community, or an individual in its environment. A SWOT Analysis is a strategic planning tool used to evaluate the Strengths, Weaknesses, Opportunities, and Threats involved in a project or in a business venture or in any other situation of an organization or individual requiring a decision in pursuit of an objective. The aim of any SWOT analysis is to identify the key internal and external factors that are important to achieving the objective
9.	Analytic Hierarchy Process (AHP)	In a business or policy setting, you have to avoid emotional confrontations and pursue a rational, common denominator, here we see the main application oh the AHP technique.

		The AHP uses the human ability to compare single properties of different alternatives and thus reach to a conclusion. It not only helps decision makers choose the best alternative, but also provides a clear rationale for the choice. It is used when making complex decisions involving multiple criteria.
10.	Buyer Decision Processes	The application of this tool lies in hands of the consumers in regard to a potential market transaction before, during, and after the purchase of a product or service. These processes are used by marketers for market analysis and reading their customers.
11.	Cost-Benefit Analysis	Cost-benefit analysis can tell us directly whether or not a given policy should be implemented. Its main application is as a governmental evaluation tool. It is used to analyze policies affecting transportation, public health, criminal justice, defense, education, the environment and many more. Calculations of discount rates.
12.	Force Field Analysis	Change management is the primary application for force field analysis. Change is a regular occurrence in many industries like the healthcare environment. Productivity improvement is the second main application of force field analysis. This universal application of how to increase employee productivity demonstrates a powerful need for the force field analysis tool Force field analysis is also a powerful decision-making tool.
13.	Monte Carlo Simulation	Simulation is very useful to draw customer attention about the system performance. It

		also provides customer support and satisfaction. Many situations are difficult to be modeled into conventional models such as linear programming, integer programming etc. Sometimes the approximation of real life parameters may not be desirable. In such cases, simulation is an efficient way to model and analyze the situations. Simulation provides modeling flexibility. Various parameters may be changed and various combinations of parameters may be evaluated. Simulation is useful to judge the system's behavior in a controlled environment. This is important when effect of changes in few parameters needs to be observed.
14.	Six Thinking Hats	Critical and Analytical Thinking, Problem-Solving, and Decision-Making Creativity Training, Meeting Facilitation and Meeting Management Team Productivity and Communication Product and Process Improvement, and Project Management Wherever High Performance Thinking is needed

Limitations of Decision Making Techniques

Some of the major limitations of the selected 14 decision making techniques have been briefed in Table 6. This may help researchers and applicators in making appropriate selection of these techniques.

Table 6: Limitations of Various Decision Making Techniques

S.No.	Decision Making Technique	Limitation of Decision Making Technique
1.	T-Chart	• This tool can be used only with smaller and non complex decision making. • During the listing of various features some features can be unthought-of. • Various features and their consequences can be misjudged.
2.	PMI	• Takes the emotion and guesswork out of complex decisions, with the side benefit of forcing a brain dump. • Some factors can be neglected or misjudged which can lead to indecision or faulty decision.
3.	Buriden's Ass	• This technique can be used only in those cases where two or more equally attractive options are cited, but these types of cases are very few. • The application area of this tool is very limited. • In this technique we completely rely on the negative aspects of the options available to take a decision, but in some cases these negative aspects are so diluted that they don't have any relevant affect on the outcome.
4.	Measured Criteria	• Indecision can occur due to misjudging the importance of some criteria. • All criteria may not be included.
5.	Pest Market Analysis Tool	• PEST relics on data, which at times is hard to come by (reliability, validity), and can hardly analyse attitudes and behavioural/ cultural issues that are also very key.

		• The factors in the context are not static • Analysis of trends assumes that future will be like the past
6.	Porter's Five Forces	• Michael Porter's five forces model, focus on the company's external competitive environment and do not attempt to look inside the company. • The model was designed for analyzing individual business strategies and it does not cope with synergies and interdependencies within the portfolio of large corporations. • The model does not address the possibility that an industry could be attractive because certain companies are in it.
7.	Brainstorming Process	• The idea is to get out before the group all ideas possible, with no thought to how practical the ideas might be. • Many of the suggestions made may not be worth anything. • Although brainstorming has become a popular group technique, researchers have generally failed to find evidence of its effectiveness for enhancing either quantity or quality of ideas generated. • Many individuals have difficulty getting away from practicalities. • In the evaluation session, it is necessary to criticize the ideas of fellow members.
8.	S.W.O.T. Analysis	• The classification of some factors as strengths or weaknesses, or as opportunities or threats is somewhat arbitrary. • The SWOT framework has a tendency to oversimplify the situation by

		classifying the firm's environmental factors into categories in which they may not always fit. • What is more important than the superficial classification of these factors is the firm's awareness of them and its development.
9.	Analytic Hierarchy Process (AHP)	• The drawback of AHP technique is that if the scale is changed from 1 to 10, to say, 1 to 100, the numbers in the end result, which we called the Value for Money Vector, will also change. • The limitations of the AHP are that it only works because the matrices are all of the same mathematical form – known as a positive reciprocal matrix. To create such a matrix requires that, if we use the number 9 to represent 'A is absolutely more important than B', then we have to use 1/9 to define the relative importance of B with respect to A. Some people regard that as reasonable, others are less happy about it.
10.	Buyer Decision Processes	• The outcome of this market analysis tool is uncertain and thus can be risky. • This tool cannot be used with all customers, thus a group or small section of customers can be targeted.
11.	Cost-Benefit Analysis	• Accuracy problem: The efficiency criteria on which cost-benefit analysis is based depend on distribution and equity and that they are relative. When the efficiency conflicts with other values, it is actually impossible, to create economic welfare criteria that integrate all values. • Another limitation is that there are no criteria for determining which costs should be included in an analysis.

12.	Force Field Analysis	• The process is subjective and requires collaborative thinking and agreement concerning forces for and against the solution to a particular problem. • May oversimplify the relationships between factors that impact a problem. • All aspects of a problem may not be identified.
13.	Monte Carlo Simulation	• Simulation requires large number of experimentations or runs under a given set of conditions. Any deviation in these conditions may not justify the simulation results. Therefore each simulation method provides a unique solution. • With increase in parameters, simulation becomes very complex to the model. • Simulation models are not precise and exact replica of reality. It is therefore not an optimizing tool. It is a descriptive tool.
14.	Six Thinking Hats	• The main limitation of this technique is its complexity. • For a sound decision making activity all the members given different roles must carry out their responsibility efficiently. Sometimes the role given to all the members are not carried out efficiently so the whole decision can be affected.

CONCLUSION

Every human being makes thousands of decisions day in and day out. Yet only few people really understand what decision making involves and about it's various parameters. This paper illustrates various decision making tools with their methodology used in the modern era to make sound decisions at personal, managerial or organizational level. Decision making is an activity to reach a conclusion which is best under the circumstances and fulfill the requirements of the decision maker to the maximum possible extent. Decision making is practiced in all facets of life be it environmental, resource management, maintenance, economic, agricultural, and manufacturing problems. In today's engineering environment, knowledge-based engineering plays an important role and is most sensible to practice. Knowledge based engineering practice involves decisions relating dispersed teams working under challenging cost and timing constraints. Under these conditions, the quality of most decisions can be improved through the application of various tools. In this paper, we propose an approach for better decision making by the use of modern tools and techniques used widely in various organization or at personal level.

REFERENCES AND BIBLIOGRAPHY

1. Cooper, L. (2000) Strategic Marketing planning for radically new products, *Journal of Marketing*, Vol. 64 Issue 1, pp.1-15.
2. Sanderson, S. (1998), New Approaches to Strategy: New Ways of Thinking for the Millennium, Management Decision, Vol. 36 issue 1, pp.9-13.
3. Dr Shankar, R., Industrial Engineering and Management, 2006, Golgotha Publications Pvt. Ltd. pp. 1-6,23-32,751-761.
4. Force Field Analysis: A New Way to Evaluate Your Strategy Thomas, Joe. Long Range Planning. London: Dec 1985.Vol.18, Is. 6; pg. 54, 6 pgs.
5. Adams, J. (2005) Analyze Your Company Using SWOTs, Supply House Times, Vol. 48 Issue 7, pp. 26-28.
6. McCaffrey, James. "The Analytic Hierarchy Process", MSDN Magazine, June 2005 (Vol. 20, No. 6), pp. 139-144.
7. Nijstad, B. A., Stroebe, W., Lodewijkx, H. F. M. (2003). Production Blocking Idea Generation: Does Blocking interfere with Cognitive Processes? *Journal of Experimental Social Psychology*, 39, 531-548.
8. Bent Flyvbjerg, Mette K. Skamris Holm, and Søren L. Buhl, "Underestimating Costs in Public Works Projects: Error or Lie?" *Journal of the American Planning Association*, vol. 68, no. 3, Summer 2002, pp. 279-295.
9. Lewin K. (1943). Defining the "Field at a Given Time." *Psychological Review*. 50: 292-310

10. Harris Robert, "Decision Making Techniques," Version Date: July 3, 1998
11. Edward de Bono, Serious Creativity, Harper Business, New York, US, 1992.
12. Byars, L. (1991) Strategic Management, Formulation and Implementation – Concepts and Cases, New York.
13. Porter, M. (1998) Competitive Strategy: Techniques for Analyzing Industries and Competitors, New York: Free Press
14. Osborn, A.F. (1963) Applied imagination: Principles and Procedures of Creative Problem Solving (Third Revised Edition). New York, NY: Charles Scribner's Sons.
15. Nicosia, F. (1966) *Consumer Decision Processes*, Prentice Hall, Englewood Cliffs, 1966.
16. Thurlby, B. (1998) "Competitive Forces are also Subject to Change", *Management Decision*, London.
17. Weihrich, H. (1982) The TOWS Matrix: A Tool for Situational Analysis, *Journal of Long Range Planning*, Vol. 15 Issue 2, pp.12-14.
18. Mullen, B., Johnson, C., & Salas, E. (1991). Productivity Loss in Brainstorming Groups: A Meta-analytic Integration. *Basic and Applied Social Psychology*. Pp. 12, 3-23.
19. Triantaphyllou, E., Decision Making in Engineering and Business: A Cost-Effective Approach, Northcon/94 Conference Record, 1994, pp. 232-237.
20. Huitt, W. (1992). Problem Solving and Decision Making: Consideration of Individual Differences Using the Myers-Briggs Type Indicator. *Journal of Psychological Type*, 24, 33-44.

Virtual Private Networks: An Overview with Performance

34

Vijay Kumar

ABSTRACT

Virtual private networks have gained immense popularity among commercial and defense organizations because of their capability to provide secure connectivity at lower costs. Several commercial and open source VPN products are now available that can be configured to provide VPN services with varying characteristics. This article studies some of the most popular Open-Source Linux-Based VPN solutions (OSLVs) and compares them with respect to network performance (measured in terms of overhead, bandwidth utilization, and latency/jitter), features and functionalities (e.g., algorithm plugins and routing), and operational concerns (defined by security and scalability). Our experiments suggest that there is no single OSLV solution that excels in all considered aspects, and a combination of different VPN products and/or trade-off among desired characteristics may be required to deliver optimal performance. Our experiments also suggest that on an average, OSLVs using UDP-based tunnels have 50 percent lower overhead, 80 percent higher bandwidth utilization, and 40–60 percent lower latency/jitter than those using TCP.

INTRODUCTION

The Internet is considered the cornerstone of connectivity for organizations to expand their operations and increase revenues. As organizations grow, different methods must be employed to provide secure and efficient connectivity among geographically distributed branch offices, strategic partners, and mobile/telecommuting employees. Although several technologies exist, most recently Internet-based virtual private networks (VPNs) have evolved as the most secure and cost-effective means of achieving these goals. VPNs belong to a family of overlay networks that use IP tunnels to form a virtual network on top of the Internet. These tunnels use cryptographic techniques to provide robust security and privacy. To a remote user, VPN provides all the benefits of a private network, while corporations benefit from the low operational costs, high security, and instant global coverage offered by it [1].

Several commercial VPN products are now widely available, drawing a lot of attention from researchers and developers alike. These are a breed of software solutions that can provide commercial-grade VPN services at commodity prices, using desktop computers running Linux. The availability of source code and open source licensing allows developers to customize and optimize (and sometimes commercialize) these products for specialized hardware to extract maximum performance; for example, SnapGear's [2] LITE+ and SME550 products use a port of FreeS/WAN (an open IPSec implementation) on □Clinux (Linux for microcon-trollers). Since Linux is used as the underlying operating system, deployment is quick and easy, circumventing the need for system administrators to learn proprietary operating systems. All this coupled with free technical support, available through newsgroups and mailing lists, presents a good alternative for small to medium businesses to operate globally at virtually zero cost. With advancements in Linux powered routers, these solutions, in our opinion, have the potential to carve a niche in the VPN market.

In this article we study and evaluate some of the most popular Open-Source Linux-Based VPN solutions (OSLVs). We present a comparative study, based on network performance, supported features/functionality, and operational concerns, for several popular OSLVs that are freely available over the Internet. From this study we seek to highlight common drawbacks that currently exist in OSLVs and underscore future research questions that need to be addressed. Recently, Pena and Evans [3] have studied different VPNs in terms of throughput and CPU usage in high-/low-speed networks. Although important, we feel that there are several aspects (overhead, security, modularity, etc.) that characterize a VPN solution and hence warrant comparison. Our work is comprehensive in terms of both the number of VPN solutions considered and the number of characteristics compared.

Our study reveals that there is no single OSLV that excels in all considered attributes; selecting an appropriate solution is a complicated procedure, involving many trade-offs depending on the company's policy and intended applications. For example, *FreeS/WAN* demonstrates low latency and jitter, making it suitable for real-time applications. However, it introduces high overhead and low bandwidth utilization. Hence, for situations where these factors are important, alternatives like *Cipe or PPTP* may be employed. In short, several factors need to be carefully evaluated before an OSLV solution is selected for deployment, and multiple solutions may be made to interwork to extract maximum performance. A condensed version of this work also appears in the proceedings of ICCCN '04.

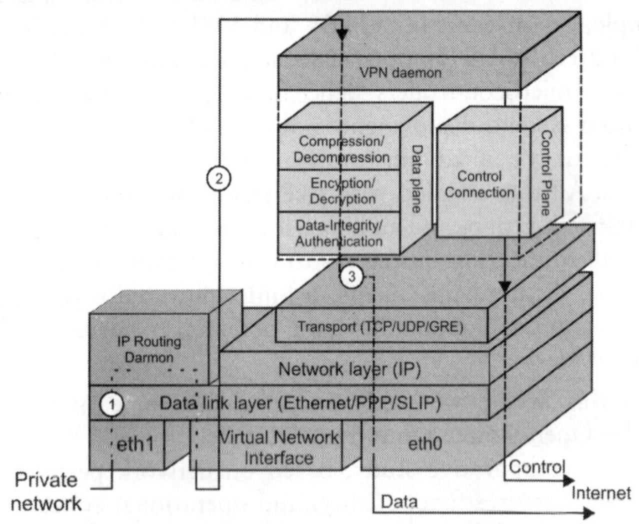

Fig. 1. The software architecture of an OSLV router.

The Software Architecture of an OSLV Router

The software architecture of a typical OSLV router is illustrated in Fig. 1. It is a modification of the TCP/IP network protocol stack with two additional components: the VPN daemon and the *Virtual Network Interface* (VNI). The VPN daemon is a user- or kernel-level process with a separate control plane for connection maintenance and a data plane for data processing. The control plane is used for peer authentication and generating session keys that are subsequently used to secure tunnels. It also maintains a mapping between IP addresses of peer OSLV routers and private subnets, which is consulted while tunneling a VPN packet. The data plane is like a serial pipeline providing encryption, authentication, and compression services. Control planes generally use TCP for transport, while the data plane may use either TCP or UDP. Later, we show that VPNs that use connection-oriented protocols (like TCP) have significantly poorer network performance than those using connectionless protocols (like UDP).

The VNI is an abstract device specifically created during VPN initialization to seamlessly exchange packets between the IP routing daemon and the VPN daemon. Any packet routed through the VNI gets automatically delivered to the VPN daemon and vice versa. Like any real network interface, a data link protocol like PPP or SLIP controls packet delivery over the VNI. The universal tun/tap driver and pseudo-terminals are some popular mechanisms for creating a VNI.

Figure 1 also outlines the data path taken by a packet as it travels from one private network to another, divided into three parts:

1. On arriving at *eth1*, the VPN packet is subsequently handed over to the IP routing daemon, which determines its next-hop router/egress interface by using a longest prefix match on its destination address.
2. Since the destination is a private address, the routing daemon will drop this packet unless the routing table is updated to route it through the VNI, or the routing daemon is modified to recognize a VPN packet and directly hand it to the VPN daemon. Although the second method eliminates an extra trip down the protocol stack, it requires changes to routing protocol,

which is much more complicated. Hence, the first method is usually preferred.

3. The VPN daemon treats all packets as data and subjects them to compression and other cryptographic functions. It then determines the public IP/port of the peer OSLV router, wraps it in a new IP header, and sends it as a normal data packet. At the receiver the exact reverse steps take place as the packet is delivered to the correct destination.

VPN Characteristics

Different VPN characteristics play a significant role in selecting an optimal solution for a given application scenario. In the discussion that follows, we classify these characteristics along the following three dimensions: network performance, supported features and functionalities, and operational concerns.

Network performance

Network performance of an OSLV is measured in terms of overhead, bandwidth utilization, and latency/jitter. It is a well-known fact that VPNs have poor network performance, implying high overhead, low bandwidth utilization, and high latency/jitter. Below, we identify some root causes of this anomaly and discuss popularly used remedies.

Overhead

The software architecture discussed earlier explains in part the large overhead added to a basic data packet as it travels through several layers of protocol. All OSLVs invariably suffer from this large overhead, 75 per cent of which is primarily contributed by the headers/ trailers added by the various protocol layers, and the remaining 25 per cent by the cryptographic algorithms employed for security. Header/trailer overhead can be reduced through compression. Some OSLVs (like *PPP_over_SSH* and *Stunnel*) use the header compression routines provided by data link layer protocols (like PPP) operating over the VNI, while others (like Tinc and Open-VPN) provide built-in compression utilities. Compression, however, introduces additional latency and, if blindly used for every packet, regardless of its size or type (compressed or encrypted), may not improve performance [4].

The overhead introduced by the cryptographic algorithms typically cannot be reduced, and is contributed by the specific cipher/medium access control (MAC) algorithm in use. Stream ciphers do not add any overhead, but the more popular block ciphers (like 3DES or blowfish) require the input to be a multiple of 8 or 16 bytes (called block size), which adds to the overhead in the form of extra padding bytes. MAC algorithms such as MD5 and SHA1 contribute an additional 16–20 bytes. Other minor contributions are from sequence numbers and timestamps used to defeat replay attacks.

Bandwidth Utilization

This is the maximum bandwidth achieved by a TCP stream and is affected by overhead, latency, and TCP stacking. While overhead reduces the amount of useful bytes transferred, latency affects the bandwidth-delay product for a TCP connection. For long fat virtual pipes (as in the present case), the latency introduced is often so large it is physically impossible to allocate the larger buffers required to support the corresponding increase in TCP window sizes to maintain the bandwidth utilization.

The last factor, TCP stacking, refers to using TCP multiple times along the packet data path. This happens if a TCP stream flows over an OSLV that uses TCP-based data channels. Interference between TCP timers at different layers causes this degradation [5]. We found this to be the most profound effect, with OSLVs using TCP performing far worse than those using UDP.

Latency/Jitter

Higher latencies occur due to the elongated packet data path (as apparent from Fig. 1), the compute-intensive nature of cryptographic functions, and multiple copying of data packets between kernel and user space. A good method to shorten data paths is to resort to layer 2 switching, as in multiprotocol label switching (MPLS) or asynchronous transfer mode (ATM), while higher computational time can be reduced by using faster hardware [6] or better cryptographic algorithms. Finally, multiple copying of data packets occurs because OSLVs exist as daemons in the user space and can be eliminated by integrating them into the operating system (OS) kernel. This, however, reduces operating flexibility, as most users are not kernel experts. Similarly increase in jitter depends on the OS scheduling scheme and can only be reduced by increasing its process priority.

Supported features/functionality

OSLVs are expected to support certain important features to enhance performance. Here, the importance of supporting two such features is discussed, while the results section presents how well equipped current OSLVs are to support such features.

Code Modularity

This refers to the flexibility of an OSLV solution when it comes to using algorithms of one's choice. Thus, code modularity can be defined as the OSLV's support for algorithm plugins, which can range from simple plugins for cryptos to more complex ones for routing or security. Algorithm plugins are an excellent way to allow quick and easy integration of newer algorithms into the OSLV solution and gives its users an option to create or buy independently developed plugins for ciphers, digests, or compression. OSLV solutions designed with plugins can survive potential security threats, thus extending their shelf life, and also allow companies to use their own proprietary code.

Routing

Routing needs to be set once the tunnels are established and the topology is set. The routing table in every OSLV router node needs to be updated with information on reaching its peer nodes. This can be done either manually or automatically. Routes can be manually updated using a command line utility like route (available on most UNIX systems). However, this presents a cumbersome and often error-prone exercise when the number of nodes is large, and often results in a full mesh topology. Automatic routing employs an independent routing daemon to exchange routing information and configure routing tables. For single-domain VPNs, where the private address space is unique, a separate routing program can be used to update private routing information. This approach allows arbitrary topologies to be created and proprietary algorithms to be used. For multidomain VPNs, where the address space is not unique, routing becomes a complicated issue. This is currently a hot area of research, and one possible solution is to have separate routing instances and routing tables (called virtual routers) for every VPN.

Operational concerns

Selecting an OSLV solution for deployment requires good background information on many operational features like security and scalability, which ultimately decide the usefulness of the VPN solution. These are qualitative parameters that are difficult to define and compare. In this section we present a number of properties for each of these aspects to get a better idea about them.

Security

Although the security offered by an OSLV solution is an important characteristic, it is highly relative and difficult to define in absolute terms. Until the recent past, secrecy and obfuscation was mainly used to provide security, which was manifested in large-scale use of proprietary non-standard algorithms (e.g., MPPE used in *PPTP*) where source code/ algorithm is kept a secret. However, this notion has long been abandoned because many such algorithms have already been broken [7]. The new and widely accepted norm is open standardized protocols where the algorithms and their implementations are widely published over the Internet, which allows extreme scrutiny on the strength of the algorithms by multitudes of experts. At this time there are no litmus tests to determine the relative security offered by different protocols, which makes it difficult if not impossible to gauge it. Hence, any preconceived comments on this topic would be inconclusive. However, we have rated standard protocols like SSH, SSL/TLS, and IPSec as more secure than nonstandard protocols. Determining the relative strength of the security offered by OSLVs belonging to the same group is out of the scope of this article.

Scalability

Clercq and Paridaens [8] have analyzed the scalability of provider provisioned VPNs in terms of *memory consumption, processing power, and configuration and management load.* We use similar lines of reasoning to address scalability concerns in this article. Memory consumption and processing power mainly depend on the number of established tunnels. Every tunnel requires certain state (session keys, certificates, routing information, etc.) to be maintained at each end. The maximum size of this state determines the memory consumption with *N* tunnels consuming *N* times the available memory. Processing power, on the other hand, is affected by the computer-intensive nature of cryptographic functions. With higher numbers of tunnels, the slice of CPU time allocated for every tunnel is reduced by the same fraction. Lastly, configuration and management load can be quantified by the total efforts required for editing configuration files, updating routing information, and distributing security keys when new tunnels are added or deleted.

Memory consumption and processing power limit the scalability of only a single OSLV node; this problem can be partially eliminated by using powerful desktops with larger main memory or higher processing power. Since OSLVs are mainly targeted for small-scale businesses (typically consisting of 10–50 sites), these factors do not play a significant role and have been neglected in this article. We only concentrate on the last factor, which in our opinion affects the scalability of the entire system.

The Experimental Testbed

The testbed used in our experiments consists of two OSLV routers (OSLV-A and -B) and creates a secure tunnel between two private networks (PN-1, PN-2) located in the same building. OSLV-A contains an Intel Pentium 4 processor at 2.0 GHz, with 512 Mbytes of RAM and running RedHat Linux 9.0. OSVL-B is a lower-end desktop using a 400 MHz Pentium II processor, with 128 Mbytes of RAM and running RedHat Linux 8.0. PC-1 (on PN-1) and PC-2 (on PN-2) are Linux desktops that are used to conduct network performance experiments. The testbed is isolated (no external congestion) and all links use 100 Mb/s Fast Ethernet.

The overhead was measured by first analyzing the OSLV solution, and later verifying it, by capturing live UDP packets of known length. These packets were generated using a simple UDP generator program and captured using a packet snooping utility like ethereal. Bandwidth and jitter were measured using *iperf*, while *ping* was used to measure latency. Each experiment was repeated 10 times in both directions, and only the average has been reported. Since there was no one common cipher/MAC that could be used with all OSLVs, experiments were performed by using one of {Blowfish, 3DES or none} for ciphers and {SHA1, MD5 or none} for MAC. Compression was disabled at all levels.

We have grouped the selected OSLV solutions based on the security protocol employed, since VPNs using the same security protocol can be expected to deliver almost similar performances. Accordingly, we have VPNs based on SSH, SSL/TLS, IPSec and other proprietary protocols, as shown in Fig. 2. All OSLVs in the top half of the figure use TCP data channels, while those at the bottom use UDP.

SSH, standardized by the *secsh* working group of the IETF, provides support for secure logins and secure file transfers. *PPP_over_SSH* is the only VPN solution that uses SSH. Both PPP and SSH are mature protocols in widespread use, and a simple VPN can be set up using a single command [9].

SSL/TLS, standardized by the *tls* working group, was initially developed by Netscape to provide secure Web transactions (versions 1 and 2), but over the past few years this protocol has matured into a standard solution for secure communications (SSLv3/TLSv1). *Stunnel, AmritaVPN*, and *LinVPN* are the OSLVs that use SSL/TLS, with *Stunnel* and *AmritaVPN* using SSLv3/TLSv1 and LinVPN using SSLv2.

IP Secure (IPSec) extends security at the network level. However, IPSec also supports a tunneling mechanism that can be utilized to provide VPN services. *FreeS/WAN* is a Linux-based

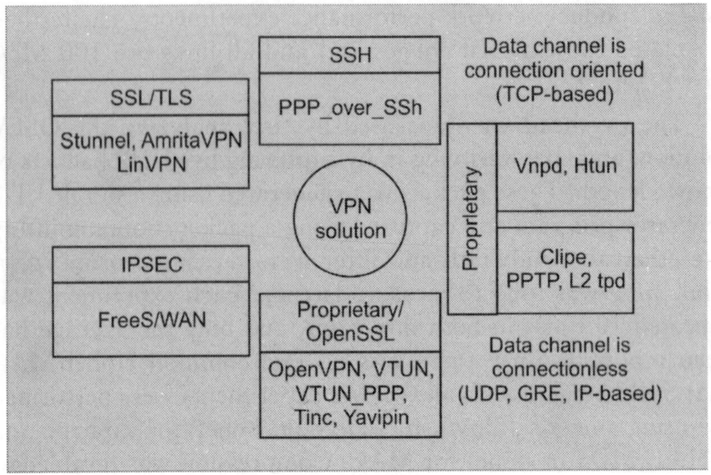

Fig. 2. VPN grouping based on security protocol.

implementation of the IPSec protocol. It consists of two components; KLIPS and PLUTO. The former offers cryptographic services to IP packets and is built as a kernel module, while the latter is an application-level program used for negotiating session keys subsequently used by KLIPS.

The remaining OSLVs use their own proprietary protocols to provide security. This group has been further divided into those that use standard cryptographic functions exported by OpenSSL (Proprietary/OpenSSL) and those that use their own proprietary implementations (Proprietary). *OpenVPN, VTUN, Tinc*, and Yavipin belong to the first group, while the second group contains Cipe, *PPTP, Vpnd, Htun*, and L2tpd. Since *VTUN* can be used with two different VNIs (tun/tap driver and pseudo-terminals), we consider both these organizations as separate OSLVs, with the first referred to as *VTUN* and the second as *VTUN_PPP*. Table 1 provides additional details on each OSLV including links to step-by-step recipes for setting up a VPN. The last column quantifies our experience with setup complexity (a lower number of asterisks imply simplified setup) evaluated against common criteria involving installation, configuration, and support.

PERFORMANCE EVALUATION RESULTS

In this section, we present the experimental results for the selected OSLVs and discuss their performances based on metrics described earlier.

Network Performance

Figure 2 plots the overhead performance normalized toward 80 bytes/packet, which was also the least overhead added by any OSLV solution. Among them, we found most OSLVs in the proprietary security group (except *Vpnd* and *Htun*) to add relatively lesser overhead than others, making them relatively suitable for applications that generate smaller packet sizes (e.g., telnet and remote login). Overall, OSLVs using UDP-based data channels (GRP_UDP) add 50 percent less overhead than those using TCP-based data channels (GRP_TCP). Smaller differences among different members of the same group are mainly due to different packet formats.

Supported Features/Functionality

Earlier, we discussed different features and functions an OSLV should provide. Here, we evaluate them based on the features that are currently supported. If a particular feature is absent, we also comment on how simple (or complex) it is to integrate it in the actual OSLV code.

Code modularity

None of the OSLV solutions strongly support algorithm plugins as defined earlier. Hence, we relax the definition and evaluate the difficulty level with which newer crypto algorithms can be used with an OSLV solution. While considering this aspect, we had to evaluate the general coding style to determine the crypto functions used internally. Accordingly, we have divided the difficulty levels into low, medium, and high as detailed below (refer to Table 2 for actual evaluation).

Low

This is the case when the OSLV uses standard third party libraries, like OpenSSL, to implement their security protocols. OpenSSL has a generic application programming interface, called, EVP API, that provides a standard access for all its ciphers.

Thus, whenever newer algorithms are invented and integrated into OpenSSL, they can be immediately used without recompiling the OSLV code.

	Version	Internet Standard	Available compression algorith ms	Available encryption/ MAC algorithms	Official Web-site	Simple recipes to set up a VPN	Setup complexity
PPP_over_SSH		Yes	ppp-ccp[1], gzip	All available with SSH, viz. bf-cbc/md5	http://www/buildinglinux vpns.net/sourcecode/	$/ssh-vpn.html	****
Stinnel	0.04	No	ppp-ccp	All available with open SSL, viz. Des/Sha1	http://www.stunnel.org/	$/ssh-vpn.html	***
Amrita VPN	0.96	No	None	Cannot specify Defaults to some value	http://aitf.amrita.edu/	$/ssh-vpn.html	***
Lin VPN	2.6-pre1	No	ppp-ccp	Cannot Specify Defaults tp some calue	http://mrtg.planetmirror. com/pub/linvpn	$/linvpn.html	******
VPnd	1.1	No	Available but buggy	bf-cbc/(md5/sha1? ripemd160)	http://sunsite.dk/vpnd/	$/linvpn.html	****
Htun	0.95	No	None	None	http://htun.runslinux.net/	$/linvpn.html	*****
Clipe	1.54	No	None	(bf-cbc?Idea)/-	http://sites.inka.de/sites/ bugred/devel/cipe.htm/	$/cipe.html	**
PPTP	1.24	Yes	ppp-ccp	MPPE	http://pptpclient.source forge.net/	$/pptpd/html	****
L2tpd	0.69	Yes	ppp-ccp	None	http://www.12tpd.org/	$/12tpd/html	***
Open VPN	1.4.2	No	Lzo	All available with] Open SSL, viz. bf-cbc/md5	http://openvpn.source forge.net/	$/openvpn.html	**
VTUN	2.6	No	zlib, lzo	Bf-cbc/md5	http://vtun.sourceforge.net/	$/vtund.html	***
VTUN_PPP	2.6	No	ppp-ccp, zlib, lzo	Bf-cbc/md5	http://vtun.sourceforge.net/	$/vtund-ppp.html	****
Tinc	Tinc-CABAL	No	zlib, lzo	All available with OpenSSL, viz. bf-cbc/md5	http://tinc.nl.linux.org/	$/tinc.html	***
Yavipin	0.9.5	No	zlib	(bf-cbc /des-cbc)/md5	http://yavipin.sourceforge. net/	$/yavipind.html	*****
FreesS/Wan	2.01	Yes	Available	3des-cbc/-	http://www.freeswan.org/	$/ipsec.html	******

([1]CCP: Compression control protocol, http://multimedia.ece.uic.edu/volans)

Table 1. Open source Linux-based VPN solutions.

Medium

The difficulty level is considered medium when new algorithms need to be manually inserted in the OSLV code. For example, *Cipe* and *Vpnd* use their own proprietary crypto implementations. Hence, newer algorithms can be used only if they are integrated with the code. This category also includes those OSLVs that directly use OpenSSL crypto APIs instead of the more generic EVP API.

High

This means newer algorithms can be used only if substantial changes are made to the source. This occurs if the OSLV did not originally support any crypto methods. Thus, to use newer algorithms one would have to start from scratch. The exception here is FreeS/WAN, included here because the source code seemed too large and complicated to locate where it needs to be modified.

Routing

Table 3 presents our evaluation of the routing mechanisms supported by the current OSLVs, again quantified into:

- **Manual:** Direct routes must be established manually, using either the route command or built-in shell scripts.
- **Automatic (for single-domain VPNs):** The routing daemon is part of the OSLV solution to handle single-domain VPNs. *Tinc* is the only solution that employs this type of routing, although it still creates a full mesh network. However, here the administrator has to configure only a single site when a new site is added, which makes the solution extremely scalable.
- **Automatic (for multidomain VPNs):** This employs virtual routing that creates a separate routing instance for every VPN domain. Unfortunately, at this time none of the OSLVs support this option.

Operational Concerns

Security

As discussed earlier, security of an OSLV cannot be measured. However, many situations can be envisioned where strong security is not a requirement, and people may just settle for weaker protocols. Accordingly, we have rated our confidence in security as:

- **Open standards**: Includes all OSLV solutions that use standardized security protocols such as SSH, SSL/TLS, and IPSec. We accept these protocols as implicitly secure because they have already been subjected to exhaustive peer review. Moreover, security lapses, if any, are widely published over the Internet with ready-made patches. From Fig. *2,PPP_over_SSH, AmritaVPN, Stunnel, Lin-VPN, and FreeS/WAN* fall in this category.

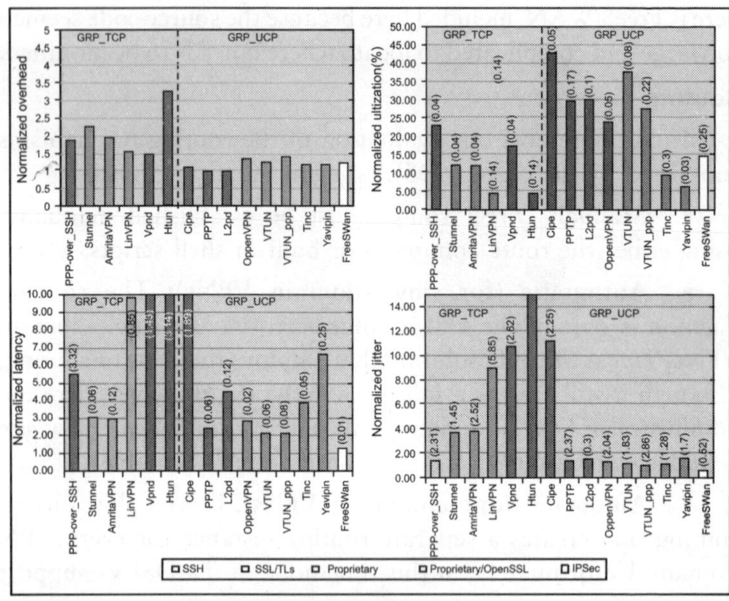

Fig. 3. a) Normalized overhead added to every packet; b) bandwidth utilization; c) normalized latency; d) normalized jitter. (The number on top of each bar presents 95 percent confidence interval).

- **Proprietary:** Includes OSLV solutions that are based on proprietary security protocols and rated lower than *open standards*. We analyze the security offered by these protocols in terms of support for basic properties including *confidentiality, data integrity, authentication/ nonrepudiation*, and *anti-replay protection*. Again, we emphasize that supporting all these properties does not necessarily mean the protocol is secure, and more exhaustive analysis clearly needs to be done. Our evaluation is presented in Table 4. OpenVPN and Tinc are the only solutions that support all four properties.

Scalability

To compare scalability of OSLV solutions, we assumed a full mesh VPN between N nodes and analyzed the total effort required for updating configuration files, editing routing information, and distributing security keys when tunnels are added/deleted. For a full mesh, it all boils down to creating $(N-1)$ additional tunnels. Since a central management infrastructure is absent, the configuration files for all N sites may need to be updated with reachability information. Similarly, since most OSLVs do not have an integrated routing daemon, routing information may need to be manually updated at every site. Finally, for distributing security keys, if the OSLV solution uses secret key or public key cryptography without a public key infrastructure, the shared secret key will need to be manually distributed to the $N-1$ peers. On the other hand, if it uses digital certificates, only the newly added site will need to acquire a signed certificate. Table 5 provides further details about the number of tasks that need to be performed for each OSLV. For example, in *PPP_over_SSH* only one configuration file (~/.ssh/config at the Nth node) needs to be updated, $2(N-1)$ routes need to be added (at both ends), and public key of the new node needs to be distributed to its peers (for passwordless login). Total efforts can then be calculated by summing up all the tasks and multiplying it by N (since this has to be repeated N times for an N-node VPN). Assigning unit effort for every task, the last

	OSLV solution	Remarks
Low	Stunnel, AmritaVPN, LinVPN	Uses Open SSL implementation of SSL/TLS/ Hence, new algorithms can be used readily without any charges to the OSLV source
	OpenVPN, Tinc,	OpenSSL EVP API is used to access different cipheres/MACs.
Medium	PPP_over_SSH	The OpenSSH implemention of SSH uses a fixed list of clophers that use the OpenSSL EVP-AP1. Hence, to use new ciphers the code for OpenSSH needs to be modified.
	Cipe, Vpnd	Uses proprietary Blowfish. Thus, new algorithms should be explicity incorporated in source.
	Yavipin, VTUN, VTUN_PPP,	Uses the OpenSSL Crypto functions for some selected ciphers. To use newer algorithms, source code will need to be modified.
High	FreeS/WAN	Uses Eric Young's DES. It is difficult to locate where modifications need to be made.
	PPTP	Uses only Microsoft P2P encryption.
	L2TPd, Htun	No ciphers used.

Table 2. The complexity of introducing proprietar algorithms

Routing	OSLV solutions	Remarks
Manual	PPP_over_SSH, Stunnel, L2tpd, Htun	Explicit route command is used.
	OpenVPN, LinVPN, Yavipin, VTUN, VTUN_PPP, PPTPD	Routing is configured by shell scripts when the VPN links is estblished.
	Cipe, AmritaVPN, FreesS/WAN, Vpnd	Routing information is included in conf. files.
Automatic, single-domain VPNs	Tinc	Supports a built-in routing daemon that establishes a full mesh network

Table 3. In-built support for routing.

column gives a good estimate of scalability. Observe that every solution is unscalable with total efforts varying as O(N2). However, for small N (say N = 10), one can see the drastic difference in the amount of work required (indicated by numbers in square brackets in the last column). Here, Tinc proves the most scalable OSLV solution.

CONCLUSIONS AND FUTURE WORK

In this article we have evaluated 15 popular OSLVs in terms of network performance, features and functionalities, and operational concerns. The relatively poor performance of OSLVs in almost all considered attributes opens new opportunities for research. One such area is improving network performance. A major bottleneck for poor network performance was found to be the compute-intensive nature of the encryption, authentication, and compression functions (called VPN functions) studiously applied to every packet sent over the VPN. Once these functions and their respective algorithms are negotiated during tunnel initialization, they remain static throughout the lifetime of the tunnel and cannot be changed without resetting it. However, this behavior may be redundant for traffic streams that are already encrypted or compressed. Many applications may also require only a subset of such functions to be applied to their streams; for example, voice over IP calls may need encryption and authentication, but can do without compression. Similarly,

	Confidentiality	Date-Integrity	Authentication/ non repudiation	Anti-replay
Vpnd	Yes	Yes	Yes	No
Htun	No	No	No	No
Cipe	Yes	Yes	No	No
PPTP	Yes	Yes	No	Yes
L2tpd	No	No	No	Yes
OpenVPN	Yes	No	Yes	Yes
VTUM	Yes	No	No	No
VTUN_PPP	Yes	Yes	No	No
Tinc	Yes	Yes	Yes	Yes
Yavipin	Yes	Yes	No	Yes

Table 4. VPN security.

not all information steams are equally important. While some may need strong cryptography, others may settle for weaker protocols that are faster and not as compute-intensive. Similar arguments hold for selecting the transport protocol for data channels. Experiments reveal that VPNs using UDP-based data channels are much better than those using TCP. None of the current OSLV solutions are flexible enough to apply such application-specific functionality and newer architectures will

	Confidentiality	Date-Integrity	Authentication/ non repudiation	Anti-replay
Vpnd	Yes	Yes	Yes	No
Htun	No	No	No	No
Cipe	Yes	Yes	No	No
PPTP	Yes	Yes	No	Yes
L2tpd	No	No	No	Yes
OpenVPN	Yes	No	Yes	Yes
VTUM	Yes	No	No	No
VTUN_PPP	Yes	Yes	No	No
Tinc	Yes	Yes	Yes	Yes
Yavipin	Yes	Yes	No	Yes

Table 5. Scalability of OSLVs.

need to be designed, that allow VPN functions to be applied at the packet level. In this regard, we are proposing a next-generation VPN architecture called Flexi-Tunes that provides a flexible tunnel implementation where within a single VPN tunnel, different VPN functions can be applied to different applications, thus offering differential and customized treatment. Flexi-Tunes empowers applications on end hosts to either specify the kind of treatment they expect for their traffic streams or take active part in applying the tunneling functions themselves.

The results presented in this article can also help end users select an optimum OSLV solution tailored to their specific needs. The simple heuristic algorithm discussed in the results section can be extended to accept weighted user requirements and output a ranked list of the best solutions. As a result, a home user interested in maximum bandwidth may settle for *Cipe* or *Vtun*, while a network administrator who is more interested in security may settle for IPSec. This method, however, requires the performance of each OSLV to be predetermined. Such results are not readily available over the Internet, and our work helps to fill this gap.

REFERENCES

1. R. Venkateswaran, "Virtual Private Networks," *IEEE Potentials*, Mar. 2001.
2. J. Epplin, "Peeking Under the Hood of SnapGear's uClinux-powered VPN Appliances," LinuxDevices.com, Jan.2003, http://www.linuxdevices. com/articles/ AT3682158384.html
3. C. J. C. Pena and J. Evans, "Performance Evaluation of Software Virtual Private Networks (VPN)," *Proc. 25th Annual IEEE Conf. Local Comp. Networks*, Nov. 2000, pp. 522–23.
4. J. P. McGregor and R. B. Lee, "Performance Impact of Data Compression on Virtual Private Network Transactions," *Proc. 25th Annual IEEE Conf. Local Comp. Networks*, 2000, pp. 500–10.
5. O. Titz, "Why TCP over TCP Is a Bad Idea," http://sitesinka.de/sites/bigred/devel/tcp-tcp.html
6. H. Lipmaa, "Crypto Hardware Pointers," http://www.tcs.hut.fi/~helger/crypto/link/practice/hardware.html
7. B. Schneier, "Security in the Real World: How to Evaluate Security Technology," excerpts from a general session presentation at CSI's NetSec Conf., St. Louis, MO, June 1999; http://www.schneier.com/essay-realworld.html
8. J. De Clercq and O. Paridaens, "Scalability Implications of Virtual Private Networks," *IEEE Commun. Mag.*, vol.40, no. 5, May 2002, pp. 151–57.
9. O. Kolesnikov and B. Hatch, "Building Linux Virtual Private Networks," New Riders, 2001

An Implementation of Handoff in Wireless Networks Using Fuzzy Logic

Manoj Sharma and *Yogesh Misra*

ABSTRACT

Handoff is the procedure changing the assignment of a mobile unit from one base station (BS) to another as the mobile moves from one cell to another. Handoff is handled in different ways in different systems and involves a number of factors. In this, the mobile switching center (MSC) transfers the call to a new channel belonging to new base station. In this paper a design methodology based on a fuzzy logic concept is used for selection of base station. In this paper we consider two input parameters namely, distance from the base station and number of users of each base station to arrive at a fuzzy handoff decision. For the simulation of fuzzy based handoff decisions Inform Software Corporation's fuzzy TECH 5.7 is used and the infrastructure of B.S of B.S.N.L Bahal is used for research work.

INTRODUCTION

Fuzzy logic control systems have been reported in a wide range of applications that include industrial processes, transportation systems, and robotics and consumer products.

A fuzzy logic based handoff mechanism is presented here with an aim of obtaining better QoS levels to the end users

Zadeh[1] proposed how one can inculcate fuzzy knowledge into the system and decisions made based on that fuzzy knowledge can be as good as human beings. However, accuracy of the decisions, of course, depends upon designed fuzzy sets and the fuzzy knowledge/expertise embedded into such a system.

Processing handoffs is an important task in any cellular radio system. The simplest scheme of choosing between several candidate base stations is to select that BS from which the received power level is the maximum. However, this can lead to overloading of the BS and cause degradation of QoS in overloaded cells or higher number of handoff failure if the number of users in a BS is restricted. The handoff scheme presented in this paper is not based only on received power level, but also on the number of users in each of the candidate BSs.

Handoff Mechanism

In a conventional handoff scheme the mobile device monitors received power levels and periodically send this information to the MSC controller via their respective BSs , which then decides whether a handoff should be performed and if yes, to which target BS. The fig (1)[2] shows how an conventional handoff is made.

In this paper we have taken an additional parameter on which the mobile switching controller bases its handoff decision, namely, the number of users i.e. user population. In this paper we considered the following handoff mechanism.

Handoff based on power level. Here, only the power levels received from candidate BSs are compared, and the BS with the highest power level above threshold is selected for handoff.

Handoff based on number of users. Here, the mobile is handed off to that BS which has its power level above the threshold and which has the minimum number of users.

Handoff based on fuzzy logic. Here, fuzzy logic is used to process the input parameters of distance from the BS (indication of the received power level from BS) and the number of users to arrive at a fuzzy handoff decision (FHD) value. The BS with the highest FHD is then chosen for handoff.

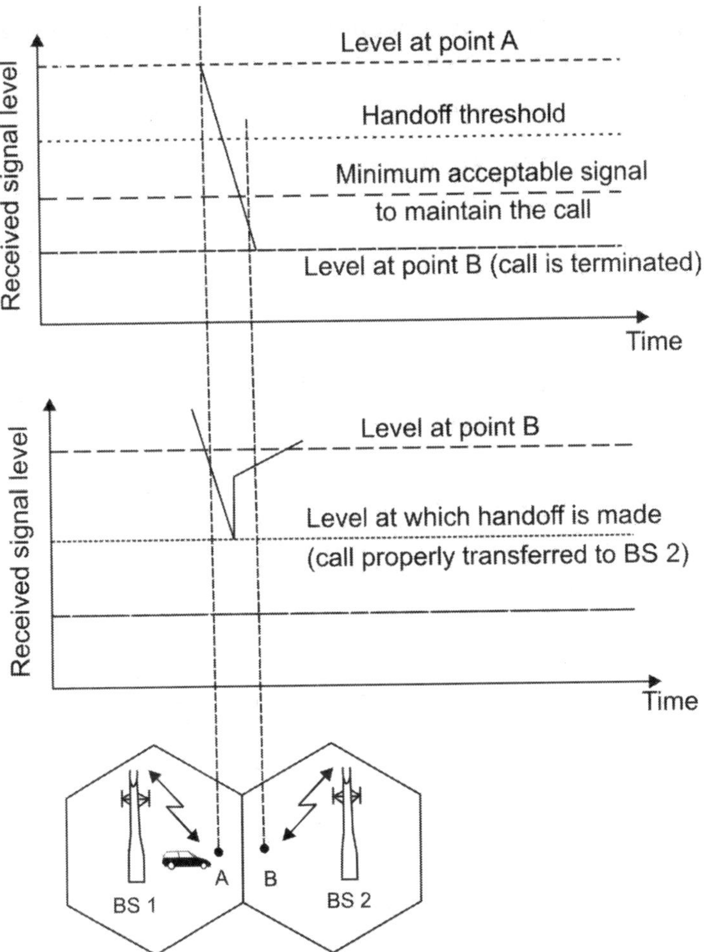

Fig.1. Conventional handoff scheme

Design Steps for Handoff Based on Fuzzy Logic Control (FLC)

In order to design a fuzzy logic system, we must describe the operation of system linguistically. Steps in designing the FL system are given below[3]

i. Identify the inputs and outputs using linguistic variables.

ii. Assign membership functions to the variables (fuzzification)

iii. Build a rule base

iv. Generate a crisp control action (defuzzification).

For this paper, we have selected two input parameters. These are-

(a) Number of users

(b) Distance from the B.S

For this paper, we have selected one output parameter. This parameter is –

"Out put Decision" which measures the degree of handoff.

Fuzzifucation: Input parameters of user population i.e. number of users and distance from BS1 are fuzzified using the pre defined input member ship functions shown in fig (2) and fig (3) respectively. The output parameter "output decision" is also fuzzified as shown in fig (4). Similarly the fuzzified input parameters and out put parameters for BS2 and BS3 are shown in fig (5)-fig (10).

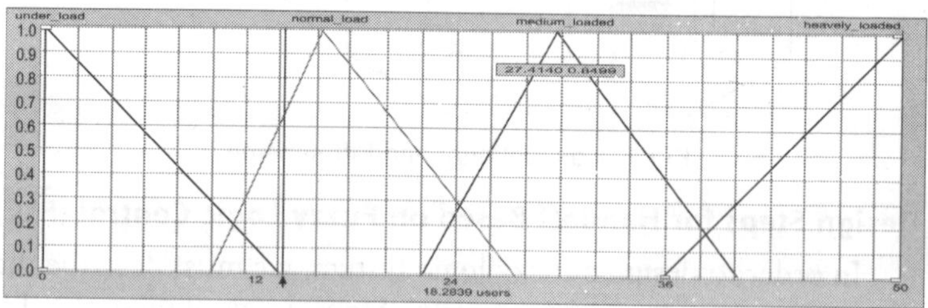

Fig. 2. No. of users for B.S 1

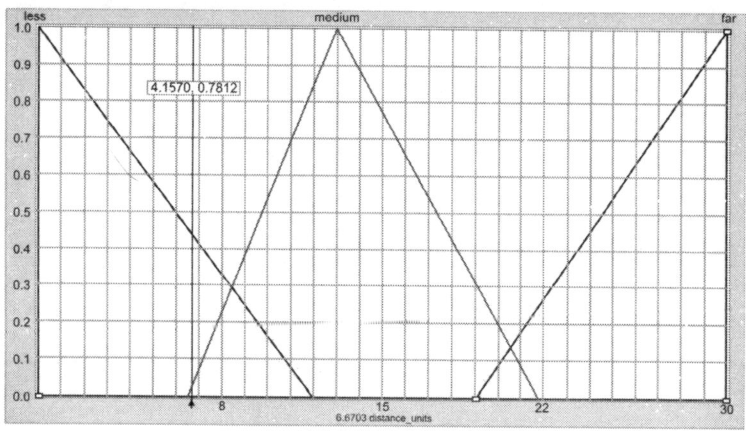

Fig. 3. Distance for B.S 1

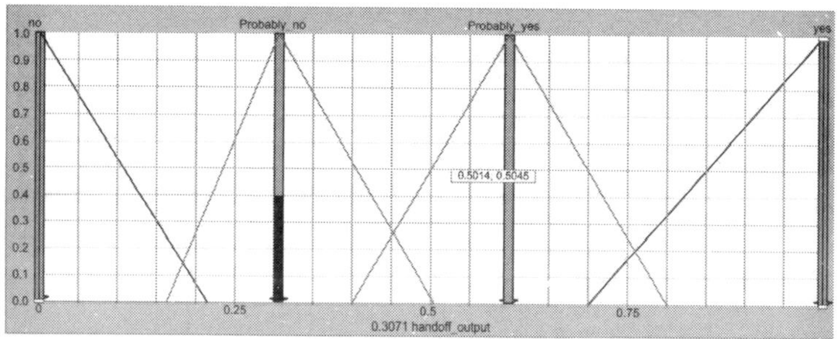

Fig. 4. Handoff "o/p decision" for B.S 1

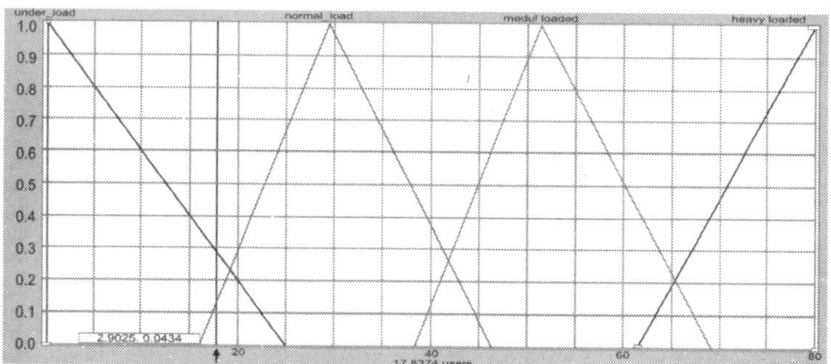

Fig. 5. No. of users for B.S 2

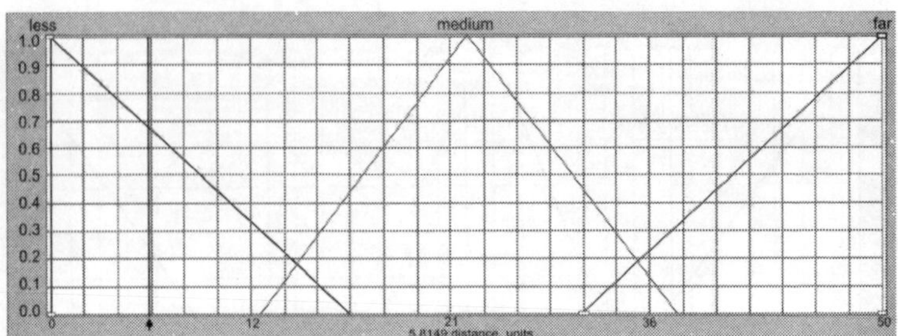

Fig. 6. Distance for B.S 2

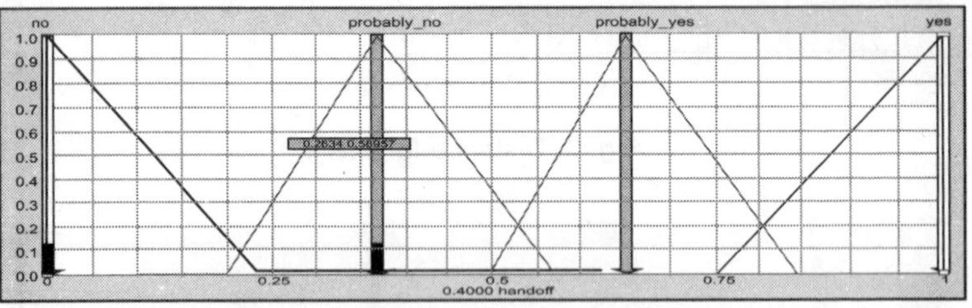

Fig. 7. Handoff "o/p decision" for B.S 2

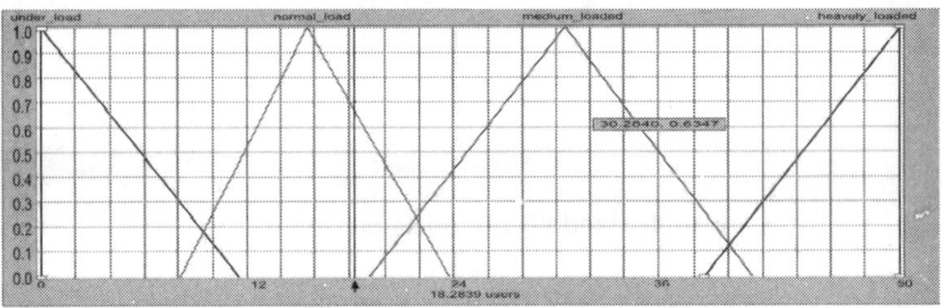

Fig. 8. No. of users for B.S 3

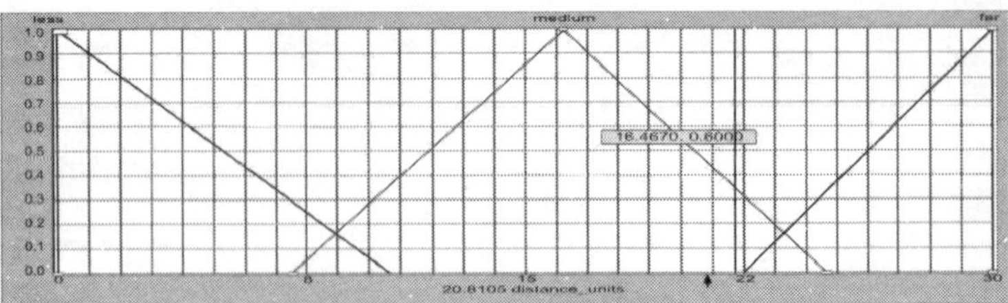

Fig. 9. Distance for B.S 3

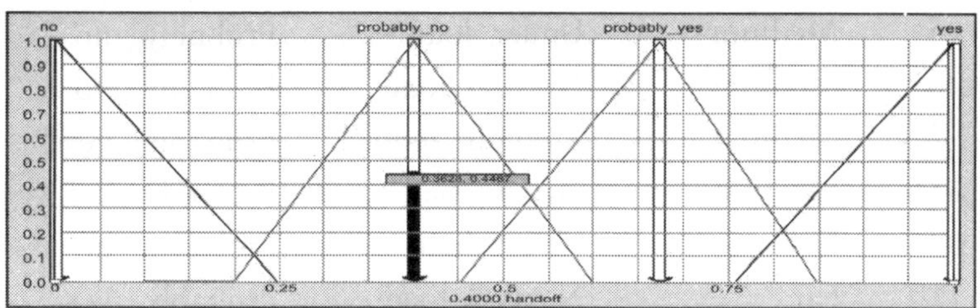

Fig. 10. Handoff "o/p decision" for B.S 3

Rule Evaluation

These fuzzified input values are used to evaluate rules for obtaining fuzzy handoff decision. These rules are summarized in Table (I) and Table (II).

Table 1. Summary of Rule Base for B.S 1 & B.S 2

#	IF DISTANCE	USERS	THEN Hndoff_output
1	Less	Under_load	No
2	Less	Normal_load	Probably_ no
3	Less	Medium_loaded	Probably_ no
4	Less	Heavy_loaded	Probably_ no
5	Medium	Under_load	Probably_ no
6	Medium	Normal_load	Probably_ no
7	Medium	Medium_loaded	Probably_ yes
8	Medium	Heavy_loaded	Probably_ yes
9	Far	Under_load	Probably_ yes
10	Far	Normal_load	Probably_ yes
11	Far	Medium_loaded	Probably_ yes
12	Far	Heavy_loaded	Yes

Table 2. Summary of Rule Base for B.S 3

#	IF DISTANCE	USERS	THEN Hndoff_output
1	Less	Under_load	No
2	Less	Normal_load	Probably_ no
3	Less	Medium_loaded	Probably_ no
4	Less	Heavy_loaded	Probably_ yes

5	Medium	Under_load	Probably_ no
6	Medium	Normal_load	Probably_ no
7	Medium	Medium_loaded	Probably_ yes
8	Medium	Heavy_loaded	Probably_ yes
9	Far	Under_load	Probably_ no
10	Far	Normal_load	Probably_ yes
11	Far	Medium_loaded	Probably_ yes
12	Far	Heavy_loaded	Yes

Deffuzifiaction: In this step we calculate the crisp value of FHD for each of the three BSs. Finally the BS with the highest FHD is chosen for handoff. Here we have used min.-max. defuzzification method for simulation of result

Results

The results of simulation carried out using Inform Software Corporation's fuzzyTECH 5.7 are given in fig. (11)—Fig. (13). By observing the figures we can find out the FHD having the highest values. The simulation result uses 12 rules. Table (III) shows summary of the results. In this system we assume that BS is placed in the center of each cell.

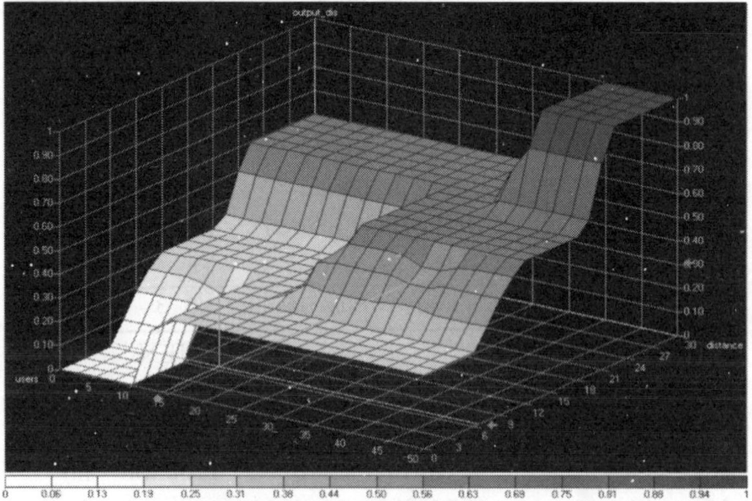

Fig. 11. The 3-D Plot draws the Transfer Surface for two i/p variable & one o/p variable Twelve Rules for B.S 1

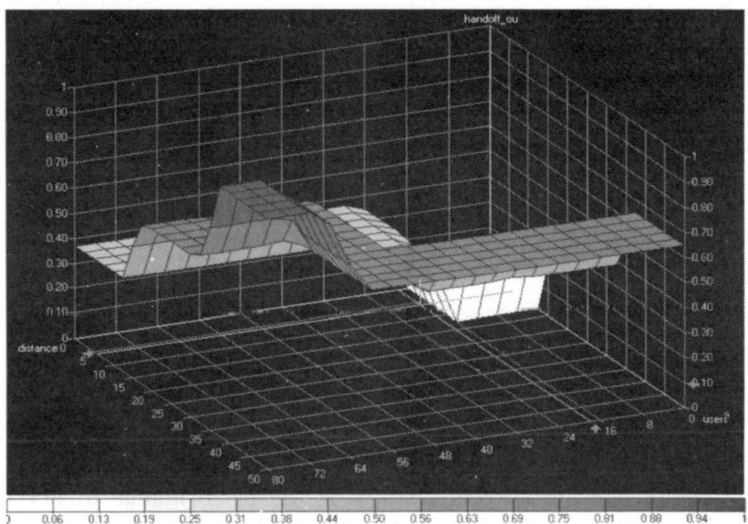

Fig. 12. The 3-D Plot draws the Transfer Surface for two i/p variable & one o/p variable Twelve Rules for B.S 2

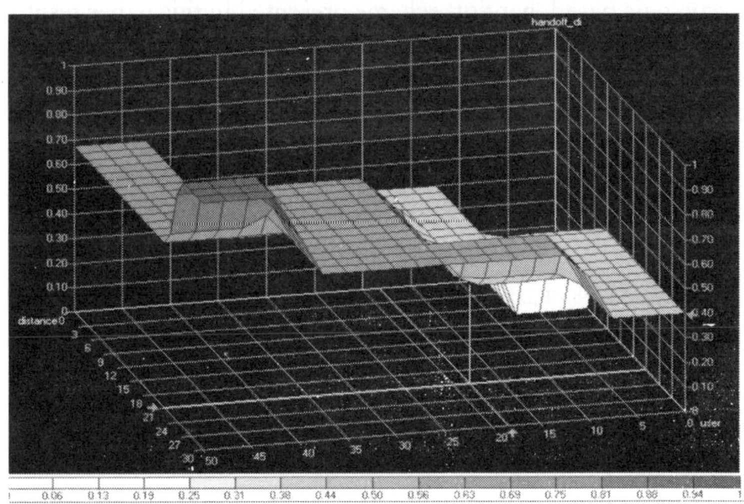

Fig. 13. The 3-D Plot draws the Transfer Surface for two i/p variable & one o/p variable Twelve Rules for B.S 3

Table 3: Summary of the Results

Base Station	Distance	User	FHD (Crisp value)	Comments
B.S.1	24	37	0.70	Recommends
B.S.2	20	38	0.37	B.S.1 for
B.S.3	21	40	0.67	Handoff
B.S.1	6.5	14	0.30	Recommends
B.S.2	33.6	64	0.73	B.S.2 for
B.S.3	9	12	0.40	Handoff

FUTURE WORK AND CONCLUSION

Here, we are currently studying the performance of FHD technique for the case when the cells in the wireless system are not identical. In this technique we may add some more input parameters so as to obtain a better fuzzy handoff decision. The fuzzy logic based handoff scheme presented in this paper resulcs in a uniform distribution of users between cells and makes switching between BSs gradual. It can therefore be used to provide fair QoS and better response time to handover requests in micro and Pico cellular networks. Fuzzy logic processing can easily be implemented through simple software procedures or dedicated fuzzy logic processing modules

REFERENCES

1. L.A. Zadeh "Fuzzy sets", Information & Control, 8, 338-353, 1965.
2. Theodore S. Rappaport "Wireless Communications: Principles and Practice" 2e.
3. Ibrahim. Ahmad. M, "Introduction to Applied Fuzzy Electronics". PHI. 2004
4. William Stallings "Wireless Communications and Networks". Pearson Education.
5. Manpreet Singh Dang, Anmol Prakash, Dinesh K.Anvekar, Manika Kapoor and Rajeev Shorey, "Fuzzy Logic Based Handoff In Wireless Networks". IEEE trans. 2000

Effect of Probe Radius for A Coaxially Fed Rectangular Microstrip Antenna

D.K. Srivastava, R.C. Saraswat, B.R. Vishvakarma and *D.C. Dhubkarya*

ABSTRACT

The rectangular microstrip antenna (RMSA) is the most popular configuration and is very easy to analyze. In the present work, the input impedance, bandwidth, VSWR and other parameters are obtained for effect of probe radius on Rectangular Microstrip antenna. The different probes like SMA connector for different radius and N-type are considered and its effect on patch RMSA is studied. The rectangular microstrip antenna is designed for resonating frequency 1.5 GHz and simulated using IE3D software which is based on method of moment.

INTRODUCTION

Microstrip antenna is also called Patch antenna and printed circuit antenna. Patch antenna offers many advantages like planar configuration, light weight, low volume, easy to fabricate but it has several disadvantages also[1,6,7]. Narrow BW is major disadvantage of Microstrip antenna which puts constraints on its applicability. Attempts are made to increase BW[3,8]. BW can be improved by increasing substrate thickness or decreasing its permittivity[6,7]. In the present work , antenna is designed for 1.5 GHz and is simulated using IE3D software[5] which is based on method of moment[4]. Analysis is done for variation of probe radius for different connectors. Single probe feed is used and feed location is optimized to keep input impedance[2] close to 50O. As the probe radius increases, probe inductance decreases for same substrate.

Theoretical Considerations

The patch in micostrip antenna can take any shape . It may be regular or irregular. The rectangular patch is the simplest configuration since it is the easiest to analyze mathematically. The patch and ground plane are separated by substrate of permittivity (er) and thickness (h). A rectangular microstrip antenna (RMSA) is defined by its length (L) and width (W) as shown in figure 1:Top View of patch and in figure 2. Side View of patch. Edges along the width are called radiating edges and that along the length are called non radiating edges[7]. To account for fringing fields in E- Field distribution , the dimensions of RMSA can be extended outwards. It can be fed by different methods like coplanar microstrip line feed, coaxial probe feed, aperture coupling, electromagnetic coupling & coplanar waveguide(CPW)[1,7] . In the present work, coaxial probe (50 ohm) feed is used . antenna is designed for 1.5 GHz. and is analyzed for different radius of probe connector. For design of Rectangular microstrip antenna, the following relationships are used to calculate the dimensions of RMSA[7].

$$\varepsilon = \frac{\varepsilon_r + 1}{2} + \frac{\varepsilon_r - 1}{2}\left[1 + \frac{10h}{W}\right]^{-1/2}$$

$$L_e = L + 2\Delta L$$

$$\Delta L = \frac{h}{\sqrt{\varepsilon e}}$$

$$f_0 = \frac{15}{L_e\sqrt{\varepsilon e}}$$

$$W = \frac{c}{2f_0\sqrt{\frac{\varepsilon_r + 1}{2}}}$$

Where, ε_r = substrate permittivity

h = thickness of substrate

ε_e = effective permittivity

L = Length of path

ΔL = increase in thickness due to

L_e = effective length
W = width of patch
c = speed of e.m. wave
f_0 = resonating frequency
r = radius of probe

Impedance of coaxial probe is obtained by adding reactance XC and probe inductance XL between patch and ground plane. The relation for XC and XL is given as [7]-

$$X_c = -\frac{1}{wC} = -\frac{h}{wL_\varepsilon W \varepsilon_r \varepsilon_0}$$

$$X_L = \frac{120\pi h}{\lambda_0}\left[Ln\left(\frac{2\lambda_0}{\pi 2r}\right) - 0.577\right]$$

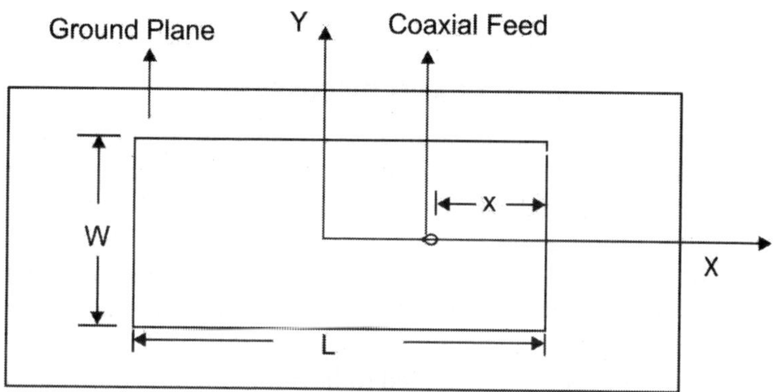

(a) Top View of RMSA with no cover

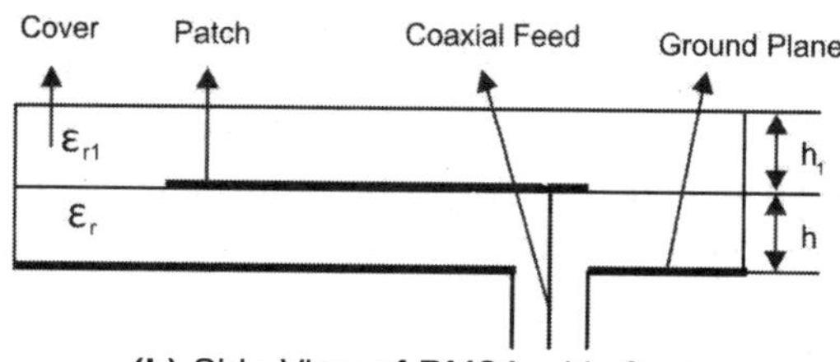

(b) Side View of RMSA with Cover

Fig 1. Rectangular Microstrip Antenna (RMSA)

Design Parameters

The dimensions for proposed antenna has been calculated. The following parameters are used for design of proposed antenna.

Design frequency (fo) = 1.5 GHz

Substrate permittivity (er1) = 2.62

Loss tangent (tand) = 0.001

Thickness of substrate (h) = 1.59 mm

Length of RMSA (L) = 60 mm

Width of RMSA (W) = 90 mm

Location of feed point (xo,yo) = (17.5, 45)

Where, xo=(L/2)-x and yo=W/2

The different sets of antennas are designed for cover of different permittivity at optimum feed location to operate in comparable resonating frequency.

RESULTS AND DISCUSSION

Using above design parameters RMSA is analyzed. The VSWR Vs. Frequency plot is shown in figure.2. By varying radius of probe, analysis is made. The minimum Return Loss with probe radius 2mm for antenna resonating at 1.51GHz is -40.63dB at optimum feed location (45,18).The optimum feed location is selected at centre axis of width, along the length of patch for proper impedance matching of 50 ohm, since the impedance of probe is considered to be 50ohm. For probe radius 0.8mm, RL claimed is -36.13dB at 1.51GHz. THE radius is varied as shown in table.1.THE output parameters like VSWR, BW, Impedance, and return loss is also shown. Feed location is changed for proper matching. Different plots between frequency and VSWR, Return Loss, Real and Imaginary Impedance is shown in Figure 2, Figure. 3 and Figure 4 respectively. The smith chart is shown in Figure 5. As probe radius increases, the probe inductance decreases and impedance plot moves in anticlockwise direction and effective impedance decreases as is clearly seen in Table 1. Return loss decreases and so the BW increases slightly, similarly VSWR decreases. For optimum feed location, resonant frequency is invariable.

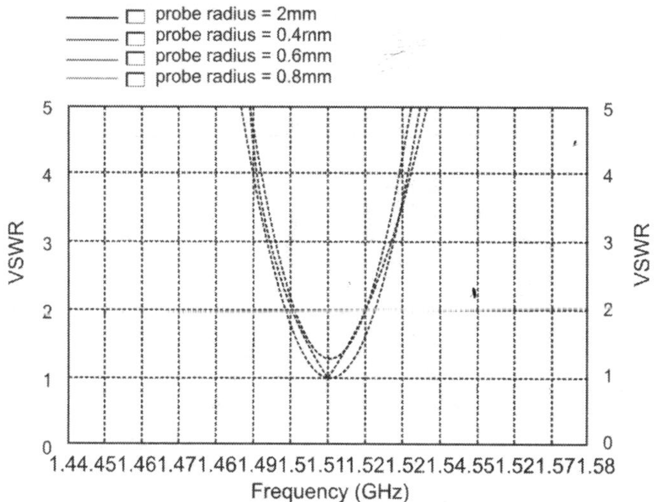

Fig 2. Freq. vs VSWR for different probe radius

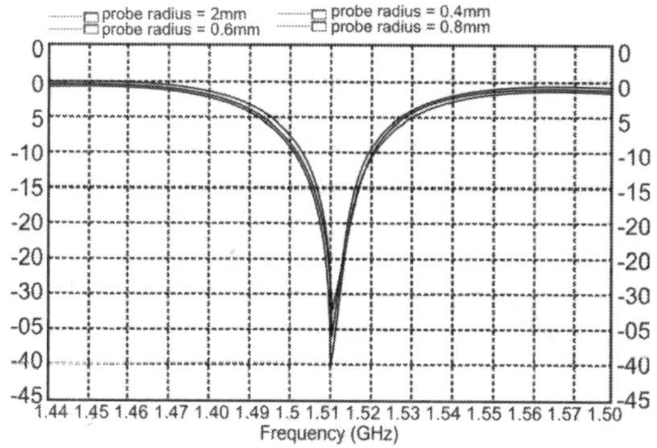

Fig 3. Freq. vs RL for different probe radius

Table 1. Variation of Cover Permittivity at Fixed Cover Thickness (h1)=1.59mm

Probe Radii (mm)	Feed Pt.(x) (mm)	R_{in} (O)	Fo (Ghz)	RL (dB)	VSWR	BW (MHz)
0.4	17.0	53.52	1.51	-23.4	1.145	18
0.6	17.25	51.99	1.51	-27.8	1.085	20
0.8	17.5	50.23	1.51	-36.1	1.032	22
2.0	18.0	49.13	1.51	-40.6	1.019	23

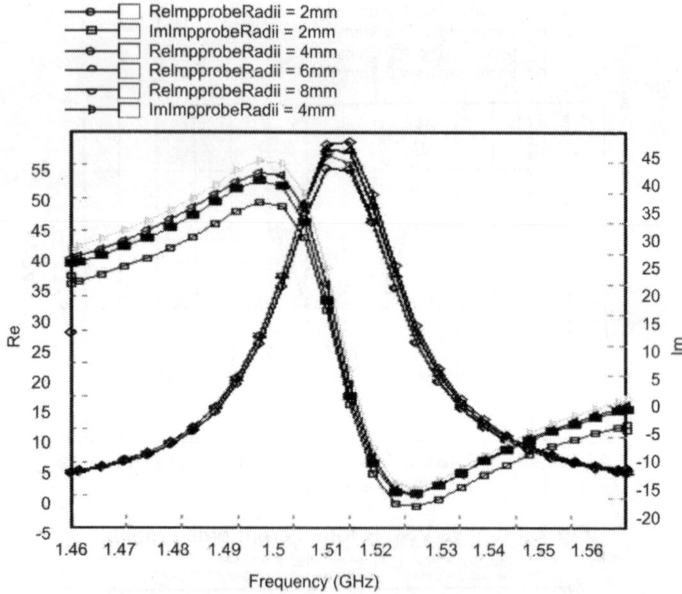

Fig 4. Freq. vs Real & Imaginary Impedance for different probe radius

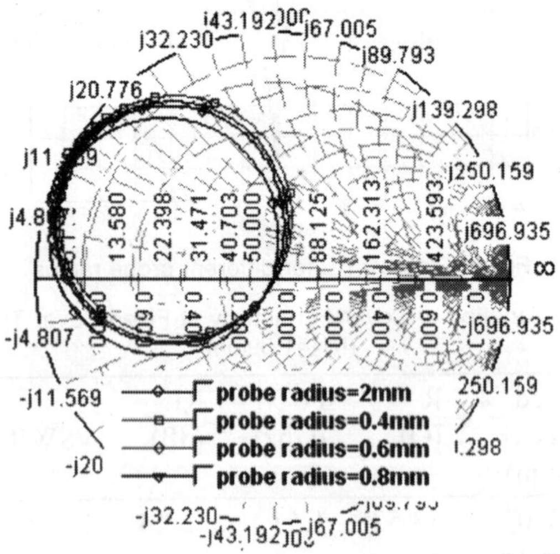

Fig 5. Impedance Curve for different probe radius

CONCLUSION

With increase in probe radius, BW increases slightly. Resonance frequency remains almost invariable. Four different values of probe radius are considered as shown in table1. The feed point is optimized to be Rin in the range 49-51O With increase in radius from 0.4mm to 2.0mm, BW increases from 18MHz to 23MHz due to decrease in inductance of probe and so effective impedance decreases and impedance plot moves in anticlockwise direction.

REFERENCES

1. Bahl, I.J. and P.Bhartiya, Microstrip Antennas, Dedham, MA:Artech House, 1980.
2. Deshpande, M.D. and M.C.Bailey, "Input Impedance of Microstrip Antennas", IEEE Trans. Antennas Propogat., Vol.AP-30, July.1982, pp.645-650.
3. F. Zavosh, and J.T.Aberle, "Improving the performance of Microstrip-Patch Antennas," IEEE Antennas and Propagation Magazine, Vol.38, No.4, August 1996.
4. E.H.Newman and P.Tulyathan, "Analysis of microstrip antenas using moment methods,"IEEE Trans.Antennas Propogation, vol. AP-30, pp. 1191-1196, Jan. 1981.
5. IE3d 12.0, Zeland Software Inc., Fremont,CA 94538, U.S.A.
6. James, J.R., and P.S.Hall, Handbook of Microstrip Antennas, Vol.1, London: Peter Peregrinus Ltd., 1989.
7. Kumar. G., and K.P.Ray, Broadband Microstrip Antennas, MA: Artech House.
8. N. Herscovici, "A Wide band Single-Layer Patch Antenna, "IEEE Trans. Antenna Propogation, Vol. AP-46, No.6, 1998, pp. 471-474.

Security Analysis of a Remote User Authentication Scheme

37

Sunder Lal and *K.K. Goyal*

ABSTRACT

In 2005 Das et al. [5] proposed a remote user authentication scheme using bilinear pairings. Fang and Huang [7] analyzed the scheme and pointed out some weaknesses. They also proposed an improvement. In 2006, Giri and Srivastava [9] observed that the improved scheme is still insecure to off-line attack and an improvement. Recently we have shown [12] that, the improved scheme is still insecure and propose an improvement. The proposed scheme also enables users to choose and change the password without the help of the remote server. In this paper we will analyze the security of our proposed scheme.

INTRODUCTION

In computer network systems, user authentication is an important mechanism for preventing unauthorized network access. The password-based authentication schemes with smart cards are usual parts of security for simpler and convenient authentication mechanisms to deal with secret data over insecure networks. In 1981, Lamport [11] proposed a well-known hash-based password authentication scheme for secure communication. His scheme resists replay attacks, but requires a verification table to verify the legitimacy of a login user. This approach also introduces risk and cost of managing and protecting the table. To avoid such problems, several authentication schemes without the verification table have been proposed [10, 14, 17]. Also, it is difficult for a user to memorize a long key or a server generated password. To overcome this problem, several schemes have been proposed [15, 17] so that the legitimate users can choose their passwords freely. Recently, some related schemes have been proposed [3, 5] for the authentication using smart cards. In 2005, Das et al. [5] proposed a scheme for smart card authentication using bilinear pairings that provides the users to choose and change their passwords freely. However, this scheme has some security flaws, which are described in [4, 8]. In 2006, Fang and Huang [7] proposed an improvement of Das et al's scheme [5] to remedy these weaknesses. In 2006, Giri and Srivastava [9] proposed an improvement on Fang and Huang [7] scheme to prevent some weaknesses. Recently we have shown that, the improved scheme is still insecure and propose an improvement. The proposed scheme also enables users to choose and change the password without the help of the remote server. In this paper we will analyze the security of our proposed scheme.

The remainder of this paper is organized as follows. Section 2, briefly introduces some mathematical concepts for our proposed scheme. Section 3, briefly reviews the scheme of Giri and Srivastava[9]. In this section we also describe a weakness of this scheme. In Section 4, we introduce our scheme and compare computational efficiency of our proposed scheme with some previously published schemes. In Section 5, we will analyze the security of our proposed scheme. Section 6, concludes the paper.

Preliminaries

In this section, we briefly review the basic concepts on bilinear pairings and a related mathematical problem.

Bilinear pairings derived from the Weil pairings or Tate pairings on elliptic curves have been used in cryptography to construct identity (ID)-based cryptographic schemes. Let $< G1 , + >$ be an additive cyclic group of order q, where q is prime and let $< G2 , X >$ be a multiplicative cyclic group of the same order. A mapping $e : G^2_1 \rightarrow G2$ is called a bilinear mapping if it satisfies the following properties:

1. Bilinear property: For all $Q, R, S \in G1$, $e(Q+R; S) = e(Q, S) X e(R,S)$ and $e(Q, R+S) = e(Q,R) X e(Q,S)$. As

a result e(a *Q, b* R) = (Q,R)a.b for all Q,R ∈ G1 and for all a,b ∈ Zq* , where a * Q means a times additions of Q, over the group < G1 , + >.

2. Non-degeneracy property: There exist Q,R ∈ G1 such that e(Q,R) ≠ 1G2 , where 1G2 is the identity element of G2.
3. Computability property: There is an efficient algorithm to compute e(Q,R) for all Q,R ∈ G1.

For implementation point of view, G1 will be the group of points on an elliptic curve and G2 will denote a multiplicative subgroup of a finite field. The mapping e will be derived from either the Weil or the Tate pairing on an elliptic curve over a finite field. We refer to [1, 6, 12] for more comprehensive description on how these groups, pairings and other parameters are defined.

Discrete Logarithm Problem (DLP): Given two elements Q, R ∈ G1, find an element x ? Zq*, such that Q = x * R whenever such an element exists.

It is known that on suitable chosen elliptic curves DLP is a computationally infeasible problem.

Brief Review of the Giri-Srivastava Scheme

In this section, we review the scheme proposed by Giri and Srivastava.

Set-up

The setup phase by the remote server(RS) proceeds as follows. The RS selects two groups: (i) G1, an additive cyclic group of order prime, say, q, and (ii) G2, a multiplicative cyclic group of the same order, a bilinear pairing e : G12 → G2 mapping and a cryptographic hash function H : {0; 1}*→G1. The RS chooses randomly a secret key (private key) s and computes the public-key as PubRS = s*P, where P is a generator of the group G1. The RS also selects a public key cryptosystem, with EPubRS (.) and Es(.) as the encryption and decryption algorithms respectively. Finally, the RS publishes the system parameters: G1, G2, q, PubRS, e(.;.), H(.) and EPubRS(.).The RS keeps the parameter s as secret.

Registration

In this phase, a user Ui submits his/her identifier IDi and password PWi (an integer in Z^*q) to the RS. These private data must be sent over a secure channel. Then RS computes:

(i) a secret parameter SPi = PWi * PubRS, and

(ii) registration identifier RegIDi = s * H(IDi) + SPi.

RS loads PubRS ; IDi ; RegIDi ; SPi and H(.) in the memory of the smart card and issues it to Ui.

Authentication

The authentication process consists of two phases: (a) the login phase and (b) the verification phase.

(a) Login Phase

If the user Ui wants to log into the RS, he/she must insert his/her smart card into a card reader and keys in his identifier IDi and password PWi. Then the smart card performs the following:

(i) computes A = PWi * PubRS, and B = RegIDi - A.

(ii) randomly selects a number r and computes Ci = EPubRS(r).

(iii) computes Di = T * B + r * PubRS, where T is the user system's current timestamp. It sends the login request message M = <IDi ; Ci ; Di ; Ti> to the RS over a public channel.

(b) Verification

On receiving the login request message M = <IDi ; Ci ; Di ; Ti> at time T', the RS and the smart card will perform the following steps for mutual authentication:

(i) RS verifies the validity of the time interval between T' and T. If $(T' - T) > \Delta T$, RS rejects the login request, where ΔT denotes the expected valid time interval for transmission delay. Otherwise, it goes for the next step.

(ii) computes X = Es(Ci) and Y = X * PubRS.

(iii) checks if e(Di - Y, P) = e(H(IDi); PubRS)T. RS accepts the login request iff the equality holds.

Password change

Our scheme also enables user to change their password freely and securely. If the user Ui wants to change his password from PWi to PW'i, he/she inserts his smart card into a card reader and keys in his identifier IDi and password PWi. Then the smart card performs the following steps:

(i) The smart card computes SP'i = PWi * PubRS and accepts the change in password request iff SP*i = SPi.

(ii) The smart card if accepts the change in request, computes Reg'IDi = RegIDi – SP'i + PW'i * PubRS = s * H(IDi) +PW'i * PubRS.

(iii) The password has been changed now with the new password PW'i and the smart card stores new SP'i and Reg'IDi in place of SPi and RegIDi respectively.

Weaknesses in the Scheme

We know that the <PubRS , IDi , RegIDi , SPi and H(.) > are stored in the memory of the smart card. If these information are revealed to an adversary X then by using RegIDi and SPi , X can easily make the new message M as follows :-

Already have A = SPi

X can compute B= RegIDi - A.

Select r' then Ci= EPubRS(r') where r' is any random number.

Di = T' * B + r' * PubRS where T' is the adversary timestamp.

Now M=< IDi ; Ci ; Di ; T' > can be sent to the RS. So the scheme of Giri and Srivastava is insecure against this offline attack.

Our Scheme

As we observed above, if all the information stored in the smart card of user Ui are revealed to an adversary X, he can make access to RS. We modify the information to be stored in the smart in such a way that the revelation of these information to do not help in the verifying equation at the RS side. In this section, we present our authentication scheme with smart cards.

The proposed scheme has four phases, namely, setup, registration, authentication, and password change phases.

Set-up phase

The system set-up proceeds as follows. The RS selects two groups: (i) G1, an additive cyclic group of order prime, say, q, and (ii) G2, a multiplicative cyclic group of the same order. A bilinear mapping e : $G_1^2 \rightarrow$ G2 and a cryptographic hash function H : {0; 1}*?G1. The RS chooses randomly a secret key (private key) s and computes the public-key as PubRS = s*P, where P is a generator of the group G1. Again, the RS selects a public key cryptosystem, where EPubRS (.) and Es(.) are the encryption and decryption algorithms respectively. Finally, the RS publishes the following system parameters: G1, G2, q, PubRS, e(.;.), H(.) and EPubRS(.).The parameter s is kept secret by RS.

Registration

In this phase, an user Ui submits his/her identifier IDi and password PWi to the RS. This data must be sent over a secure channel. Then RS computs:

(i) a secret parameter SPi=PWi * PubRS, and

(ii) registration identifier RegIDi = (s + PWi)H(IDi).

RS loads PubRS ; IDi ; RegIDi ; SPi and H(.) in the memory of the smart card and issues it to Ui .

Authentication

The authentication phase has two phases: (a) the login phase and (b) the verification phase.

(a) **Login Phase.** If the user Ui wants to log into the RS, he/she must insert his/her smart card into a card reader and keys in his identifier IDi and password PWi. Then the smart card performs the following:

(i) computes A = RegIDi – PWi.H(ID).

(ii) randomly selects a number r and computes Bi = EPubRS(r).

(iii) computes Ci = T * A + r * PubRS, where T is the user system's current timestamp.

It sends the login request message M = <IDi ; Bi ; Ci ; Ti> to the RS over a public channel.

(b) Verification. On receiving the login request message M = <IDi ; Bi ; Ci ; Ti> at time T', the RS and the smart card will perform the following steps for mutual authentication:

(i) RS verifies the validity of the time interval between T' and T. If (T'- T) >?T RS rejects the login request, where ΔT denotes the expected valid time interval for transmission delay. Otherwise, it goes for the next step.

(ii) computes X = Es(Bi) and then Y = X * PubRS.

(iii) checks if e(Ci - Y, P) = e(H(IDi); PubRS)T. RS accepts the login request if the equality holds.

Password change

Our scheme also enables user to change their password freely and securely. If the user Ui wants to change his password from PWi to PW'i, he/she insert his smart card into a card reader and keys in his identifier IDi and old password PWi. Then the smart card performs the following:

(i) computes SP*i = PWi * PubRS and accepts the change in password request iff SP*i = SPi.

(ii) If accepts the change in request then computes A = PWi * H(IDi), B = PW'i * H(IDi), and Reg'IDi = RegIDi – A+ B, where PW' is the new password.

The smart card now stores Reg'IDi and SP'i in place RegIDi and SPi respectively.

To compare our scheme computationally with the previous schemes with respect to time complexity we use the following notations:

Table 1: Time Complexity for Different Phases

Items Schemes	registration	Login	Verification	Password Change
Das et al	2tH + tAG	2tAG + tH	tH + 2te + tMG + t+	2tH + 2t+
Fang et al	2tH + tAG	tAG + tE	tH + tE + 2te + tMG	2tH

Giri et al	tH + 2tAG + t+	3tAG + 2t+ + tE	tH + tAG + t+ + tE + 2te + tMG	2tAG + 2t+
Our	tH + 2tAG+ t+	3tAG + 2t+ + tE+ tH	tH + tAG + t+ + tE + 2te + tMG	3tAG + 2t+

t+ is the time for addition of two elements in the additive group < G1 ; + >.

tAG is the time for x ∈ Z*q times additions in the additive group < G1 ; + >.

tMG is the time for x ∈ Z*q times multiplication in the multiplicative group < G2 ; X >.

te is the time for bilinear pairing operation.

tH is the time for executing the one-way hash function.

tE is the time for encrypting/decrypting a message.

We observe that in our scheme in the registration phase and the verification phase the computational time is same as to Giri and Srivastava[9] scheme but in login phase our scheme takes just tH more time than the Giri and Srivastava[9] scheme and in password change phase computation time is 3tAG + 2t+ . This is the cost that we pay in our scheme to achieve more security as compared to the scheme of Giri and Srivastava[9] and the scheme of Fang and Huang[7].

Security Analysis

This section provides the proof of correctness of the proposed scheme. Here, seven security properties: replay attack, on-line password guessing attack, off-line password guessing attack, server data eavesdropping, server spoofing attack and perfect forward secrecy should be considered for the proposed scheme.

Replay attack: Replay attack fails because RS generates RegIDi and SPi independently. If an adversary intercepts in login phase and uses it to impersonate Ui to login into the server, he can not do it. He has no knowledge of A and therefore he cannot compute s.H(IDi) which is required in login phase for verification.

On-line password guessing attack: The proposed scheme enables user to choose and change the password without the help of the remote server and so, the on-line password guessing attack does not succeed in our proposed scheme.

Off-line password guessing attack: To avoid the off-line password guessing attack we verify the password at the time of user login. If adversary obtains login request message M = <IDi ; Bi ; Ci ; Ti> and guesses a password PW* but in the memory of smart card secret parameter SPi is stored with PWi. So there is no match with SPi and SPi*. Therefore, our proposed scheme can resist off-line password guessing attack.

Server data eavesdropping: Without knowing server's secret key s, adversary cannot forge a login request to pass the authentication. The PWi is not stored on server and to find s by RegIDi is a case of Discrete Logarithm Problem. It is known that on suitably chosen elliptic curves DLP is a computationally infeasible problem.

Server spoofing attack: Since the proposed scheme provides mutual authentication, the server spoofing attack can be resisted.

Perfect forward secrecy: Perfect forward secrecy is provided in the situation that even though user's password pwi or server's secret key s is compromised, an adversary still cannot derive any previous session keys. In our proposed scheme, suppose that an adversary knows user's password pw, he tries to find server private keys from the information collected by passive attack in past communication sessions. However, it is difficult due to the hardness of DLP. Therefore, our proposed scheme can provides the property of perfect forward secrecy.

CONCLUSIONS

In this paper we analyzed the Giri and Srivastava[9] scheme and observed some weakness in it. We propose an improvement to remove this weakness. We modified the password change protocol, which remains offline. We also compare our proposed scheme with previously published schemes. We have proved that our scheme is more secure as compared to previously published schemes by security analysis and retains the flexibility in password change.

REFERENCES

1. Boneh D., M. Franklin, "Identity-based encryption from the Weil pairing," In J. Kilian, editor, *Advances in Cryptology-CRYPTO* 2001, Springer-Verlag, LNCS, #2139, pp.213- 229, 2001.
2. Boneh D., B. Lynn and H. Shacham, "Short signatures from the Weil pairing," *Advances in Cryptology - Asiacrypt 2001*, LNCS #2248, Springer-Verlag, pp. 514-532, 2002.
3. Chien H., J. Jan and Y.Tseng, "An efficient and practical solution to remote authentication: smart card," *Computers and Security*, 21(4), 372-375, 2002.
4. Chou J.S., Y. Chen, and J.Y. Lin, "Improvement of Manik et al. remote user authentication scheme," http://eprint.iacr.org/2005/450.pdf, 2005.
5. Das M.L., A. Saxena, V.P. Gulati and D.B. Phatak, "A novel remote user authentication scheme using bilinear pairings," *Computers and Security*, 25(3), pp.184-189, 2005.
6. Frey G. and H. G. Ruck, "A remark concerning m-divisibility and the discrete logarithm in the divisor class group of curves," Math. Comp., 62(206), pp. 865-874, 1994.
7. Fang G. and G. Huang, "Improvement of recently proposed remote user authentication schemes," http://eprint.iacr.org/2006/200.pdf.
8. Goriparthi T., M.L. Das, A. Negi, and A. Saxena, "Cryptanalysis of recently proposed remote user authentication schemes,"http://eprint.iacr.org/2006/028.pdf, 2005.
9. Giri Debasis and P.D. Srivastava, "An improved remote user authentication scheme with smart card using billinear pairings." http://eprint.iacr.org/2006/274.pdf.
10. Hwang M. and L. Li, "A new remote user authentication scheme using smart cards," *IEEE Trans Consumer Electron*, 46(1), pp. 28-30, February 2000.
11. Lamport L., "Password authentication with insecure communication," Commun ACM, 24, pp. 770-772, 1981.
12. Lal Sunder, K.K.Goyal,"An improved remote user authentication scheme using bilinear pairing",
13. Menezes A.J., T. Okamoto and S.A. Vanstone, "Reducing elliptic curve logarithms to logarithms in a finite field," *IEEE Trans. Inf. Theory*, 39(5), pp.1639 1646, 1993.
14. Sun H., "An efficient remote user authentication scheme using smart cards," *IEEE Trans Consumer Electron*, 46(4), pp. 958-961, November 2000.

15. Tan K. and H. Zhu, "Remote password authentication scheme with smart cards," Comput Commun,18, pp. 390-393, 1999.
16. Thulasi G., Manik Lal Das and Ashutosh Saxena," Cryptanalysis of recently proposed remote user authentication schemes," http://eprint.iacr.org/2006/028.pdf
17. Yang W. and S. Shieh, "Password authentication schemes with smart cards," *Computers and Security*, 18(8), pp. 727-733, 1999.

Virtualization Effects on the Security

38

Dinesh Kumar Agarwal and *Garima Singh*

ABSTRACT

Virtualization is a technology which provides the efficient and effective usage of computing system. The computing system is not only a single personnel system but also a system consisting of multiprocessors systems. To use the system efficiently & effectively. we will be using virtualization technology. Now a days business world is very competitive. Customers demanding new products this technology will provide opportunity to produce new products with the same resources with the existing infra structure.Within this technology one important issue is the "security". It has changed the classical definition of security. The classical definition suggest to try to detect the security violations at the first place and then take the action, but with the virtualization we can create the separate environment for security related application that would not effect the trusted information with the system. The concept has changed the scenario of security related solutions by inviting the malicious from the communication system & executing them with the separate virtualization machine environment that would not affect the trusted information with the same system.

INTRODUCTION

Madnick and Donovan first proposed the use of virtual machines to increase security in multiprogrammed operating systems. They recognized that the complexity of such systems increased the probability that an exploit could be found that allowed a malicious user to disturb the operating system. Such an exploit would allow the user to directly affect another user's data, by passing the operating system's built-in protection. They proposed running a VM per user, each with a private copy of the operating system. This increases security because now a malicious user would have to exploit vulnerability in both the operating system and the VMM in order to violate protection. Assuming independent failures in both the operating system and the VMM, this probability is vastly smaller that that of the OS alone.The IBM KVM/370 [33] and the VAX VMM Security Kernel [40] utilized virtual machines in a similar manner. Each was designed to support military-level security, which mandated separate physical machines for work on different security classifications. These projects demonstrated that equivalent security could be gained using VMs. Despite these benefits, interest in VMs for security. The use of virtual machines with the introduction of the Disco project revived the notion of using virtual machines for strong isolation. Their goal was to support the multiplexing of diverse Internet services on the same physical machine. In this setting, strong isolation is desired, services potentially require different operating environments, and no sharing of data is required between services.

VMs is the perfect solution under such conditions.VMs is able to scale the number of simultaneous VMs on a single machine to the hundreds through the extensive use of Para-virtualization, modifying the virtual architecture (which requires changes to guest operating systems) to allow for increased scalability.

What Is Virtualisation?

When computer systems were first invented they were mammoth systems that were large & expensive to operate. Due to their size, expense & demand for their usage, Computer systems quickly involved to become time sharing systems so that multiple users could use them simultaneously. As computers became more prevalent however, it became apparent that simply time sharing a single computer was not ideal. For example: misuse of the system could easily bring the computer system to a halt for all users. For organizations that could afford it, they simply purchased multiple computer systems to solve these problems. Having multiple Computer systems proved beneficial for the following reasons:

Isolation: - In many situations it is beneficial to have certain activities running on separate system. For example, an application may be known to contain bugs to interfere with other applications on the same system. Placing the application on a separate system guarantees it will not effect the other applications.

Performance

Placing an application on its on system allows it to have exclusive access to the system's resources and thus have better performance than if it have to share the system with other applications. Most organizations at the time were not capable to purchase multiple computer systems. It was also recognized that purchasing multiple computer systems was often wasteful, as it is hard to keep them busy all the time. However, having multiple computers obviously had it's benefits, so taking cast & waste into consideration IBM in 1960's began developing the first virtual machines that allowed one Computer to be shared as if it were several.

Virtual Machines

IBM defined the virtual machine as a fully protected and isolated software abstraction with the looks of a computer system's hardware (Fig 3.1). IBM designed their virtual machine systems with the goal that applications, even operating systems, run in the virtual machine would behave exactly as they would on the original hardware. Now, the term encompasses a large range of abstractions for example J.V.M. That does not watch an existing real machine

Application Programs
Operating System
Hardware layer

Fig. 1: Modern Computer System Structure

Levels of Virtualization

A modern computer system is composed of layers beginning with hardware & including layers of an operating system and application Programs running on top of the operating system .

Virtualization software abstracts virtual machines by interposing a layer at various places in the system. According to position of virtualization layer in the computer system we are having following types of virtualization:-

Hardware–level virtualization

Here the virtualization layer sits right on top of the hardware exporting the virtual machine abstraction. Because the virtual machine looks like the hardware, all the software written for it will run in the virtual machine.

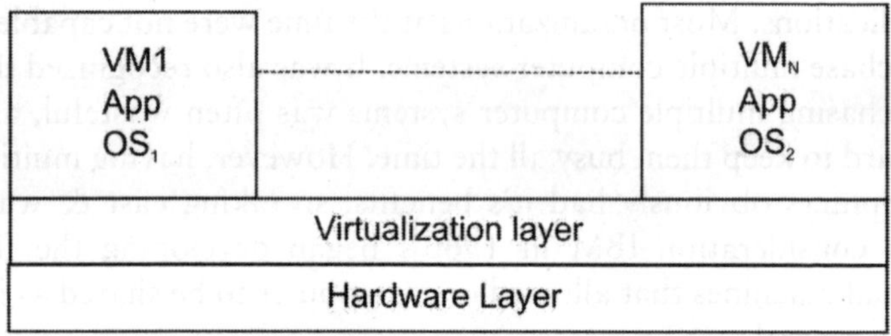

Fig.2 Hardware Level Virtualization

Operating system-level virtualization

In this case the virtualization layer sits between the operating system and the application programs that run on the operating system. The virtual machine runs applications, or sets of applications, that are written for the particular operating system being virtualized.

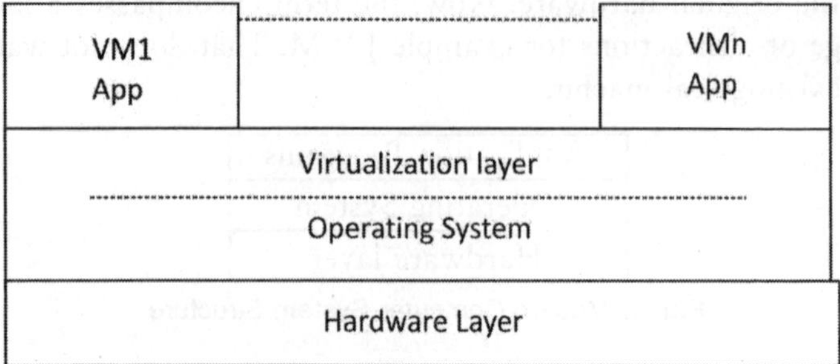

Fig. 3: Operating System Level Virtualization

High-level language-virtualization

In high level language virtualization, the virtualization layer sits as an application program on top of an operating system. The layer exports an abstraction of the virtual machine that can run programs written & compiled to the particular abstract machine definition. Any program written in the high level language & complied for this virtual machine will run in it.

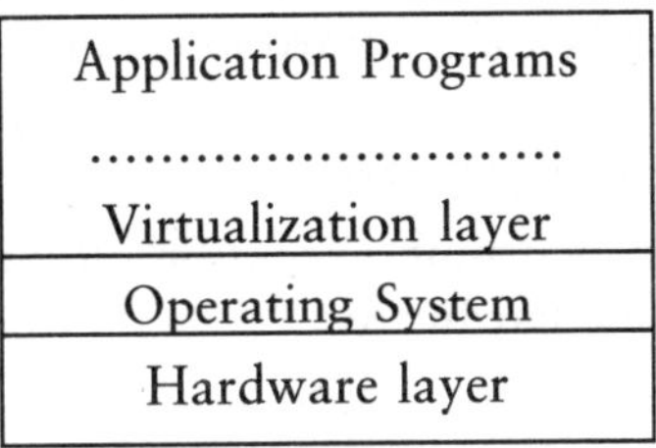

Fig. 4: High-Level languages Level Virtualization

General Advantages of Virtual Machines

There are different types of Virtual Machines providing different types of characteristics. But all of them share the following advantages.

Software compatibility

The Virtual machine provides a compatible abstraction so that all software written for it will run on it. For example, a hardware level virtual machine will run all the software, operating systems & applications written for the hardware.

Isolation: The virtual machine abstraction isolates the software running in the virtual machine from other virtual machines & real machine. This isolation provides that bugs or hackers can be contained within the to virtual machine & can not adversely effect other parts of the system.

Encapsulation: The software layer exporting the virtual machine abstraction is an example of level of indirection this layer can be used to manipulate & control the execution of the software in the virtual machine. It can also use this indirection to enhance the software or to provide a better execution environment.

Performance: Adding a software layer to a system adds overhead, which can adversely affect the performance of the software running in the virtual machine. But the benefits of the virtual systems outweigh any overhead that they introduce.

Virtual machine monitor benefits

Virtual Machine Monitors normally allow a system manger to configure the environment in which a VM will run. VM Configurations can be different from real machine. For example, a real Machine may have 32 MB of Memory, but a Virtual Machine may have only 8 MB.

They allow concurrent execution of different operating systems on the same hardware.

They allow users to isolate untrusted applications. For example, a program downloaded from internet could be tested in a VM. If the program contained a virus the virus would be isolated to that VM. When upgrading an operating system or migrating to a different operating system, it is common that some applications do not work on the new operating system. VMM allows both the new & old operating system on the same hardware.

VMM allows multiple copies of an operating system running on a scalable computer.

It also allows these operating systems to share resources each other.

Virtualization Impact on the Security

Virtual machine and security

Security is an important factor if the programs of Independent and possibly malicious users are to coexist on the same computer system. A combined virtual machine monitor/operating system (VMM/OS) approach to Information system isolation provides substantially better software security than a conventional multi programming operating system approach. This added protection is derived from redundant security using Independent mechanisms that are inherent in the design of most VMM/OS systems. During the past decade the technique of multiprogramming (the concurrent execution of several independent programs on the same computer system) has been developed to take full advantage of medium- and large-scale computer systems (cost economics, flexibility, easy of operation, hardware reliability and redundancy, etc.). Unfortunately, in transferring physically isolated information systems. Fig. 5a to physically shared information systems Fig. 5b, we must cope with the problems of operating system compatibility, reliability, and security. The Virtual Machine approach provides effective solutions to these problems.

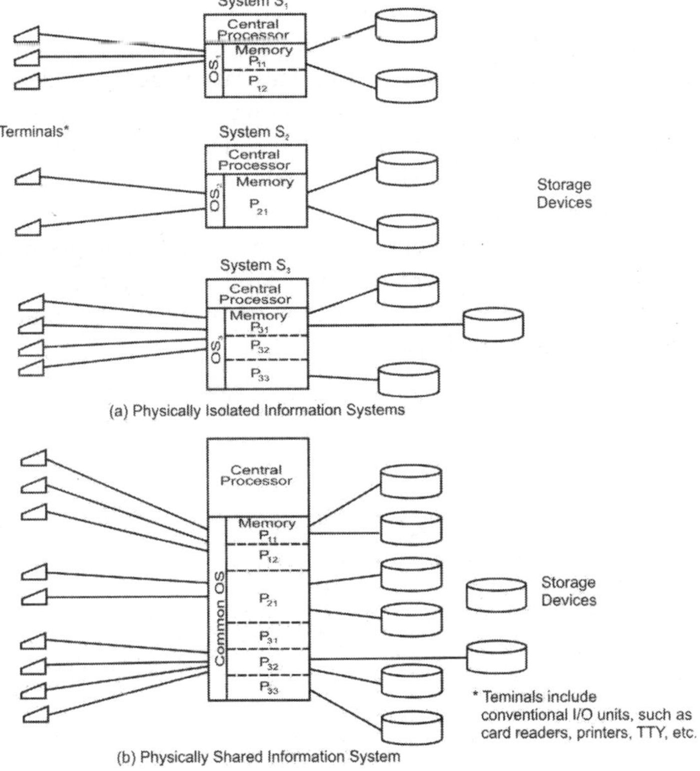

Fig. 5: Isolated & Share Information System

Virtual Machine Approach for Isolation and Compatibility

Virtual machine may be defined as a replica of a real computer and real computer System simulated by a combination of a Virtual Machine Monitor (VMM) software program and appropriate hardware support. Thus, a VMM can make one computer system function as a multiple physically isolated systems Fig. 6. A VMM do this by controlling the multiplexing of the physical hardware resources such that the telephone company multiplexes communications enabling separate and, hopefully, Isolated conversations over the same wires.

VMM is different from a conventional operating system. A VMM restricts itself to the task of multiplexing and allocating the physical hardware, this presents an interface that appears identical to a "bare machine". In fact, it is necessary to load a conventional operating system into each virtual machine in order to accomplish useful work. This latter fact provides the basis for the solution to the operating system compatibility problem. Each virtual machine is controlled by a separate, and If necessary, different operating system. This solution need the extra additional overhead in information system operation, but this overhead can be kept rather low. Depending upon the precise economics and benefits of a large-scale system. VMM approach is often preferable to the operation of the multiple physically isolated real systems.

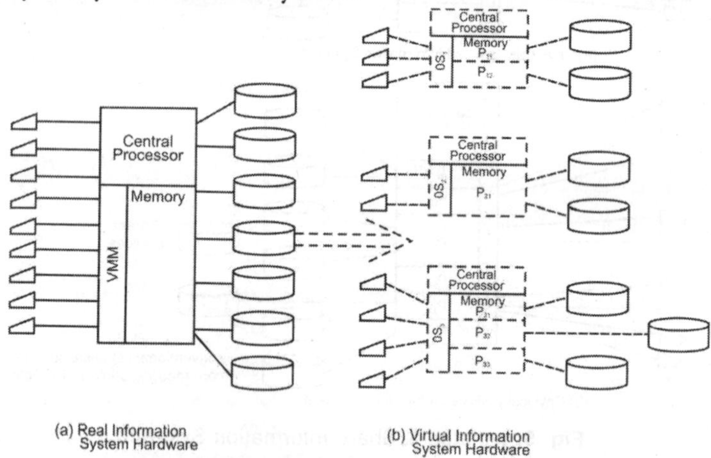

Fig. 6: Real and Virtual Information Systems

Security & Reliability in a Virtual Machine Environment

In the above virtual machine approach solves the OS compatibility problems by allowing different operating systems to run and coexist on the same computer at the same time. In the view of security and reliability in a virtual machine environment we can show that the virtual machine approach results in a system that is much less susceptible to such failures than a conventional multiprogramming operating system. The problems of software reliability and security are quite similar. A reliability failure is any action of a user's program that causes the system to cease correct operation (e.g., "stops" or "crashes"). A security failure is a form of reliability failure that allows one user's program to access or destroy the data or programs of another Isolated user or gain control of the entire computer system.

Contemporary Operating System Environment

Most contemporary operating systems, in conjunction with appropriate hardware support, provide mechanisms to prevent reliability and security failures. In this project, I am only concerned about isolation security (no user is allowed access to any other user information). The problem of generalized controlled access (a user is allowed restrictive access to another user's information) is much more difficult but, such facility is not needed for this environment illustrated in Figure I. Under "Ideal" circumstances, most current operating systems can provide isolation security. 0S/360, for example, uses the System/360's lock and key protection to insulate users from each other and from the operating system. The supervisor/problem state modes further prevent users from "gaining control" of the system. Thus, it should be possible to isolate users.

Figure 3.3(a) illustrates the coexistence of multiple programs on the same information system. Such a system is susceptible to security violations if a single hardware or software failure were to occur. Typical modern operating systems consist of thousands, possibly millions, of instructions. The user programs interface with the operating system through hundreds of parameters (e.g; supervisor calls, program Interrupts, I/0 requests and interrupts,). At the current time there is no known way to systematically validate the correct functioning of the operating system for all possible parameters. In fact, most systems tend to be highly vulnerable to invalid parameters. The operating system, running with protection disabled and assuming that the address parameter corresponds to a user's data areas transfers the return data to that location. If the address provided actually corresponds to locations with in the time the operating system, the system can be made to destroy or disable itself. Host system attempt to detect this kind of error but there are many other techniques. Fig 7 see some of the factors contributing to the problem. In order to provide sufficient functionality to be effectively for a large and heterogeneous collection of programs, the operating system must be quite comprehensive and, thus, more error. In general, a single logical error in the operating system software can invalidate the entire security mechanism. Furthermore, as depicted in Figure 4.3(a), there is no more protection between the programs of differing user groups or the operating system than there is between the application programs of a single user group.

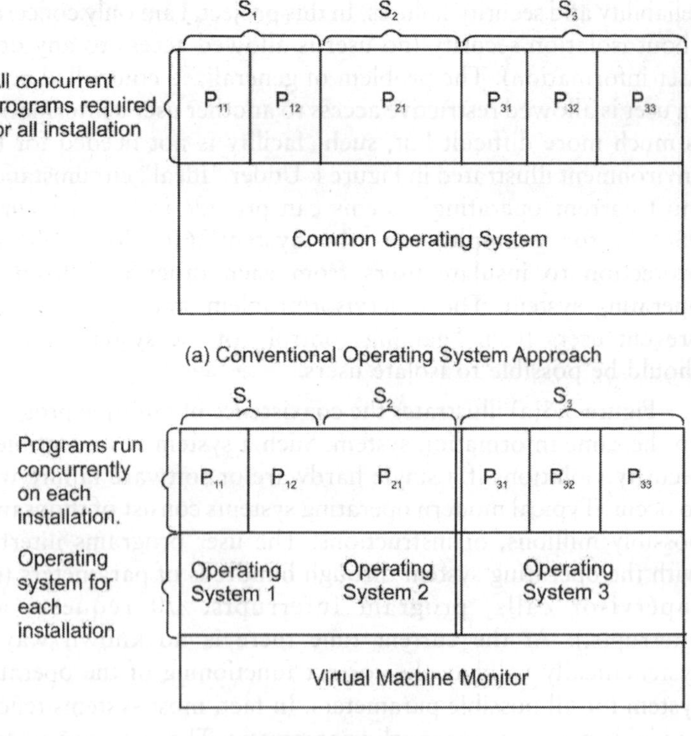

Fig. 7: Comparison of Conventional OS and VMM / OS Approach

Virtual Machine Environment

Fig. 7 shows the virtual machine approach to a physically shared system. This arrangement has numerous security advantages. If we define Ps(P) to be the probability that a given run of program P will cause a security violation to occur, the following conditions would be expected to hold:

Ps(PlOS(n)) < Ps(PlOS(m)) for k<m

OS (I) refers to a conventional operating system multiprogramming at level I the probability of system failurc tends to increase with the load on the operating system.In particular, a monoprogrammlng system, 0S (1), tends to be much simpler and reliable than a comprehensive. Multiprogramming system. Furthermore, the m-degree multiprogramming system often requires intricate alterations to support the special needs of the m users, especially if m is large. These problems have been experienced in most large-scale multiprogramming systems. These problems remove in the VM systems each virtual machine may run a separate, each operating system may be simpler and less a single comprehensive all-encompassing operating system

Ps(OSIVMM(k)) < Ps(PlOS(m)) for k<m

VMM (1) means a virtual machine monitor. The operating system, OS, on a particular virtual machine has the same relationship to the VMM (k) as a user's. Program, P, has to a conventional multiprogramming operating system, OS(m). Using the same rationale as In A above, the smaller the degree of multiprogramming (I.e., k<m), the smaller the probability of a security violation. Furthermore, since virtual machine monitors tend to be shorter, simpler, and easier to debug than conventional multiprogramming operating systems, even when k=m, the VMM is less error-prone. For example, since the VMM is defined by the hardware specifications of the real machine, the field engineer's hardware diagnostic software can be used to checkout the correctness of the VMM.

Redundant Security Mechanisms

If the Individual operating systems, OS, and the virtual machine monitor, used identical security mechanisms and algorithms, then any user action that resulted in penetration of one could also penetrate the other. That is, first take control of the OS and then, using the same technique, take control of the VMM. This is 1oglcally analogous to placing one safe Inside another safe - but having the same combination on both safes. To remove this danger, the OS and VMM must have redundant security based upon Independent mechanisms.

In a VMM/OS environment using VM/370 and 0S/360 as example systems, let us consider main memory security first. 0S/360 uses the System/360-370 lock and key hardware to isolate one user's memory area from invalid access by another user's program.VM/370, on the other hand, the Dynamic Address Translation (DAT) hardware to provide a separate virtual memory for each virtual machine - Independent of the locks and keys. Thus, a malicious user would have to overwhelm both the lock and key and the DAT mechanisms to violate the Isolation security of another coexisting program on another virtual machine.

REFERENCES

1. R.J. Creasy, "The origin of the VM/370 Time sharing system," *IBM Journal of Research & Development*, Vol. 25, No. 5. p. 483, 1981
2. "The Reincarnation of Virtual Machines," by Mendel Rosenblum, Stanford University and VMWare from *Virtual Machines* Vol. 2, No. 5, July / August 2004
3. G.J. Popek & R.P. Goldenberg, "Formal Requirements for Virtualizable Third Generation Architectures" Communication ACM Vol. 17, No. 7, pp. 412-421, 1974

   T.V. VleeK, "the IBM 360/67 & CP/CMS,"
4. A. Whitaker, M. Shaw, & S. Gribble, " Denali: Light Weight Virtual Machines for Distributed & Networked Applications," The University of Washington.
5. P. Barham, B. Dragovic et, "Xen & the Art of Virtualization," in SOS P'o3, ACM.
6. John Scott Robin, Cynthia E.Iruine, "Analysis of the Intel Pentium's Ability to xxxsupport a Virtual Machine Monitor," *Proceedings of the 9th USE NIX security xxxsymposium*, pp. 129-144, 2000 Denver, Colorado, U.S.A.
7. Poul Henning Kamp & Robert Watson's, "Building Systems to be shared".

8. "Interview: James Gosling" Eric Allman interviews the creator of Java.

9. Application and analysis of Virtual Machine Approach to information system security and isolation Stuart E. Madnlck(*) and John D. Donovan(**) Massachusetts Institute of Technology Cambridge, Massachusetts 02139.

10. Buzen, D.P., Peter P. Chen, and Robert P. Goldberg, "Virtual Machine Techniques for Improving System Relablity", *The ACM Wqrkshop on Vlrtual Computer Systems*, (March 26-27, 1973).

11. *Cryptography and Network Security* William Stalling (Book).

12. Popek, G.J., and Kline, C. Verifiable secure operating system software. Proc. NCC 1974, AFIPS Press, Montvale, N.J., pp. 145-151.421 *Communications* July 197 of Volume 17 the ACM Number 7.

13. How virtualization can improve securityAlessandroperili,CISSP.MVP 06.28.200647.

Broadband Wireless Communication System—An Emerging Future

S.K. Pandey

ABSTRACT

Communication System has always been playing a crucial role in the society, organizations, individual, etc. But due to high installation cost & monthly rate, it was not much popular up to last decade (1990). The rapid pace at which the technological innovations are being introduced in the world poses a potential growth of communication system especially wireless communications.

In 1991 less than 1% of the world's population had access to a mobile phone where as by the end of 2001, an estimated one in every five people had a mobile phone. During the same period the number of countries worldwide having a mobile network increased from just 3% to over 90%. In 2002, the number of mobile subscribers overtook the no. of fixed phone subscribers. By this growth It may be predicted that this growth will continue to rise and by 2010 there will be more than 1700 million mobile phone (wireless communication) subscribers worldwide.This explosive growth shows the great future of wireless communication system in the world. In this competitive & fast life era, communication systems have been playing a crucial role in general and wireless communication systems in particular. The Term 'Time is money' has now become 100% true as people are ready to pay any amount for getting the services within no time and without moving from their place.

Wireless communication systems have proved its importance through its service. Due to the ease of installation, wireless systems are the first choice of the customer in all types of systems such as Mobile (Wireless) phones, WLL fixed phones, remote controlled doors, remote controlled vehicle locking systems, Wireless LANs, Wireless Internet connections, wireless computer keyboards, mouse, wireless mice, etc. Wireless data transferring systems such as Bluetooth, infrared, wi-fi, etc incorporated in computers, Laptops, mobile phones, etc. are the most preferred devices in all around the world. This success has been achieved due to the introduction of Broadband Wireless Communication Systems. Broadband Wireless Communication Systems is one of the most growing technologies in the communication sector today and will be in future also.

INTRODUCTION

The term *wireless* is normally used to refer to any type of electrical or electronic operation which is accomplished without the use of electrical conductors or wires. The distances covered by the system may be short (a few meters as in television remote control) or very long (thousands or millions of Km for radio communications). Wireless communication is generally considered to be a branch of Telecommunications. The term broadband also refers to telecommunication in which a wide band of frequencies is available to transmit information. Because a wide band of frequencies is available, information can be Multiplexed and sent on many different frequencies or channels within the band concurrently, allowing more information to be transmitted in a given amount of time (much as more lanes on a highway allow more cars to travel on it at the same time). Related terms are wideband (a synonym), baseband (an onechannel band), and narrowband (sometimes meaning just wide enough to carry voice, or simply "not broadband," and sometimes meaning specifically between 50 cps and 64 Kpbs).

Wireless came into public use to refer to a radio receiver or transceiver (a dual purpose receiver and transmitter device), establishing its usage in the field of wireless telegraphy early on, now the term is used to describe modern wireless connections such as in cellular networks, satellite communication and wireless broadband Internet. It is also used in a general sense to refer to any type of operation that is implemented without the use of wires, such as "wireless remote control", "wireless energy transfer", etc. regardless of the specific technology (radio, infrared, ultrasonic, etc.) that is used to accomplish the operation. Communication system has created its own identity by its functionality and has been playing a vital role from the day of its development and introduction in the market (aprox 1946 First interconnection of mobile users to public switched telephone network (PSTN)). Electronic communication system has always been the first preference for communication in the world but due to high cost and less availability it could not be popular more specially in the middle level community. But continuous research and development in this field has made it possible to be affordable by the middle level community. Introduction of Wireless communication systems (television remote control, CD players with remote control, remote control car locking systems, WLL phones, mobile phones, cellular phones, remote controlled door systems, etc.) has attracted a large portion of world population. By the development of Broadband, wireless communication system has become popular like anything in all around the world. The first generation (1G) systems were analogue and commissioned in 1980s. In 1990s, second generation (2G) digital systems such as Global System for Mobile communication (GSM) came into existence. The GSM standard has been extremely successful providing national as well as international coverage. Today, the GSM is the most preferred stream of mobile communication system.

A brief History of Wireless (Mobile) Telephony

1946 - Introduction of first interconnection of mobile users to public switched telephone network (PSTN)

1949 - FCC recognizes mobile radio as new class of service

1940s - Number of mobile users > 50K

1950s - Number of mobile users > 500K

1960s - Number of mobile users > 1.4M

1960s - Improved Mobile Telephone Service (IMTS) introduced (full-duplex, auto dial, auto trunking supporting)

1976 – Introduction of Bell Mobile Phone (543 pay customers using 12 channels in the New York City area, waiting list was 3700 people, service is poor due to blocking)

1979 - Japan deploys first cellular communication system

1983 - Advanced Mobile Phone System (AMPS) deployed in US in 900 MHz band: supports 666 duplex channels.

1989 - Group Special Mobile defines European digital cellular standard, GSM

1991 - US Digital Cellular phone system introduced

1993 - IS-95 code-division multiple - access (CDMA) spread-spectrum digital cellular system deployed in US

1994 - GSM system deployed in US, relabeled Global System for Mobile Communications

1995 - FCC auctions off frequencies in Personal Communications System (PCS) band at 1.8 GHz for mobile telephony

2000 - Third generation cellular system standards, Bluetooth standards.

Common examples of wireless equipment which are in use today include:

Cellular phones and pagers:

Provide connectivity for portable and mobile applications, both personal and business.

Global positioning system (GPS):

It allows drivers of cars and trucks, captains of boats and ships, and pilots of aircraft to ascertain their location anywhere on earth.

Cordless computer peripherals:

The cordless mouse is a common example; keyboards and printers can also be linked to a computer via wireless.

Cordless telephone sets:

These are limited range devices, not to be confused with cell phones.

Satellite television:

Allows viewers in almost any location to select from hundreds of channels.

Scope of Growth

With the emergence of broadband wireless communication systems, new business opportunities have appeared for operators, content provides, and manufacturers.

Broadband wireless communications technologies promise the freedom of constant access to the Internet at high speeds, without the limitation of connection cables. Broadband Wireless Communications Business provides comprehensive coverage of the present status and future evolution of these technologies, giving vital practical cost and benefit advice on design, construction and implementation For the past decade or so, telecommunication activities have gained momentum in the world. Efforts have been made from both governmental and nongovernmental platforms to enhance the infrastructure. The idea is to help modern telecommunication technology penetrate India's socio-culturally diverse society, and to transform it into a nation of technology aware people. Broadband Wireless systems are used to meet a variety of needs. The most common use is to connect laptop users who travel from location to location. Another common use is for Phones, mobile networks that connect via satellite. A wireless transmission method is a logical choice to network a LAN segment that must frequently change locations. The following situations justify the use of wireless technology:

To span a distance beyond the capabilities of typical cabling,

To avoid obstacles such as physical structures, EMI, or RFI

To provide a backup communications link in case of normal network failure

To link portable or temporary workstations

To overcome situations where normal cabling is difficult or financially impractical

To remotely connect mobile users or networks It is the broadband which makes possible to get the phone as well mobile connections on demand which was not possible 5 years back even. But due to continuous research & development in the field of wireless communication system it has become possible to get multiple connections of fixed phone as well as mobile phone on the same day at cheaper rates.

Brief information about the subscribers in India in different forms is as under [2]:

Telephony Subscribers (Wireless and Landline): 264.8 million (November 2007)

Cellphones: 225.5 million (November 2007)

Land Lines: 39.31 million (November 2007)

Yearly Cellphone Addition: 100 million (2007)

Monthly Cellphone Addition: 8.3 million (November 2007)

Teledensity: 23% (September 2007)

Projected teledensity: 500 million, 40% of population by 2010

Broadband Connection:

2.67 million (September 2007). The telecommunications system in India is the fourth largest in the world and it was thrown open to private players in the 1990s. The country is divided into multiple zones, called circles (roughly along state boundaries). Government and several private players run local and long distance telephone services. Competition has caused prices to drop and calls across India are one of the cheapest in the world. The rates are supposed to go down further with new measures to be taken by the concerned ministry, Govt. of India [3]. This explosive growth rate of broadband wireless communication systems users in different form shows the tremandous scope of the sector in near future.

SUGGESTIONS & CONCLUSION

After economic liberalization (1992), many private Internet Service Providers (ISPs) have entered the market, many with their own local loop and gateway infrastructures. However the customer service of most of these private ISPs is pathetic as the critical mass of customers have not yet been reached. In addition the speed that one can get from these ISPs is questionable and rarely exceeds the broadband definition of 256 kbit/s. Right now the market is infinite and competition is fierce to lure prospective customers into buying their services, broadband law of 2004, changed the definition for broadband to 256 kbit/s always on, most ISPs found that they can provide broadband with a capping of data that can be downloaded. Though the people are approximately happy with the services provided by the various governmental & non-governmental organizations in this sector but there are few points highlighted below are being suggested to be taken care of on priority as these are the major problems of most of the sevice providers :

Bandwidth Enhancement

Prevention of the privacy of a subscriber

Prevention of Call overlapping

Prevention of Call Taping

Unwanted messages barring etc. it is high time that the industry should concentrate seriously on the above highlighted points to maintain & increase the gowth rate of the industry.

REFERENCES

1. http://www.investintech.com/purchasea2e.html
2. http://www.wikipedia.org
3. http://www.Google.com
4. http://www.tutorial-reports.com
5. http://www.webopedia.com
6. J. Thornton, D. Grace, C. Spillard, T. Konefal, T.C. Tozer, Broadband Communications from a High Altitude Platforms, *IEE Electronics and Communications Engineering Journal*, Vol 13, No. 3, pp. 138-144, June 2001 (through net).

Bibliography

Acharya S.; Franklin M.J.; Zdonik A.B., *Balancing Push and Pull for Data Broadcast,* In SIGMOD Conference, pp. 183-94, 1997.

Acharya S.; Franklin, M.J.; Zdonik S.B., *Disseminating Updates on Broadcast Disks,* In *VLDB*, pp. 354-65, 1996.

Alberto Leon Garcia, *Communication Networks Fundamentals Concepts and Key Architectures*, New Delhi: TMH.

Alberto Leon: Gracia, *Communication Networks Funamentales Concepts and Key Architectures,* New Delhi: TMH.

Alonso R.; Barbara D.; Garcia-Molina, *Data Caching Issues in an Information Retrieval System ACM Transactions on Database Systems (TODS)*, 5(3): 359-84, September 1990.

Andresen D.; YangT.; Ibarra O.H., *Toward a Scalable Distributed WWW Server on Workstation Clusters*, Journal of Parallel and Distributed Computing, 42:91-100, 1997.

Andrew J. Viterb, *Principles of Digital Communication & Coding*, McGraw Hill.

Annadurai, *Fundamentals of Digital Image Processing*, Pearson Education India.

Backes M.; Jacobi C.; Pfitzmann B., *Deriving Cryptographically Sound Implementations Using Composition and Formally Verified Bisimulation.* In proceedings of Formal Methods Europe (FME) 2002, pp. 310-29.

Bagli S.; Soille P., *Morphological Automatic Extraction of Coastline from Pan-European Landsat on Images*, In

Proceedings of the Fifth International Symposium on GIS and Computer Cartography for Coastal Zone Management, Volume 3, pp. 58-59, Geneva, 2003.

Bahl I.J.; P. Bhartiya, Dedham M.A., *Microstrip Antennas*, Artech House, 1980.

Bakhtiari S.; Safavi, *Cryptographic Hash Functions*, Naini Piperzyk J. 1995.

Behrouz A. Farouzan, *Data Communication and Networking*, New Delhi: Tata McGraw Hill.

Biala J., Friedr, *Mobilfunk und Intelligente Netze*, Vieweg & Sohn Verlagsgesellschaft, 1994.

Bingham, J.A.C., *Multicarrier Modulation for Data Transmission: An Idea whose Time has Come*, May 1990, IEEE Communications Magazine, Vol. 28, No. 5, pp. 5-14.

Bishop, *Computer Security: Art And Science*, Pearson Education India.

Blum E.K., *Journal of Computer and System Sciences*, Vol. 48 (1-3), 1994, New York: Academic Press Inc.

Bo G.; Delleplane S.; Laurentiis R. De, *Coastline Extraction in Remotely Sensed Images by means of Texture Features Analysis*, International Geosciences and Remote Sensing Symposium, 2001, IGARSS '01, Volume 3, pp. 1493-95, Sydney, NSW, Australia, 2001.

Boneh D.; Lynn B.; Shacham H., *Short Signatures from the Weil Pairing*, Advances in Cryptology—Asiacrypt 2001, LNCS #2248, Springer-Verlag, pp. 514-32, 2002.

Boneh D.; Franklin M., In J. Kilian, *Identity-based Encryption from the Weil Pairing*, Advances in Cryptology-CRYPTO 2001, Springer-Verlag, LNCS, #2139, pp. 213-29, 2001.

Bragg R.; Rhodes-Ousley; Strassberg K., *The Complete Reference: Network Security*.

Bratko, *Prolog: Programming for Artifical Intelligence,* Pearson Education India.

Buchmann J.A., *Introduction to Cryptography*, Springer-Verlag.

Charnick, *Introduction to Artificial Intelligences,* Addision Wesley.

Chien H.; Jan J.; Tseng Y., *An Efficient and Practical Solution to Remote Authentication: Smart Card*, Computers and Security, 21(4), pp. 372-75, 2002.

Christopher T., *Artificial Intelligence*, New Age International.

Cichocki A.; Unbehauen R., *Neural Networks For Optimization & Signal Processing,* John Wiley.

Cioffi J.M., *A Multicarrier Primer, in ANSI T1E1.4 Committee Contribution*, No. 91-157 Nov. 1991, Boca Raton, FL.

Clark A.P.; Jayasinghe S.G., *Channel Estimation for Land Mobile Radio Systems*, IEE Proceedings Part F, Vol. 134, No. 4, pp. 383-93, July 1987.

Comer, *Hands-on-Networking with Internet Technology*, Pearson Education India.

Cooke J.C.; Brewster R.L., *Cryptographic Security Techniques for Digital Mobile Telephones.*

Cosentino, *Essential PHP for Web Professionals*, Pearson Education India.

Cosman P.C.; Gray R.M.; Olshen R.A., *Evaluating Quality of Compressed Medical Images: SNR, Subjective Rating, and Diagnostic Accuracy,* Proceedings of the IEEE, Volume, 82 6, June 1994, pp. 919-32.

Cowling J., *Dynamic Location Management in Heterogeneous Cellular Networks,* MIT Thesis.

Cummings M., *FPGA in Software Radio,* IEEE Communication Magazine, 1999.

Dang M.S.; Prakash A.; Anvekar D.K., Kapoor M.; Shorey R., *Fuzzy Logic Based Handoff in Wireless Networks,* IEEE trans. 2000.

Das M.L.; Saxena A.; Gulati V.P.; Phatak D.B., *A Novel Remote user Authentication Scheme using Bilinear Pairings,* Computers and Security, 25(3), pp. 184-89, 2005.

David J., Skyrme, *Knowledge Networking: Creating the Collaborative Enterprice*, Oxford: Butterworth-Heinemann.

Deo Nar Singh, *Graph Theory with Applications to Engineering and Computer Science*, New Delhi: Prentice Hall.

Derfler Frank: Freed LES, *Practical Networking Cabling*, P.H.I.

Deshpande M.D.; Bailey M.C., *Input Impedance of Microstrip Antennas*, IEEE Trans. Antennas Propogat., Vol. AP-30, July, 1982, pp. 645-50.

Deva V., *E-Banking*, Commonwealth Publishers.

Dixon R.C., *Spread Spectrum Communications*, Second Edition, John Wiley and Sons, New York, 1984.

Dr. Feher K., *Wireless Digital Communications, Modulation and Spread Spectrum Applications*, U.S. addition.

ed. by Shubhash Bhatnagar; Robert Schware, *Information and Communication Technology in Devolopment: Cases from India*, New Delhi: Sage Publications.

Egger W. Li.; Kunt M., *Very Low Bit Rate Image Compression Using an Adaptive Morphological Sub band Decomposition,* Proceedings of the IEEE, Special Issue on Advances in Image and Video Compression, Early 1995.

Eikelboom R.H.; Yogesan K.; Barry C.J., *Methods and Limits of Digital Image Compression of Retinal Images for Telemedicine*, 2000, Invest. Ophthal. Vis. Sci. In Press.

Emillia M., *Web Engireering*, New Age International.

Epplin J., *Peeking Under the Hood of SnapGear's uClinux-powered*, VPN Appliances.

Fausett L., *Fundamentals of Neural Network*, PHI.

Forouzen, *Data Communication and Networking*, T.M.H. Publiction.

Frank J. Derfler Jr.:Les Freed, *Practical Networking Cabling*, N. Delhi, PHI.

Freeman, *Neural Network*, Pearson Education India.

Frey G.; Ruck H.G., *A Remark Concerning M-divisibility and the Discrete Logarithm in the Divisor Class Group of Curves*, 62(206), pp. 865-74, 1994.

Furber S., *ARM System-on-chip Architecture in English Language*, Second Edition published by Addison Wesley.

Garacia L.; Widjaja, *Communication Network: Fundamentals Concepts and Key Architectures*, New Delhi, TMH.

Garcia-Molina; Wiederhold, *Read-Only Transactions in a Distributed Database. ACM Transactions on Database Systems,* 7(2): 209-34, June 1982.

Gersho A.; Gray R.M., *Vector Quantization and Signal Compression,* Kluwer Academic Press, 1992.

Gilbert Hild, *Digital Networking and T-Carrier Multiplexing*, New York: John Wiley.

Gill P.S., *Data Communication and Computer Networks,* Peepee.

Goldreich, *Foundations of Cryptography,* Cambridge Press, 2001.

Goncalves M.; Niles, K., *IPv6 Networks,* McGraw Hill, 1998.

Gonzalez R.C.; Woods R.E., *Digital Image Processing,* Addision-Wesley, Reading, MA, 1992.

Goralski Walter J., *Optical Networking and WDM,* Tata McGraw Hill.

Gracia Alberto Leaon:Widjaja Indra, *Communication Networks*, TMH.

Grossglauser M.; Tse D., *Mobility Increases the Capacity of Ad-hoc Wireless Networks,* Proceedings of IEEE Infocom 2001, Anchorage, Alaska, April 2001.

Gupta P.; Kumar P.R., *The Capacity of Wireless Networks,* IEEE Transactions on Information Theory, Vol. 46, No. 2, pp. 388-404, March 2000.

Hallberg Bruce, *Networking: A Beginner's Guide*, TMH.

Handel, *ATM Networks*, Pearson Education India.

Herbert Taub, Principles of Communications System, New Delhi: Tata McGraw Hill Publishing Company Ltd.

Hodges, M.R.L., *The GSM Radio Interface,* British Telecom Technology Journal, Vol. 8, No. 1, January 1990, pp. 31-43.

Huitema, C., *IPv6: The New Internet Protocol*, Prentice Hall, 1997, 2nd edn.

Hykin, *Communication System,* John Wiley.

Ibrahim Ahmad M., *Introduction to Applied Fuzzy Electronics*, PHI, 2004.

Information System for Banks, Indian Institute of Banking & Finance, Taxman Publications (P) Ltd.

J. Serra, *Image Analysis and Mathematical Morphology*, Academic Press, New York, N.Y., 1982.

Jackson, *Introduction to Expert System*, Pearson Education India.

Jain A.K., *Image Data Compression: A Review*, Proc. IEEE, Vol. 69, pp. 349-89, 1981.

Jain Satish, *Computer Fundamentals and C++ Programing V.II*, New Delhi: BPB Publication.

Jakobsson M.; Sako K.; Impaliazzo K.R., *Designated Verifier Proofs and Their Applications*. Eurocrypt 1996, LNCS #1070, Springer-Verlag, 1996, 142-154.

James, J.R.; Hall P.S., *Handbook of Microstrip Antennas*, Vol. 1, London: Peter Peregrinus Ltd., 1989.

Jeremiah F. Hayes, *Modelling and Analysis of Communications Network*, Delhi, Khanna Pub.

Jesse Liberty, *Learning Visual basic.Net*, Navi Mumbai, Shroff Publishers.

Jobmann K., *Wireless Networks—Location Management in Cellular Networks.*

Johansson P., *Rasmus—A Spread Spectrum and Modulation Evaluation System*, Report FOA-R- -00-01439-504- - SE, Defence Research Establishment, Sweden 2000.

Johnson N.F.; Jajodia S., *Exploring Steganography: Seeing the Unseen*, Computer 31, No. 2, pp. 26-34, 1998.

Joseph, *Grid Computing*, Pearson Education India.

Juan X.L.; Liang X.Q.; Zheng Z., *Identity Based Designated Verifier Threshold Signature Scheme*, Journal of Computer Applications, 1058-61, Vol. 27 (05), 2007.

K.R. Bojokvic Rao; Dragorad A. Milovanovice, *Multimedia Communication Systems: Technicals, Standards*, New Delhi: Prentice Hall of India.

Katz E.D.; Butler M.; McGrath R., *A Scalable HTTP Server: The NCSA Prototype*, Computer Networks and ISDN Systems, 27:155-164, 1994.

Keshav S., *An Engineering Approach on Computer Networking,* Addision Wesley.

Keshav S., *Computer Networking: An Engineering approach To,* Singapore: AWP.

Keshav S., *Engineering Approach to Computer Networking*, Pearson.

Khate A., *Cryptography and Networks Security.*

Kim S.; Park S.; Won D., *Proxy Signatures Revisited,* Proc. Information and Communication Security (ICICS '97), LNCS#1334, Springer-Verlag, 1997, 223-32.

Kumar K.P.; Shailaja G.; Saxena A., *Identity Based Strong Designated Verifier Signature Scheme. Cryptography eprint Archive*, Report 2006/134.

Kumar R., *Communication Systems (For VII Sem ECE): Text Book ON.*

Kurose James F. Ros Kith W., *Computer Networking: A Top-Down Approach Featuring the Internet,* Pearson Education.

Kurose James F., *Computer Networking: A Top-Down Approach Featuring the Internet,* Addison Wesley.

Lewis, *Fundamentals of Embedded Software,* Pearson Education India.

Linda M. Harasim, *Globles Networks: Computers and International Communication,* Cambridge, MIT.

Lynnette R. Porter; William Coggin, *Rearch Strategies in Technical Communication,* New York, John Wiley.

McGregor J.P.; Lee R.B., *Performance Impact of Data Compression on Virtual Private Network Transactions,* Proc. 25th Annual IEEE Conf. Local Comp. Networks, 2000, pp. 500-510.

Mehrotra K., Mohan C.K., *Elements of Artificial Neural Networks,* MIT Press.

Miller Michael A., *Data and Network Communications*, New Delhi, Vikas Publishing House Pvt. Ltd.

Mitola J., *The Software Radio Architecture,* IEEE Communications Magazine, May 1995, pp. 26-37.

Murthy C.S.V., *E-Commerce*, Himalaya Publishing House.

Nalink Sharda, *Multimedia Information Networking,* New Delhi: Prentice-Hall of India Pvt. Ltd.

Natarajan A.M., *Theory of Automata & Formal Languages,* New Age International.

Natarajan A.M., *Theory of Computation,* New Age International.

Newman E.H.; Tulyathan P., *Analysis of Microstrip Antenas using Moment Methods,* IEEE Trans. Antennas Propogation, Vol. AP-30, pp. 1191-96, Jan. 1981.

O. Kolesnikov and B. Hatch, *Building Linux Virtual Private Networks,* New Riders, 2001.

Onana V.P.; Ngono J.M.; Trebossen H.; Rudant J.P.; Tonye E., *Coastline Detection in SAR Images using Texture Analysis in Textural or Geometrical Multi-resolution.*

International Geosciences and Remote Sensing Symposium, 2001. IGARSS '01, Volume 3, pp. 1549-51, Sydney, NSW, Australia.

Pennell Andrew, *Master Your ZX Microdrive Programs, Machine Code and Networking,* Sunshine.

Peter M., *Embedded System Design,* New Age International.

Pitoura E.; Chrysanthis P.K., *Exploiting Versions for Handling Updates in Broadcast Disks,* In VLDB, pp. 114-25, 1999.

Pitoura E.; Chrysanthis P.K., *Scalable Processing of Read-only Transactions in Broadcast Push,* ICDCS, pp. 432-39, 1999.

Pitoura E.; Chrysanthis P.K., *Multiversion Data Broadcast. IEEE Trans. Computers,* 51(10): 1224-30, 2002.

Prabhu S., *Data Mining and Warehousing,* New Age International.

R. Venkateswaran, *Virtual Private Networks,* IEEE Potentials, March 2001.

Rajaraman V., *Fundamentals of Comptures,* New Delhi, Prentice Hall of India.

Rajiv Rai; A. Rajindran, *Computer Science,* Delhi, S.K. Kataria & Sons.

Rekik A.; Zribi M.; Hamida A.B.; Benjelloun M., *Review of Satellite Image Segmentation for an Optimal Fusion System Based on the Edge.*

Richard H. Baker, *Network Security: How to Plan for it and Achieve it,* New Delhi: McGraw Hill.

Runtong Z., *Fuzzy Control of Queueing Systems*, New Age International.

Rupert B., *The DSP Bottleneck*, IEEE Communication Magazine, May 1995, pp. 46-54.

S. Jaiswal, *Networking Technologies,* New Delhi, Galgotia.

Sadiku M.; Akujuobi C., *Software Defined Radio—A Brief Overview,* IEEE Potentials, 2004.

Satyanarayanan M., *The Evolution of Coda. ACM Trans. Comput. Syst B72,* 20(2): 85-124, 2002.

Scaling the internet web servers, Cisco System. November 1997. White Paper.

Schiener B., *Applied Cryptography.*

Schiller J., *Mobile Communications,* Low Price Edition.

Schneier, B., *Applied Cryptography,* J. Wiley & Sons, 1994.

Seal D., *ARM Architecture Reference Manual*, Addison-Wesley.

Security Related Network Functions, European Telecommunications Standards Institute, Recommendation GSM 03.20.

Senoo T.; Girod B., *Vector Quantization for Entropy Coding Image Sub Bands,* IEEE Transactions on Image Processing, 1(4): 526-533, Oct. 1992.

Shelswell P., *The COFDM Modulation System: The Heart of Digital Audio Broadcasting,* 1996/8, BBC Research and Development Report, BBC RD.

Shrinivasan T.M., *Computer Applications,* Jaipur: Aavishkar Publishing.

Singhal M., Niranjan G., *Advanced Concepts in Operating Systems*, Tata McGraw Hill Edition.

Siyan, *TCP/IP Unleashed,* Pearson Education India.

Smith, *Internet Cryptography*, Pearson Education India.

Snayder A. Randall: Gallagher D. Michael, *Wireless Telecummunications Networking With ANSI-4*, McGraw Hill Int. Editions.

Stalling W., *Cryptography and Network Security: Principals and Practice*, Prentice Hall.

Stalling W., *Data and Computer Commuincation,* Prentice Hall.

Stallings W., *High Speed Networks & Internet*, Pearson Education India.

Stallings W., *Wireless Communications and Network,* Pearson Education.

Stallings William, *Computer Networking with Internet Protocols and Networkig,* Pearson Education.

Stott J., *The Effects of Phase Noise in COFDM,* Summer 1998, EBU Technical Review.

Sun H., *An Efficient Remote user Authentication Scheme using Smart Cards,* IEEE Trans Consumer Electron, 46(4), pp. 958-61, November 2000.

Tan WH; Bister M., *Uncommitted Morphological Merging of Watershed Segments,* International Conference on Image Processing (ICIP2003), 2003.

Taur J.S.; Tao C.W., *Medical Image Compression using Principal Compont Analysis.*

International Conference on Image Processing, Volume: 1, 1996, p. 903-06, Vol. 2.

Tenenbaum A.M., *Computer Network*, Prentice Hall.

Theodore S., *Wireless Communications Principles and Practice*, Rappaport2e.

Thomas Steven V., *Windows NT Heterogeneous Networking,* Techmedia.

Thornton J.; Grace D.; Spillard C.; Konefal T.; Tozer T.C., *Broadband Communications from a High Altitude Platforms,* IEEE Electronics and Communications Engineering Journal, Vol. 13, No. 3, pp. 138-44, June 2001 (through net).

USC: 'Internet Protocol', Information Sciences Institute, RFC 791, IETF, September 1981.

Uyless D. Black, *Computer Network: Protocols Standards and Interfaces,* New Delhi, PHI.

Van Valkenburg M.E., *Networking Analysis (Van Valkenburg),* Prentice Hall of India Pvt. Ltd.

Walr: Jean:Varaiya Pravin, *High Performance Communication Networks,* Harcourt.

Wan Hee Kim and Robert Tien when Chien, *Topological Analaysis Synthesis of Communication Network,* New York; Columbia University Press.

Waterman, *A Guide to Expert System,* Pearson Education India.

Weinstein, S.B.; Ebert, P.M., *Data Transmission by Frequency-Division Multiplexing Using the Discrete Fourier Transform,* October 1971, IEEE Transactions on Communication Technology, Vol. COM-19, No. 5, pp. 628-34.

Williamson, J., *GSM Bids for Global Recognition in a Crowded Cellular World,* Telephony, Vol. 333, No. 14, April 1992, pp. 36-40.

Wireless Communications, Principles and Practice, Rappaport T.S. Prentice Hall, New Jersey, 1996.

Wireless Communications—Principles and Practices, Rappaport T.S. 2nd edition.

Wong S.; Zaremba L.; Gooden D.; Huang H.K., *Radio Logic Image Compression—A Review,* Proc. IEEE, Vol. 83, No. 2, pp. 194-219, 1995.

Wu Y.G.; Tai S.C., *Medical Image Compression by Discrete Cosine Transform Spectral Similarity Strategy,* IEEE Trans. Information Technology in Biomedicine, Vol. 5, No. 3, pp. 236-43, September 2001.

Y. Desmedt, *Verifier-Designated Signatures,* Rump Session, Crypto'03 (2003).

Yao A., *How to Generate and Exchange Results,* FOCS, pp. 162-167, 1986.

Yegnanarayana, *Artificial Neural Network,* PHI.

Yiu J., *The Definitive Guide to the ARM Cortex-M3.*

Zacker C., *The Complete Reference: Networking.*

Zadeh L.A., *Fuzzy Sets,* Information & Control, 8, pp. 338-53, 1965.

Zavosh F.; Aberle J.T., *Improving the Performance of Microstrip-Patch Antennas,* IEEE Antennas and Propagation Magazine, Vol. 38, No. 4, August 1996.

Zeadally, S.; Raicu, I., *Evaluating IPv6 on Windows and Solaris,* IEEE Internet Comput., 2003, 7, (3).

Zhu X, *Remote Sensing Monitoring of Coastline Change in Pearl River Estuary,* 22nd Asian Conference on Remote Sensing, pp. 19-22, November, Singapore, 2001.

Contributors

Abdaheer, S., Deptt. of E & CE, Z.H. College of Engg. & Tech., AMU, Aligarh.

Agarwal, Abha, Sr. Lecturer, Ideal Institute of Technology, Ghaziabad.

Agarwal, Abhinav, Add. Manager, Tata Teleservices Ltd, Delhi.

Agarwal, B.B., C.E.T., I.F.T.M., Moradabad.

Agarwal, D.K., Lecturer, SRM Engineering Group, SRM University.

Agrawal, I., Lecturer, E & CE Deptt. GLAITM, Mathura.

Agrawal, S., Student of MCA, GLAITM, Mathura.

Ahmad, M., Student of CS Department, AMU, Aligarh.

Alam, M.S., Faculty of Engg. & Technology, AMU, Aligarh.

Ali, R., Student of CS Department, AMU, Aligarh.

Beg, Mohd. Salim, Coordinator, Center for Wireless Networks, Deptt. of Electronics Engineering, Z.H. College of Engg. & Technology, AMU, Aligarh.

Bhardwaj, D., Senior Lecturer, GLAITM, Mathura.

Bhardwaj, K., Research Scholar, Dr. B.R. Ambedkar University, Agra.

Bhat (Kaul), S., Asst. Prof., Dept. of MCA, AKG, Engineering College, Ghaziabad.

Bhat, H.J., Lecturer, Dept. of Comp and Mgmt Science, IMSIT, c/o Vivekand College Campus Smarth Nagar, Aurangabad, Maharashtra.

Bhatnagar, Charul, HOD, Computer Science, GLA ITM, Mathura.

Bhattacharyya, B., Department of Computer & System Sciences, Visva-Bharati University, Santiniketan.

Chandra, R., Dept of Comp Applications, Azad Instt. of Engg. & Tech., Lucknow.

Chaturvedi, A., Department of EC, GLAITM, Mathura.

Chaudhary, P., B.Tech. Final Year, Deptt. Computer Science, GLAITM, Mathura.

Chaurasia, B.K., Department of CSE, ITM, Gwalior.

Deolia, V.K., Reader, Department of ECE, GLAITM, Mathura.

Dhubkarya, D.C., Department of ECE, BIET, Jhansi.

Dutt, V., C-106 Top Floor Sector 33, Noida.

Gangwar, D.S., Lecturer, Department of ECE, GLAITM, Mathura.

Garg, G., B.Tech. Final Year, Deptt. of Computer Science, GLAITM, Mathura.

Ghose, U., Lecturer, University School of Information Technology, G.G.S. Indraprastha University, Kashmere Gate, Delhi.

Goyal, K.K., Faculty of Mgmt. & Computer Application, R.B.S. College, Khandari, Agra.

Gupta, B., College of Engg. and Tech., IFTM, Moradabad.

Gupta, P., Z.H. College of Engg. & Technology, AMU, Aligarh.

Haleem, A., Prof. of Mech. Engg. Coordinator MBA evening program, Faculty of Engg. and Technology, Jamia Millia Islamia, New Delhi.

Israil, Mohd., Department of Electronics Engineering, Z.H. College of Engg. and Tech., Aligarh Muslim University, Aligarh.

Jain, A., Lecturer, University School of Information Technology, G.G.S. Indraprastha University, Kashmere Gate, Delhi.

Kafeel, A., Lecturer, Electronics Engg. Section, University Women's Polytechnic, Faculty of Engg., AMU, Aligarh.

Kaushik, C., Student of MCA, GLAITM, Mathura.

Khan, M.E., Department of Electronics Engineering, Z.H. College of Engg. and Tech., Aligarh Muslim University, Aligarh.

Kumar, M., Department of CSE, GLAITM, Mathura.

Kumar, Rakesh, B.Tech final year EC, GLAITM, Mathura.

Kumar Ravi, Department of ECE, Z.H. College of Engg. and Tech., AMU, Aligarh.

Kumar, S., Dept. of Mech. & Automation Engg., Guru Prem Sukh Memorial College.

Kumar, V., Lecturer, Shekhawati Engineering College, Dundlod.

Kushwah, Rajendra Singh, Department of CSE, ITM, Gwalior.

Lal, Sunder, Head, Dept. of Mathematics, Dr. B.R. Ambedkar (Agra) University, Agra.

Misra, Y., B.R.C.M. College of Engg. and Technology, Bahal.

Mukhopadhyay, T., Department of Computer & System Sciences, Visva-Bharati University, Santiniketan.

Narendra Mohan, Lecture, Department of ECE, GLAIPS, Mathura.

Pandey, B.P., Student of EC Department, GLAITM, Mathura.

Pandey, S.K., Asst. Professor, Comp Sc. & Mgmt., Indian Institute Carpet Technology, Bhadohi.

Pareek, Saurabh.

Rafiq, M.Q., Dept. of Computer Engg., Z.H. College of Engg. & Tech., AMU, Aligarh.

Rajni, Deptt. of E&C Engg., SBS College of Engg. & Tech., Ferozepur.

Rastogi, A., Lecturer, Deptt. of MCA, MIET, Meerut.

Rathi, A., Student of EC Dept., GLAITM, Mathura.

Rihan, Mohd., Faculty of Engg. & Tech., AMU, Aligarh.

Saraswat, R.C., Lecturer, VBSPU, Jaunpur.

Sawhney, A., Deptt. of Mech. and Automation Engg., Guru Prem Sukh Memorial College of Engg.

Shaheen, S., Reader & Head, Computer Engg. Section, University. Women's Polytechnic, Faculty of Engg., AMU, Aligarh.

Sharma, A., Lecturer, Deptt. of MCA, GLAITM, Mathura.

Sharma, M., B.R.C.M. College of Engg. and Technology, Bahal.

Sharma, S., Lecturer, Department of ECE, GLAIPS, Mathura.

Singh, G., Lecturer, SRM Engineering Group, SRM University.

Singh, J.P., Lecturer, Deptt. of BCA, GLAIPS, Mathura.

Singh, Manu Pratap, Department of Computer Science, Dr. B.R.A. University, Khandari, Agra.

Sinha, P., Deptt. of IT, A.B.E.S. Engineering College, Ghaziabad.

Srivastava, D.K., Department of ECE, BIET, Jhansi.

Srivastava, V., Department of Computer Applications, Azad Institute of Engineering & Technology, Lucknow.

Surabhi, Deptt. of E&C Engg., JSS Academy of Tech Edu, Noida.

Tayal, S.P., Tata Technologies Ltd., Pune.

Tiwari, U.K., MEIT, Meerut.

Varshney, N., Lecturer, Deptt. of BCA, GLAIPS, Mathura.

Verma, A.K., Student of EC Department, GLAITM, Mathura.

Verma, G., Lecturer, Deptt. of MCA, MIET, Meerut.

Verma, P., Lecturer, Deptt. of MCA, MIET, Meerut.

Verma, Vandani, Department of Mathematics, Dr. B.R.A. (Agra), University, Agra.

Verma, Vijeta, College of Engg. & Tech., IFTM, Moradabad.

Vishvakarma, B.R., Deptt. of IT, ECE, BHU, Varanasi.

Yadav, M., Department of MCA, GLAITM, Mathura.

Yadav, Santosh Kumar, Research Scholars, Dr. B.R. Ambedkar University, Agra.

Zuaib, Mohd., MCA, GLAITM, Mathura.